Historical and Cultural Dictionaries of Asia
edited by Basil C. Hedrick

1. *Saudi Arabia,* by Carroll L. Riley, 1972.
2. *Nepal,* by Basil C. and Anne K. Hedrick. 1972.
3. *The Philippines,* by Ester G. and Joel M. Maring. 1973.
4. *Burma,* by Joel M. and Ester G. Maring. 1973.
5. *Afghanistan,* by M. Jamil Hanifi. 1976.
6. *Thailand,* by Harold Smith. 1976.
7. *Vietnam,* by Danny J. Whitfield. 1976.
8. *India,* by George Kurian. 1976.

Historical and Cultural
Dictionary of
INDIA

by

George Thomas Kurian

Historical & Cultural Dictionaries of Asia, No. 8

The Scarecrow Press, Inc.
Metuchen, N.J.   1976

Books by the same author:

Dictionary of Indian English
Directory of American Book Publishing

Library of Congress Cataloging in Publication Data

Kurian, George Thomas.
    Historical and cultural dictionary of India.

    (Historical and cultural dictionaries of Asia ;
no. 8)
    Bibliography: p.
    1.   India--Dictionaries and encyclopedias.
I. Title. II. Series: Historical and cultural
dictionaries of Asia series ; no. 8.
DS405.K87   954'.003   76-16186
ISBN 0-8108-0951-6

to
CLARENCE LEWIS BARNHART
The Greatest Editor I Have Known

TABLE OF CONTENTS

PREFACE

THE HISTORICAL AND CULTURAL DICTIONARY OF INDIA
is designed as a book of Indian facts and as a guide to
the understanding of India.

THE PAST 28 YEARS since independence have witnessed a
renaissance of Indian historical scholarship. This is due
partly to a renewed interest in Indian studies by Western
and particularly American scholars and partly to the re-
surgence of regional and local studies under the auspices
of Indian states and universities. The result has been a
vast body of historical literature which though poorly covered bibliographically is available for the most part in the
English language. I have drawn liberally on these resources and my debt is acknowledged in the form of an
extensive bibliography at the end of this book. Confronted
with this immense apparatus criticus on the one hand and
the stark limitations of space on the other I have tried to
achieve in each entry a brevity which in the words of
Lytton Strachey excludes everything that is redundant and
nothing that is significant.

THE WORK lists over 2000 entries, of which less than a
quarter are biographical. The bulk of the entries relates
to terms of native provenance, an understanding of which
is absolutely essential for a student of India. Some of
these words in their Anglicized form have already found
a domicile in the English language and may be regarded
as part of that fascinating sublanguage known as Indian
English. But the majority of the words are still unfamil-
iar to Western readers. This dictionary could therefore
be useful not only to historians but also to linguists, ety-
mologists, and anthropologists.

FROM A LEXICOGRAPHER'S point of view the spelling of Indian words in English provides a source of unending des-
pair. Not only does it require what should be unnecessary
cross-referencing but also frequently leads to wrong pro-

nunciation. Indian orthography has not yet recovered from the ravages inflicted upon it by three centuries of Western Hobson-Jobsonizers. There is hardly any Indian term they have not either shrunk or pulled out of its phonetic shape. But some kind of a consensus has begun to emerge in Indian newspapers and books and as a native-born Indian I have tried to follow contemporary Indian usage in most cases. I have conformed to official Indian usage in the case of all geographical names (Tiruchirapally, Kozhikode, Kanpur, Machilipatnam, etc.). Where there is no consensus I have tried to exercise the author's right of following his own personal preferences (Mughal, Muslim, Punjab, etc.).

ALL DATES in the Dictionary are A.D. unless "B.C." is specified. Throughout the entries "the Company" is used to mean the East India Company.

THE ALPHABETIZATION and citation of Indian names may present some difficulties to Western readers familiar with the conventional manuals of style. The main problems are: (1) In India the last name is not always the surname; particularly among Hindus it is the nomen or caste indicator, as Iyer, Das, Shastri, or Menon; among Muslims it is the rank or pedigree indicator, as khan or shah. (2) Some names may be made up of two or more elements which may or may not be combined according to usage as Nandkumar or Nanda Kumar. (3) Each caste and each region has its onomastic peculiarities. (4) Dynastic names, titles, and assumed names present difficulties of a different order. In this class must be included persons whose titles have a better recognition quotient than their real names (e.g., Gautama Buddha rather than Siddhartha). The general guiding principle adopted in this book for entry headings has been to treat caste and rank indicators and dynastic names as secondary elements of a name. However, there are exceptions to this rule based on evidence of usage, such as with the name Lal Bahadur Shastri, which is listed under Shastri rather than Lal Bahadur.

FINALLY I must express my grateful thanks to all who have assisted in the compilation of this work. I will also be grateful for any word of omissions or corrections and for suggestions of new entries in future editions.

New York : July 10 1975   George Thomas Kurian

CHRONOLOGY OF INDIAN HISTORY

B. C.

c3102	The war between the Kurus and the Pandavas (--Mahabharata)
c2700	The Indus Valley civilization
c544	Nirvana of Gautama Buddha
c527	Nirvana of Mahavira
327-326	Invasion of India by Alexander the Great
c322	Foundation of Maurya Dynasty by Chandragupta Maurya
c305	Invasion of Seleucos Nikator
c273	Accession of Asoka the Great
c187	Foundation of the Sunga Dynasty
c58	Foundation of the Vikrama Era
c50	Foundation of the Satavahana Dynasty

A. D.

c51	Saint Thomas in India
c66	Arrival in China of the Indian Buddhist missionary monks, Kasyapa, Matanga, and Gobharana
78	Commencement of the Saka Era
c78	Accession of Kadphises II
c120	Accession of Kanishka
c162	Accession of Huvishka
c182	Accession of Vasudeva I
320	Commencement of the Gupta Era
405	Fa-Hien arrives in India

ix

455	Accession of Skandagupta
476	Birth of the astronomer Aryabhata
c566	Accession of the Chalukya king Kirtivarman I
606	Accession of Harshavardhana
629	Hiuen Tsang arrives in India
637	Arab invasion of Sind
c642	Accession of the Pallava king Narasimhavarman
643	Sixth quinquennial assembly at Prayag
674	Accession of Vikramaditya I, king of the Chalukyas, and Paramesvaravarman I, king of the Pallavas
710-11	Arab invasion of Sind under Muhammad bin Kasim
712	Battle of Alor--Arab conquest of Sind
713	Fall of Multan to the Arabs
753	Foundation of the Rashtrakuta Dynasty
783	Foundation of the Pratihara Dynasty
871	Accession of the Chola king Aditya I
973	Foundation of the Chalukya Dynasty of Kalyani
985	Accession of Rajaraja the Great
986-7	First invasion of India by Sabuktigin
1001	Defeat of Jaipal
1012	Accession of Rajendra Chola I
1018	Raid on Kanauj by Sultan Mahmud of Ghazni
1026	Sack of the temple of Somnath by Sultan Mahmud
c1076	Accession of Anantavarman Choda Ganga of Orissa
1175	Invasion of the Punjab by Shibab-ud-din Muhammad Ghuri
c1185	Accession of Lakshmana Sena in Bengal
1191	First Battle of Tarain--Defeat of Shihab-ud-din
1192	Second Battle of Tarain--Defeat of Prithviraj by Shihab-ud-din
1192-3	Fall of Delhi to the Muslim forces
1194	Battle of Chandwar--Defeat of Jayachandra of Kanauj

c1200	Conquest of Bihar and Bengal by Muslim forces under Bakhtiyar Khalji
1206	Foundation of the Delhi Sultanate--Accession of Qutb-ud-din
1210-11	Accession of Iltutmish
1221	Invasion of Chingiz [Genghis] Khan
1228	Ahom conquest of Kamarupa or Assam
1231	Foundation of Qutb Minar
1236	Accession of Raziya
1246	Accession of Nasir-ud-din
1266	Accession of Balban
1288	Marco Polo visits Kayal
1290	Foundation of the Khalji Dynasty
1294	Sack of Devagiri by Alauddin Khalji
1296	Accession of Alauddin Khalji
1297	Muslim conquest of Gujarat
1302	Fall of Chitor to Alauddin--Mongol invasion
1310	South Indian expedition of Malik Kafur
1317-18	Fall of the Yadavas
1320	Accession of Ghiyas-ud-din Tughluq
1325	Accession of Muhammad bin Tughluq
c1327	Imperial capital moved from Delhi to Daulatabad
1336	Foundation of the Vijayanagar kingdom
1338-39	Foundation of the Sultanate of Bengal
1339	Establishment of kingdom of Kashmir by Shah Mir
1347	Foundation of the Bahmani kingdom of the Deccan
1351	Accession of Firuz Shah Tughluq
1393	Establishment of the Jaunpur kingdom
1398	Invasion of India by Timur
1420	Visit of Vijayanagar by Nicolo Conti
1429	Transfer of the Bahmani capital to Bidar
c1430	Accession of Rana Kumbha of Mewar

1451	Accession of Bahlul Lodi--Foundation of Lodi Dynasty
1469	Birth of Guru Nanak
1484	Secession of Berar from the Bahmani Empire
1489	Accession of Sikander Lodi--Establishment of the Sultanate of Bijapur
1490	Establishment of the Sultanate of Ahmednagar
1493	Accession of Husain Shah of Bengal
1497-98	First voyage of Vasco da Gama to India
1509	Accession of Krishnadeva Raya of Vijayanagar--Accession of Rana Sanga of Mewar--Appointment of Affonso de Albuquerque as governor of Portuguese possessions
1510	Portuguese capture of Goa
1512	Establishment of the Sultanate of Golkonda
1526	First Battle of Panipet--Foundation of the Mughal Dynasty--Accession of Babur
1527	Battle of Khanua--Defeat of Rana Sanga by the Mughals
1529	Battle of Gogra--Defeat of the Afghans by the Mughals
1530	Accession of Humayun
1539	Battle of Chaunsa--Defeat of Humayun by Sher Khan
1540	Battle of Kanauj--Defeat of Humayun by Sher Shah--Accession of Sher Shah as emperor of Delhi--Establishment of the Sur Dynasty
1555	Recovery of the throne of Delhi by Humayun
1556	Accession of Akbar the Great--Second Battle of Panipet
1560	Fall of Bairam Khan
1561	Conquest of Malwa by Akbar
1565	Battle of Talikota and the fall of Vijayanagar
1568	Fall of Chitor
1571	Foundation of Fatehpur Sikri
1572	Annexation of Gujarat to the Mughal Empire
1576	Conquest of Bengal by Akbar

1582	Promulgation of Din-Ilahi
1586	Conquest of Kashmir by the Mughals
1591	Conquest of Sind by the Mughals
1592	Akbar's annexation of Orissa
1595	Annexation of Baluchistan and Kandahar
1600	Establishment of the English East India Company in London
1602	Establishment of the Dutch East India Company
1605	Accession of Jahangir
1606	Execution of Arjan, fifth Guru of the Sikhs
1609	Establishment of the Dutch trading settlement at Pulicat
1611	Establishment of the English factory at Machilipatnam
1612	Establishment of the English Factory at Surat
1613	Grant of farman to the English East India Company of Jahangir
1615	Arrival of Ambassador Sir Thomas Roe in India
1620	Revolt of Malik Ambar
1625	Establishment of the Dutch factory at Chinsura
1628	Accession of Shah Jahan
1633	Fall of the Nizam Shahi Dynasty of Ahmadnagar
1639	Foundation of Fort St. George at Madras
1649	Fall of Kandahar to the Persians
1651	Establishment of the English factory at Hughli
1657	Beginning of the War of Succession of Shah Jahan's sons
1658	Battles of Dharmat and Shamugarh
1659	Battles of Khajwah and Deorai--Coronation of Aurangzeb--Execution of Prince Dara
1661	Bombay ceded to the English--Execution of Prince Murad
1662	Mughal conquest of Assam under Mir Jumla
1664	Establishment of the French East India Company --Coronation of Shivaji

1669	Revolt of the Jats under Gokla
1670	Sack of Surat by Shivaji
1672	Satnami and Afridi revolts
1674	Foundation of the French settlement at Pondicherry
1675	Execution of Tej Bahadur, Sikh Guru
1679	Reimposition by Aurangzeb of the jiziya on non-Muslims
1680	Death of Shivaji
1681	Assam throws off Mughal yoke
1686	Aurangzeb's conquest and annexation of Bijapur
1687	Aurangzeb's conquest and annexation of Golkonda
1689	Accession of Rajaram to the Maratha throne
1690	Foundation of Calcutta by Job Charnock
1691	Suppression of the Jats by Aurangzeb
1698	East India Company ceded the zamindari of Sutanati, Kalikata, and Govindapur
1707	Accession of Bahadur Shah I
1708	Accession of Shahu to the Maratha throne
1712	Accession of Jahandar Shah
1713	Accession of Farrukhsiyar
1714	Appointment of Balaji Viswanath as Peshwa
1716	Execution of the Sikh leader Banda
1717	Grant of farman to the English East India Company by Farrukhsiyar
1719	Accession of Muhammad Shah
1720	Baji Rao I appointed Peshwa
1724	Appointment of Sa'adat Khan as governor of Oudh --Establishment of the Sultanate of Oudh
1725	Appointment of Shuja-ud-din as governor of Bengal
1739	Sack of Delhi by Nadir Shah
1740	Accession of Balaji Baji Rao as Peshwa and Alivardi Khan as Nawab of Bengal

1742	Appointment of Dupleix as governor of Pondicherry
1744-8	First Carnatic War
1747	Invasion of India by Ahmad Shah Abdali
1748	Accession of Ahmad Shah
1750-4	Second Carnatic War
1751	Robert Clive's capture and defense of Arcot
1754	Accession of Alamgir II
1756	Accession of Siraj-ud-daulah as Nawab of Bengal --Capture of Calcutta by Siraj-ud-daulah--Third Carnatic War
1757	Recovery of Calcutta by the English forces-- Battle of Plassey and the defeat and execution of Siraj-ud-daulah--Installation of Mir Jafar as Nawab of Bengal--Sack of Delhi and Mathura by Ahmad Shah Abdali
1758	Punjab occupied by the Marathas
1759	Battle of Bedara
1760	Battle of Wandiwash--Battle of Udgir--Appointment of Vansittart as governor of Bengal--Mir Kasim replaced Mir Jafar as Nawab of Bengal
1761	Third Battle of Panipet--Accession of Shah Alam II--Accession of Madhava Rao as Peshwa
1764	Battle of Buxar
1765	Return of Robert Clive as governor of Bengal-- Treaty of Allahabad--Grant of the Diwani of Bengal, Bihar, and Orissa to the Company by Shah Alam II
1766	Cession of Northern Circars to the Company
1767-9	First Mysore War
1770	Bengal famine
1772	Appointment of Warren Hastings as governor of Bengal
1773	Enactment of the Regulating Act
1774	Appointment of Warren Hastings as governor general--Establishment of Supreme Court at Calcutta--Rohilla War

1775	Trial and execution of Nanda Kumar
1775-82	First Maratha War
1776	Treaty of Purandhar
1779	Convention of Wadgaon
1780-4	Second Mysore War
1782	Treaty of Salbai
1783	Fox's India Bill
1784	Treaty of Mangalore--Pitt's India Act
1786	Appointment of Lord Cornwallis as governor general
1790-2	Third Mysore War
1792	Treaty of Seringapatam--Ranjit Singh assumed leadership of a Sikh misl
1793	Permanent Revenue Settlement in Bengal--Appointment of Sir John Shore as governor general
1795	Battle of Kharda
1796	Accession of Baji Rao II as Peshwa
1798	Appointment of Lord Wellesley as governor general--Nizam joined subsidiary alliance
1799	Fourth Mysore War--Fall of Seringapatam and the death of Tipu Sultan--Establishment of the Wadiyar Dynasty of Mysore--Foundation of the Baptist mission at Serampore by William Carey
1801	Annexation of Carnatic to the British territories
1802	Battle of Poona--Treaty of Bassein
1803-5	Second Maratha War--Battles of Delhi, Assaye, Laswari, and Argaon--Treaties of Deagaon and Surji-Arjungaon
1805	Recall of Lord Wellesley--Appointment of Lord Cornwallis as governor general--Death of Lord Cornwallis--Appointment of George Barlow as governor general
1806	Vellore mutiny
1807	Appointment of Lord Minto as governor general
1809	Treaty of Amritsar
1813	Appointment of Lord Hastings as governor general

1814-6	Anglo-Nepali War
1816	Treaty of Sagauli
1817-8	Third Maratha and Pindari Wars--Battles of Kirkee, Sitabaldi, and Mahidpur
1818	Battle of Ashti--Surrender of Peshwa Baji Rao II
1819	Abolition of the peshwaship--Rajput states joined protective alliance
1823	Appointment of Lord Amherst as governor general
1824-6	The First Burmese War
1826	Fall of Bharatpur--Treaty of Yandabo--Annexation of Assam, Arakan, and Tennasserim
1828	Appointment of Lord Bentinck as governor general
1829	Abolition of sati
1829-37	Suppression of Thuggee
1830	Annexation of Cachar
1832	Annexation of Jaintia
1834	Annexation of Coorg--Appointment of Lord Maucalay as Law Member
1836	Appointment of Lord Auckland as governor general
1839-42	First Afghan War
1842	Appointment of Lord Ellenborough as governor general
1843	Battles of Miani and Dabo--Annexation of Sind--Suppression of slavery
1844	Appointment of Lord Hardinge as governor general
1845-6	First Sikh War--Battles of Mudki and Ferozeshah
1846	Battles of Aliwal and Sobraon--Treaty of Lahore
1848	Appointment of Lord Dalhousie as governor general--Revolt of Mulraj--Promulgation of the Doctrine of Lapse
1848-9	Second Sikh War
1849	Battles of Chillianwalla and Gujarat--Annexation of Jaitpur, Sambalpur, and Punjab

1852	Second Burmese War--Annexation of Pegu
1853	Inauguration of the first railway line in India from Bombay to Thana--Opening of telegraphic link between Calcutta and Agra--Annexation of Nagpur and Jhansi--Cession of Berar by the Nizam--Adoption of competition system for the Indian Civil Service
1854	Sir Charles Wood's Education Despatch
1855	The Santal revolt
✓ 1856	Annexation of Oudh--The Indian Universities Act --Hindu Widow's Remarriage Act--Religious Disabilities Act--Appointment of Lord Canning as governor general
✓ 1857	Outbreak of the Sepoy Mutiny at Meerut--Occupation of Delhi by the rebels and the proclamation of Bahadur Shah as emperor--Recapture of Delhi, Lucknow, and Kanpur--Foundation of the universities of Madras, Calcutta, and Bombay
1858	Recapture of Jhansi, Bareilly, and Gwalior--Proclamation of peace by Lord Canning--Act for the Better Government of India--Queen's proclamation--Appointment of Lord Canning as viceroy
✓ 1860	Promulgation of the Indian Penal Code
✓ 1861	Enactment of the Indian Councils Act, Civil Service Act, and the Code of Criminal Procedure--Establishment of High Courts in the presidencies
1862	Appointment of Lord Elgin as viceroy
1864	Appointment of Sir John Lawrence as viceroy--Bhutan War
1865	Orissa famine
1869	Appointment of Lord Mayo as viceroy
1872	Appointment of Lord Northbrook as viceroy
1873-4	Bihar famine
1876	Appointment of Lord Lytton as viceroy--Deccan famine
1877	Delhi durbar--Proclamation of Queen Victoria as Empress of India
1878	Vernacular Press Act

1878-80	Second Afghan War
1880	Appointment of Lord Ripon as viceroy--Battle of Maiwand
1881	First general census
1882	Repeal of the Vernacular Press Act--Hunter Commission
1883	Enactment of Ilbert Bill
1884	Appointment of Lord Dufferin as viceroy
1885	First session of the Indian National Congress--Third Burmese War
1886	Annexation of Upper Burma
1888	Appointment of Lord Lansdowne as viceroy
1891	Manipur insurrection
1892	Enactment of Indian Councils Act
1893	Henry Durand's delimitation of the Indo-Afghan frontier
1894	Appointment of Lord Elgin as viceroy
1899	Appointment of Lord Curzon as viceroy
1901	Creation of the North-West Frontier Province
1904	Enactment of the Indian Universities Act and the Cooperative Society Act
1905	Partition of Bengal--Appointment of Lord Minto as viceroy
1906	Foundation of the Muslim League--Adoption of Purna Swaraj as goal of the Indian National Congress
1908	Enactment of Newspapers Act
✓1909	Enactment of Minto-Morley Reforms--Appointment of first Indian member of viceroy's executive council
1910	Appointment of Lord Hardinge as viceroy
✓ 1911	Delhi Durbar--Visit to India of King George V--Modification of the partition of Bengal--Transfer of the capital of India from Calcutta to New Delhi
1912	Creation of a new province of Bihar and Orissa
✓ 1913	Award of Nobel Prize for literature to Rabindranath Tagore

1915   Defence of India Act

1916   Appointment of Lord Chelmsford as viceroy--
            Foundation of the Home Rule League

1918   Publication of the Montague-Chelmsford Report

1919   Enactment of the Government of India Act of 1919

1920   Khalifat Movement--Mahatma Gandhi launches the
            noncooperation movement

1921   Foundation of the Chamber of Princes--Moplah
            revolt--Appointment of Lord Reading as viceroy

1923   Establishment of the Swaraj Party

1926   Appointment of Lord Irwin as viceroy

1927   Appointment of Simon Commission

1928   Publication of the (Motilal) Nehru Report--For-
            mation of the Independence League within the
            Congress

1930   Launching of the Civil Disobedience Movement--
            Publication of the Report of the Simon Commis-
            sion--Round Table Conference

1931   Irwin-Gandhi Pact--Appointment of Lord Welling-
            ton as viceroy

1932   Gandhi's imprisonment and fast--Communal
            Award--Poona Pact

1934   Civil Disobedience Movement suspended--Crea-
            tion of Royal Indian Navy

1935   Enactment of Government of India Act

1936   Appointment of Lord Linlithgow as viceroy

1937   Inauguration of provincial autonomy and the for-
            mation of Congress ministries in six provinces

1940   Adoption by the Muslim League of the goal of a
            separate Muslim state known as Pakistan

1941   Escape of Subhas Chandra Bose to Germany

1942   Launching of the Quit India Movement--Outlawing
            of the Indian National Congress and imprison-
            ment of its leaders--Cripps mission

1943   Bengal famine--Appointment of Lord Wavell as
            governor general

1945   General Elections held

1946   Cabinet Mission to India--Communal riots in
            Calcutta, Dacca, Noakhali, Tipperah, and Bihar
            --Formation of the Interim government with Con-
            gress and Muslim League as members--First
            session of Constituent Assembly

1947   Appointment of Lord Mountbatten as governor
            general--Grant of independence to India and the
            partition of India into two dominions (India and
            Pakistan)--Enactment of the Independence of India
            Act--Accession of Kashmir--Pakistani invasion
            of Kashmir

1948   Assassination of Mahatma Gandhi--Appointment
            of C Rajagopalachari as first Indian governor
            general--Police action in Hyderabad and the
            merger of Hyderabad in the Indian Union

1949   Enactment of the Indian Constitution Act

1950   Proclamation of India as a sovereign democratic
            republic--Election of Rajendra Prasad as Presi-
            dent and Jawaharlal Nehru as prime minister--
            Finalization of the integration of princely states

1952   First general election on the basis of universal
            adult suffrage

1953   Formation of Andhra Pradesh on the basis of
            linguistic reorganization of states

1954   Signing of the Pancha Shila agreement

1956   Enactment of the States Reorganization Act--
            Cession of French territories in India by France

1957   Second general election--Introduction of the deci-
            mal system of coinage

1960   Bifurcation of the state of Bombay into Maha-
            rashtra and Gujarat

1961   Liberation of Goa and its merger with the Indian
            Union

1962   Third general election--Formation of Nagaland as
            a separate state and Goa as a Union Territory--
            Indo-China War

1964   Death of Jawaharlal Nehru--Election of Lal
            Bahadur Shastri as prime minister

1965-6   Three-week Indo-Pakistani War ended by accord
            at Tashkent--Death of Lal Bahadur Shastri--

Election of Indira Gandhi as prime minister

1969   Power struggle in Congress Party following election of V. V. Giri as president--Split of the ruling party into New Congress and Old Congress

1971   Landslide victory of Indira Gandhi in general elections--Occupation of East Pakistan by Indian Army and establishment of the state of Bangladesh

1974   India explodes a nuclear device

1975   Merger of Sikkim into the Indian Union

THE DICTIONARY

ABASTANOI. Warlike tribe who lived near the Chinab River in NW India at the time of the invasion of India by Alexander the Great. From Sanskrit, Ambastha.

ABDUL HAMID see BADSHAH-NAMAH

ABDUS SAMAD, KHWAJA see DASTAN-I-AMIR HAMZAL

ABHANGA see PADA

ABHIDHANA. Wordbook or dictionary by the Jain writer, Hemachandra, who flourished in the 13th century.

ABHIRAS. Tribe living in the lower Indus Valley and western Rajasthan in the early Christian Era. Noticed in Periplus (q. v.) and Patanjali's Mahabhasya.

ABHISARAS. Tribe living in parts of Kashmir and North-West Frontier Province at the time of the invasion of India by Alexander the Great.

ABHISHEKA. Consecration of a king during his coronation with 17 kinds of liquids, usually performed by a Brahmin priest.

ABKARI. Tax or excise duty on the production and sale of alcoholic liquors, as arrack and toddy.

ABOR. A hill tribe of Assam.

ABU-L FAZL. Minister and historian at the court of Akbar; author of Ain-i-Akbari and Akbar-namah.

ACHARYA. Literally, one who observes the rules of his order; title of a Vedic preceptor or teacher.

ACT FOR THE BETTER GOVERNMENT OF INDIA. 1858 Act of British Parliament taking over the administration of the government of India from the East India Company.

1

The governor general became the viceroy; the Board of Control, the Council of India; and its president, the Secretary of State for India.

ADALAT AKBAR. The court of final appeal established by the Company in 1793 as part of the sadr [chief] adalat, or supreme court.

ADALAT AL-QASI. Civil court settling disputes relating to Muslim law presided over by the qasi.

ADALAT ASHGAR. A subordinate court of justice established by the Company in 1793 as part of the sadr adalat

ADBHUTASAGARA see BALLAL SENA

ADHIKARI. Title of a rural headman in South India.

ADHIPA. (In ancient India) Governor of a province.

ADHYAKSHA. Head of department in ancient India. The nagaradhyaksha was in charge of cities while the baladhyaksha was in charge of military affairs.

ADI GRANTH. Literally, First Sacred Book. The Sikh scripture compiled in 1604 by the fifth Guru, Arjan. It is sometimes referred to, respectfully, as Granth Sahib.

ADIL SHAHI. Dynasty founded in 1489 by Yusuf Adil Khan, a Georgian slave, which ruled over Bijapur until 1685 when the last Adil Shahi ruler was defeated and the kingdom annexed by Aurangzeb. The Adil Shahis were great builders and their principal monuments include the Bijapur mosque and the tombs of Ibrahim II and Muhammad. The dynasty consisted of nine kings (with dates of accession):

Yusuf Adil Khan (1490)	Ibrahim II (1580)
Ismail (1510)	Muhammad (1627)
Mallu (1534)	Ali II (1657)
Ibrahim (1534)	Sikander (1672)
Ali (1558)	

ADIVARAHA. Literally, Primeval Boar. Title assumed by King Mihira Bhoja (840-90) of the Gurjara-Pratihara dynasty of Kanauj.

ADIVASIS. Literally, aboriginals. Term applied to the primitive hill tribes who were outside the Hindu social system.

ADVAITA. School of Vedanta philosophy founded by a series
of philosophers including Gaudapada, author of Mandukya
karika in the eighth century, Shankara, author of Atmabodha, Vacaspati Mishra, author of Bhamati, and Bharatitirtha. Advaita is a monist system of epistemology and
ontology and holds that the phenomenal universe as viewed
by man is maya or illusion.

AFGHANS. Term loosely applied to the Sultans of Delhi who   ✳
ruled from 1200 to 1526. Sultan Mahmud was the first
Afghan to invade India and Shihab-ud-din Muhammad
Ghori was the founder of Afghan rule in India. The sultans of the Lodi dynasty (1450-1526) were true Afghans.
Sher Shah reestablished Afghan rule for a brief period
from 1540-55.

AFRIDI. Warlike frontier tribe inhabiting the Khyber region.
They led a revolt against Aurangzeb in 1667.

AGA KHAN. Title of the religious head of the Bora Ismaili
Muslims; first conferred on Hasan Aly Shah who claimed
descent from Prophet Muhammad. At one time he held
temporal authority under the Shah of Persia but fled to
India after a quarrel. The third Aga Khan was a member
of the Viceroy's Executive Council.

AGALASSOI. Tribe who inhabited the lower Indus Valley at
the time of the invasion of India by Alexander the Great.
According to classical accounts they were defeated by
Alexander.

AGAMA. Scriptures of Hindu sects.

AGNI. God of fire; one of the lokapalas or guardians of the
world represented as driving a chariot with seven wheels
standing for the seven winds.

AGNIKULA. Literally, fire-born. A term applied to any
one of the four Rajput clans--the Pawar (Pramara),
Parihar (Pratihara), Chauhan (Chahumana), and Solanki
(Chalukya)--or to all collectively--who, according to
Chand Raisa, originated from a fire-pit in Mount Abu.

AGNIMITRA. Sunga ruler who succeeded Pushyamitra in 149 B.C. He extended Sunga dominion to the Warda River. Kalidas' Malavikagnimitra is based on his life and loves.

AGNI PURANA. One of the 18 Puranas; contains a systematic record of historical traditions.

AGRONOMOI. Magistrates in the time of Chandragupta Maurya who, according to Strabo, "had the care of the rivers, measured the land, collected taxes, superintended public roads, and had the charge of the hunters."

AHADI. Literally, single men. A grade of troops in the Mughal service under the immediate orders of the emperor.

AHALYA BAI, Rani. Ruler of Holkar State who ascended the gadi on the death of her father-in-law, Malhar Rao Holkar in 1764. She is remembered as an able administrator and as a builder. She died in 1795.

AHARGANA see BRAHMAGUPTA

AHICHCHATRA. Ancient city, capital of Northern Panchala; visited by Hiuen Tsang in the seventh century. Identified with modern Ramnagar in Bareilly District.

AHIMSA. Doctrine of non-violence and non-injury to living things, considered as an element of spiritual perfection.

AHMADABAD. (1) City founded by Ahmad Shah, the ninth Bahmani sultan, who transferred his capital from Gulbarga to Bidar and renamed it Ahmadabad.
(2) City founded by Ahmad Shah of Gujarat near the site of the old city of Aswal. It was conquered by Akbar in 1572 and by the Marathas in 1758. Present capital of the state of Gujarat and center of Indian textile industry. The city's most prominent monument is the Jumma Masjid, built by Ahmad Shah.

AHMADNAGAR. City in western India; capital of the Nizam Shahi dynasty founded by Ahmad Nizam Shah. It was annexed to the Mughal dominions by Shah Jahan in 1637.

AHMAD NIZAM SHAH. Original name: Malik Ahmad (q.v.). He defeated the last Bahmani sultan, Muhammad Shah, and established a sovereign state with his capital at Ahmadnagar. He assumed the title of Ahmad Nizam Shah and the dynasty that he thus founded is known as Nizam Shahi. He ruled till 1508.

[1]AHMAD SHAH. Third sultan of the independent kingdom of Gujarat who founded the city of Ahmadabad. His reign lasted for 30 years from 1411 to 1441.

[2]AHMAD SHAH. The 20th Mughal emperor who succeeded Muhammad Shah in 1748; his empire was weakened by Ahmad Shah Abdali's invasions in 1750 and 1751; blinded and deposed by Wazir Gazi-ud-din in 1754.

AHMAD SHAH ABDALI see PANIPAT ... (3)

AHMAD SHAH BAHMANI. Ninth Bahmani sultan who ruled from 1422 to 1435. He transferred the capital from Gulbarga to Bidar. His rule was marked by incessant wars with Vijayanagar, Warangal, Konkan, Malwa, and Gujarat.

AHOMS. Tribe inhabiting NE India related to the Shans of upper Burma. Led by Sukapha they invaded Assam about 1228 and gradually extended their dominion over the modern districts of Lakhimpur, Sibsagar, Darang, Nowgong, and Kamrup. The Ahom rule spanned six centuries (1228-1825) and 39 kings who bore the title of Svargadeo or Lord of Heaven. The Ahom capital was Garhgaon, near modern Jorhat. The Ahoms had their own language and religion in the early days but later adopted Hinduism as their religion and Assamese as their language.

AHSAN SHAH see MA'BAR

AHSAN SHAH, JALALUDDIN. Founder of the independent kingdom of Ma'bar in 1335. He was a governor under Sultan Muhammad Tughluq and was one of many provincial rulers who successfully revolted against the Sultan. Ahsan Shah's dynasty ruled Ma'bar until 1378 when the region was absorbed by Vijayanagar.

AIN-I-AKBARI. History and description of Akbar's reign written in Persian by Abu-l Fazl. Translated by Blochmann and Jarratt in 1873.

AIX-LA-CHAPELLE, TREATY OF. Ended the First Carnatic War (1746-48) and restored Madras to the English
after its French capture.

AJANTA. Place in Andhra Pradesh; site of 29 Buddhist
caves excavated in rock consisting of chaityas (chapels),
viharas (monasteries), and galleries; a few date from
150 but the majority belong to the seventh century.
Five caves belong to the Hinayana sect and the others
to the Mahayana.

AJATASATRU (also known as Kunika). King of Magadha;
son of Bimbisara and contemporary of Gautama Buddha
and Mahavira. According to tradition Ajatasatru killed
his father and seized the throne in 516 B.C. He conquered the kingdoms of Vaisali and Kosala and laid the
foundation of Pataliputra. He died in 489 B.C.

AJAYADEVA. Chouhan king who founded Ajmer about 1100.

AJIT SINGH. Rana of Marwar who successfully defied
Aurangzeb. Through his influence at the court of Farrukhsiyar he became the ruler of Ajmer and Gujarat.

AJIVIKAS. Religious sect founded by Gosala, a contemporary of Gautama Buddha and Mahavira. Their doctrines
are contained in two scriptures: Samanna-phala-Sutta
and Bhagavati-Sutra. They believed in fate and denied
free will and human responsibility.

AKALI. Member of a body of Sikh zealots distinguished by
blue clothing and steel armlets. From Sanskrit a-kal,
one without time, or eternal one.

AKBAR. 1542-1605. Third and the most famous Mughal
emperor; assumed the throne on the death of his father
Humayun in 1556. At the time of his death in 1605 his
empire extended from Kabul in the west to Bengal in
the east and the Himalayas in the north to the Narmada
River in the South. Akbar was also a great administrator; he divided his empire into 15 subas or provinces, each under a subadar or Nawab Nazim. With
the help of Raja Todar Mal he organized an efficient
land-revenue system with uniform standards of measurement and assessment. To gain the loyalty of Hindus
he adopted a policy of tolerance and conciliation in matters of religion. To bring all his subjects together he pro-
mulgated a new syncretic religion called Din-Ilahi in 1581.

AKBAR II. The 25th and penultimate Mughal emperor
    (1806-37); a titular ruler under the shadow of the East
    India Company.

AKBAR-NAMAH. Historical account of the reign of Akbar
    by his courtier Abu-l Fazl.

AKESINES. Classical name for the Chinab River. From
    Sanskrit Asikni.

AKHBAR. Periodic reports containing general news and
    news of princes' affairs, decrees, and proceedings of
    courts sent from the capitals of other Indian states
    by intelligence agents maintained by rulers in medieval
    India.

AKHO. 1591-1656. Gujarati goldsmith-poet who wrote
    700 chhapas, or six-line stanzas.

AKHYANA. (In Sanskrit literature) a long historical story.

AKHYAYIKA. (In Sanskrit literature) a short story based
    on fact, tradition, or history.

AKSHAUHINI. In the Hindu army of Vedic times, a corps
    consisting of 21,870 elephants, 21,870 chariots, 65,610
    cavalry, and 109,350 foot soldiers under a maha-sena-
    pati or commander-in-chief.

ALAM SHAH II see SHAH ALAM II

ALAMGIR. Literally, Conqueror of the World. Title as-
    sumed by Aurangzeb.

ALAMGIR II. Original name: Aziz-ud-din. The 21st
    Mughal emperor (1754-59); placed on the throne by
    Wazir Ghazi-ud-din who had blinded and deposed his
    predecessor, Ahmad Shah. Alamgir was in turn mur-
    dered by the Wazir in 1759.

ALAUDDIN HUSAIN SHAH. Founder of the Husain Shahi
    dynasty of Bengal; sultan of Bengal from 1493 to 1518.
    A Sayyid of Arab descent, he is remembered as a tol-
    erant and popular king.

ALAUDDIN KHALJI. Sultan of Delhi (1296-1316). He as-
    cended the throne on the murder of his uncle and

father-in-law, Jalal-ud-din Khalji.   He carried his
arms to Cape Comorin and became the paramount ruler
of the Indian subcontinent.   He repulsed the Mongols in
1308.   His other conquests included Gujarat, Ranthambhor, Chitor, Malwa, Ujjain, Dhar, Mandu, Chanderi,
Devagiri, and Warangal.

🖎 ALBERUNI.   Original name: Abu-Rihan Muhammad.   Took
the name of Alberuni, meaning "the master."   Accompanied Sultan Mahmud of Ghazni to India and lived in
the Punjab for several years where he learned Sanskrit
and Indian philosophy.   Wrote Tahkik-i-Hind (An Inquiry
into India), a sourcebook on Indian history and culture
on the eve of Muslim invasions.

ALBUQUERQUE, AFFONSO DE.   1453-1515.   Portuguese
navigator and administrator; founder of the Portuguese
empire in the East.   On his second expedition to India
he carried secret orders from King Emmanuel to replace Almeida, Portuguese viceroy in India by whom he
was imprisoned until the grand marshal's fleet came to
his support in 1509.   He conquered Goa in 1510, Malacca and the Malabar Coast in 1512, and Ceylon, the
Sunda Islands, and Ormuz in 1515.

ALEXANDER THE GREAT.   356 B.C.-323 B.C.   King of
Macedon and conqueror of the world; invaded India in
326 B.C.   With the help of King Ambhi, king of Taxila,
he crossed the Jhelum, the Chinab, and the Ravi until
he reached the banks of the Bias or Hyphasis, the border of the Magadha Empire.   He met stiff resistance
from certain chieftains (e.g., Poros and Assakenians).
Alexander retraced his steps to the Jhelum and marched
down that river until he reached the mouth of the Indus,
subduing the many tribes of the lower Punjab and Sind
(including the Malavas, the Khudrakas, and the Brahmanas of the kingdom of Mousikanos).   Alexander left
India in 325 B.C. after a 19-month campaign.   The
Greek Empire in India did not long outlive Alexander's
death at Babylon in 323 B.C.

AL-HAJJAJ.   Governor of Iraq under the Caliphate of Walid;
dispatched the army that, under his nephew and son-in-
law, Muhammad-ibn Kasim, defeated King Dahir at the
Battle of Raor in 712 and established Muslim rule in
Sind.

ALI ADIL SHAH I. Fifth sultan of the Adil Shahi dynasty
of Bijapur, 1557-80. Took part in the destruction of
Ahmadnagar in 1558 and the destruction of Vijayanagar
in 1565.

ALIGARH. Town and district in Uttar Pradesh; seat of
Aligarh Muslim University, founded in 1875 by Sir Syed
Ahmad as the Anglo-Oriental College.

ALIGOL. Irregular foot soldiers in the Maratha army under Shivaji and his successors.

ALINAGAR, TREATY OF. Treaty in 1757 between Nawab
Siraj-ud-daulah of Bengal and the East India Company
restoring to the Company all the trading rights granted
by the imperial farman. Violation of this treaty led to
the famous Battle of Plassey and the defeat and murder
of the Nawab.

ALIVARDI KHAN. Original name: Mirza Muhammad Khan;
also known as Allahvardi Khan. Became Nawab of Bengal following the Battle of Giria, near Rajmahal, in
which he defeated Sarfaraz Khan, son of Shuja-ud-din
in 1740. He ruled for 16 years until 1756.

ALIWAL, BATTLE OF. Battle, in 1848, between the English and the Sikhs in which the latter were routed.

ALLAHABAD (also, Triveni). City in Uttar Pradesh, known   ✴
in ancient times as Prayag, on the confluence of the
Ganges and the Yamuna. It was capital of the Gupta
Empire in the fourth and fifth centuries. Two famous
monuments are found here: a pillar containing an Asokan edict and the commemorative inscription of Samudragupta. Renamed Allahabad by Akbar who built a fort
here in 1583. It was the headquarters of a Mughal
suba. It was ceded to the British in 1801.
     Allahabad is also one of the sacred cities of the
Hindus and contains the akshya-bat or the tree of im-
mortality. Every year a mela or religious fair known
as Magha mela is held here; once in 12 years it be-
comes the kumbh mela, a super festival.

ALLAHABAD, TREATY OF. Treaty in 1765 between Robert   ✴
Clive representing the East India Company and Shah
Alam II granting the Company the Diwani of Bengal,
Bihar, and Orissa in return for an annual tribute of

26 lakhs of rupees [i. e. , 2,600,000 rupees] and the districts of Kora and Allahabad.

ALL INDIA FINE ARTS AND CRAFTS SOCIETY.   Association founded in 1928 in New Delhi for the promotion of Indian fine arts and crafts. Publishes Roop Lekha.

ALL INDIA RADIO. State broadcasting agency, also known as Akashvani, under the Ministry of Information and Broadcasting.

AL-MASUDI. Arab traveler and writer who visited India in 915 and left an account of the Pratihara kingdom under King Mahipala I.

ALMEIDA, FRANCISCO DE. 1450-1510. First viceroy of the Portuguese possessions in India (1505-09); defeated the combined naval fleet of Egypt and Venice in 1509.

ALOR. Capital of Sind during Hindu rule before the Muslim conquest in 712.

ALTAMGHA. A royal grant under the seal of a native prince.

ALVAR. A group of Tamil Vaishnava poets who flourished between the seventh and ninth centuries. Of the 12 chief alvars Nammalvar is the most famous.

AMALDAR. Collector of revenue in a district especially under the Marathas.

AMARAKOSHA see AMARA SINGHA

AMARA SINGHA. Sanskrit lexicographer, poet, and grammarian of the Gupta age who flourished in the court of Vikramaditya in the seventh century; author of Amarakosha (also called Trikanda), a three-volume vocabulary in 1500 verses of Sanskrit roots arranged in meter to facilitate memorizing.

AMARAVATI. City in Guntur district in Andhra Pradesh; a center of Hindu culture under the Satavahana Kings. Famous for its school of art, architecture, and sculpture.

AMARDAS. Third Sikh Guru (1552-74).

AMARKOT see UMARKOT

AMAR SINGH. Rana of Mewar (1597-1620) who was defeated by Akbar in 1599 after a gallant resistance. He
submitted to Jahangir in 1614.

AMATYA. Title of a high official in the administration of
the Gupta Empire and later under Shivaji.

AMBEDKAR, BHIMRAO RAMJI. 1892-1956. Indian leader
of the Depressed Classes or Untouchables. He was one
of the principal framers of the Indian Constitution.

AMBHI. King of Taxila, ally of Alexander the Great, and
rival of Poros. Appointed by Alexander as the governor
of the valley of the Indus up to its confluence with the
Chinab. Overthrown by Chandragupta Maurya who lib-
erated Punjab from the Greeks.

AMBUR, BATTLE OF. Battle in 1749 between Chanda
Sahib and Nawab Anwaruddin of the Carnatic in which
the latter was defeated and killed.

AMHERST, Lord. Full name: William Pitt Amherst; official name: Earl Amherst of Arakan. 1758-1857.
Governor general of India (1823-28). His administration
was marked by the successful First Burmese War
(1824-26).

AMIL. An official under Muslim rulers with various func-
tions. Under Akbar he was a collector of revenue. In
the 18th century he was a governor in charge of the
general administration.

AMIN. A civil court official and land survey assistant in
the Mughal administration.

AMIRS OF MIRPUR. A branch of the Amirs of Sind (q. v.),
whose last amir, Muhammad, was defeated by Sir
Charles Napier at Dabo in 1843.

AMIRS OF SIND. Rulers of Sind in the last quarter of the
18th century; members of a Baluchi tribe known as Tal-
pura. Though technically under Afghan rule, the Amirs
were compelled to accept British protection through the
Treaty of 1832, renewed in 1834 and 1838. They were
also forced to pay tribute to the British Indian

government. A harsher treaty was imposed on the
Amirs in 1842, leading to war in 1843. The Amirs
were defeated in the Battles of Miani and Dabo and Sind
was annexed to the British Empire.

AMITRAGHATA. Literally, One Who Slays Enemies. Title
of Bindusara, son of Chandragupta Maurya.

AMOGHAVARSHA. Name of three kings of the Rashtrakuta
Dynasty of the Deccan. The most famous of the three
was Amoghavarsha I, who ruled from 814 to 877. He
moved his capital from Nasik to Manyakheta. Sulaiman,
the Arab traveler, described him as one of the four
great princes of the world. He was also a patron of
Jainism.

AMRITSAR. City in Punjab state; holy city of the Sikhs.
Granted to the fourth Guru Ramdas in 1577 by Emperor
Akbar. Site of the Golden Temple.

AMRITSAR, TREATY OF. (1) Treaty in 1809 between Ranjit Singh and East India Company recognizing Ranjit
Singh as king of Punjab west of the Sutlej and acknowledging British suzerainty over cis-Sutlej states.
    (2) Treaty in 1846 concluding the First Anglo-Sikh
War granting Kashmir to Golab Singh in return for ten
million rupees.

AMSAM. Part of a taluk in Malabar constituting the smallest revenue division (a unit of land under the British
administration).

ANANDAPAL. Hindu ruler of Shahiya Dynasty of Udbhanda-
pur (or Waihand or Ohind) on the Indus who organized
a league of Indian princes to repel Sultan Mahmud of
Ghazni. The allies were defeated by Mahmud in 1008.

ANANDA RANGA PILLAI. Dubash of Dupleix whose Diary
recorded, in 12 volumes, historical events in French
India.

ANANDA-TIRTHA see ¹MADHAVA

ANANDA VIKRAMA ERA. An Indian era used by the poet
Chand Bardai in his Chand-Raisa (or Prithviraj-Raisa).
It is dated from 33.

ANANGAPALA.   A king of the Tomara Dynasty, circa 11th
century, who built the Red Fort in Old Delhi.

ANANTAVARMAN CHODA GANGA.   1076-1147.   Kalinga
ruler of the Eastern Ganga Dynasty.   His dominion extended from the Ganges to the Godavari.   He built the
temple of Jagannath at Puri and the temple of the Sun-
God at Konarak in Orissa.   He was also a patron of
Sanskrit and Telugu literature.

ANARYA.   Literally, non-Aryan.   Broad term for the autochthonous people of India at the time of the Aryan
conquest of India, variously referred to as dasas (servants), rakshasas (ogres), or melechchhas (barbarians).

ANDAMAN AND NICOBAR ISLANDS.   (1) Island group in
the Bay of Bengal.   The Andaman Islands comprise five
islands known as the Great Andamans and the island of
Little Andaman.   The Nicobar Islands comprise 19
islands of which the chief are Great Nicobar, Car Nicobar, and Nancowrie.   The British occupation dates from
1850s.   From 1857 until 1947 the islands were used as
a penal settlement.   From 1942 until 1945 the islands
were under Japanese occupation.
    (2) A Union Territory in the Indian Union.   Capital:
Port Blair.

ANDAMANESE.   Family of languages spoken in the Andaman
and Nicobar Islands.   Divided into Great Andamanese
(Ba, Chari, Kora, Yeru, Juwoi, Kede, Kol, Puchikvar,
Bale, and Bea) and Little Andamanese (Onga and Yara-
va).

ANDHRA.   (1) Territory extending from the Godavari River
to the Krishna River on the eastern coast of India inhabited by predominantly Telugu-speaking people.
    (2) See SATAVAHANA.

ANDHRA HISTORICAL SOCIETY.   Learned society founded
in Rajahmundry, Andhra Pradesh, in 1922.   It maintains
a library of over 7700 palm-leaf books in Sanskrit and
Telugu and a museum of copper plates and archaeological exhibits.   Publishes Journal of Historical Research
and Histories of Telugu Dynasties.

ANDHRA PRADESH.   State of the Indian Union constituted in
1953 comprising the Telugu-speaking areas of the

former Madras state.   In 1956 the state was enlarged
by the addition of the Telingana area of the former Hyderabad state, consisting of the districts of Hyderabad,
Medak, Nizamabad, Karimnagar, Warangal, Khammam,
Nalgonda, and Mahbubnagar and parts of Adilabad,
Raichur, Gulbarga, Bidar, and Nanded districts.   Capital: Hyderabad.

ANGA.   Ancient name of East Bihar with its capital at
Champa near modern Bhagalpur on the Ganges.   It was
annexed to the kingdom of Magadha in the fifth century
B. C.

ANGAD.   Second Guru of the Sikhs (1438-52).

ANGAMI.   A hill tribe of NE India who were until recent
times head hunters.

ANGLO-AFGHAN WARS.   (1) First Anglo-Afghan War (1838-
42).   Waged by Lord Auckland and Lord Ellenborough
against Amir Dost Mohammad and his son Akbar Khan.
   (2) Second Anglo-Afghan War (1878-80).   Waged by
Lord Lytton and Lord Ripon against Sher Ali and his
sons Yakub Khan and Ayub Khan.   Concluded by a
treaty with the new Amir Abdur Rahman Khan.
   (3) Third Anglo-Afghan War (1919).   Waged against
King Amanullah.   Concluded by the Treaty of Rawalpindi.

ANGLO-INDIAN.   Indian citizen of mixed British and Indian
descent; represented as a special group in the Indian
Parliament by a nominated member.

ANHILWARA.   Principal city in Gujarat from the eighth to
the 15th century.   Now known as Patan.

ANNA.   Formerly, a monetary unit and coin worth one-
sixteenth of a rupee.

ANTHROPOLOGICAL SURVEY OF INDIA.   Department of the
government of India conducting anthropological field work
and research.   Publishes Bulletin, Memoir, and Anthropology in India.

ANWARUDDIN.   Nawab of the Carnatic (1743-49); appointed
to that post by Asaf Jha, the Nizam-ul-mulk, in 1743.
Defeated and killed in the Battle of Ambur in 1749.

APABHRAMSA.   Literally, deviation.   Vernacular languages
(i. e. , spoken by the common people) that developed between the sixth and tenth centuries.

APARAJITA PALLAVA.   Last Pallava king of Kanchi.   Defeated the Pandya king Varaguna Varman at the Battle
of Sri Purambiya in 862-63 and was himself defeated
and killed by the Chola king Aditya I.

APPA SAHIB.   Regent of Nagpur; brother of Raghuji II, the
Bhonsla Raja; entered into an alliance with the British
in 1816; joined Peshwa Baji Rao II against the British
in 1817; defeated at the Battle of Sitabaldi; spent his last
days as an exile in Jodhpur.

AQUAVIVA, Father RIDOLFO.   Jesuit missionary and
scholar at the court of Akbar (1580).

ARAM SHAH.   Sultan of Delhi (1210-11); successor of Qutb-
ud-din.   He was deposed in favor of Iltutmish.

ARANYAKA.   Class of Vedic writings attached to the Brahmanas consisting of speculative texts for meditation by
anchorites; from Sanskrit aranya, forest.

ARAVIDU.   Dynasty, also known as Karnata, founded by
Tirumala, brother of Ram Raja, following the destruction of Vijayanagar at the Battle of Talikota in 1565.
He established his capital at Penugonda.   The Aravidu
Dynasty ruled in the Deccan until 1684 restoring to some
degree the power of Vijayanagar.   The most famous
king of this line was Venkata II who transferred his
capital to Chandragiri and patronized Telugu poets and
writers.   A later ruler, also known as Venkata, granted
the site of the present-day Madras to the East India
Company.

ARCHAEOLOGICAL SURVEY OF INDIA.   Department of the
government of India founded in 1902 for conducting
archeological excavations and conserving monuments and
artifacts.

ARCOT.   Town in Tamil Nadu; capital of the Carnatic principality of Nawab Anwaruddin.   It was taken by Robert
Clive in 1751 during the Second Carnatic War and successfully defended by him against the French-backed
army of Anwaruddin.   It was finally ceded to the British
in 1801.

ARDHA MAGADHI. Semi-Magadhi Prakrit spoken in Oudh and used in Asokan pillar inscriptions. It is the language of Jain scriptures and the parent of Eastern Hindi.

ARGAON, BATTLE OF. Battle in 1803 between Bhonsla Raja of Nagpur and Arthur Wellesley during the course of the Second Maratha War in which the former was defeated.

ARHAT. A Buddhist or Jain saint who has attained nirvana in this existence through spiritual perfection. From Sanskrit arhant, deserving.

ARJAN. The fifth Sikh Guru (1581-1606), son and successor of Ramdas. Compiled the Adi Granth, the Sikh scripture. Executed by Emperor Jahangir on a treason charge for helping the rebel Prince Khusrav.

ARJUNA. One of the warrior heroes of the Mahabharata; son of King Pandu and his queen Kunti. Krishna was Arjuna's charioteer and counselor and their dialogue in the field of battle constitutes the Bhagavad-Gita.

ARTHASASTRA. Treatise on political science and administration attributed to Kautilya (or Chanakya), chief minister of Chandragupta Maurya.

ARTHAVANA see TELUGU

ARUNACHAL PRADESH. A Union Territory of the Indian Union comprising the major portion of the former North-East Frontier Agency.

ARYABHATA. Indian mathematician and astronomer; born 476. He is credited with discovering the diurnal motion of the earth and the elliptical orbits of the earth and the planets; author of Aryabhata-Tantra. He was also one of the first known users of algebra.

ARYADEVA. Buddhist author of the second century; one of the earliest exponents of Mahayana Buddhism.

ARYAN. Name used by Hindus to designate speakers of Indo-Iranian languages; also used to describe the Caucasian invaders of India in prehistoric times.

ARYA SAMAJ. Hindu social reform organization founded by
Swami Dayananda Saraswati in 1875 advocating a return
to Vedic ideals. It condemned polytheism, the use of
images, caste restrictions and child marriage. It supported widow remarriage and female education. Through
the suddhi movement it attempted to propagate Hinduism
among non-Hindus. One section of the Samaj under
Lala Hansraj favored Westernization and English education and founded the Anglo-Vedic College at Lahore for
that purpose. Another section favored the revival of
Vedic studies and founded the Gurukul in Hardwar in
1902.

ARYAVARTA. Literally, land of the Aryans. Term de-
scribing northern India between the Himalayas and the
Vindhyas; first used in the Institute of Manu.

ASAF JHA. Original name: Mir Qamar-ud-din Chin Qilich
Khan. A member of a Turani noble family who was
appointed governor of the Deccan by Emperor Farrukhsiyar in 1713, with the title of Nizam-ul-mulk. Emperor Muhammad Shah conferred upon him the title of
Asaf Jha. As the independent ruler of the Deccan he
founded the dynasty of the Nizams of Hyderabad. He
died in 1748.

ASANGA. Buddhist scholar and saint of the Gupta period in
the fourth century; author of Yogacharya Bhumi Shastra,
an important Mahayana text.

ASAWAL. Town in Gujarat in ancient and medieval times;
site of the modern city of Ahmadabad.

ASHTADHYAYI see PANINI

ASHTANGA-SAMGRAHA see VAGABHATA

ASHTAPRADHAN. The Council of Eight Ministers, an ad-
visory cabinet created by Shivaji. The eight ministers
were (1) the peshwa, or prime minister, (2) amatya,
or finance minister, (3) mantri, or chronicler, (4)
sachiva, or secretary in charge of correspondence, (5)
samanta, or foreign affairs minister, (6) senapati, or
commander-in-chief, (7) pandit rao (or dandadhyaksha),
or royal chaplain (or almoner), and (8) nyayadhisa (or
shastri), or chief justice.

ASHTI, BATTLE OF. Battle in 1818 between the East India
  Company and Peshwa Baji Rao II during the Third Anglo-
  Maratha War in which the Peshwa was defeated.

❋ ASIATIC SOCIETY OF BENGAL. Learned society for the
  promotion of Oriental studies founded in 1784 by Sir
  William Jones. Known from 1857 until 1947 as the
  Royal Asiatic Society of Bengal.

ASIRGARH. Fortress on the Tapti River in Khandesh;
  originally held by the Hindu rajas of Malwa. Later it
  passed into the hands of the sultans of Delhi from whom
  it was captured by the Faruqi Dynasty of Khandesh. It
  was taken by Akbar in 1601. For a while it belonged
  to the Sindhias but finally fell to the British after the
  Battle of Assaye.

❊ ASOKA. Full name: Asokavardhana. Third emperor of
  the Maurya Dynasty of Magadha; succeeded his father
  Bindusara in 273 B. C. In his inscriptions he is variously referred to as Devanampiya (beloved of the gods)
  or Piyadarshin (he who looks after the welfare of his
  subjects). In the 13th year of his reign, following a
  bloody war with Kalinga, he renounced all violence and
  embraced Buddhism. The next 31 years of his reign
  were devoted to the propagation of the dhamma. He
  appointed dhamma-mahamatras for propagating and ex-
  pounding Buddhism to the people. He also sent missionaries to lands and kingdoms outside his empire:
  south India, Ceylon, Burma, Syria, Egypt, Cyrene,
  Macedonia, and Epirus.
       He had the doctrines of the dhamma permanently in-
  scribed on rocks, pillars, and caves all over his
  dominions which extended from the Himalayas in the
  north to the Pennar River in the south and from Hindu-
  kush in the west to Bengal in the east. Asoka also built
  1000 stupas of which only one survives--at Bhilsa.
  According to Tibetan tradition he died at Taxila in 232
  B. C.

ASOKA CHAKRA. Wheel motif in the Lion Pillar at Sarnath;
  adopted as the national emblem of India in 1947.

ASPASIANS. Tribe who inhabited the valley of the Kunar
  River or Chitral in NW India at the time of the invasion
  of India by Alexander the Great.

ASSAKENOIS. Tribe who inhabited the Malakand Pass at the
time of the invasion of India by Alexander the Great.
Their fortress at Massaga fell to Alexander after a
fierce battle.

ASSAM. (1) Region in NE India extending along the valley
of the Brahmaputra River. It was called Pragjyotisha
in the Epics and Kamarupa in the Puranas. The modern name of Assam is derived from the Ahoms who
ruled the land for six centuries (1228-1825).
(2) State in the Union of India with capital at Dispur.

ASSAMESE. Indo-Aryan language of Assam which evolved
from Middle Sanskrit and Prachya Magadh Prakrit.

ASSAYE, BATTLE OF. Battle in 1803 between the British
Army led by Arthur Wellesley and the combined armies
of Sindhia and Bhonsla during the course of the Second
Anglo-Maratha War in which the Maratha Army was
routed.

ASUR. An Austric aboriginal tribe living in Central India;
sometimes identified with the Asuras of the Vedas.

ASURAS. Pre-Aryan race of people who inhabited India in
prehistoric times.

ASVAGHOSHA. Buddhist saint and scholar born in Magadha
sometime in the second century; spent most of his life
at the court of Kanishka, the Kushan king at Peshawar.
Among his works are the dramas, Rastrapala and Sari-
putra Prakasha; lyrics, such as Sutralankara; the epic,
Buddha-charita; and the doctrinal exposition, Awakening
of the Faith. He attended and took a leading part in the
Buddhist Council at Peshawar.

ASVALAYANA. Author of Grihya-Sutra, a treatise on the
rituals and customs of Brahminical Hindus.

ASVAMEDHA. Rite performed by a monarch to signalize
his undisputed imperium. An asva or horse belonging
to the ruler was allowed to roam the country for a
period of time and if it returned safe was sacrificed by
its master to celebrate the universal submission to his
power.

ATISHA. Original name: Chandragarbha. Buddhist monk

and scholar, born in Bengal in 981. Entered the Sangha at the age of 31; spent the next 12 years visiting Burma and Ceylon. On his return he became the head of the Vikramasila Vihara. He spent the last years of his life at the monastery of Thalong in Tibet. He is reputed to have composed more than 100 books in Tibetan and Sanskrit. In acknowledgment of his learning and piety the title Dipankara Sri Jhana, (roughly, "torchbearer of wisdom") was conferred on him.

ATMABODHA   see   ADVAITA

AUCKLAND, Lord. Full name: George Eden. 1784-1849. Governor general of India (1836-42). His administration was marked by the first Anglo-Arghan War and the annexation of Karnul.

✳ AURANGZEB. Full name: Muhyi-ud-din Muhammad Aurangzeb. 1618-1707. Ninth Mughal emperor (1659-1707). Third son of Shah Jahan; became governor of the Deccan in 1638; usurped the throne in 1658 after having murdered his two elder brothers, Dara and Shuja, and imprisoned his father and younger brother; assumed the title Alamgir (conqueror of the world); extended the Mughal empire to its furthest boundaries in the west, east, and south. The Marathas, the Jats, the Ahoms, the Sikhs, the Bundellas, the Satnamis, and the Mewaris all rose in revolt against him at one time or other. His policies alienated the non-Muslim communities while his ruinous wars sapped the financial strength of the empire. A zealous sunni he dreamed of converting his empire into a dar-ul-Islam or an Islamic state. In pursuance of this policy he reimposed the jiziya, forbade the recruitment of Hindus to public offices and destroyed their temples.

AUROBINDO GHOSH. 1872-1950. Revolutionary and spiritual leader. Ghosh began his career as an extremist and became leader of the Bengal revolutionary movement (1905-10); prosecuted in the Alipore Bomb Case; later abandoned politics and founded an ashram at Pondicherry; author of many religious and literary works including The Life Divine.

AVADANA. (In Buddhist literature) a moral tale.

AVAMUKTA. State in the Deccan mentioned in the Allahabad Pillar inscription of Samudragupta.

AVANTI. State in ancient India whose capital was Ujjain. It was one of the 16 states into which India was divided in the pre-Buddhist period and later one of the four great states. In the fourth century B. C. Chandragupta Maurya annexed Avanti to his empire.

AVATAR. An incarnation of the Supreme Being for the purpose of destroying the wicked and impious and saving the virtuous. According the Hindu tradition there have been nine avatars of Vishnu since creation and a tenth one is expected. From Sanskrit avatara, descent.

AWADHI. The literary dialect of Eastern Hindi.

AYODHYA. Ancient city on the banks of the Saraju located near modern Fyzabad. Capital of the kingdom of Koshala. It is considered one of the seven sacred Hindu cities.

AYURVEDA (also, ashtanga). Literally, life knowledge, from Sanskrit ayus, life. One of the Upavedas attributed to the sage Dhanvantari. The study of medicine and healing was known as ashtanga after the eight divisions of the subject. It included chikitsa, or medical lore.

AYURVEDA-DIPIKA see CHAKRAPANI

AZES I. Indo-Parthian prince who ruled Taxila, first as a viceroy of Mithridates and later as an independent monarch. He is considered to have instituted the Vikrama Era.

- B -

BABHAN. A Kshattriya subcaste in Bihar now primarily engaged in agriculture.

BABU. (Under the East India Company) a native clerk who writes English; often used as a term of disparagement.

BABUR. 1483-1530. The first Mughal emperor (1526-30); founder of the Mughal Dynasty; descended on his father's side from Timur or Tamarlane and on his mother's side from Chingiz [Genghis] Khan; conquered Kabul in 1504 at the age of 21; foiled in attempt to take

Samarkand and turned attention to India; defeated Sultan
Ibrahim Lodi in the First Battle of Panipat in 1526;
overwhelmed the Rajput leader Rana Sangram Singh of
Mewar at the Battle of Khanua and took the fortress of
Chanderi in 1527; effectively destroyed Afghan power in
Bengal and Bihar at the Battle of Gogra; died in 1530
before he could consolidate his victories. Babur's
Memoirs, written in Turki, is considered a delightful
work of some literary merit.

BACTRIA. In ancient geography, a region in Central Asia
between the Hindu Kush and the Oxus, nearly corresponding to the modern district of Balkh in Afghanistan.
It was part of the Seleucid Empire until 256 B. C.,
when it became independent under Euthydemos, whose
successor, Demetrios, annexed NW India and assumed
the title King of the Indians. Bactria was an intermedi-
ary between Greek and Indian civilizations and was the
center of the Indo-Greek school of sculpture known as
Gandhara.

BADAGA. (1) Telugu people who invaded Tamil country
from the Vijayanagar Empire. From Tamil vadaga,
northerner.
(2) An aboriginal tribe living in the Nilgiris Hills.

BADAJENA, BRAJNATH see ORIYA

BADAL. Rajput hero of Mewar who died in the defense of
Chitor against Alauddin Khalji.

BADAMI. City in Bijapur district known in ancient times as
Vatapi; capital of the Chalukya Dynasty founded by
Pulakeshin I in the sixth century; famous for its cave
temples.

BADAN SINGH. Founder of the Jat state comprising Agra
and Mathura districts.

BADAONI, ABDUL KADIR AL. Muslim historian; author of
Muntakhabu-t-Tawarik, an account of Akbar's reign.

BADR-I-CHACH. Muslim historian of the reign of Muhammad Tughluq.

BADRINATH. Mountain peak and village in Kumaon district
in Uttar Pradesh; site of a famous temple and center of
pilgrimage.

BADSHAH-NAMAH.   History of the reign of Aurangzeb written by Abdul Hamid.

BAGH.   Town near Gwalior in Central India noted for its
fresco paintings dating from 400 to 700.

BAGHELA.   A Rajput tribe of Gujarat who gave their name
to Baghelkhand.

BAHADUR.   Literally, hero, or champion.   Title of Mongol
origin introduced by the Mughals into India and used extensively in British India.   At the Mughal court there
were four gradations of this title: Bahadur, Bahadur
Jang, Bahadur-ud-Daulah, and Bahadur-ul-Mulk.

BAHADURPUR, BATTLE OF.   Battle in 1658 between Sulaiman, eldest son of Prince Dara Shukoh, and Prince
Shuja, second son of Shah Jahan, in which the latter
was defeated.

BAHADUR SHAH I.   Full name: Muazzam Shah Alam I.
Twelfth Mughal emperor (1707-12).   Second son of
Aurangzeb who emerged victorious in a war of succession in which his brothers Azam and Kam Baksh were
killed.   During his short reign he conciliated the Rajputs
and Marathas but ruthlessly suppressed the Sikhs.

BAHADUR SHAH II.   Full name: Muhammad Bahadur Shah.
1768-1862.   Last Mughal emperor (1837-58).   Proclaimed Emperor of India by the sepoys during the
Mutiny of 1857.   When the Mutiny was quelled the
British arrested the emperor and after a summary trial
exiled him to Rangoon where he died in 1862 at the age
of 87 years.

BAHAR.   Unit of weight used in trading transactions throughout India and the East, generally reckoned as equal to
400 lbs.   From Sanskrit bhara, weight.

BAHLOL LODI.   Founder of the Lodi Dynasty; sultan of
Delhi from 1451 to 1489.   Seized the throne on the ab-
dication of Alam Shah of the Sayyid Dynasty.   He subdued Jaunpur, Mewat, Sambhal, Rewari, and Gwalior
and managed to restore the territorial integrity of the
Delhi Sultanate.

BAHMANI.   Dynasty founded in 1347 by Hasan or Zafar

Khan, an official of the Tughluq administration. After
he seized power he assumed the title of Alauddin Bahman Shah with his capital at Gulbarga. At his death
in 1358 his realm extended from Wainganga River in the
north to Krishna River in the south and from Goa in the
west to Bhongir in the east. The Bahmani history was
marked by chronic conflicts with its Hindu neighbor,
Vijayanagar, and by internal hostility between the Sunni
and the Shia Muslims which culminated in the assassination of chief minister Muhammad Gawan in 1481. Under
the last sultan, Mahmud, the provincial governors as-
serted their independence and the kingdom broke into
five independent states: Berar, Bidar, Ahmadnagar,
Golkonda, and Bijapur. The dynasty consisted of 18
rulers:

Alauddin Hasan Bahman Shah (1347)	Ala-ud-din Ahmad II (1436)
Muhammad I (1358)	Humayun (1458)
Mujahid (1375)	Nizam (1461)
Daud (1378)	Muhammad III (1463)
Muhammad II (1378)	Mahmud (1482)
Ghiyas-ud-din (1397)	Ahmad III (1518)
Shams-ud-din (1397)	Ala-ud-din (1521)
Firuz (1397)	Wali-ullah (1522)
Ahmad I (1422)	Kalim-ullah (1525-7)

BAHRAM, MUIZZ-UD-DIN see KAITHAL, BATTLE OF

BAIGA. A Kolarian aboriginal tribe living in Central India.

BAIRAM KHAN. Guardian of Akbar appointed by Emperor
Humayun. In 1556 he was instrumental in proclaiming
Akbar emperor on the death of Humayun and later his
valor enabled Akbar to win the Second Battle of Panipat
and to recover the throne of Delhi. For the next four
years Bairam Khan acted as the regent, engaging in
successful wars with Gwalior, Ajmer, and Jaunpur.
His exercise of imperial power offended Akbar who dismissed him in 1560. Bairam thereupon led a revolt
which was soon quelled. He was pardoned by Akbar
and allowed to proceed to Mecca but was assassinated
on his way in 1561.

BAJI RAO I. The second Peshwa (1720-40); succeeded his
father Balaji Viswanath. Spurred by the vision of a
Hindu empire (Hindu-pad-Padshahi) that would supplant
the declining Mughal power he decided to carry the

Maratha arms to Delhi so that he could "strike at the
trunk of the withering tree. " He conquered Malwa in
1723 and Gujarat in 1724; defeated and killed the dissi-
dent Maratha leader Trimbak Rao Dhabade at the Battle
of Dhaboi; routed the army of the Nizam and forced him
to make peace by a treaty which left Marathas in control
of all territories between the Narmada and the Chambal.
He also took Salsette and Bassein from the Portuguese.
He finally founded the Maratha Confederacy consisting
of four loyal chieftains: Sindhia of Gwalior, Holkar of
Indore, Bhonsla of Nagpur, and Gaekwad of Baroda.
This Confederacy eventually proved to be the instrument
of Maratha disintegration.

BAJI RAO II. Eighth and last Peshwa (1796-1818). On the
     death of the Peshwa's chief minister Nana Fadnavis in
     1800 Daulat Rao Sindhia and Jaswant Rao Holkar began
     jockeying for power. Baji Rao sided with Sindhia but
     their combined army was defeated by Holkar. Baji Rao
     thereupon fled to the English at Bassein where he
     signed the Treaty of Bassein in 1802 entering into a
     subsidiary alliance with the East India Company by
     which he was given the protection of its army in return
     for territorial concessions. The Treaty of Bassein was
     denounced by the other Maratha chieftains and in the
     ensuing Anglo-Maratha War British supremacy was es-
     tablished. In 1870 Baji Rao led a revolt against the
     British. He was defeated and forced to surrender. The
     English abolished the Peshwaship and deposed Baji Rao
     who ended his days in exile in Kanpur.

BAKSHI. Title of the military paymaster-general under the
     Mughals.

BALA-CHARITA see BHASA

BALAHI. Traditional bard and genealogist of Madhya Pra-
     desh, belonging to the untouchable weaver caste.

BALAJI BAJI RAO. Third Peshwa (1740-61). Pursued the
     plans of Baji Rao I to establish Maratha hegemony in
     northern and southern India. He defeated the Nizam at
     the Battle of Udgir in 1760 and forced him to cede
     Bijapur and parts of Aurangabad and Bidar. In the
     north the Marathas overran the Doab and expelled Ab-
     dali's forces from the Punjab. But Abdali invaded India
     again and defeated the Marathas at the Battle of Barari

Ghat in 1760. The Marathas were defeated again at the Third Battle of Panipat in 1761. The defeat hastened Balaji Baji Rao's death, which took place a few months later.

BALAJI VISWANATH. First Peshwa (1713-20). Appointed Peshwa in 1713 by Raja Shahu. He made the Peshwaship the center of Maratha power. In 1714 he made a treaty with the Mughal emperor by which he agreed to pay the imperial treasury one million rupees in return for the right to collect chauth and sardeshmukhi from the six provinces of the Deccan. He thus recovered all the territories over which Shivaji's writ had run as well as Khandesh, Gondwana, Berar, and parts of Hyderabad and Karnataka.

BALARAMAYANA see RAJASEKHARA

BALASORE. Original name: Balesvara. Town in Orissa; site of one of the earliest English factories in the Bay in 1642.

BALBAN, GHIYAS-UD-DIN. Ninth sultan of the Slave Dynasty (1266-87). A Turki slave of Sultan Iltutmish who became minister when Sultan Nasir-ud-din married his daughter. He succeeded to the sultanate under the name of Ghiyas-ud-din on the death of his son-in-law in 1266. He restored peace and order to the land and proved to be one of the strongest sultans of the dynasty. He suppressed the restless Hindus of the Doab and defeated and killed Tughril Khan, the rebel governor of Bengal.

BALHARA. Title applied by Arab historians to the Rashtrakuta kings of Malkhed. Corruption of the Sanskrit term, vallabharaja.

BALI. Land tax imposed by the Maurya kings in addition to the bhaga or one-sixth of the produce.

BALLAL SENA. Ruler of the Sena Dynasty of Bengal (1158-79); credited with the destruction of the Pala Dynasty. He was also a Sanskrit scholar and is the author of at least two books extant, Danasagara and Adbhutasagara. He revived and patronized orthodox Hinduism and founded the system of elitism known as kulinism among the brahmins and kayasthas of Bengal.

BALOCHPUR, BATTLE OF. Battle in 1623 between the
armies of Jahangir and Prince Khurram in which the
latter was defeated.

BALUCHI. Native inhabitant of Baluchistan related to the Afghans and Brahoes.

BALUCHISTAN. NW region of the Indian subcontinent; part
of the Maurya empire; conquered by Akbar and annexed
to the Mughal empire in 1595; became a part of the
British Indian empire in 1843 though Quetta, the capital,
was not annexed until 1847.

BANA. Court-poet of Harshavardhana; author of Harsha
Charita, a chronicle of the reign of Harsha. He was
also the author of Kadambari, a Sanskrit classic.

BANDA. Leader of the Sikhs from 1708 to 1715. He led a
Sikh force that captured Sirhind and killed its faujdar,
Wazir Khan, the murderer of the children of Guru Govind. He brought under Sikh control the territory between the Sutlej and the Jumna and built the fort of
Lohgarh at Mukishpur. He assumed royal powers and
had coins struck in his name. In 1715 he was besieged
and captured and tortured to death by the Mughals.

BANDAR. Landing place or quay; seaport or harbor; often
used with a name as in Machili-bandar.

BANDEL. Old Portuguese settlement in Bengal about a mile
above Hooghly; site of the oldest church in Bengal.

BANDH. A nationwide or statewide paralysis of work and
business as an instrument of mass protest.

BANERJEE, W. C. 1844-1906. First president of the Indian National Congress. In 1902 he settled in England
where he died.

BANIA (or, banya). Name applied by the Europeans to Gujarati Hindu merchants and brokers and sometimes by
extension to all Hindus. From Sanskrit vanijya, trade;
Gujarati vaniyo, trader.

BANJARA. Itinerant dealers in grain and salt who followed
the armies in the Deccan with supplies and provisions.
They spoke a Marathi or Hindi patois.

BANKSHALL. (1) A warehouse. (2) Office of a harbor
   master or other port authority.

BANNERJEE, SURENDRANATH. 1848-1925. Moderate Indian nationalist leader. Twice president of Indian National Congress in 1895 and 1902; editor of the influen-
   tial The Bengalee; opposed the Partition of Bengal and
   led the successful movement that modified it.

BANSRI. Bamboo flute--in religious texts called a murali
   or venu--used according to popular mythology by
   Krishna while tending his goat herd.

BANSWARA. Rajput state on the border of Rajasthan and
   Gujarat formerly ruled by an offshoot of the Ranas of
   Udaipur.

BAPA. Founder of the Guhilot Rajput dynasty of Chitor to
   which the Ranas of Mewar belonged.

BARANI, ZIAUDDIN. Muslim historian; author of Tarikh-i-
   Firoz Shahi, an account of the reign of Firoz Shah
   Tughluq.

BARARI GHAT, BATTLE OF. Battle in 1760 between Ahmad Shah Abdali and the Maratha forces led by Dattaji
   Sindhia in which the Marathas were defeated.

BAR BARUA. Title of the administrator of upper Assam
   east of Kaliabar in Ahom times.

BARBOSA, EDOARDO. Jesuit traveler who came to India
   in 1560 and left a detailed account of Vijayanagar, Bengal, and northern India.

BARDAI, CHAND see CHAND-RAISA

BARGIR. Maratha cavalryman equipped with horses and
   arms by the state. Distinguished from silahdar.

BARGIT. Simple Vaishnavite devotional hymns in Assamese. They dealt with legends and folklore and included aphorisms and proverbs.

BAR GOHAIN. Title of a high official under the Ahom rulers of Assam. The office was by tradition hereditary
   and was held exclusively by one of 15 Ahom noble
   families.

BARHUIS. A Dravidian-speaking people in Baluchistan.

BARHUT. Place in central India, noted for Buddhist sculptures of the Sunga period.

BARID SHAHI. Dynasty founded in 1492 by Qasim Barid
that ruled Bidar until overthrown by the Sultan of Bijapur in 1619. The line consisted of eight rulers:

Qasim I (1487)	Qasim II (1586)
Amir I (1504)	Amir Barid Shah (1589)
Ali (1542)	Mirza Ali (1601)
Ibrahim (1579)	Ali Barid Shah (1609)

BARLOW, Sir GEORGE. Acting governor general of India
from 1805 to 1807. He followed a policy of noninterven-
tion in native state affairs. He quelled with great sev-
erity the Sepoy Mutiny of Vellore which occurred during
his administration.

BARODA. (1) City on the Viswamitri River in Gujarat;
capital of the Gaekwads from 1732 to 1947.
(2) State founded in 1721 by Pilaji Gaekwad, now part
of Gujarat state.

BARRACKPORE. Military cantonment and former country
seat of the governor general on the Hooghly River.
Scene of two sepoy mutinies against the British, first
in 1824 during the First Anglo-Burmese War and the
second in 1857, sometime before the Great Mutiny.

BARTOLI, F. Jesuit priest and traveler who visited India
during the time of Akbar.

BARUA. Title of any of several high officials in the administration of the Ahom kings of Assam; originally restricted to 20 persons recruited from Ahom noble families.

BARYGAZA. Classical Greek name for present day Broach;
corruption of the Sanskrit name Bhrigucachha.

BASSEIN. Port on the west coast of India near Bombay and
chief town of Thana district; part of Portuguese possessions in the 16th century; captured by the Marathas in
1770 and later ceded to the British.

BASSEIN, TREATY OF. Treaty of alliance in 1802 between

Peshwa Baji Rao II and the British under which the latter restored the Peshwa to his throne from which he had been dislodged by Jaswant Rao Holkar. The treaty also provided that the Company should station a force of six battalions in Poona for the protection of the Peshwa. In return the Peshwa agreed to pay an annual subsidy of 26 lakhs of rupees [i. e. , 2,600,000 rupees] to give up his claims to Surat, and to accept British hegemony in foreign relations.

BATTA.   Field allowance or extra pay granted to the officers of the East India Company in Bengal; stopped by Clive in 1766; restored in 1795; finally suspended during the governor generalship of Lord William Bentinck (1828-35).

BAUL.   Peripatetic rustic bard of Bengal who traveled from village to village singing devotional hymns and folk songs on small drums and one-stringed fiddles known as ektaras.

BAY.   Elliptical name for the Bay of Bengal in the records of the East India Company; applied by extension to the Company's settlements on the east coast.

BEDARA, BATTLE OF.   Battle in 1759 between the Dutch and the English in which the former were routed.

BEGARI.   Type of forced or unpaid labor or labor for token payment formerly prevalent in some parts of India.

BEGUM.   Title of Muslim ladies of rank; feminine of beg, chief or lord.

BEGUMS OF OUDH.   Mother and grandmother of Nawab Asaf-ud-daulah of Oudh who by the Treaty of Faizabad had agreed to pay a large subsidy to the British for the support of a British force of protection in Oudh.   The nawab soon fell into arrears and when the Company demanded payment he requested British help in collecting the amount from his mother and grandmother who controlled the purse strings.   Warren Hastings acceded to his request and ordered the British resident to use force against the Begums.   The Begums finally surrendered and yielded their wealth in 1782.   This incident formed one of the articles of impeachment against Hastings at the time of his trial.

BENARES see VARANASI

BENARES, TREATY OF. (1) Treaty in 1773 between Nawab
  Shuja-ud-daulah of Oudh and the East India Company by
  which he was given the districts of Kora and Allahabad
  in return for an annual subsidy of 5 million rupees.
  (2) Treaty of 1775 between Chait Singh, Raja of
  Benares, and the East India Company by which the
  former accepted the suzerainty of the Company and
  agreed to pay an annual tribute of 2.25 million rupees.

BENGAL. Region bounded by the Bay of Bengal, Orissa,
  Bihar, and Assam. East and Central Bengal was known
  as Vanga and west and NW Bengal as Gauda in Epic
  times. It was part of both Maurya and Gupta Empires.
  Pala and Sena Dynasties held sway over Bengal until the
  Muslim conquest of the 13th century. The Ilias Shahi
  and Sayyid were two of the more important Muslim
  dynasties that ruled Bengal in the middle ages.
      In 1576 Akbar annexed the kingdom to his dominions.
  In the 17th century five European nations--the Portuguese, Dutch, Danes, French, and English--established
  trading factories in Bengal. In 1740 Nawab Alivardi
  Khan threw off the yoke of Delhi and became an independent ruler. His grandson Siraj-ud-daulah was defeated by the East India Company in 1757 at the Battle
  of Plassey. In 1765 the Company was granted the
  Diwani of Bengal, Bihar, and Orissa by the Mughal
  emperor Shah Alam II. In 1773 Warren Hastings was
  appointed as governor general of Bengal with Calcutta
  as the capital.
      In 1905 Lord Curzon partitioned Bengal with West
  Bengal, Bihar, and Orissa as one province and East
  Bengal and Assam as another. The resulting agitation
  led to the annulment of the partition in 1911 but the
  state was divided again into West Bengal and East Bengal in 1947 following the partition of India. East Bengal became a part of Pakistan under the name East
  Pakistan with its provincial capital at Dacca. A separatist political movement known as Awami League led
  by Mujibur Rahman gained strength in East Pakistan in
  the 1960s and led to civil war in 1971 and the establishment of an independent nation of Bangladesh in 1972.
      See Pala and Sena for lists of rulers until 1336.
  From 1336 until its annexation by Akbar in 1576 Bengal
  was ruled by 36 kings--the first two of Eastern Bengal
  Dynasty, and the others of Western and all Bengal Dynasty:

Fakhr-ud-din Mubarak Shah (1336)
Ikhtiyar-ud-din Ghazi Shah (1346)
Ala-ud-din Ali Shah (1339)
Haji Shams-ud-din Ilyas Shah (1345)
Sikander Shah (1357)
Ghiyas-ud-din Azam Shah (1393)
Saif-ud-din Hamza Shah (1410)
Shihab-ud-din Bayazid (1412)
Ganesh of Bhaturia (1414)
Jadu or Jalal-ud-din Muhammad Shah (1414)
Danuja-mardana (1417)
Mahendra (1418)
Shams-ud-din Ahmad Shah (1431)
Nasir-ud-din Mahmud Shah (1442)
Rukn-ud-din Barbak Shah (1460)
Shams-ud-din Yusuf Shah (1474)
Sikander Shah II (1481)
Jalal-ud-din Fath Shah (1481)
Barbak the Eunuch, Sultan Shahzada (1486)
Malik Indil Firuz Shah (1486)
Nasir-ud-din Mahmud Shah II (1489)
Sidi Badr Shams-ud-din Muzaffar Shah (1490)
Sayyid Ala-ud-din Husain Shah (1493)
Nasir-ud-din Nusrat Shah (1518)
Ala-ud-din Firuz Shah (1533)
Ghiyas-ud-din Mahmud Shah (1533)
Humayun Emperor of Delhi (1538)
Sher Shah Sur (1539)
Khizr Khan (1540)
Muhammad Khan Sur (1545)
Khizr Khan Bahadur Shah (1555)
Ghiyas-ud-din Jalal Shah (1561)
Taj Khan Kararani (1564)
Sulaiman Kararani (1572)
Bayazid Khan Kararani (1572)
Daud Khan Kararani (1572)

The dynasty of the independent Nawabs of Bengal
founded by Murshid Quli Jafar Khan consisted of nine rulers:
Murshid Quli Jafar Khan (1703)
Shuja-ud-din (1727)
Sarfaraz Khan (1739)
Ali vardi Khan (1740)
Siraj-ud-daulah (1756)
Mir Jafar (1757 and 1763)
Mir Qasim (1760)
Najm-ud-daulah (1765)
Said-ud-daulah (1766)

BENGAL GAZETTE. First newspaper in India (founded
1780), published and edited by James Augustus Hicky.

BENGALI. Also called Banga-bhasa. An Indo-Aryan language descended from the ancient Magadh Prakrit. It
has two dialects: the literary speech called Sadhu-bhasa
and the colloquial speech called Colit-bhasa. The alphabet is a variety of Devanagiri.

BENI ISRAEL. Small Jewish community in Maharashtra
around Bombay, believed to be descendants of refugees
from Muslim persecution in Persia and Iraq in the 18th
and 19th centuries. They were originally oilmen by
profession and hence are called Shanwar tellis, Saturday
oilmen.

BENTINCK, Lord. Full name: William Cavendish Bentinck. 1774-1839. The last governor general of Bengal and the first governor general of India (1828-35).
He came to India as governor of Madras (1803-07) and
was appointed to succeed Lord Amherst as governor
general. His peaceful administration was marked by
far-reaching administrative and domestic reforms. He
encouraged the policy of recruiting Indians to higher
civil positions. He abolished the barbarous sati and
suppressed the Thugs. His most revolutionary reform
was his decision to introduce English as the medium of
instruction in Indian schools and colleges in 1832. He
also established the first medical college at Calcutta in
1835.

BERAR. Region in central India known as Vidarbha in ancient times. It was once part of the Maurya Empire.
Later it came under the rule of the Chalukyas from
whom it was wrested by the sultans of Delhi. It constituted one of the main provinces of the Bahmani kingdom until 1484 when it became independent under the
Imad Shahi kings. From 1574 to 1596 it was part of
the Ahmadnagar kingdom. In 1596 it was ceded to Akbar and became a suba of the Mughal Empire. It came
under Maratha sway under Peshwa Balaji Viswanath.
Bestowed on Raghuji Bhonsla as a jagir, it became
the nucleus of the Bhonsla state. Following the defeat
of the Bhonsla raja in the Second Anglo-Maratha War
Berar was assigned to the Nizam by the Treaty of
Deogaon. During this period it was known as Hyderabad
Assigned Districts. In 1902 the region reverted to the

Paramount Power and on independence became part of
the state of Madhya Pradesh.

BERNIER, FRANÇOIS. French traveler who traveled in India from 1656 to 1668 and left an account of the country under Shah Jahan and Aurangzeb. Bernier is also
remembered as court physician to Aurangzeb.

BESNAGAR. City in Malwa called Vidisa in ancient times;
important in the reign of the Sunga Dynasty. Heliod-
oros, the ambassador of the Greek king Antialkidas,
erected a monolithic column here in honor of the god
Vasudeva.

BETAL-PANCHAVIMSATI see VIDYASAGAR

BETAT. Stringed musical instrument played by plucking
strings with a mizrab or plectrum.

BHADRABAHU. Jain saint, contemporary of Chandragupta
Maurya, who introduced Jainism to south India.

BHAGA. Land tax in ancient India considered the king's
share; usually one-sixth of the produce of the land.

BHAGAT. A Vaishnavite devotee.

BHAGAVAD GITA. The sixth book of the Mahabharata, assigned by scholars to the fourth century; a dramatic
poem in the form of a dialogue between Arjuna and
Krishna on the field of battle at Kurukshetra. Its
philosophy is eclectic, combining elements of the
Sankhya, Yoga, and Vedanta systems with the later
theory of bhakti.

BHAGAVATA PURANA. Epic poem in the Puranas of 18,000
verses attributed to the grammarian Vopadeva who
flourished in the 13th century.

BHAGAVATAS. Hindu sect that practiced bhakti or total
devotion to Vishnu and therefore also known as Vaishnavas. The doctrines of this sect were propagated by
a number of acharyas, or teachers, of whom Sri
Chaitanya and Ramanuja were the most famous.

BHAGAVATI-SUTRA see AJIVIKAS

BHAGAWAN DAS. Raja of Amber who entered the service
of Akbar and rose to be a general. He was also a
Hindi poet of note.

BHAJAN. Song of devotional love accompanied by drums
and strings; called kirtan in Bengal.

BHAKTA MALA see NABHADAS

BHAMATI see ADVAITA

BHANA. (In Sanskrit drama) monologue with mime.

BHANDARI. A Maharashtrian class of toddy tappers.

BHANDARKAR ORIENTAL RESEARCH INSTITUTE. Institu-
tion founded in Poona in 1917 for the promotion of
Indological studies. Publishes Annals of the Bhandarkar
Oriental Research Institute, Bhandarkar Oriental Series,
Bombay Sanskrit and Prakrit Series, critical editions of
Mahabharata and Harivamisa, and other books. It also
sponsors the All-India Oriental Conference.

BHANGI. Member of a low Panchama class employed as
sweepers in north India.

BHANUMATI see CHAKRAPANI

BHAR. An aboriginal tribe in Rajasthan who became Rajputs through intermarriage.

BHARAT. Full form: Bharatavarsha. Literally, the land
of the descendants of the sage Bharata. Term
applied to the Indian subcontinent in Hindu traditions;
alternative official name for India in the Indian Constitution.

BHARATA. Semilegendary author of a treatise on drama,
music, and dance entitled Natya-Sastra, who flourished
between 100 and 300. The name is believed to be an
acronym derived from the first syllables of bhava
(emotion), raga (melody), and tala (rhythm).

BHARATA ITIHASA SAMSHODHAKA MANDAL. Learned
society founded in 1910 in Poona for collecting, conserving, and publishing historical materials. Its collection includes 5200 coins, 27,500 Persian, Sanskrit, and

Marathi manuscripts, 1,500,000 documents, 1200 paint-
ings, 1000 copperplates and other antiquarian objects.
Publishes Journal, the Sviya Granthamala series, and
Puraskrita Granthamala.

BHARATA NATYAM. Modern form of South Indian dance
which originated as a temple dance; hence also called
devadasi attam, dance of the courtesans. It combines
mime, rhythm, and gesture.

BHARATITIRTHA see ADVAITA

BHARATIYA VIDYA BHAVAN. Institution founded in Bombay
in 1938 by K. M. Munshi to conserve, develop, and
diffuse Indian culture. It publishes Bharatiya Vidya,
Samvid, Bhavan's Journal, Bharati, Samarpan, History
and Culture of the Indian People in 11 volumes, the
Singhi Jain series, and the Bharatiya Vidya series.

BHARATPUR. Town and kingdom founded during the early
18th century by the Jat leader Badan Singh. He and
his successor Suraj Mal extended their dominion over
the districts of Agra, Dholpur, Mainpuri, Hathras,
Aligarh, Etawah, Gurgaon, and Mathura. During this
time the famous fort was built in the town. In 1826
the British subdued the kingdom and placed their protégé
on the throne.

BHARAT RATNA. Highest civil award of honor in the Indian
Union.

BHARAVI. Author of Kiratarjuniya, a Sanskrit maha kavya
in 18 cantos based on an episode in the Mahabharata.

BHARGAS. Pre-Mauryan hill people who lived in the region
of Sumsumara Hill.

BHARI. The East India Company's Arcot rupee worth 3 1/2
per cent less than the sicca rupee.

BHARTRIDAMAN. The last great satrap of Ujjain, who
ruled from 289 to 295. During the closing years of his
reign his kingdom was invaded by the Sassanians, of a
dynasty of Persian kings who ruled from 226 until 641.

BHARTRIHARI. Sanskrit poet, grammarian, and philosopher
who lived in the seventh century. The Bhattikavya is
sometimes attributed to him.

BHASA.   Sanskrit dramatist of the fourth century; author of
Bala-charita and, possibly, of Mrichchhakatika.   His
dramas show traces of Greek influence.

BHASHYA.   (In Sanskrit literature) a commentary on a classic work.

BHASKARACHARYA.   Indian astronomer and mathematician;
born 1114 at Bijapur; author of Siddhanta Siromani, a
treatise in verse on arithmetic and logic.

BHASKARAVARMAN.   King of Kamarupa in the seventh century; a contemporary of Harshavardhana.   He received
the Chinese traveler Hiuen Tsang who has left an account of his kingdom.

BHAT.   Member of a tribe of Rajasthani bards.   They
usually accompanied travelers and guaranteed them
security against thieves.

BHATARKA see MAITRAKA

BHATTA.   Bearer of great wisdom; title of a religious
teacher, generally combined with another title, as in
Bhattacharya, or with another name, as in Kumarilab-
hatta.

BHATTI.   A Rajput tribe of Jaisalmer.

BHATTIKAVYA.   An artificial epic poem by Bhatti celebrating the exploits of Rama and illustrating Sanskrit grammar by the employment of all possible forms of con-
structions.   Sometimes attributed to Bhartrihari (q. v.).

BHAVABHUTI.   Sanskrit dramatist and court poet of king
Yasovarman of Kanauj in the eighth century; author of
Uttaracharita, Mahaviracharita, and Malatimadhava.

BHAVE, VINOBA see BHOODAN

BHIKSHU.   Male mendicant.   A female bhikshu is known as
a bhikshuni and the alms given to a bhikshu is known as
bhiksha.   From Pali bhikku.

BHIL.   A Kolarian aboriginal tribe of west central India
noted for their skill as archers and horsemen.   They
were known as Nishadas in Vedic times.

BHILI. Dravidian language belonging to the Gondi group
spoken in central India.

BHILLAMA see YADAVA

BHIMASENA (also, Bhima). Pandava prince of enormous
physical strength and voracious appetite whose exploits
are related in the Mahabharata.

BHIMSEN. Hindu historian; author of Nushka-i-Dilkusha, a
record of the reign of Aurangzeb written in Persian.

BHITPALO see PALA SCHOOL; DHIMAN

BHOGA. Tribe mentioned in the Buddhist traditions as a
member of the Vrijian confederacy based at Vaisali from
the fifth century B. C. to the fourth century A. D.

BHOI. Dynasty founded by Govinda that ruled Orissa from
1542 to 1559. So called because Govinda belonged to
the Bhoi or writer caste.

BHOJA. (1) A royal appellation designating a consecrated
monarch. (2) A tribe that inhabited Bihar in Asokan
times.

BHOJA I. Original name: Mihira. Gurjara-Pratihara king
of Kanauj in the ninth century. His empire extended
from the Himalayas to the Narmada and from Bengal
to the Sutlej.

BHOJPURI. One of the three dialects of Bihari.

BHONSLA. Dynasty of Maratha rulers of Nagpur founded
about 1730 by Raghuji Bhonsla. Raghuji was related to
Raja Shahu and the Bhonslas bore the same surname
as Shavji's descendants. The line consisted of eight
rulers:
Shivaji I (1674)	Shahu (1708)
Shambuji (1680)	Ram Raja (1749)
Rajaram (1689)	Shahu (1777)
Tara Bai (1700)	Pratap Singh (1810)

BHOODAN. A movement launched by Acharya Vinoba Bhave
in the 1950s for redistributing land by gifts of individual
holdings to village groups and landless peasants.

BHOPAL. (1) State in central India; fief carved out of the
    kingdom of Rani Durgavati of Gondwana and placed under
    a Nawab by Akbar; became independent in 1761 but later
    submitted to the British Raj.
    (2) Town in central India; capital of the former state
    of Bhopal and the modern state of Madhya Pradesh.

BHOTIYA. A member of an ethnic group in the Himalayan
    states.

BHRIGU. Sage who, according to tradition, compiled the
    Manava-Dharma-Shastra or the Institutes of Manu.

BHRIGU-KACHHA. Pre-Mauryan port on the west coast of
    India; corresponds to modern Broach.

BHUBANESWAR. City in Eastern India; capital of the state
    of Orissa. It was the capital of the Kesari kings of
    Orissa from the fifth to the tenth century. It is believed
    that 7000 shrines once surrounded its sacred lake.
    Famed for the Lingaraja and Rajarani temples built in
    the seventh century.

BHUIYAS. Petty landlords in Bengal and Assam who wielded
    semi-independent powers. They were suppressed by
    Akbar in Bengal and by King Nara Narayan in Assam
    in the 16th century.

BHUKTI. Administrative province of the Gupta Empire un-
    der an uparika. A bhukti was divided into vishayas or
    mandalas.

BHUMAKA. Founder of the Kshaharata Dynasty of the first
    century with its capital at Nasik.

BHUTAN. State in eastern Himalayas bounded by Tibet,
    Sikkim, and India. Name derived from Bhotanta, which
    means "End of Bhot [Tibet]." Bhotiyas form the racial
    majority. The form of government from the middle of
    the 16th century until 1907 consisted of a dual govern-
    ment by the Deb Raja (secular head) and Dharma Raja
    (spiritual head). Since 1907 the country has been ruled
    by a maharaja with the title of Druk Gyalpo. District
    administration is based on dzongs or forts.
    The majority of the people are Mahayana Buddhists
    of the Druk Kargue or "Red hat" sect. Tashi-Cho
    Dzong, the chief monastery, contains over 1000 monks.

Bibigarh 40

The official language is Dzongkha, which is related to
Tibetan. The capital is at Thimphu. Under the terms
of the treaties of 1774, 1910, and 1949, Bhutan is
recognized as an independent feudatory state subject only
to the government of India in its foreign relations.

BIBIGARH. Building in Kanpur; site of the massacre of 211
British women and children during the Sepoy Mutiny on
the orders of Nana Sahib and Tantia Topi.

BIDAR. City in the Deccan; conquered by Alauddin Khalji
and later annexed to the Delhi Sultanate. Part of the
Bahmani kingdom from 1347 to 1492 and its capital
from the reign of Sultan Ahmad Shah. Became independent under the Barid Shahis, who ruled from 1492
until 1619 when it was overrun by Bijapur.

BIDRI. Type of ornamental metalwork made in the Deccan;
so called from the town of Bidar where it was formerly
made. The basic material in bidri is pewter alloyed
with one-fourth copper which is then damascened with
patterns in silver with the pewter ground blackened.

BIGHA. Unit of land measurement varying in different parts
of India but generally 3025 square yards or 5/8 of an
acre. Divided into pukka ("full" or "complete") bigha
and kutcha ("rough" or "approximate") bigha.

BIHAR. (1) Region bounded by Uttar Pradesh, Bengal,
Orissa, and the Himalayas. Known as Magadha until
the 12th century when the invading Muslims adopted the
present name, derived from vihara, monastery. Bihar
was a suba in Akbar's time. It was annexed to the
suba of Bengal under Murshid Quli Jafar Khan and
passed under the Company's rule in 1765. In 1911 it
was constituted as a separate province.
(2) State in the Union of India with capital at Patna.

BIHARI. Regional form of Hindi spoken in Bihar with three
branches: Bhojpuri, Magadhi, and Maithili.

BIHARILAL. 1603-1663. Hindi poet born in Jaipur. His
Satsai and shorter poems are famous in Hindi literature.

BIHAR RESEARCH SOCIETY. Learned society founded in
Patna in 1915 for the promotion of historical studies and
research. Publishes a Journal.

BIJAPUR. (1) City in Maharashtra; former capital of the
sultanate of Bijapur. Its architectural monuments include the famous jumma masjid, the Gagan Mahal
(audience hall), and the mausoleums of Ibrahim II and
Muhammad.
(2) Sultanate of Deccan founded by Yusuf Adil Shah
in 1489. From 1347 until 1489 it formed part of the
Bahmani Empire. Bijapur allied with Vijayanagar to
defeat and sack Ahmadnagar in 1558 and seven years
later combined with Bidar, Ahmadnagar, and Golkonda
to defeat Vijayanagar at the Battle of Talikota. The
kingdom surrendered independence to Aurangzeb in 1686.
The Adil Shahis were patrons of art, architecture, and
literature. The Muslim historian Muhammad Qasim,
surnamed Firishta, flourished under Sultan Ibrahim II.

BIJJALA KALACHURYA. The founder, who reigned from
1156 to 1167, of the Kalachurya Dynasty of Kalyani;
remembered as a patron of Jainism.

BIKANER. (1) Town in Rajasthan.
(2) Former state in Rajputana founded by the Rathor
chief Bika; part of the Mughal Empire from 1570 to 1818
when it became a protected state under the Company.

BILABANDI. Account of the revenue settlement of a district
specifying the name of the mahal or estate, the name of
the owner, and the amount of the rent.

BILHANA. Kashmiri court-poet of the Chalukya king Vikramaditya VI of Kalyani; author of Vikramaditya-charita.

BIMBISARA (also, Srenika). King of Magadha who belonged
to either the Saisunaga or Haryanka Dynasty; contemporary of Gautama Buddha; ascended the throne c546 B. C.;
extended the Magadha dominion by annexing Anga (East
Bihar); established a new capital at Rajagriha, the
present-day Rajgir.

BIN. Snake charmer's gourd.

BINDUSARA. Second Maurya emperor and father of Asoka
(300-273 B. C.). He assumed the title of Amitraghata,
or One Who Slays Enemies.

BIRBAL, Raja. Rajput general and poet at the court of Akbar; bore the title of Kavi Priya; died in a Mughal foray
against the Yusufi tribe in NW India.

BIRHOR. A Kolarian aboriginal tribe living in Chota Nagpur.

BISHAN DAS. Noted Hindu painter at the court of Jahangir.

BISNAGA. Name by which Vijayanagar was known to the Portuguese.

BISWA SINGH. Founder in 1515 of the Koch kingdom, whose capital was the modern Cooch Behar.

BITHUR. Town in Uttar Pradesh where Nana Sahib proclaimed himself Peshwa on the outbreak of the Sepoy Mutiny in 1857.

BITIKCHI. Title of the financial superintendent of a suba.

BITTIGA see HOYSALA

✱ BLACK HOLE OF CALCUTTA. Garrison strongroom measuring 18' x 14' 10" in Fort Williams in Calcutta where probably about 40 English prisoners were confined in 1756 on the orders of Nawab Siraj-ud-daulah. The next morning probably about 15 were dead of suffocation. These figures of imprisoned and dead are the result of modern scholarship and stand in contrast to the long-purported figures of 123 dead of 146 confined based on probably unreliable and probably chauvinistically-motivated reports of one survivor, writing many years after the event.

BLACK TOWN. (In Anglo-Indian usage) the city of Madras as distinguished from the English settlement and Fort St. George.

BOARD OF CONTROL. Board established by the Pitt's India Act of 1784 to "superintend, direct, and control all acts relating to the civil or military government or revenues of India." Commercial matters were outside its purview. The board consisted of six privy councilors plus the president, who had a casting vote. Henry Dundas was the first president and Lord Ellenborough the last. In 1858 with the transfer of power to the Crown the Board of Control was abolished and its powers were assumed by the Council of the Secretary of State for India.

BOARD OF REVENUE. Administrative body set up by

Warren Hastings in 1772 when the East India Company
was granted the Diwani of Bengal, Bihar, and Orissa.
It was primarily concerned with revenue settlement and
collection of taxes. Lord Cornwallis appointed Sir John
Shore as the first president of the Board of Revenue.

BOARD OF TRADE.   Agency of the East India Company devoted to the supervision of trade and commerce.   It was
abolished in 1833.

BODH-GAYA.   Buddhist holy place six miles south of modern Gaya in Bihar where Gautama Buddha received enlightenment under a Bo-tree; site of a Buddhist monastery in ancient times.   The Bo-tree was dug up and
destroyed by Sasanka, the Hindu king of Gauda, to
signify his hatred of Buddhism.

BODHISATTVA (also, boddhisattva).   (In Mahayana Buddhism)
an arhat (saint) who has attained nirvana in this life or
is considered likely to become, in a future incarnation,
a Buddha.

BODO.   Language spoken by an Assamese tribe of upper
Assam called Chutiya.

BOLAN PASS.   Historic pass connecting Sind with Afghanistan.

BOMBAY.   (1) City in western India; capital of the state of
Maharashtra; also known as Gateway of India.   It was a
Portuguese possession from 1510 to 1661, when it was
ceded to Charles II as part of the dowry of Princess
Catharine of Braganza.   In 1668 Charles II transferred
the place to the East India Company for an annual rent
of ten pounds.   Under Governor Gerald Aungier (1669-
1677) Bombay developed into a prosperous town and
soon supplanted Surat as the principal settlement of the
English on the west coast and later became capital of
the Bombay Presidency.   With the opening of the Suez
Canal in 1869 it became the first port of call for ships
coming from Europe.
    (2) Former presidency and state which at one time
included modern Maharashtra, Gujarat, and Sind.

BOPADEVA (also, Vopadeva).   Sanskrit grammarian who
flourished under the Yadavas of Devagiri; author of
Mugdhabodha.

BORA (or, Bohra).   A Muslim community of traders and
peasants in Maharashtra and Gujarat belonging to both
the Shia and Sunni sects.   The Shia Boras are believed
to be of foreign descent while the Sunni Boras are descendants of Hindu converts.

BOSE, SUBHAS CHANDRA.   1897-1945.   Indian and Bengali
nationalist leader.   Twice president of the Indian National Congress and spokesman of its extremist section
--known as the Forward Bloc--which advocated violent
means to expel the British; imprisoned 11 times; fled
India in 1941 during World War II and secured German
and Japanese support for an Indian Provisional Government called Azad Hind; organized the Indian National
Army in Singapore in 1943 and led a military campaign
against British India; died in an air accident in 1945.

BRAHMA.   Major Hindu deity considered as the creator of
the universe; also called Vidhatri (ordainer) or Prajapati (lord of creatures).   Along with Siva and Vishnu
he constitutes the Hindu trinity.

BRAHMAGUPTA.   c598-c660.   Hindu mathematician and
astronomer; author of the Ahargana, translated into
Arabic as Arkand.

BRAHMAN.   The Universal Soul or the Absolute that according to the Upanishads and the Vedanta dwells in
every living thing and guides every being.   Also called
Paramatman.

BRAHMANAS.   Prose texts containing directions on sacrificial rites.   The principal Brahmanas are: Aitareya
and Kausitaki in Rig Veda, Tandya and Jaiminiya in
Sama Veda, Tattiriya and Satapatha in Yajur Veda and
Gopatha in Atharva Veda.

BRAHMAPALA.   Founder of the Pala Dynasty of Kamarupa
that ruled Assam from about 1000 to 1200.

BRAHMAPURANA.   One of the 18 Puranas so called because
it was revealed by Brahma to Daksha.   This Purana
is sometimes placed first and hence called Adipurana.

BRAHMAPUTRA.   Also Matsang, Tamchok, Tsangpo (in
Tibetan); Dihang or Dihong (in Assamese); Dyardanes,
Oedanes (in classical Greek).   River that rises near

Lake Manasarowar in Tibet and flows through Assam
and Bangladesh into the Bay of Bengal. Its junction
with the Ganges and the Meghna is sometimes called the
Padma.

BRAHMARSHI-DESHA. Literally, the land of the sages.
(In Manu's works) region including Thaneswar, Mathura,
eastern Rajasthan, and the doab between the Ganges and
the Jamuna.

BRAHMA SABHA. A monotheistic Hindu society founded by
Raja Ram Mohan Roy in Calcutta in 1828. It stood for
the abolition of caste and image worship. After the
departure of Ram Mohan Roy for England the Sabha was
directed by Maharshi Devendranath Tagore, whose strict-
er interpretation of Vedic orthodoxy led to various
schisms.

BRAHMA SAMAJ. Schismatic movement that had its roots
in the Brahma Sabha, a society of theistic reformers
who advocated monotheism, the abolition of caste, and
the emancipation of women. In course of time this
movement was divided into three branches: Adi Brahma
Samaj under Maharshi Devendranath Tagore, which
represented the orthodox group; the Nava Vidhana under
Keshab Chandra Sen, which represented the radical
group; and the Sadharan Brahma Samaj. In Maharashtra the movement spread under the name Prarthana
Samaj.

BRAHMI. Ancient Indian script from which current Indian
alphabets are derived. According to tradition Brahmi
is derived from the hieroglyphs of Mohenjo-Daro and
Harappa.

BRAHMIN. One of the four Hindu castes created from the
mouth of Purusha so that they may instruct mankind.
Strictly speaking, every Brahmin is a descendant of the
seven or eight patriarchs, or rishis, who are called
gotrakaras, or family (tribe, clan)-makers. His duties
include the performance of sacrificial rites and the
teaching of the Vedas and among his privileges were
archa (veneration), dana (gifts), ajeyata (freedom from
oppression), and avadhyata (immunity from capital pun-
ishment). There are 1800 subdivisions of the Brahmin
caste, including the Panchagauda or the five classes of
the White Brahmins of north India, and the

Panchadravida, or the five classes of the dark-skinned Brahmins of the south.   See also TOL.

BRAHMINISM.   Hinduism as practiced in pre-Buddhist times.

BRAHUI.   Dravidian language spoken in Baluchistan.

BRAJBHASA.   A variety of Hindi popularized by the disciples of Vallabhacharya (q. v.).

BRAJBHUMI.   Region of the Yamuna Valley including the Hindu sacred cities of Mathura and Vrindaban.

BRIHADRATHA.   Founder of the first dynasty of Mauryan kings who ruled Magadha until the sixth century B. C.

✶ BRIHASPATI.   Ancient India lawgiver of the Gupta age; author of Brihaspati Smriti.

BRIHATKATHA.   The "Great Narration," a collection, no longer extant, of Sanskrit tales by Gunadhya, of uncertain date but of the 1st or 2nd century A. D.   Somadeva's Kathasaritsagara and Kshemendra Vyasadasa's Brihat-kathamanjari are derived from this classic.

BRIHAT-SAMHITA.   Literally, the Great Collection.   An astrological work by Varahamihira of the sixth century, who also wrote Hora-Sastra.

BRINDAVAN DAS   see   CHAITANYA

BUCKINGHAM, JOHN SILK   see   CALCUTTA JOURNAL

BUDDHA, GAUTAMA.   Also called Siddhartha (He Who Has Accomplished His Purpose); Sakya-Muni (Sage of the Sakyas); Tathagata (He Who Has Arrived at the Truth). c563 B. C. -c483 B. C.   Founder of Buddhism.   Born in a princely Sakya family at Kapilavastu in the Tarai in Uttar Pradesh.   Married at the age of 16.   At the age of 29 he renounced his life of luxury and became a wandering monk to find out a way of escape from the sufferings of disease, old age, and death.   He spent the next six years studying philosophy and practicing austerities.   One day enlightenment (buddhi) came to him as he sat under a Bo-tree near Bodh-Gaya on the bank of the Nairanjana.   Henceforth he was known as Buddha

or the Enlightened One. He delivered his first sermon
at the Deer Park in Sarnath where he gained his first
five disciples. He spent the next forty-five years
preaching and converting thousands to the new faith and
organizing the Sangha or Buddhist Order. His parinirvana or death occurred at the age of 80 at Kusinagara,
identified with Kasia in Gorakhpur district. The dates
of his birth and death have not been exactly determined.
According to tradition he died in 483 B. C.

BUDDHISM. Religion founded by Gautama Buddha. It is
based on the Four Noble Truths and the Noble Eightfold
Path. The Four Noble Truths are: (1) There is suffering in life, (2) This suffering has a cause, (3) Suffering
must be caused to cease, and (4) Suffering can cease if
one knows the right way. Buddhism holds that suffering
is caused by desire or tanha (thirst) and that the extinction of desire will cause the cessation of existence
through endless rebirth. The Noble Eightfold Path or
the Middle Path consists of (1) right beliefs, (2) right
aims, (3) right speech, (4) right conduct, (5) right
means of livelihood, (6) right endeavor, (7) right mind-
fulness, including self-mastery and self-knowledge, and
(8) right meditation. The highest goal of Buddhism is
nirvana. It affirms the Hindu concepts of karma and
rebirth but denies the existence of a soul or god and
the efficacy of prayers and sacrifices. It has no priest-
hood and claims that any one who follows the Four Noble
Truths and Noble Eightfold Path can become a bodhisattva. Centuries after the death of Buddha, Asoka sent
missionaries to many countries outside India eventually
making Buddhism a world religion. But it never struck
deep roots in the land of its birth.

BUDDHIST COUNCILS. First Council at Rajagriha was attended by the theras or elders, including Mahakassapa,
who presided. It is believed to have been held soon
after Buddha's death. Three of Buddha's disciples--
Kasyapa, Ananda, and Upali--put in writing Buddha's
teachings.
        Second Council was held at Vaisali sometime in the
fourth century.
        Third Council was held in the reign of Asoka and was
presided over by monk Tissa Moggaliputta. The Council
drew up the Tripitaka, the Buddhist canon.
        Fourth Council was held at Peshawar in the reign of
Kanishka.

BUDGROOK. A low-denomination coin current at Goa and the west coast in the 16th and 17th centuries, particularly in Portuguese India, worth 1/840 of a cruzado.

BUKKA I. Cofounder with his brother Harihara I of the city of Vijayanagar in 1336. Ruled Vijayanagar from 1354 to 1377.

BULWAND DARWAZA. Literally, lofty portal. Triumphal arch built by Akbar in 1575-76 at Fatehpur Sikri to commemorate the conquest of Gujarat.

BUNDELKHAND. Region between the Yamuna on the north and the Vindhyas on the south; named after the Bundellas who established a state here in the 14th century. From the 9th to the 14th centuries it was known as Jijhoti or Jejakabhukti and was ruled by the Chandellas. It is now part of Madhya Pradesh.

BUNDELLAS. Warlike Rajput clan who inhabited the region known as Bundelkhand in the 14th century. They were subdued by Akbar but under their leader, Chhatrasal, became independent again in the reign of Aurangzeb.

BUNDI. Rajput state which was under the control of the Mughals and later the Holkars. It was a protected native state under the British until 1947; now part of Rajasthan.

BURANJIES. Official records of the Ahom kings of Assam written in both the Ahom language and in Assamese.

BURHA GOHAIN. Title of a hereditary officer under the Ahom kings of Assam.

BURHAN-I-MAASIR. Historical chronicle of the Bahmani sultans written by Sayyid Ali Taba-taba, a court historian in the service of Burhan Nizam Shah II, sultan of Ahmadnagar (1591-1595).

BURUSHASKI. Language spoken in NW India unrelated to any known language family.

BUSSY, Marquis de. Full name: Charles Joseph Patissier. French general. Adviser to Nizam Salabat Jang who assigned him the revenues of Northern Circars in return for his services. He was recalled on the outbreak of

the Third Anglo-French War and taken prisoner by the
English at the Battle of Wandiwash in 1760.   He was
later released and sent back to France.

BUTLER REPORT.   Report submitted in 1929 by the Indian   ✶
States Committee under the presidency of Sir Harcourt
Butler on the relationship between the Paramount Power
and the native states.

BUXAR, BATTLE OF.   Battle in 1764 between the forces of
the East India Company under Major Hector Munro and
the combined armies of Emperor Shah Alam II, Nawab
Shuja-ud-daulah, and Nawab Mir Qasim, in which the
latter armies were defeated.

- C -

CABRAL, ANTONIO.   Portuguese envoy at the court of Akbar; negotiated a treaty of peace in 1573.

CACHAR.   District in Assam with headquarters at Silchar;
a protected state under the Ahoms; annexed to the British dominions in 1830 on the death of the last reigning
raja, Govinda Chandra.

CALCUTTA.   City on the Hooghly River; capital of West   ✶
Bengal; former capital of Bengal Presidency and Indian
Empire.   Founded by Job Charnock, agent of the East
India Company, in 1690.   The original factory at Sutanati was expanded eight years later through the acquisition of three adjacent villages: Sutanati, Kalikata, and
Govindapur and the settlement came to be known as Calcutta, an anglicized form of Kalikata.   In 1700 it became the seat of the Bengal Presidency and in 1716 Fort
William was completed.   In 1772 Calcutta became the
capital of British possessions in India and remained so
until 1912.

CALCUTTA JOURNAL.   One of the earliest English period-
ical publications in India, founded in 1818 and printed
and published by John Silk Buckingham.

CALICUT see KOZHIKODE

CANARA (also, Kanara).   Region and district in Karnataka
north of Malabar and south of Goa.   Usually divided into
North Canara and South Canara.

K. R. CAMA ORIENTAL INSTITUTE. Founded in 1916 in
Bombay for the promotion of Indological studies. Publishes a Journal.

CAMBAY. Original name: Khambavati, or City of the Pillar. Seaport at the head of the Gulf of Cambay, capital
of a former native state and of a former kingdom in the
fifth century.

CAMPBELL, Sir COLIN. Later, Lord Clyde. Commander-
in-chief of the British forces that suppressed the Sepoy
Mutiny.

CANDY. Unit of weight in South India, approximately 500
lbs.

CANNING, Earl of. Full name: Charles John Canning.
1812-62. Governor general of India (1856-62) and Viceroy of India (1858-62). His administration was marked
by the outbreak and suppression of the Sepoy Mutiny and
the transfer of power from the Company to the Crown.
His many reforms include: introduction of a paper currency and income tax; enactment of the Indian Penal
Code in 1860 and the Criminal Procedure Code in 1861;
and replacement of the adalats with high courts in Bombay, Madras, and Calcutta. He passed the Rent Act
giving greater security to tenants and corrected abuses
in the European indigo plantations. The Indian Councils
Act of 1861 was also passed during his viceroyalty. In
1857 he founded the three major universities at Calcutta,
Bombay, and Madras. His leniency toward the sepoy
rebels earned him the nickname of Clemency Canning.

CAPE COMORIN. The land's end of the Indian subcontinent.
From Tamil, Kumari, a goddess to whom a temple is
dedicated here.

CARERI, GEMELLI. Italian traveler who visited India during the reign of Aurangzeb.

CAREY, WILLIAM. 1761-1834. English missionary and
scholar. Came to Bengal in 1793 and settled at Serampore. Translated the Bible into Bengali and published
two Bengali journals. He was the author of grammars
of Marathi, Sanskrit, Punjabi, and Telugu and dictionaries of Marathi and Bengali. His works in Bengali include Kathopakathan.

CARNATIC.   The plains below the Eastern Ghats in penin-
    sular India; former kingdom ruled by the Nawabs of Ar-
    cot.   From Tamil, kar nadu, black country.

CARNATIC WARS.   Wars between the French and the Eng-
    lish for supremacy in the Carnatic.
        First Carnatic War (1746-48).   Madras was captured
    by the French who defeated the forces of Nawab Anwar-
    ud-din.   Ended by the Treaty of Aix-la-Chapelle in
    1748, which restored Madras to the English.
        Second Carnatic War (1751-54).   Unofficial war be-
    tween Dupleix and the East India Company marked by
    early French successes.   The French-backed Chanda
    Sahib became the Nawab and drove his rival, Muhammad
    Ali, the ally of the English, to Tiruchirapally to seek
    refuge in the fort.   In Hyderabad Dupleix's protégé
    Muzaffar Jang became the Nizam with the help of the
    French.   In 1751 Muzaffar Jang was killed but was suc-
    ceeded by another French puppet, Salabat Jang.   To
    relieve Muhammad Ali in Tiruchirapally Captain Robert
    Clive of the Company's army adopted a brilliant diver-
    sionary tactic.   He attacked Arcot, Chanda Sahib's
    capital, with an army of only 500 soldiers.   Chanda
    Sahib thereupon dispatched a large part of his force to
    recapture Arcot.   Clive withstood the siege for 53 days
    and with the help of reinforcements defeated the Nawab.
    The fortunes of war had turned in favor of the British.
    Dupleix was recalled to France in 1754 and peace was
    restored between the two nations.
        Third Carnatic War (1756-63).   Followed the Seven
    Years' War in Europe.   Count de Lally, the French
    governor of Pondicherry, captured Fort St. David but
    failed in his attempt to take Madras.   An English army
    under Sir Eyre Coote captured Northern Circars and
    defeated the French at the Battle of Wandiwash.   Pondi-
    cherry was besieged and forced to surrender in 1761.

CARON, FRANÇOIS.   Founder of the first French factory
    in India, in 1667, at Surat.

CASTE.   Quadruple social hierarchy established by the law-
    giver Manu dividing Hindu society into four classes:
    Brahmins (priests), Kshattriyas (warriors), Vaisyas
    (traders), and Sudras (menials), each with its own rigid
    code of dharma, usage, and caste marks.   The first
    three castes are known as dvija or twice-born because
    they are regarded as born again through the ritual of

tying a sacred thread, while the Sudras are known as
Panchamas.   Caste was based according to some scholars on jata or race.   There are about 3000 castes in
India within the chatur varna or the four-caste system
and nearly 25,000 subcastes.   In rare cases caste may
be lost or one may move to a higher caste through
merit.   Outside Hinduism caste is sometimes found
among Muslims and Sikhs; Musalis are lowcaste Muslims
and Mazhabis are lowcaste Sikhs.

CASTE MARK.   A mark (tilaka) on the forehead, chest, or
arms with white, red, or yellow pigment, sindura (red
lead), sandal wood paste, or ashes, which signifies
one's caste.   There are also various sect marks used
by the Vaishnavites and Saivites.

CATAMARAN.   A raft formed of three or four logs lashed
together.   From Tamil kattu maram, bind wood.

CAUVERY.   River in Tamil Nadu flowing into the Bay of
Bengal.   Length, 475 miles.

CEDED DISTRICTS.   Territory in Andhra south of the
Tungabhadra River ceded to the Company by the Nizam
in 1800.   It included the districts of Bellary, Cuddapah,
Kurnool, and part of Kistna.

CENTRAL PROVINCES.   Former province in British India
containing four divisions: Nagpur, Jabalpur, Narbada,
and Chhattisgarh.   Berar became a part of the province
in 1903.   Name changed to Madhya Pradesh in 1950.

CHACH.   Founder of a dynasty of Hindu kings in Sind in the
seventh century.

CHAHAMANA   see   CHAUHAN (1)

CHAIN OF JUSTICE.   A chain of 60 bells set up by Emperor
Jahangir in Agra, near the fort, which could be shaken
by any subject to bring grievances to the Emperor's
notice.

CHAITANYA.   1485-1527.   Founder of Vaishnavism in Bengal.   He renounced secular life at the age of 24 and for
the next 20 years preached the cult of bhakti to all ir-
respective of caste or creed.   His followers came to
regard him as Krishna incarnate.   His life and teachings

are described in several biographies, the most impor-
tant of which are Chaitanya Bhagavata by Brindavan
Das, Chaitanya-Charitamrita by Krishnadas Kaviraj, and
Chaitanya Mangal by Jayananda.

CHAIT SINGH. Raja of Benares. By the Treaty of Benares,
     1775, he placed himself under the suzerainty of the
     Company, agreeing to pay an annual tribute of 22 1/2
     lakhs of rupees [i. e. , 2,500,000 rupees].   Further
     exactions were levied on the raja and when in 1780 he
     was unable to meet them in full Hastings marched to
     Benares and occupied that city.   Chait Singh fled to
     Gwalior and Hastings bestowed the principality on his
     nephew in return for an annual tribute of 40 lakhs of
     rupees.   Hastings' treatment of Chait Singh was one of
     the articles of impeachment against him at the time of
     his trial.

CHAITYA.   Originally a funeral mound or tumulus.   Later
     a Buddhist sanctuary for monks and still later a horse-
     shoe-shaped rock-cut Buddhist temple.   The temple
     may be circular or semicircular with a stupa, or statue
     of Buddha, at the apsidal end.   A typical chaitya was a
     long hall with a rounded apse divided by a row of pillars
     into a broad nave and two side aisles.   Light was ad-
     mitted by a sun-window in the center of the archway
     over the entrance.

CHAKKS.   Ruling tribe of Kashmir from 1555 to 1586.

CHAKLA.   A large division of a suba introduced by Shah
     Jahan.

CHAKRA.   (1) Disk or circle representing the sun, the cy-
     cle of seasons, or power.
           (2) A sharp, disk-shaped weapon used by the Sikhs
     for throwing.

CHAKRAPANI.   11th-century Sanskrit writer on medicine;
     author of Ayurveda-Dipika, Bhanumati, and Chikitsa-
     Samgraha.

CHAKRAVARTIN.   Literally, wheel mover, or ruler of all
     regions over which chariot wheels traversed.   Title
     assumed by Hindu emperors.

CHALANI.   Current rupee of account in which the East India

Company's accounts were kept.   116 chalani rupees
were equal to 100 sicca rupees.

CHALUKYA.   Dynasty of South Indian kings established in
the middle of the sixth century by Pulakeshin I with
Vatapi as his capital.   They were also known as Solankis and are presumed to be Rajputs in origin.   This
dynasty known as Early Chalukyas ruled from 550 to
753 with a short interregnum of 13 years from 642 to
655.   At the time of king Pulakeshin II the Chalukya
Empire extended from the Narmada River in the north
to Kaveri River in the south.   The last king in this line
was Kirttivarman II who was overthrown by the Rashtrakuta king Dantidurga in 753.

The Early Chalukyas consisted of nine kings:

Pulakeshin I (550)	Vinayaditya (680)
Kirttivarman I (566)	Vijayaditya (696)
Mangalesha (597)	Vikramaditya II (733)
Pulakeshin II (609)	Kirttivarman II (746)
Vikramaditya I (655)	

In 973 Taila or Tailapa overthrew the Rashtrakuta king
Kakka II and founded a new Chalukya Dynasty with Kalyani as his capital.   This line ruled until 1200.   Their
rule was marked by intermittent wars with the Chola
kings of Tanjore or Thanjavur.   Somesvara I inflicted a
severe defeat on the Chola king Rajadhiraja at the Battle
of Koppam.   Vikramaditya VI, also known as Vikramanka, captured Kanchi but Chalukya power declined after
his death.   In the 13th century the Chalukya dominions
were carved up by the Yadavas of Devagiri and Hoysalas
of Dvarasamudra.

The Chalukyas of Kalyani consisted of 12 kings:

Taila II or Tailapa (973)	Someshvara II (1068)
Satyashraya (997)	Vikramaditya VI (1076)
Vikramaditya V (1008)	Someshvara III (1127)
Ayyana (1014)	Jagadekamalla II (1138)
Jayasimha or Jagade-	Taila III (1151)
kamalla (1015)	Someshvara IV (1184)
Someshvara I (1042)	

CHALUKYA OF VENGI (also, Eastern Chalukya).   An offshoot of the Chalukyas of Vatapi.   Founded by Kubja
Vishnuvardhana, a brother of king Pulakeshin II, in 615,
when he became independent ruler of Vengi, with capital
at Pishtapura, the modern Pithapuram.   Rajendra III,
the last king of this line, was born of a Chola princess
and he married the daughter of the Chola king Rajendra

IV.   He thus united the two kingdoms and established the
new dynasty of Chalukya-Chola.

CHALUKYA-CHOLA.   Dynasty founded in 1070 by Rajendra
III, surnamed Kulottunga Chola, the 28th king of the
Chalukya Dynasty of Vengi who united the Eastern
Chalukya and Chola crowns through inheritance and mar-
riage.   This dynasty ruled until 1527.

CHAMBER OF PRINCES.   A consultative organization of Indian native states set up in 1921 to implement a recom-
mendation of the Montague-Chelmsford Report.

CHAMBIALI.   A Western Pahari dialect spoken in the old
Chamba state.

CHAMPA.   Capital of the ancient kingdom of Anga on the
confluence of the Champa River and the Ganges.

CHAMPU.   (In Sanskrit literature) a composition in mixed
prose and verse.

CHAMU.   In the Hindu army of Vedic times, a division commanded by a chamu-natha (general), consisting of 729
elephants, 2187 cavalry, and 3645 infantry soldiers.

CHANAKYA   see   KAUTILYA

CHANDA SAHIB.   Son-in-law of Nawab Dost Ali of the Carnatic who proclaimed himself nawab after defeating and
killing Nawab Anwaruddin with the help of the French.
He was subsequently defeated in battle by Robert Clive.

CHANDELLA.   (1) Rajput clan believed to have descended
from the aboriginal Gonds, or Bhars, but which later
assumed the kshattriya caste.   Their land, known as
Jejakabhukti, corresponds to Bundelkhand in Madhya
Pradesh.   They are famous for their architecture, of
which the prime example is found at Khajuraho.
    (2) Dynasty founded in the ninth century by Nannuka
Chandella by displacing the Pratihara chieftains and
gaining control of south Jejajabhukti or modern Bundelkhand.   The seventh king of this line, Yasovarman,
who captured the fortress of Kalanjar, was the first
truly independent king.   The Chandellas were in power
until the 14th century.

CHANDERNAGORE. Town in West Bengal; assigned by
    Nawab Shaista Khan to the French in 1674; site of a
    factory established by the French East India Company
    in 1690-92.   Captured by Robert Clive in 1757 and re-
    stored to the French in 1763.   Remained in French
    hands until 1950, when it was merged with the Indian
    Union.

CHANDIGARH.   A Union Territory of the Indian Union com-
    prising the city of Chandigarh and a 26-sq. km. area
    around it.

CHANDRADEVA.   Founder of the Gahadvala Dynasty of Kan-
    auj in the 11th century.   The dynasty remained in power
    until the 13th century.

CHANDRAGUPTA I.   Founder in 320 of the Gupta Dynasty;
    a minor king of Magadha who extended his territories
    by conquest and by marriage to the Lichchhavi princess
    Kumara Devi.   He established his capital at Pataliputra
    and assumed the title Maharajadhiraja.

CHANDRAGUPTA II.   Third Gupta emperor (c375-c413); son
    and successor of Samudragupta.   He conquered Malwa,
    Gujarat, Kathiawar, and Ujjain and annexed them to the
    Gupta Empire.   Assumed the title of Vikramaditya.
    Believed to be the patron of Kalidasa, the great Sanskrit
    poet.

CHANDRAGUPTA MAURYA.   Founder of the Maurya Dynas-
    ty.   According to Buddhist tradition he was born to the
    Moriyas, a kshatriya clan of Pippalivana.   He began
    his career as the leader of a band of robbers.   He
    overthrew the last king of the Nanda Dynasty and crowned
    himself as ruler of Magadha with the help of a wily
    Brahmin named Kautilya (or Chanakya).   Between 324
    and 321 B. C. he wiped out the Greek dominions in India.
    With a large army of nearly 30,000 cavalry, 9000 ele-
    phants, 600,000 infantry, and hundreds of chariots, he
    conquered all of India north of the Narmada River.
    Seleucus invaded his empire but was defeated and forced
    to conclude a humiliating peace, ceding all his posses-
    sions in Punjab and NW India.
        Within the course of 18 years Chandragupta Maurya
    built up one of the largest empires of his time.   He is
    believed to have abdicated about 298 B. C. and to have
    committed suicide about 286 B. C.   Arthasastra by

Kautilya and Indica by the Greek ambassador, Megasthenes, describe his career and rule.

CHAND RAISA (or, Prithviraja Raso). Hindi epic by Chand
    Bardai, court-poet of Prithviraj, the Chauhan king of
    Delhi and Ajmer.

CHANDRAS. Petty chieftains who ruled Eastern Bengal af-
    ter the decline of the Palas in the 11th century.

CHANDWAR, BATTLE OF. Battle in 1194 between Shihab-
    ud-din Muhammad Ghori and Jayachandra, Raja of
    Benares and Kanauj, in which the raja was defeated.

CHANNADAM. Travel guides in Malabar who escorted tra-
    velers from one place to another guaranteeing their
    security with their own lives.

CHARAKA. Hindu physician and writer on medicine of the
    second century.

CHARAN. Hereditary court bard of Gujarat who belonged
    to the Brahmin caste.

CHARANDAS. 1703-82. Bani poet and disciple of Kabir
    who founded the sect of Charandasis in Delhi.

CHARITA. (In Sanskrit literature) biography of a ruler or
    saint, such as Harshacharita or Vikramankadevacharita.

CHARKHA. The spinning wheel, used as a symbol of the
    Indian National Congress; used to emphasize the impor-
    tance of cottage industries and swadeshi goods.

CHAR MINAR. Tower in Hyderabad City so called because
    it had four towers (char = four; minar = towers).

CHARNOCK, JOB. Founder of Calcutta; arrived in India
    from England between 1655 and 1656, as a servant of
    the East India Company. In 1690 he secured the grant
    of the tract of land on which Calcutta now stands. He
    died in 1693.

CHARTER ACTS. 1813: Act of British Parliament throwing
    open the Indian trade to all British citizens. 1833:
    Act of British Parliament divesting the East India Com-
    pany of its trading privileges. 1853: Act of British

Parliament introducing open competition based on merit for entry into the Indian Civil Service.

CHARVAKA. Indian philosopher who was a major exponent of the lokayata or materialist school of philosophy, which denied the existence of a soul.

CHARYA. Short lyrical Bengali song embodying the tenets of the Buddhist Sahajiya sect; popular from the 10th to the 12th century.

CHASTHANA. Founder of the dynasty of Great Satraps of Malwa in the first century.

CHATTERJI, BANKIM CHANDRA. 1834-94. Bengali novelist; author of the nationalist anthem Bande Mataram; founder of the Bengali journal, Bangadarsan.

CHATUR-ANGA. In the Hindu army of Vedic times, a platoon consisting of one elephant, one chariot, three soldiers on horseback, and five foot soldiers.

CHATURVARGACHINTAMANI see HEMADRI

CHATURVEDI. Title bestowed on a Vedic scholar who is versed in all the four Vedas.

CHAUHAN (1) (also, Chahamana). An agnikula Rajput tribe or clan claiming origin from a firepit in Mount Abu in Rajasthan; believed by historians to be Hinduized foreign immigrants, such as the White Huns, who invaded India during the fifth and sixth centuries.
    (2) Dynasty of rulers of Sambhar (Sakambhari) in Rajasthan with Ajmer as their capital. This dynasty came to an end with the defeat and death of its last king Prithviraj II in the Second Battle of Tarain in 1192.
    (3) Dynasty of rulers of Malwa that succeeded the Tomaras. They were overthrown by Muslim invaders in 1401.

CHAUK. Open place or wide street in the middle of a city where the bazar is held. The most famous example is the Chandni Chauk of Old Delhi.

CHAUKIDAR. Rural policeman also employed for watch and ward in smaller towns.

CHAUNSA, BATTLE OF.   Battle in 1539 between Emperor
Humayun and Sher Shah Sur in which Humayun was defeated and forced to flee.

CHAUTH.   Forced levy equal to one fourth of the revenue
assessment; first collected by Raja of Ramnagar and
regularly levied by Shivaji and his successors.

CHEDI.   Region between the Yamuna (or, Jumna) and the
Narmada, one of the 16 great states, or mahajanapadas,
of Buddhist times.   It was under the Kalachuri Dynasty
from 1015 to 1070.

CHEDI ERA (or, Traikutaka Kalachuri Era).   Hindu era
dated from 248.

CHELA.   A pupil, especially a novice studying with a Buddhist teacher.

CHELMSFORD, Viscount.   Full name: Frederick John
Napier Thesiger.   1868-1933.   Viceroy and governor
general of India (1916-1921).   Coauthor with Edwin
Montague, secretary of state for India, of the Montague-
Chelmsford Report on Indian Constitutional Reforms on
which the Government of India Act of 1919 was based.
His administration was marked by great civil unrest.

CHENNAIPATTINAM.   Tamil name for Madras city.

CHERA.   Dynasty that ruled Malabar in the middle ages.

CHERAMAN PERUMAL   see   PERUMAL

CHERO.   A Kolarian aboriginal tribe who claim Rajput descent.

CHERUMAN.   A Panchama class of South Canara and Malabar related to the Tamil Paraiyans.

CHERUSSERI   see   MALAYALAM

CHETTY (also, shetti).   Member of a trading class in South
India.

CHHATRAPATI.   Imperial title assumed by Shivaji on his
coronation in 1674, and continued by his successors.

CHHATRASAL. Founder of the independent Hindu principality of Bundelkhand in 1671 with its capital at Panna.

CHHAU. An all-male dance in honor of Siva popular in
Orissa; so called from the chhaus or masks worn by
the actors. Variations of this dance include the Tanda-
va, a fierce war dance, Mayura, a peacock dance, and
Sabara, a hunter's dance.

CHIKITSA-SAMGRAHA see CHAKRAPANI

CHILLIANWALLA, BATTLE OF. Battle in 1849 between
the Sikhs and the British in which both sides lost heav-
ily.

CHINSURA. Dutch settlement in Bengal established in 1653.
It remained under Dutch control until 1825 when it was
exchanged for English settlements in Sumatra.

CHITOR. Fort and capital of the Ranas of Mewar. It fell
thrice to Muslim invaders, first to Alauddin Khalji in
1303, second to Sultan Bahadur Shah of Gujarat in 1534,
and finally to Akbar in 1568. Akbar removed the gates
of the fortress. The walls were rebuilt by Rana Jagat
Singh but Shah Jahan razed it in 1654.

CHITRAL. Valley dividing Afghanistan and Pakistan; placed
in 1893 inside the Indian border by the Durand Line.
The so-called Chitral campaign of 1895 was directed at
subduing the fierce tribes that inhabited this valley.

CHITTAGONG. (1) District in Bangladesh ceded to Aurangzeb in 1666 by the king of Arakan; passed under the
control of the Nawabs of Bengal; granted to the East
India Company in 1760 by Nawab Mir Qasim.
(2) Town in Bangladesh, also known as Islamabad;
capital of Chittagong district.

CHOGYAL. Title of the former ruler of Sikkim.

CHOLAS. Tamil-speaking people who inhabited Cholamanda-
lam or the land of the Cholas which extended along the
Coromandel coast from Nellore to Pudukottai. The first
historical king of the Cholas was Karikkal whose dynasty
disappeared from history after a brief rule in the first
century. When they reappeared in the seventh century
the Cholas were subject to the Pallava paramountcy.

But with the defeat of the Pallavas by the Chalukya
king Vikramaditya in 740 and the sack of their capital
Kanchi the Cholas reasserted themselves. Parantaka I
overthrew the Pallava power, captured Madurai, the
Pandya capital, and founded the Chola Dynasty with
capital at Thanjavur. The tenth king of this line Rajaraja I became the paramount sovereign of South India
and Ceylon. He also built the great temple at Thanjavur. His son Rajendra I conquered territories beyond
the sea: Pegu, Martaban, and Andaman and Nicobar
Islands and led an expedition to north India. For carrying his arms to the bank of the Ganges he took the
title of Gangaikonda. The throne eventually passed to
Rajendra Kulottunga I who founded the dynasty of
Chalukya-Cholas. His successors ruled for more than
four centuries until the kingdom was absorbed by Vijayanagar.

The Chola Dynasty consisted of 24 kings:

Vijayalaya (846)	Rajendradeva II (1052)
Aditya I (871)	Rajamahendra (1060)
Parantaka I (907)	Virarajendra (1063)
Rajaditya I (947)	Adhirajendra (1067)
Gandaraditya (949)	Rajendra III (1070)
Arinjaya (956)	Vikrama Chola (1118)
Parantaka II (956)	Kulottunga Chola II (1133)
Aditya II (956)	Rajaraja II (1146)
Madhurantaka Uttama (969)	Rajadhiraja II (1163)
Rajaraja (985)	Kulottunga III (1178)
Rajendra I (1012)	Rajaraja III (1216)
Rajadhiraja I (1044)	Rajendra IV (1246)

CHOUK   see   CHAUK

CHOULTRY.   Hall or shed used by travelers in South India
as a resting place.

CHOWDHRY.   (1) Headman of a village or craft guild
through whom supplies and workmen are obtained for
public purposes.
(2) Landowner next in rank to a zamindar; district
revenue officer in Orissa.

CHUNGAM.   Toll or customs duties levied in Malabar.

CHURAMAN SINGH.   Jat military hero who led the Jats in
revolt against the Mughals after the death of Emperor
Aurangzeb with his center of operations at Mathura.

He committed suicide in 1721 after the capture of his
stronghold, Thun, by Sawai Man Singh.

CHUTIYA. Assamese tribe of upper Assam speaking a language called Bodo.

CHUTU. Dynasty that ruled the Satavahana Empire with
capital at Vanavasi in the third century.

CIVIL DISOBEDIENCE MOVEMENT. Begun by Mahatma
Gandhi in 1930 to paralyze the British Raj by breaking
civil laws and thus force it to grant complete independence to India. Gandhi himself marched from his
Sabarmati Ashram to Dandi to break the Salt Act by distill-
ing salt. The movement was renewed in 1932 and 1940.

CIVILIAN. Member of the Indian Civil Service.

CIVIL SERVICE see INDIAN CIVIL SERVICE

CLIVE, ROBERT. 1725-1774. British soldier and empire
builder. Clive came to India as a young boy. He
gained fame during the Second Carnatic War (1751-54)
when he planned and directed the capture of Arcot and
the defeat of Chanda Sahib. By this one stroke he established British predominance in the Carnatic. In
1756 he was placed in command of an expedition against
Siraj-ud-daulah. Within the next two years he elimi-
nated the Dutch power at Chinsura; defeated and killed
Nawab Siraj-ud-daulah at the Battle of Plassey; installed
the Company's protégé, Mir Jafar, as the Nawab of
Bengal; obtained the zamindari of 24 Parganas; and
wrested Northern Circars from the French.
     In 1758 he was appointed governor of Bengal but fail-
ing health forced him to leave for England in 1760 where
he was created Baron Clive of Plassey. He returned to
India as governor and commander in chief soon after the
Battle of Buxar and obtained the Diwani of Bengal,
Bihar, and Orissa from Emperor Shah Alam II. Clive
also instituted reforms in the civil and military administration.
     He returned to England in 1767 where he was sub-
jected to attack for the corruption and venality of his
acts. A Parliamentary motion condemned his illegal
acquisition of vast wealth but acknowledged his services
to England. He died by his own hand in 1774.

COCHIN.   Port and former native state on the Malabar
coast; now part of Kerala.   It was settled by the Portuguese in 1503 and was held by the Dutch from 1663
to 1796.

COLBERT   see   FRENCH EAST INDIA COMPANY

COLIT-BHASA   see   BENGALI

COLLECTOR.   Official entrusted with the administration of
a district in India; post first created in 1772; also
sometimes vested with magisterial powers.

COMATY.   Member of a trading class in Andhra Pradesh
corresponding to the Chetty in Tamil Nadu.   From
Sanskrit go-mushti, eye-fist, a reference to their vigilant
habits.

COMMISSIONER.   Official in charge of a division comprising several districts; post first created in 1829.

COMMUNAL REPRESENTATION.   Special legislative representation accorded to such various religious and racial
minorities as Muslims, Anglo-Indians, and scheduled
castes and tribes; embodied in the Communal Award of
1932.

"COMPANY JOHN"   see   "JOHN COMPANY"

COMPETITION-WALA.   Member of the Indian Civil Service selected through a qualifying competitive examination.   The term was popularized by G. O. Trevelyan,
author of Letters of a Competition-wala.

CONSTITUTION OF INDIA.   Constitution passed by the Indian Constituent Assembly on November 26, 1949, by
which India became a sovereign democratic republic on
January 26, 1950.   Under the Constitution India is a
Union of States comprising (in 1976) 22 states administered by governors and 10 Union Territories administered
by the President through an administrator.   The head of
the Union is the rashtrapati who is elected by an elec-
toral college consisting of all the elected members of
parliament and of the state legislative assemblies.
      The parliament consists of Rajya Sabha, or Council
of States, and the Lok Sabha, or House of the People.
The Rajya Sabha consists of not more than 250 members

elected indirectly of whom one third retire every second
year. The Lok Sabha consists of not more than 500
members directly elected for a period of five years.

The state legislatures of Andhra Pradesh, Jammu
and Kashmir, Madhya Pradesh, Tamil Nadu, Maharashtra, Karnataka, Punjab, Uttar Pradesh, and West Bengal consist of two houses and in other states, one.

The various subjects of legislation are enumerated in
three lists in the seventh schedule to the Constitution.
The Union list consists of 97 subjects (including defense, foreign affairs, communications, currency, and
customs); the State list consists of 66 subjects (including police, agriculture, education, public health, and
local government); the Concurrent list consists of 47
subjects (including planning and labor). Two chapters
of the Constitution deal with fundamental rights and Di-
rective Principles of State Policy. It also provides
that the official language of the Union shall be Hindi in
the Devanagiri script, with English as an associate official language until 1965.

CONTI, NICCOLO DE. Italian traveler who visited south India in 1420 and left an account of the kingdom of Vijayanagar.

CONVENTION OF WADGAON. Treaty in 1779 in the course
of the First Maratha War between an English force led
by Col. James Cockburn and a Maratha army following
an English reverse at Telegaon. Its terms included the
surrender by the British of all territories acquired by
the English since 1773. The convention was later repudiated by the governor general.

COOCH BEHAR (also, Kuch Behar). Town and district in
West Bengal; former native state. The name is derived
from the Koches, a tribe that lived in the territory.
The state was founded by a Koch chief named Biswa
Singh in the 16th century. It became a feudatory of the
Mughal Empire under Akbar and in 1772 it accepted the
suzerainty of the British.

COORG. District in Karnataka; former native state and chief
commissionership with capital at Mercara. In medieval
times it formed part of the Ganga, Chola, Hoysala, and
Vijayanagar Empires. It was a protected native state
until 1834 when the last ruler was deposed for misgov-
ernment and the territory became a chief commissionership. Known for its gold mines.

COOTE, Sir EYRE. 1726-1783. British commander who led the British forces in a decisive victory over the French at Wandiwash in 1760 and thus assured British supremacy in the Northern Circars.

CORNWALLIS, Marquis CHARLES. 1738-1805. Governor general and commander in chief of India (1786-93; 1805). His administration was marked by the annexation of the territories ceded by Tipu Sultan by the Treaty of Seringapatam at the conclusion of the Third Mysore War and by the introduction of far-reaching domestic reforms. By the Cornwallis Code, Bengal was divided into a number of districts and each district was placed under the charge of a collector assisted by a district magistrate and a district superintendent of police. Each district was divided into a number of thanas under the supervision of a darogha. The Sadr Nizamat Adalat was created to administer criminal justice and was presided over by the governor general in council. Four provincial courts of appeal were established at Calcutta, Patna, Dacca, and Murshidabad in addition to four courts of circuit. All the district officers above the darogha were to be exclusively recruited from among Englishmen. Cornwallis also introduced the Permanent Settlement of land revenue by which zamindars were assigned land in perpetuity in return for a guaranteed payment of taxes.

COSMAS INDICOPLEUSTES. Egyptian monk and traveler in India in the sixth century; author of Topographia Christiana, a record of his travels from 535-547.

COTTON, Sir HENRY JOHN STEDMAN. 1845-1915. Member of the Indian Civil Service; chief commissioner of Assam (1896-1902); president of the Indian National Congress (1904).

COUNCIL OF STATE. Upper house of the bicameral legislature established by the Government of India Act of 1919. Now the Rajya Sabha.

COURT OF DIRECTORS. Governing body, of 24 members, of the East India Company, elected annually by the Court of Proprietors, who controlled the commercial affairs and the administration of the Company's territories in India.

COVENANTED CIVIL SERVICE see INDIAN CIVIL SER-
VICE

CRANGANORE. Ancient city and port of Malabar now in
ruins; identified with the Muziris of Pliny; capital of
the Perumal Dynasty of Kerala; site of the earliest
Jewish and Christian settlements and of one of the seven
churches founded by St. Thomas. It was already in
decay when the Portuguese arrived. They eventually
established themselves there with a strong fort in 1523
which the Dutch took in 1662. The fort was destroyed
by Tipu Sultan's troops in 1790.

CRIMINAL CASTES AND TRIBES. Aboriginal tribes that
hereditarily engage in criminal activities: for example,
Sansiya in Rajasthan and Korava in Tamil Nadu.

CRORE. The number 10,000,000 (or, 100 lakhs).

✳ CROWN REPRESENTATIVE. Title and office created by the
Government of India Act of 1935 to replace that of viceroy. The last two were Earl Wavell (1943) and Viscount Mountbatten (1947).

CUDDALORE. Town in Tamil Nadu; site of the English settlement of Fort St. David (1682).

CUNNINGHAM, Sir ALEXANDER. 1814-93. First archaeological surveyor to the government of India; authority
on Indian numismatics and ancient Indian history; author
of Book of Indian Eras.

CURZON, GEORGE NATHANIEL, Marquess of Kedleston.
1859-1905. Viceroy and governor general of India (1899-
1905). His administration was marked by the inauguration of the Northwest Frontier Province, the victorious
Waziri campaign, the victorious Tibet campaign, the
Partition of Bengal, the Coronation Durbar of 1902,
and such measures as Official Secrets Act, the Indian
Mines Act, the Ancient Monuments Preservation Act,
and the Cooperative Credit Societies Act. He resigned
in 1905 following differences with the commander in
chief, Lord Kitchener.

CUTCHERRY. An administrative office or court house.

CUTTACK. Town in Orissa on the Mahanadi River; former
capital of Orissa province.

- D -

DABO, BATTLE OF.   Battle in 1843 between the Company
forces under Sir Charles Napier and the Amir of Mirpur, Sind, in which the Amir was defeated.

DADHABHAI NAOROJI.   1825-1917.   Parsi businessman and
nationalist leader; thrice president of Indian National
Congress (1886, 1893, 1906); first Indian to be elected
to the British House of Commons on a Liberal ticket.

DADRA AND NAGAR HAVELI.   A Union Territory of the
Indian Union constituted in 1961 with headquarters at
Silvassa.

DADU.   1544-1603.   Hindu mystic and teacher; follower of
Kabir.   Dadu founded a Hindu sect with Muslim overtones and his followers are known as Dadupanthis.   His
doctrines are set out in Bani or oracles consisting of
5000 poems and aphorisms.

DAFLAS.   Tribe in NE India in Darang district in Assam.

DAGOBA.   Receptacle of sacred relics or ashes in a Buddhist stupa.   From Sanskrit dhatu-garbha, relic-recep-
tacle.

DAHIR, King   see   AL-HAJJAJ

DAK.   Properly, transport by relays of men and horses and,
by extension, mail so transmitted.

DAK BUNGALOW.   Rest house for travelers maintained by
the state.

DALA'IL-I FIRUZ SHAHI.   Translation in Persian verse of
Sanskrit books found in the temple of Jwalamukhi in
Nagarkot by A'aaz-ud-din Khalid Khani, court-poet of
Sultan Firuz Shah Tughluq.

DALAVA.   Title of the commander in chief of a South Indian
army, in the 17th-19th centuries.   From Sanskrit dala,
army, and vah, to lead.

DALHOUSIE, Lord.   Full name: James Andrew Broun Ram-
say.   1812-60.   Governor general of India (1848-56).
Extended British territory by annexing Punjab and Oudh;

formulated the Doctrine of Lapse and applied it to annex
Satara, Jaitpur, Sambalpur, Jhansi, and Nagpur; established the public works department; built railways and
a system and post and telegraph offices; opened the
Ganges Canal; and improved the civil service by opening
it to all natural-born British subjects (i. e. , native Indians).

DALPATRAM.   1820-98.   Gujarati poet, satirist, and social reformer.

DALWAI.   Title of the chief minister of former Mysore
state.

DAM.   Copper coin in the time of Akbar equal to 1/40 of
a rupee; divided into 25 jetals.

DAMAJI GAEKWAD.   Founder of the house of Gaekwad of
Baroda and member of the Maratha Confederacy.

DAMRU (or, damaru).   Small, double-sided, narrow-waisted
drum.

DANASAGARA   see   BALLAL SENA

DANAVAS.   Non-Aryan people who inhabited northern India
in prehistoric times.

DANDA.   A unit of length in ancient India equivalent to six
feet.

DANDANAYAKA.   Commander in chief of Vijayanagar Empire.   Title.

[1]DANDIN.   An ascetic who carries a staff.

[2]DANDIN.   Sanskrit poet and critic of the sixth century;
author of Kavyadarsa and Dasakumaracharita and, possibly, of Mrichchhakatika.

DANDY.   A type of litter used in the Himalaya region consisting of a strong cloth slung like a hammock between
two bamboo staffs carried by two or more men.

DANGUR.   A collective name for the hill tribes of Chota
Nagpur.

DANISH EAST INDIA COMPANY. Founded in 1618; dissolved in 1634; reorganized in 1670; established the first factory in Tranquebar in 1620; a settlement in Serampore followed in 1755; finally dissolved in 1729 when its possessions were ceded to the Crown of Denmark.

DANTIDURGA (also, Dantivarman). Founder of the Rashtrakuta Dynasty in the eighth century who overthrew the Chalukyas of Vatapi.

DARA SHUKOH. Eldest and favorite son of Shah Jahan defeated by Aurangzeb in the war of succession in three battles at Dharmat, Samugarh, and Deorai. Captured and brought to Delhi as a criminal and beheaded.

DARGAH. Shrine of a Muslim saint regarded as a place of congregation and prayer.

DARJEELING. Town and hill station in West Bengal in the eastern Himalaya region. Elevation, 7500 feet. It was purchased by the East India Company from the Raja of Sikkim in 1835. The name is derived from Dorje-glin, or land of Dorje, the ritual scepter of the lamas.

DAROGA. Title of Mongol origin applied in earlier times to the governor of a province or city and later to the head of a department in a native state and still later to the head of a police or excise station.

DARSHAN. Spiritual experience or blessing conferred by the sight of a great personality or teacher.

DARU see KUCHIPUDI

DAS, CHITTARANJAN. 1870-1925. Surnamed Desabandhu (Friend of the Country). Bengali nationalist leader; one of the founders of the Swaraj Party; president of the Indian National Congress in 1922 and first mayor of Calcutta.

DAS, SARALA see ORIYA

DASAKUMARACHARITA see 2DANDIN

DASARATHA. King of Ayodhya and father of Rama, the hero of Ramayana.

DASAS (also, Dasyus).   Pre-Aryan inhabitants of the Indus Valley described as a dark-skinned, flat-nosed people.

DASTAK.   Authorization issued by the East India Company to their servants to trade within the province of Bengal without paying the 2 1/2 per cent customs duty; the abuse of this privilege by the Company's servants led to the war with Mir Qasim; abolished by Lord Cornwallis.

DASTAN-I-AMIR HAMZAL.   Album of miniature paintings by Mir Sayyid Ali and Khwaja Abdus Samad, court painters at the court of Humayun.

DASTUR (or, dasturi).   Literally, custom or customary. Commission; or percentage of the money passing in any cash transaction that sticks to the fingers of the agent. According to Ibn Batuta public officials at the court of Delhi deducted 10 per cent of all sums paid out of the treasury.

DASWANATH see MUGHAL SCHOOL

DATTATREYA see TANTRAS; TANTRISM

DAUD KHAN.   Ruler of Bengal who defied Akbar and was defeated and slain at the Battle of Rajmahal in 1576.

DAULATABAD.   Muslimized name of Devagiri, the Yadava capital in central India; made capital of the Imperial Sultanate by Muhammad Tughluq in 1327.   It later became the capital of one of the four provinces of the Bahmani Empire in the state of Ahmadnagar.   Aurangazeb was buried here.

DAULAT RAO SINDHIA.   The second ruler of the Sindhia Dynasty of Gwalior (1794-1827); engaged unsuccessfully in battle with Jaswant Rao Holkar; defeated by the British in the Second Maratha War and finally bound to protected status by the Treaty of Surji-Arjungaon.

DAY, FRANCIS.   Founder of the British settlement at Fort St. George, Madras, in 1640.

DAYABHAGA.   A commentary on the Manusamhita compiled by Sanskrit legal scholar Jimutavahana in the 15th century; believed to be part of a larger work known as Dharma-ratna.   The Dayabhaga forms the basis of the Gauriya school of law prevalent in Bengal and Assam.

DAYANANDA SARASWATI, Swami. 1824-83. Founder of
the Arya Samaj, which advocated the revival of Vedic
ideals as a means of combating the spread of Christianity; also sponsored the Suddhi movement for prose-
lytizing non-Hindus and condemned certain social abuses
in Hindu society.

DECCAN. Term used variously to denote either the whole
peninsular India south of the Vindhyas or particularly
the plateau between the Narmada and the Krishna Rivers.
From Sanskrit dakshina, south, or dakshinapada, southern region.

DECCAN COLLEGE POST-GRADUATE AND RESEARCH IN-
STITUTE. Institution founded in 1939 in Yervada,
Poona, for research in Indian linguistics and history.
Publishes a Quarterly Bulletin, Monograph Series, Dis-
sertation Series, Handbook Series, and Sources of Indian
Lexicography.

DEFENSE OF INDIA ACT. Act vesting the Government of
India with extensive powers of arrest and preventive
detention to deal with subversion and civil unrest.

DEH. A village considered as an administrative unit.

DELHI. (1) City on the Yamuna River; ancient capital of
India; built on the site of Indraprastha, the Pandava
capital in Mahabharatha. In historical times it appears
as the stronghold of Anangapala, the Tomara king who
built a Red Fort here. Later it passed under the rule
of the Chauhans of Ajmer. It was conquered by Muhammad Ghori in 1193 and remained the center and focus
of Muslim power until 1857 when the last Mughal emperor Bahadur Shah was deposed and exiled to Rangoon.
According to tradition, seven cities have been built
around Delhi: Siri, Indraprastha, Tughluqabad, Jahan-
pannah, Firozabad, Purana Kila, and Shahjahanabad.
Delhi was sacked many times during its history: by
Timur in 1398, by Nadir Shah in 1739, and by Ahmad
Shah Abdali in 1757. The principal monuments of Delhi
are the Red Fort, the Jumma Masjid, the tomb of
Humayun and the Qutb Minar.
     (2) A Union Territory administered by a chief com-
missioner.

DELHI DURBARS. Imperial assemblies held in Delhi in

1877, 1903, and 1911. The first coincided with the assumption of the title of Empress of India by Queen Victoria; the second and third marked the coronations of Edward VII and George V respectively.

DELHI SULTANATE. The five Muslim dynasties that ruled northern India from 1206 to 1526 with Delhi as their capital: the Slaves, the Khaljis, The Tughluqs, the Sayyids, and the Lodis.

DEOGAON, TREATY OF. Treaty concluded in 1803 between Raghuji Bhonsla II and the British by which the former accepted the tutelage of the Company and yielded all territories west of Warda River.

DEPRESSED CASTE (also, Scheduled caste). Official term for untouchable Hindu caste.

DESAI. Title of hereditary petty chiefs in Maharashtra and Gujarat.

DESARI. Head of a village, especially in Gujarat and the Deccan.

DESH. Region in Maharashtra lying to the east of Maval and west of Warda River.

DESHMUKH. A hereditary official with police and revenue authority in a district.

DEVABHUTI see VASUDEVA

DEVADASI. A woman serving as a dancer and courtesan in a Hindu temple.

DEVADATTA. Cousin of Gautama Buddha and founder of a rival sect.

DEVANAGIRI (also, Nagari). Literally, script of the divine city (Nagari: city script). Popular Indian script believed to have been derived from the Naga mode of writing and hence also called Naga-lipi. It is also related to the earlier Brahmi and Harsha scripts and was perfected in its present form in the early centuries of the Christian era, though the first inscription extant dates from 754 and the first manuscript from the 11th century. Variants include Balbodh (Marathi); Modi, or

the "twisted" (also Marathi); Nandinagari (Deccani),
Rajasthani, Marwari, and Mahajani.

DEVANAMPIYA PIYADASI.   Literally, the darling of the
gods who cares for all men's welfare.   Title of Asoka.

DEVAPALA.   Third king of the Pala Dynasty of Bengal
(810-50), a Buddhist ruler who ruled Bengal and Bihar
for 35 years and extended Pala power to its zenith.

DEVARSHI.   A sage who is exalted as a demigod after attaining perfection on earth.

DEVI.   The mother goddess of India.   See SHAKTI.

DHAMMA.   (In Pali scriptures) dharma.

DHANADHAKSHA.   One of the eight ministerial positions in
Shivaji's cabinet; the royal chaplain or almoner; also
known as pandit rao.

DHANGA.   950-999.   Powerful ruler of the Chandella Dynasty; member of the confederacy of Hindu princes who
were defeated by Sabuktigin.

DHAR.   Town in Madhya Pradesh; capital of the ancient
kingdom of Malwa and a center of Hindu learning from
the 9th to the 14th century.

DHARMA.   Moral code of conduct leading to virtue and
righteousness.   Dharma comprehended ritual obligations
of one's caste, duties toward family and community,
and professional ethics. (also, dhamma).

DHARMACHAKRA.   Literally, wheel of the law.   Symbol of
Buddhist dogma.

DHARMAPAL.   Second and greatest king of the Pala Dynasty
of Bengal (752-794); waged wars with the Rashtrakutas
and the Pratiharas and became a dominant power in
northern India; traditionally celebrated as a pious Buddhist.

DHARMAPALA.   Fl. 6th century.   Buddhist metaphysician,
born in Kanchipuram, South India, as the son of powerful minister of state.   On the eve of his marriage he
escaped to a remote mountain temple where he spent
many years mastering Hinayana and Mahayana philosophy;

he soon gathered many disciples and gained a reputation
as a skillful polemicist and apologist for Buddhism.
He is regarded as one of the most important commenta-
tors on the Vijnapti Maitraka school of Buddhism.   He
was also for some time the head of the Buddhist university at Nalanda.   He died at the age of 32.

[1]DHARMARATNA (also, Dharma-raksha).   Indian Buddhist
monk and missionary who traveled to China in 65 with
Kashyapa Matanga and established the White House
monastery at Lo-yang; believed to have begun the
preaching of Buddhism in China.

[2]DHARMA-RATNA   see   DAYABHAGA

DHARMASALA.   Resthouse for wayfarers in North India
corresponding to the choultry or chuttram of South India.

DHARMASASTRAS.   Body of Hindu law, particularly the
laws ascribed to Manu, Yajnavalkya, and other sages.
These texts are generally in three parts: (1) achara,
or rules of conduct, (2) vyavahara, or litigation, and
(3) prayashchitta, or penance.

DHARMAT, BATTLE OF.   Battle in 1658 between Dara
Shukoh and the two rebel sons of Shah Jahan, Aurangzeb
and Murad, in which Dara was defeated.

DHIMAN.   Bengali artist and sculptor who lived in the time
of the Pala Dynasty in the ninth century and founded a
school of fine arts.

DHOLAK.   Cylindrical double-headed drum played with one
hand and a stick.

DHRUPAD.   Devotional song or hymn with evocative cadences
developed by Tansen.   A variation is the dhamar or
hori.

DIG, BATTLE OF.   Battle in 1804 between Holkar and the
English during the Second Maratha War in which the
former was defeated.

DIGAMBARA.   A Jain sect whose tenets required its members to go without clothes.

DIGNAGA.   Buddhist sage of the fourth century.

DIGVIJAYIN.   Literally, sovereign of the four quarters.
Title assumed by Hindu emperors.

DIKSHITAR, GOVIND.   1614-40.   Founder of a famous
school of music under the Nayyaka kings of Thanjavur;
author of Sangita Sudha.

DILRUBA.   Fretted musical instrument introduced by the
Muslims and popular in the Deccan.

DIMA.   (In Sanskrit drama) a play generally in four acts
dealing with the supernatural.

DINGALA.   An old form of Rajasthani, now extinct, in
which the medieval bardic songs were written.

DIN-ILAHI.   Literally, the Divine Faith.   Syncretic faith established by Akbar in 1582 that fused the monotheism
of Islam with certain universally valid elements in Hinduism and other religions.   It did not outlive Akbar.

DIODOROS (surnamed Siculus).   Greek historian of the first
century B. C. who wrote an account of the invasion of
India by Alexander the Great.

DIPAVAMSA see   MAHENDRA

DIU.   Island on the west coast in Gujarat which along with
the villages of Simbor and Gogola constituted the former
Portuguese settlement.   The Portuguese built a fort on
the island in 1535-36.   It successfully withstood as-
saults by Indian armies in 1538 and 1546.   In 1670 it
was raided by Arabs of Muscat.

DIVALI.   Properly, Dipa-vali, or row of lights.   One of the
most important festivals of the Hindu year lasting for
five days in October-November.

DIWAN.   (1) Official in the Mughal administration responsible
for revenue and finances.   He was subordinate to the
subadar in the provinces.
    (2) Chief minister of a native state.

DIWAN-I.   "Department," as in diwan-i-'am, "office of the
emperor"; diwan-i-amir kohi, "department of agriculture"; diwan-i-'arz, "war department"; diwan-i-bandagan,
"department of slaves"; diwan-i-insha, "department of

correspondence"; diwan-i-istiqaq, "department of pensions"; diwan-i-khairat, "department of charity"; diwan-i-khas, "hall of private audience"; diwan-i-mustakraj, "department of revenue collections"; diwan-i-qazi-i-mamalik, "department of intelligence, post, and justice"; diwan-i-risalat, "department of appeals"; and diwan-i-riyasat, "department of market superintendency. "

DIWANI ADALAT.   The civil court of the diwan, the head of the revenue administration of a province.

DIWANI OF BENGAL.   Right to collect revenues in Bengal, Bihar, and Orissa granted in 1765 to the East India Company by Emperor Shah Alam II in return for the cession of Allahabad and an annual rent of 26 lakhs [i. e. , 2,600,000] of rupees to the emperor and 53 (later 32) lakhs of rupees to the Nawab of Bengal.

DOAB.   Fertile land between two rivers, as between the Ganges and the Yamuna and between the Krishna and the Tungabhadra.

DOAR.   Low, partially cultivated land at the foot of the Himalayas near Bhutan.   It corresponds to the terai farther west.

DOCTRINE OF LAPSE.   Principle formulated in 1834 and applied extensively by Lord Dalhousie by which the sovereignty of a native state reverted to the Paramount Power, i. e. the East India Company, when the ruler died without leaving a natural heir.   The British government did not recognize the right of adoption.   Under this Doctrine the British government annexed the states of Satara (1848), Jaitpur and Sambalpur (1849), Jhansi (1855), and Nagpur (1854).

DOGRA.   A Kshattriya subcaste of partial Hun descent, dominant in Kashmir and northern India.

DOGRI.   A dialect of Punjabi spoken in Kashmir.

DOLI.   A type of litter consisting of a frame suspended by the four corners from a bamboo pole and carried by two or four men.

DRAVIDA MUNNETRA KAZHAGAM.   A Tamil political party

founded by C. N. Annadurai as an exclusively Dravidian movement against North Indian and Brahmin hegemony; dominant in Tamil Nadu since 1966.

DRAVIDIAN.   (1) Semi-Negroid race who inhabited India in pre-Aryan times.   Their descendants constitute a substantial segment of the population of South India.
(2) Family of languages whose main branches are Tamil-Kurukh (Tamil, Malayalam, Kanarese, Tulu, and Kurukh), Kui-Gondi (Kui, Gondi, Bhili, Kolimi, and Naiki), Telugu, and Brahui.

DRONOSIMHA   see   VALABHI (2)

DRUK GYALPO.   Title of the maharaja of Bhutan.

DUAL SYSTEM.   Administrative system established by the Treaty of Allahabad (1765) under which the East India Company as the Diwan was responsible for the collection of revenues of Bengal, Bihar, and Orissa, and the Nawab of Bengal for civil and criminal administration. It was abolished in 1772.

DUBASH.   Literally, man of two languages.   Interpreter attached to European mercantile houses who acts as broker in transactions with natives.

DUFFADAR.   A petty police officer or a noncommissioned officer in the irregular cavalry.

DUFFERIN, Marquis of.   Full name: Frederick Temple Hamilton-Temple Blackwood.   1826-1902.   Viceroy and governor general of India (1884-88).   Administration marked by the passing of Tenancy Acts and the annexation of upper Burma.   He delimited the Northwest Frontier and pacified the amir of Afghanistan.

DUFTARY.   An official in charge of public records.

DUFTER.   Originally, a register or public record.   By extension, an office where the records are kept.

DUFTERDAR.   Title of the head revenue officer in the office of a district collector.

DULHA RAI.   Kachwaha Rajput leader who founded Jaipur State in 1128.   He is said to have been a native of Gwalior.

DUMDUM.   Military cantonment near Calcutta; headquarters
of the Bengal Artillery where the treaty between Robert
Clive and Siraj-ud-daulah was signed in 1757.   The ex-
panding bullet which bears the same name was invented
here.

DUN.   A flat valley parallel to the base of the Himalayas
and lying between the mountains and the tertiary ranges
known as the Siwalik Hills.   The dun of Dehra below
Mussoorie is known as Dehra Dun.

DUNDUBHI.   Kettledrum used in battle and on ceremonial
occasions.

DUPLEIX, JOSEPH FRANÇOIS.   1697-1763.   Governor general of the French East Indies (1741-54).   Worked to
extend French dominion in India; toward that end captured Madras in 1746; established French dominance at
the court of Muzaffar Jang and Salabat Jang, Nizams
of Hyderabad; backed the claims of Chanda Sahib to
throne of the Carnatic; all his efforts were foiled by the
English in two Carnatic Wars; recalled to France in
1754 and died in poverty.

DURAND LINE.   Boundary line between Afghanistan and
North West Frontier Province drawn up by Sir Henry
Durand in 1893.

DURBAR.   The court or levee of a native prince.

DURGA.   In Hindu mythology, one of the malignant forms
of Devi, wife of Siva.   Often identified as Kali (q. v.).

DURGADAS.   Rathor leader of Marwar; took up arms
against Aurangzeb on behalf of Ajit Singh, the minor
son of Raja Jaswant Singh.

DURGA PUJA   see   NAVARATHRI

DURGAVATI.   Widowed rani of Raja Dalpat Sa of Gondwana
and regent of her son Bir Narayan.   Defeated and slain
by Akbar's general Asaf Khan in 1564.

DURLABHAVARDHANA.   Founder of the Karkota Dynasty
that ruled Kashmir from the seventh to the ninth century.

DVADASA SASTRA   see   [1]NAGARJUNA

DVARASAMUDRA.   Capital of the Hoysala kingdom and the
   center of Vaishnava sect of Hinduism; identified with
   modern Halebid.

DVIJA.   Literally, twice-born.   Term formerly applied to
   the first three superior castes and now restricted to
   the Brahmins.   The second birth was considered to take
   place through the ritual of tying a sacred thread around
   the body.

DYARCHY.   Constitutional system set up under the Government of India Act of 1919 under which the departments
   of provincial administration were divided into Transferred and Reserved.   The Transferred departments
   included education, local self-government, public health,
   public works, agriculture, and cooperation while Reserved departments included land revenue, law, justice,
   police, irrigation, labor, and finance.   The Transferred
   departments were assigned to elected ministers responsible to the legislatures while Reserved departments
   were under the control of executive councilors responsible to the governor.

DYER, General REGINALD   see   JALLIANWALLA BAGH

DZONGKHA.   Official language of Bhutan, akin to Tibetan.

- E -

EASTERN CHALUKYA   see   CHALUKYA OF VENGI

EASTERN GANGA.   Kalinga Dynasty founded by Rajaraja I,
   which ruled Orissa from the middle of the 11th to the
   end of the 14th century.   The Eastern Ganga consisted
   of 15 rulers:

Rajaraja I	Narasinha I
Anantavarman Chodaganga	Bhanudeva I
Kamarnava	Narasinha II
Raghava	Bhanudeva II
Rajaraja II	Narasinha III
Anangabhima I	Bhanudeva III
Rajaraja III	Narasinha IV
Anangabhima II	

EASTERN HINDI.   Regional form of Hindi, also called
    Kosali, including the dialects Bagheli, Purbi, Chhatis-
    garhi, and Baisvari (or Awadhi).

EAST INDIA COLLEGE.   College established at Haileybury,
    England, in 1805 for training the Company's covenanted
    civil servants (exclusively Anglo).

EAST INDIA COMPANY.   Trading company chartered by
    Queen Elizabeth I in 1600 as "Governor and Company
    of Merchants of London Trading with the East Indies,"
    and granted exclusive rights of commerce.   In 1608
    the first trading vessel of the Company reached Surat.
    In 1613 the Company received its first farman.   In 1615-
    18 Sir Thomas Roe, ambassador of James I to the
    Mughal court, obtained for the Company some trading
    privileges.   Before the end of the 17th century the Com-
    pany had established settlements, known as presidencies,
    in Madras, Bombay, and Calcutta, each ruled by a
    governor.   At the turn of the century a rival company
    known as "The English Company Trading to the East
    Indies," was formed in London; it later merged with the
    older firm under the name of "The United Company of
    the Merchants of England Trading to the East Indies."
    By the end of the Second Carnatic War the Company had
    eliminated the French from the Carnatic; the victories
    of Plassey and Buxar established its power in Bengal,
    Bihar, and Orissa.   The Marathas were subdued during
    the governor generalship of Lord Hastings and the Mug-
    hal emperor became a pensioner of the Company.   As-
    sam came under the Company's rule in 1829, Sind in
    1843, Punjab in 1849, and by 1857 when it was liquidated
    its writ ran from Peshawar to Rangoon and from Kash-
    mir to Ceylon.

EDWARDS, WILLIAM.   Ambassador of King James I to
    Emperor Jahangir in 1615.

EKANATH.   Maratha saint and poet who flourished in the
    16th century.

EKTARA.   One-stringed fiddle used by wandering minstrels.

ELEPHANTA.   Native name: Gharapuri.   Island in Bombay
    harbor famous for its magnificent excavated temples
    dating from the middle of the eighth century.

ELGIN, Earl of and Earl of KINCARDINE.   (1) Full name:
    James Bruce.   1811-1863.   Viceroy and governor gen-
    eral of India (1862-63).
        (2) Full name: Victor Alexander Bruce.   1849-1917.
    Viceroy and governor general of India (1894-99).   Ad-
    ministration marked by famines and uprisings.

ELLENBOROUGH, Lord.   Full name: Edward Law.   1790-
    1871.   Governor general of India (1842-44).   Adminis-
    tration marked by the annexation of Sind, the invasion
    of Gwalior, and the pacification of the Marathas at the
    battles of Maharajpur and Paniar.   He was recalled by
    the Court of Directors in 1844.

ELLORA.   Town in Maharashtra containing Dravidian rock-
    cut temples from before the 10th century.   The central
    sanctuary is enclosed by a porch of 16 columns.   The
    court is surrounded by a peristyle containing a number
    of cells.   The sculptured decoration combines elaborate
    geometrical motifs and figures.

ENGLISH BAZAR.   Town in West Bengal; headquarters of
    Malda district; site of an English settlement in the
    17th century.

ENGLISH COMPANY TRADING TO THE EAST INDIES.
    Rival trading company founded in 1698 in London;
    merged with the East India Company in 1702.

ESRAJ.   Fretted musical instrument used in Bengal for
    solo accompaniment.

EZHUTTACHAN see MALAYALAM

- F -

FACTOR.   Designation of the middle category of East India
    Company's civil service during the period from the fifth
    to the eighth year of service.

FACTORY.   European trading settlement in India in the 17th
    and 18th centuries.

FADNAVIS.   Maratha official through whom all orders and
    grants were issued and to whom all accounts were sent.

FA HIEN (or, Fa-Hsian). Chinese Buddhist monk who made a pilgrimage to India, 401-410, to carry back to China complete copies of the <u>Vinaya-pitaka</u>. He wrote a valuable account of his travels.

FAKHR-UD-DIN MUBARAK SHAH. Founder of an independent kingdom in Bengal in 1336 during the reign of Sultan Muhammad Tughluq.

FAKHR-UL-TUJJAR. Literally, the pride of merchants. Title granted by the Mughal government to an eminent banker or merchant.

FAKIRMOHAN see ORIYA

FANAM. Ancient Indian coin bearing various local values and made of gold, silver, or other metals. In the early 18th century 42 fanams made a star pagoda (a local monetary unit used in parts of South India). It was used in the state of Travancore until 1947.

FARMAN. Mandate or order issued by a ruler granting certain rights or special privileges.

FARRUKHSIYAR. Fifteenth Mughal emperor (1713-19). Ascended the throne after deposing his uncle, Jahandar Shah. Soon after his accession he executed his chief minister, Zulfiqar Khan, who had helped him to become emperor. During his reign the Sikh leader, Banda, and his followers were captured and killed. In 1715 he granted trading privileges in Bengal to the East India Company through William Hamilton, a surgeon who had cured his daughter.

FARSALA. Former unit of weight used in Indian trade generally equivalent to ten small maunds or between 20 and 30 lbs.

FARUQI. Dynasty established in 1382 in Khandesh by Malik Raja Faruqi, governor of Khandesh under Sultan Firoz Shah Tughluq. The dynasty consisted of 16 rulers:

Malik Raja (1382)	Ghazni Khan (1508)
Malik Nasir (1399)	Hasan Khan (1508)
Adil Khan I (1437)	Adil Khan III (1509)
Mubarak Khan (1441)	Miran Muhammad (1520)
Adil Khan II (1457)	Ahmad Shah (1537)
Daud (1501)	Miran Mubarak II (1537)

Miran Muhammad II   Hasan Shah (1576)
(1566)   Ali Khan (1577)
                              Bahadur Shah (1597)

FASLI.   Solar era established by Muslim rulers for use in
    revenue and revenue transactions to offset the inconven-
    ience of the lunar Hijra calendar which did not corres-
    pond with the natural seasons.   At least three of these
    eras were established by Akbar and one by Shah Jahan.
    Two fasli years are still in use in some parts of India:
    the fasli of northern India beginning on April 2 and the
    fasli of Tamil Nadu beginning on July 1.

FATEHCHAND   see JAGAT SETH

FATEHPUR SIKRI.   City in Uttar Pradesh near Agra; for-
    merly Sikri; built by Akbar in 1569 in honor of the
    Muslim saint Shaikh Salim Chishti; renamed Fatehpur,
    or Victory Town, to celebrate the conquest of Gujarat;
    Akbar's capital for 15 years but later abandoned because
    of the difficulty of obtaining water supplies; many of its
    edifices, built of red sandstone, survive in lonely
    splendor.

FATHULLAH.   Founder of the Imad Shahi Dynasty; governor
    of Berar under the Bahmani sultan Mahmud; proclaimed
    himself independent in 1484 under the title of Imad-ul-
    Mulk.   His successors ruled Berar until 1568.

FATWA.   A written and usually binding opinion of a qasi on
    a question of Islamic law.

FAUJDAR.   (1) (In the 14th century) a military officer in
    command of a division subordinate to the commander
    in chief.
        (2) (In the 16th and 17th centuries) an official in
    charge of the general administration of a district.
        (3) (In the 18th century) an official concerned with
    general, as distinct from revenue, administration and
    with criminal, as distinct from civil, justice.
        (4) (In modern times) a police subinspector.

FAUJDARI ADALAT.   (Until 1862) the chief criminal court
    under the East India Company at Madras and Bombay,
    equivalent to the nizamat adalat in Calcutta.

FEDEA.   A former copper coin current on the west coast in

the 16th century. Its value is given variously as 1/4
of a silver tanka or 1/50 of a rupee.

FEDERAL COURT OF INDIA. Supreme court established by
the Government of India Act of 1935 with Sir Maurice
Gwyer as the first chief justice.

FEROZESHAH, BATTLE OF. Battle in 1845 between the
Sikhs and the British during the course of the First
Sikh War in which the Sikhs were defeated.

FIRINGI. Term, a corruption of "Frank," applied to the
Portuguese throughout Asia with local variations in
spelling. In Tamil it is Parangi, as in Parangi Malai
or Portuguese Hill. The name was applied by extension
to the straight cut and thrust swords introduced by the
Portuguese.

FIRISHTA. Full name: Muhammad Kasim Hindushah.
Persian-born historian of the 16th century who became
court historian to Sultan Ibrahim Adil Shah II of Bijapur;
author of Tarikh-i-Firishta in 1609, translated as The
History of the Rise of Muhammadan Power in India, one
of the most trustworthy sources for this period.

FIROZ SHAH TUGHLUQ. Third sultan of the Tughluq Dynasty (1352-88). Reduced Sind to submission but failed in
attempts to regain Bengal and the Deccan; considered
as a benevolent and peaceloving king who built many
cities and mosques, pacified the army, and abolished
harsh taxes, except the jiziya.

FIRUZ SHAH BAHMANI. The eighth and the greatest Bahmani sultan (1397-1422); captured Vijayanagar in 1406;
great builder of mosques.

FITCH, RALPH. English merchant who visited India (1583-
91) and left an account of his travels.

"FIVE K's". Objects to be worn by every member of the
Sikh brotherhood or khalsa: kesh (long hair and beard);
kungha (hair-comb); kuchcha (shorts); kara (iron bangle);
and kirpan (sword).

FLAG. Tricolor with deep saffron, white, and dark green
bands and an Asoka Chakra in navy blue in the center
of the white band.

FORT ST. DAVID. Fort built by the English East India
    Company on the Coromandel Coast, south of Pondicher-
    ry.

FORT ST. GEORGE. Fort built on the site granted to
    Francis Day in 1640 by the raja of Chandragiri; nucleus
    of the modern city of Madras.

FORT WILLIAM. Fort built in Calcutta (1696-1715); cap-
    tured by Nawab Siraj-ud-daulah in 1756; recaptured by
    Clive in 1757; original fort was torn down later and re-
    built on a different site.

FRANCIS, PHILIP see HASTINGS, WARREN

FRENCH EAST INDIA COMPANY. Trading company founded
    by Jean Baptiste Colbert in 1664. Unlike the English
    East India Company it was a state agency. It estab-
    lished four main trading centers in India: Pondicherry
    in 1673; Chandernagore in 1674; Mahe in 1725; and Kari-
    kal in 1739. French attempts under Dupleix to gain
    supremacy over the English ended ingloriously and
    Dupleix was recalled to France. The Company was dis-
    solved in 1769 when its possessions were ceded to the
    Crown. The French colonies were merged with the
    Union of India in 1950.

FRYER, JOHN. British traveler who visited India in the
    17th century and wrote an account of his travels.

- G -

GADADHAR SINGH. 29th Ahom king who ruled Assam (1681-
    96). In 1682 he recovered Gauhati from the Mughals.

GADI. The throne of an Indian ruler; a cushion or padded
    seat on which the king sits regarded as the seat of
    royalty.

GAEKWAD. Dynasty of Maratha rulers of Baroda founded
    by Damaji I. His nephew Pilaji was a supporter of
    Senapati Khande Rao Dabade and then of his son, Trim-
    bak Rao Dabade. After the death of his latter patron
    Pilaji set himself up in Baroda as a semi-independent
    ruler. The line consisted of 14 rulers:
        Damaji I   Pilaji (1721)

Damaji II (1732)	Anand Rao (1800)
Govind Rao (1768)	Sayaji Rao II (1818)
Sayaji Rao I (1771)	Ganpat Rao (1847)
Fateh Singh (1771)	Khande Rao (1856)
Manaji (1789)	Malhar Rao (1870)
Govind Rao (1793)	Sayaji Rao III (1875)

GAHADVALA (also, Gaharwar). Rajput dynasty of the 11th century founded by Chandradeva; ruled over modern Uttar Pradesh and Bihar. Its most famous kings were Govinda Chandra and Raja Jayachandra, who was defeated by Shihabuddin Muhammad Ghori in the Battle of Chandwar in 1194.

GAJAPATI. Literally, the lord of the elephants. Title of the rulers of Orissa. According to Buddhist legends the title was that of one of four great kings who ruled the earth in prehistorical times: Gajapati, the ruler of the south; Asvapati (lord of horses), ruler of the north; Chhatrapati (lord of the umbrella), ruler of the west; and Narapati (lord of men), ruler of the east.

GAKKAR. Tribe in the Punjab who resisted the Muslim invaders from the 13th to the 16th centuries.

GAMA, VASCO DA. 1469-1524. Portuguese navigator; the first European explorer to make a sea voyage to India; founder of the Portuguese Empire in the east. His historic voyage, celebrated in the Lusiad of Camões, arrived at Calicut or Kozhikode on May 20, 1498.

GAMELLI-CARRERI. Italian traveler who visited India in the reign of Emperor Aurangzeb and left an account of his travels.

GANDHARA. (1) Region in modern Pakistan comprising the districts of Rawalpindi and Peshawar. It was held by the Indo-Bactrian princes and later became part of the Kushan Empire. Its two great cities were Taxila and Pushkaravati.
   (2) Name of the Indo-Greek school of art and architecture developed here.

GANDHI, INDIRA. 1917- . Third prime minister of India (1966-); daughter of Jawaharlal Nehru; married in 1942 to Firoz Gandhi, a Parsi politician. She broke away from the conservative faction of the Indian

National Congress and established the New Congress;
directed the victorious war with Pakistan which ended
in the creation of Bangla Desh; stopped the privy
purses paid to Indian princes since 1947; promoted nuclear development, which led to the explosion of a nuclear device in 1974.

GANDHI, MOHANDAS KARAMCHAND, Mahatma.   Surname:
Bapu.   1869-1948.   Indian nationalist leader and architect of Indian independence.   Gandhi studied law in
London (1888) and practiced in India until 1893.   He
went to South Africa and championed the rights of the
Asiatic settlers, applying for the first time the technique of passive resistance that later came to be known
as satyagraha (holding onto truth).   He aided the British
cause in the Boer War and again in World War I but
became a severe critic of British rule in India after
the Rowlatt Act of 1919 and made common cause with
the Muslims during the Khilafat movement.
     Again and again he urged the boycott of British goods
and the promotion of swadeshi (one's own country) or
home industries.   As the head of the Indian nationalist
movement and as president of the Indian National Congress (1924-34; 1940-41) he set the goal of Purna
Swaraj or full independence from Great Britain.   Gandhi
rejected not only the British Empire but also much of
western civilization and sought to reconstruct Indian society on the basis of Ram Rajya, the ideal Hindu social
and religious polity.
     His ethical and political principles, popularly known
as Gandhism, constituted the dominant ideology of India
from 1919 until 1947.   He captured the imagination of
the Indian masses through his extreme asceticism, his
several fasts of protest, his use of the spinning wheel
as a symbol of economic independence, and his campaign
to eliminate caste untouchability.   He was assassinated
in New Delhi in 1948 by a Hindu fanatic enraged at
Gandhi's conciliatory attitude toward Muslims.   Gandhi's
works include his autobiography, Story of My Experiments with Truth.

GANESA-CHATURTI.   Hindu festival of Dravidian origin
celebrated in August-September in commemoration of
the birthday of Ganesa, the elephant-headed god of good
luck.

GANESH.   Bengali baron who assumed the throne of Bengal

in 1414 under the title of Danuja-mardana-Deva.   His
successors accepted Islam and ruled as Muslim kings
until 1442.

GANGA.   Dynasty founded by Konganivarma which ruled modern Mysore from the second to the 11th century.   They
were patrons of Jainism and the colossal statue of
Gomata at Sravana Belgola was made under their auspices.

GANGAIKONDA.   Title of the Chola king Rajendra Choladeva
I; assumed on the occasion of his forces' reaching the
bank of the Ganges after defeating Mahipala of Bengal.
He built a new city to celebrate his feat called Gangaikonda Cholapuram.

GANGANATH JHA RESEARCH INSTITUTE.   Institution
founded in Allahabad in 1943 for conducting research
into Sanskrit and other Indian languages.   Publishes a
Quarterly Research Journal.

GANGES (also, Ganga).   Sacred river of India, 1557 miles
long.   It rises under the name of the Bhagirathi in the
Himalayas and is called the Ganges after its junction
with the Alakanada.   It flows southeast across one of
the most densely peopled plains of the world, finally
entering the Meghna estuary of the Bay of Bengal.   Its
chief tributaries are the Yamuna, Ramganga, Gumti,
Gogra, Gandak, Kosi, Atrai, Son, and the Jamuna.

GANGEYADEVA KALACHURI.   King of Chedi (1015-1040)
who assumed the title of Vikramaditya on accession to
the throne.   He successfully consolidated Kalachuri
suzerainty over the Gangetic plains by repelling the
Palas of Bengal and the rulers of Malwa.

GARHGAON.   Ahom capital of Assam on the banks of the
Dikhu River in Sibsagar district.   It was under Mughal
occupation from 1662-67.

GAT (or, gati).   A mixed instrument-voice composition developed by Feroz Khan and Masiyat Khan.

GATEWAY OF INDIA.   Monument erected in Bombay pier
in honor of the visit in 1921 of Edward, Prince of Wales.
Applied by extension to the whole city of Bombay.

GAUD.   Headman of a village in Karnataka.

GAUDA.   (1) Capital of Bengal under the Sena kings in the
11th and 12th centuries.   It fell to the Muslims in 1203
and became the capital again in 1220 under Ghyas-ud-
din Iwaz.   Repeated plunder by invading armies, epide-
mics, and a change in the course of the Ganges resulted in the complete desolation of the city.   It is now
in ruins.
    (2) State comprising west and northwest Bengal with
Karnasuvarna as capital.   It came into power with the
fall of the Guptas and its primacy lasted through the
reigns of the Pala and Sena Dynasties well into the
12th century.

GAUDAPATA   see   ADVAITA

GAUHATI.   Town in Assam on the Brahmaputra River; modern name for Pragjyotishapura, the ancient capital of
the kingdom of Kamarupa (variant name, along with
Pragiyotisha, for modern Assam).   It was the capital
of Assam again for a brief period in the 18th century.

GAURIYA.   Adjectival form of Gaur, or Gaud, the ancient
name for Bengal.

GAURJARI (also, Old Gujarati).   A lesser Prakrit language
from which modern Gujarati, Marwari, and Rajasthani
are derived.

GAYA.   City and district in Bihar; place of Hindu and Buddhist pilgrimage.   Buddha attained enlightenment in
nearby Bodh-Gaya.

GAZ.   Unit of length varying from 18 inches to 52.   The
Ilahi gaz of Akbar was intended to provide a uniform
standard of 33 inches.

GENTOO.   Term, a corruption of gentile, applied to Hindus
by European writers in the 17th and 18th centuries.

GHAIRWAJH.   Irregular troops in the army of Sultan Firoz
Shah Tughluq.

GHARI.   (In ancient India) a unit of time equal to 1/60 of
a day, or 24 minutes.   Eight gharis made a pahar, or
quarter day.

GHAT.   A landing place; the path of descent to a river; the holy stairs into the Ganges; the quay of a ferry boat.

GHATS.   Literally, passes, or landing stairs.   Two mountain systems in South India enclosing the Deccan plateau and uniting near Cape Comorin.   They are not properly mountain ranges but rather the rugged fringes of the Deccan plateau.   The Western Ghats extend for about 800 miles from the Tapti Valley to Kerala, rising abruptly from the coastal plain and covered generally by dense monsoon forests.   The Eastern Ghats are a series of broken mountain spurs running parallel to the Coromandel coast for about 700 miles with an average elevation of about 2000 ft.

GHAZAL.   Amorous ode in Hindi and Urdu literature.

GHAZI.   Holy warrior; title assumed by certain Muslim rulers including Aurangzeb.

GHAZI-UD-DIN, IMAD-UL-MULK.   Son of Ghazi-ud-din Khan and grandson of Asaf Jah, the first Nizam of Hyderabad.   On the murder of his father in 1752 Ghazi-ud-din sought refuge in the court of Emperor Ahmad Shah who made him paymaster general.   He became powerful enough to depose his master in 1754 and five years later murdered Ahmad Shah's successor, Alamgir II, in order to set up Shah Jahan III on the throne.   He made common front with the Marathas and the Jat ruler Suraj Mall against Ahmad Shah Abdali, and after the latter's decisive victory in the Third Battle of Panipat in 1761, Ghazi-ud-din retired from public life and lived in relative obscurity until his death in 1800.

GHILZAIS.   Afghan tribe who revolted against the British in 1840 and 1841.

GHIYAS-UD-DIN TUGHLUQ.   Also, Tughluq Shah.   Original name: Ghazi Malik.   Founder of the Tughluq Dynasty and sultan of Delhi (1320-25).   His father was a Turkish slave of Sultan Balban and he earned his stripes as Warden of the Marches under Sultan Alauddin Khalji. He overthrew Sultan Nasir-ud-din Khusrav and was acclaimed sultan in 1320.   Within five years he ably re-established the power of the sultanate by defeating the Kakatiya king Prataparudradeva II of Warangal and Ghiyas-ud-din Bahadur of Bengal.   He also improved the collection of revenue and the administration of justice.

GHULAM AHMAD, MIRZA. 1839-1908. Founder of the
   Ahmadiya sect, a heretical Muslim denomination.

GHULAM HUSAIN KHAN TABATABA, SYED. An 18th-cen-
   tury historian (also known as Mirza Ghulam Hossain)
   in the service of Nawab Mir Qasim; author of Siyar-al-
   Mutakharin (or, Siyar-ul-Mutagherin), an account of the
   decline and fall of Muslim power in India.

GHURI. Independent dynasty of Malwa founded by Dilawar
   Khan Ghuri in 1392. It ruled until 1436 when its last
   king, Ma'ud, was murdered and the throne usurped by
   Mahmud Khalji, founder of the Khalji line of Malwa.
   Rulers: Dilawar Khan Ghuri (1392), Hushang Shah
   (1405), Muhammad (1435), Ma'ud (1436).

GILGIT. (1) Tributary of the Indus flowing into Kashmir.
      (2) Town in the valley of the Gilgit River; headquart-
   ers of a British agency established in 1889 under Lord
   Lytton to check Russian designs in the area.

GINGEE (also, Jinji). Strong fortress in the Deccan in the
   province of Golkonda; captured by Shivaji; citadel of
   Shivaji's second son, Raja Ram (1689); besieged by the
   Mughal Army from 1690 until 1698, when it fell.

GIRIA. Town in Bihar near Rajmahal; site of a battle in
   1740 between Alivardi Khan and Sarfaraz Khan, in which
   the latter was defeated, and of another battle in 1763
   between the Company and Nawab Mir Qasim, in which
   the nawab was defeated.

GIRIVRAJA. Town, known in ancient times as Rajagriha
   and in modern times as Rajgir, built by King Bimbisara
   about 550 B. C. The First Buddhist Council was held
   here in 486 B. C.

GITA GOVINDA. Book of Sanskrit lyrics composed by Jayadeva, Bengali poet who lived in the court of Lakshmana
   Sena.

GLAUKANIKOI. Tribe, also known as Glausi, inhabiting the
   Indus region west of the Chinab River at the time of the
   invasion of India by Alexander the Great.

GOA. Former Portuguese settlement on the west coast
   (1510-1961), with capital at Panjim. The colony included

the port of Marmugao and the ruined city of Old Goa, capital from 1510 until 1759. Invaded and annexed by India in 1961.

GOA, DAMAN AND DIU. A Union Territory of the Indian Union constituted in 1961. Capital: Panjim.

GODAVARI. River in the Deccan rising in the Western Ghats and flowing into the Deccan; one of the sacred rivers of India. Length: 900 miles.

GOGUNDA, BATTLE OF. Battle in 1576 between the armies of Akbar and Rana Pratap Singh of Mewar in which the rana was defeated.

GOKHALE, GOPAL KRISHNA. 1866-1915. Moderate nationalist leader who campaigned for educational and social reforms; founder of the Servants of India Society; president of the Indian National Congress in 1905.

GOKLA. Jat leader who led a revolt against Emperor Aurangzeb but was defeated and killed.

GOLAB SINGH. A horseman in the service of Ranjit Singh who rose from the ranks to become ruler of Jammu; annexed Ladakh; elected minister of the Khalsa; obtained Kashmir from the British in return for £1 million and set himself up as maharaja of Jammu and Kashmir in 1846.

GOLKONDA. City, fort, and former kingdom in the Deccan between the Godavari and the Krishna; in ancient times it was part of the Kakatiya kingdom of Barmangal (Warangal). In 1424-25 it was annexed to the Bahmani Empire. In 1518 it became independent under Sultan Quli Qutb Shah, founder of the Qutb Shahi Dynasty, which ruled over it until 1687 when it fell to Aurangzeb. It was once famous for its diamond mines.

GOND. A Kolarian aboriginal tribe living in Gondwana in Central India. Some Gonds claim to be Rajputs and Kshattriyas. The Chandellas are believed to be of Gond descent. They also established dynasties in Orissa and remained comparatively independent until modern times.

GONDI. Language belonging to the Kui-Gondi family spoken by the Gonds of central India.

GONDOPHERNES. Indo-Parthian king who ruled over a
    large empire that included Kandahar, Kabul, and Taxila.
    According to legend St. Thomas visited his court and
    converted him to Christianity.

GONDWANA. Territory of the Gonds, also known as Garha-
    Katanga, in northern Madhya Pradesh. It was annexed
    by Akbar in 1564.

GOPALA I. Founder of the Pala Dynasty of Bengal.

GOPURAM. Literally, city-gate. Pyramidal tower over
    the entrance gate to the precinct of a temple. Accord-
    ing to the Silpa-sastra it was adopted for purposes of
    defense in the Middle Ages.

GOSAIN. Religious sect of the 19th century whose members
    served in the army.

GOSALA. Founder of the Ajivikas (q.v.) sect, a contempo-
    rary of Gautama Buddha.

GOSHA. Literally, corner. Secluded, as women in purdah
    or in a zenana.

GOTRA. A Vedic community who followed the sacrificial
    custom of a particular rishi or patriarch. All Brahmin
    families are said to have descended from seven or eight
    gotrakaras or family-makers, who were generally
    rishis. These gotras were divided into 49 gotrakula
    (i.e., subgotras), which were again subdivided into
    clans, or ganas. A direct gotra line is called vamsa
    while the collateral branches are called vargas.

GOVERNMENT OF INDIA ACTS. 1909: Act of British
    Parliament popularly known as Minto-Morley Reforms.
    It authorized the appointment of Indians to the viceroy's
    executive council and the provincial executive councils;
    raised the membership of the Central Legislative As-
    sembly to 60 and the provincial legislatures to 50; in-
    creased the proportion of nonofficial elected members
    elected indirectly on communal representation system;
    and permitted the legislatures to discuss budgets and
    matters of general interest.
        1919: Act of British Parliament popularly known as
    the Montague-Chelmsford Reforms. It gave India for the
    first time an elected parliament with two chambers in

which elected members were in a majority. This Central Legislature was a bicameral body with two houses
called the Legislative Assembly and the Council of
State.   Also, the powers of the legislature were extended. The Act made far-reaching changes in provincial governments by introducing the principle of dyarchy
or dual government.   Under this system the administrative departments were divided into Reserved Subjects
(such as police, justice, land revenue) and Transferred
Subjects (such as local self-government, education, public health). The Reserved Subjects were to be under
the authority of the governor in council while the Transferred Subjects were administered by the governor with
the help of ministers appointed from among the elected
members of the legislature.   Bills on Transferred Subjects could be passed only with the approval of the
Legislature.   The Act also provided for the appointment
of an Indian high commissioner in London.

1935: Act of British Parliament that created two
new provinces--Sind and Orissa--which, along with
North West Frontier, were made governor's provinces.
Burma was separated from India.   British India, now
administered directly by the Crown, consisted of 11
provinces and four chief commissionerships--Ajmer,
Coorg, Delhi, and Andaman and Nicobar.   The Act
abolished dyarchy in the provinces; the lower houses
were to consist entirely of popularly elected members
and all departments were placed in charge of ministers
responsible to the legislature.   Communal representation
was reaffirmed and six provinces were given bicameral
legislatures.   The Act also provided for a federal bicameral parliament; the majority of the members were
to be directly elected by voters; the Indian princes were
to nominate one-third of the lower house and two-fifths
of the upper.   The dyarchical principle was introduced
at the Center and defense and foreign affairs were declared as Reserved Subjects.

GOVERNOR GENERAL.   Title and office created by the
Regulating Act of 1773; Warren Hastings was the first
to hold the office.   Until 1834 the office was known as
governor general of Fort William; in that year the name
was changed to governor general of India.   From 1848
until 1943 the title was governor general and viceroy of
India; from 1943 until 1947, governor general of India
and crown representative.   See VICEROY for list of
governors general and viceroys.   From 1774 until 1858

British India was ruled by 13 governors general:
(names of acting governors general are in parentheses):

Warren Hastings (1774)
(Sir John Macpherson 1785)
Marquess Cornwallis (1786)
Sir John Shore (1793)
(Sir A. Clarke 1798)
Marquess Wellesley (1798)
Marquess Cornwallis (1805)
(Sir George Barlow 1805)
Earl of Minto (1807)
Marquess of Hastings (1813)
(John Adam 1823)
Earl Amherst (1823)
(William Butterworth Bayley 1828)

Lord William Cavendish-Bentinck (1828)
(Sir Charles Metcalfe 1835)
Earl of Auckland (1836)
Earl of Ellenborough (1842)
(William Wilberforce Bird 1844)
Viscount Hardinge (1844)
Marquess of Dalhousie (1848)
Earl Canning (1856)

GOVINDA I.   Founder of the Bhoi Dynasty which ruled Orissa from 1542 to 1559.

GOVINDA III.   Rashtrakuta king (793-815) who through the conquest of Malwa, Kanchi, Gujarat, Bengal, and Kanuaj, extended the Rashtrakuta Empire to its furthest limits.

GOVINDA CHANDRA   see   GAHADVALA

GOVINDA SINGH, GURU.   The tenth and last Sikh Guru from 1675 to 1708.   He was the founder of Sikh military power and waged constant wars with the Mughals.   He was murdered at Nander.

GRAECO-BACTRIAN.   Dynasty founded by Diodotos, the Greek governor of Bactria, in the middle of the third century B.C.   It lasted until the middle of the second century B.C.   Demetrios (200-190 B.C.) was the most famous king of this line.

GRAM (or, grama).   Village, especially considered as a unit of local self-government.

GRAMANI.   Village chief in Indo-Aryan times.

GRAMDAN.   Movement related to the bhoodan whose goal is the donation of entire villages so that the land may belong to the village community as a whole.

GRANTHA. Script from which Tamil, Telugu, Kanarese, and Malayalam are derived. Vatteluttu in Tamil and Koleluttu in Malayalam are forms of grantha.

GRANTH SAHIB see ADI GRANTH

GREAT SATRAPS (also, Mahakshatrapas). Saka rulers who belonged to two main lines, (1) Western Great Satraps, founded by Bhumaka with capital at Nasik; its greatest king was Nahapana; it was overthrown around 124; and (b) Great Satraps of Ujjain, founded by Chastana which ruled Ujjain from 130 until 388; Rudradaman I was the greatest ruler of this branch.

GRIERSON see LINGUISTIC SURVEY

GRIHYA-SUTRA see ASVALAYANA

GROUND. A unit of land measurement in Tamil Nadu equal to 100 sq. ft.

GUHILA. A Rajput tribe of Mewar, Chitor, and Udaipur to which the Sesodiyas belonged.

GUJAR. A subgroup of the Gurjaras.

GUJARAT. (1) Region in west central India; named derived from the Gurjaras who settled in the area in the beginning of the fifth century. The kingdom prospered under the Gurajara-Pratiharas. It was conquered by Alauddin Khalji in 1297 and annexed to the Delhi Sultanate. In 1401 Zafar Khan, the governor of Gujarat, proclaimed his independence, assuming the title Nasiruddin Muhammad Shah. The dynasty founded by him ruled Gujarat until 1572 and then was part of the Mughal Empire from 1572 to 1720. It passed under the control of the Maratha Gaekwads in the 18th century. It was yielded to the British after the Third Maratha War and joined to the Bombay Presidency. It became a state of the Indian Union as a result of the Bombay Reorganization Act of 1960. The dynasty founded by Zafar Khan consisted of 14 rulers:

Zafar Khan Muzaffar I   Daud (1458)
   (1396)   Mahmud I (1458)
Ahmad I (1411)   Muzaffar II (1511)
Muhammad Karim (1442)   Sikandar (1526)
Qutb-ud-din Ahmad (1451)   Nasir Khan Mahmud II

(1526)   Mahmud III (1537)
Bahadur (1526)   Ahmad II (1554)
Miran Muhammad (1537)   Muzaffar III (1562)
(2) State of the Indian Union consisting of Saurashtra, Kutch, Banas Kantha, Mehsana, Sabar Kantha, Ahmadabad, Kaira, Panch Mahals, Baroda, Broach, Surat, Dangs, Amreli, Surendranagar, Rajkot, Jamnagar, Junagadh, Bhavnagar and certain parts of Thana and West Khandesh, with capital at Ahmadabad.

GUJARAT, BATTLE OF.   Battle in 1849 between the British and the Sikhs, during the course of the Second Sikh War, in which the latter were defeated.

GUJARATI SCHOOL.   School of painting, also called Jain school, which flourished from 1100 until 1600.   This school specialized in illustrations on palm leaves.

GUJARAT RESEARCH SOCIETY.   Association founded in Bombay in 1936 to organize and coordinate research in social and cultural history.   Publishes a Journal.

GULAB SINGH   see   GOLAB SINGH

GULBARGA.   City in Karnataka; capital of the Bahmani kingdom (renamed Ahsanabad by Sultan Ala-ud-din Hasan Shah in 1347) from 1347 to 1425.

GULNA.   In the Hindu army of Vedic times, a company led by a nayaka or captain consisting of 9 chariots, 27 horses, and 45 foot soldiers.

GUMASTA.   Native agent or factor in an European trading establishment in South India, usually a clerk handling vernacular correspondence.

GUMTI.   River rising in the Shahjahanpur district, flowing past the cities of Lucknow and Jaunpur, and joining the Ganges between Varanasi and Jaunpur.   Length 500 miles.

GUNAVARMAN.   Kashmiri prince and Buddhist monk who preached Buddhism in Ceylon, Java, and China, where he died in 431.

GUPTA.   (1) Dynasty founded in 320 by Chandragupta I who by conquest and by marriage to the Lichchhavi princess

Kumara Devi created a large kingdom that included Magadha, Tirhut, and Oudh. He assumed the title of maharajadhiraja. His immediate successors are notable in their efforts to extend the empire and to ward off such enemies as the Sakas, Huns, and Pushyamitras. The imperial Guptas began to decline after the reign of Skandagupta, though the line survived for a longer time in Malwa and Magadha. The Gupta Age is known as the golden age of Indian architecture, art, sculpture, and metallurgy. The imperial Gupta Dynasty consisted of five rulers: Chandragupta I (320), Samudragupta (330), Chandragupta II or Vikramaditya (380), Kumara-gupta (415), and Skandagupta (455).

(2) Script which evolved from Kushana. It included two forms, a lapidary for monumental inscriptions and a cursive.

GUPTA ERA.   Era established by Chandragupta I dated from 319-20.

GURJARA.   Tribe, believed to be immigrants related to Huns, who established themselves in Punjab, Marwar, and Broach in the sixth and seventh centuries.

GURJARA-PRATIHARA.   Dynasty founded about 725 by Nagabhata who claimed descent from the Pratihara or Parihara clan of the Rajputs, a sept of the Gurjaras. Nagabhata's successor Vatsaraja assumed the title of Samrat and the next ruler Nagabhata II conquered Kanauj and transferred his capital to that imperial city. The Gurjara-Pratiharas ruled an extensive empire from their new capital until 1018 when Sultan Mahmud Ghazni overran the country.   The greatest ruler of the line was Bhoja I (or Mihira Bhoja) who ruled for half a century from 836 to 886 and extended the Pratihara Empire from Bengal to the Sutlej.   The Gurjara-Prati-hara Dynasty consisted of 13 kings:

Nagabhata I (750)	Mahipala (914)
Devaraja (?)	Bhoja II (?)
Vatsaraja (783)	Vinayakapala (?)
Nagabhata II (815)	Mahendrapala (946)
Ramabhadra (?)	Devapala (948)
Bhoja I (836)	Vijayapala (960)
Mahendrapala (893)	

GURKHA WAR.   Campaign waged by the East India Company under Lord Hastings against the Gurkhas of Nepal

(1814-16).   Concluded by the Treaty of Sangauli ceding
to the British the districts of Garhwal and Kumaon.

GURU.   A spiritual preceptor or mentor.

GURUDASPUR.   Fortress in the Punjab where the Sikh leader Banda took refuge in 1715.   The fortress was besieged by the Mughals and fell after a fierce battle.
Banda and his followers were captured and taken to
Delhi and killed.

GURUDEV.   A common greeting, but especially a name of
honor bestowed on poet Rabindranath Tagore.

GURUDWARA.   Sikh temple.

GWALIOR.   (1) Former state in central India; named derived from Gopagiri or Godpadri.   The region was ruled
by the Hun chief Toramana and his son Mihiragula in
the sixth century; later it passed into the hands of the
Gurjara-Pratiharas.   From 1196 to 1210 and from 1232
to 1398 it was under the sultanate of Delhi.   It was recovered by the Rajputs in 1398.   It fell again to Ibrahim Lodi in 1518, to Babur in 1526, to Sher Shah in
1542, and to Akbar in 1558.   The Marathas wrested the
land from the Mughals in 1751 and it became the Sindhia
state.   The Sindhia rule came to an end in 1947 when
the state merged with Madhya Pradesh.
      (2) City in Madhya Pradesh; known for its Jain and
Hindu antiquities and for its fortress, below which, on
the faces of a sandstone cliff, are groups of colossal
rock sculptures done in the 15th century.   The Rajput
ruler Raja Man Singh made Gwalior a center of culture
and built a monumental palace.   It became the capital
of the Sindhias in 1771 but passed under British rule
after the Sepoy Mutiny.   It was returned to the Sindhias
in 1886 in return for Jhansi district.

GYMKHANA.   Place of public resort where facilities are
provided for athletics and games.   (From Hindi gend-
khana, racket court, influenced by English gymnasium.)

- H -

HABSHIES.   Muslim Abyssinian negroes who became a very
powerful group in the Bahmani kingdom.   A band of

Abyssinians established a pirate center at Jinjee and terrorized the Arabian Sea until destroyed by Shivaji in 1677. One slave of Abyssinian descent became the tyrant of Bengal under the name of Sams-ud-din Muzzaffar Shah.

HAFIZ. A title of honor bestowed on a Muslim who has memorized the Koran.

HAIDER ALI KHAN (also, Hyder Ali). 1722-1782. Soldier of fortune who overthrew the Hindu raja of Mysore and became the maharaja in 1766. He extended his sway over Canara but soon came into conflict with the English who formed a league with the Marathas against him in 1767. A war ensued resulting in the defeat of the English, who were compelled to sue for peace in 1769. In 1779 he joined a confederacy against the English with the Marathas and the Nizam and invaded the Carnatic but was decisively defeated by Sir Eyre Coote at Porto Novo in 1781. He recovered sufficiently to beat a British force under Col. Braithwaite but died in 1782, leaving the throne and his unfinished campaigns to his son Tipu Sultan.

HAIHAYAS see KALACHURIS

HALEBID. Ancient capital of the Hoysala kings of Dvarasamudra.

HAMID LAHORI, ABDUL see PADSHAHNAMA

HAMILTON, WILLIAM. Surgeon in the employ of the East India Company who accompanied John Surman's embassy to the Mughal court in 1715. Hamilton gained the favor of Emperor Farrukhsiyar by curing his daughter and obtained in return a farman that granted trading concessions to the Company.

HAMIR DEVA. Chauhan king of Ranthambhor from 1282 to 1301; expanded his dominions but finally succumbed to the Muslim power after a fierce struggle with Sultan Alauddin Khalji.

HARAPPA. Place in Montgomery district in West Punjab in Pakistan; site of excavations of an ancient Indus Valley civilization in prehistoric times.

HARAVIJAYA. Poem in 50 cantos by the Kashmiri poet
   Ratnakaran who flourished in the ninth century.

HARDINGE, CHARLES, Baron of Penhurst. 1858-1944.
   Viceroy and governor general of India (1910-16). Administration marked by the Delhi Durbar of 1911, the
   reunion of Bengal and the creation of a new province
   of Bihar and Orissa, the proclamation of New Delhi as
   the capital, and the outbreak of World War I.

HARDINGE, HENRY, First Viscount Hardinge of Lahore.
   1785-1856. Governor general of India (1844-48). Administration marked by the expansion of the railway
   system and the suppression of barbarous native customs
   such as sati, infanticide, and human sacrifices. He
   also successfully conducted the First Sikh War which
   ended with the Treaty of Lahore.

HARDWAR (also, Gangadwara). Ancient city in Uttar Pradesh on the right bank of the Ganges where the river
   comes out of the Himalayas into the plain at the foot
   of the Siwalik Hills; known in Vedic times as Magapur
   or Kapila. It is one of seven sacred Hindu cities and
   an important place of pilgrimage where a kumbh mela
   takes place every three years.

HAR GOVIND. The sixth Guru of the Sikhs (1606-45). Imprisoned by Jahangir for 12 years; on his release gathered his forces and defeated the imperial army at
   Sangram in 1628 but was eventually compelled to flee to
   Kashmir where he died.

HARIHARA I. One of the five sons of Sangama who founded
   in 1336 the city of Vijayanagar and helped to establish
   the famous Hindu kingdom of that name.

HARIJAN (sing. and pl.). Literally, children (or child) of
   god. Term coined by Mahatma Gandhi and used to re-
   fer to members of the untouchable class. See also
   PANCHAMA.

HARISCHANDRA. 1850-85. Founder of modern Hindi drama, also known by the title of Bharatendu or Moon of
   India. He wrote over 175 works including 18 plays.

HAR KISHAN. The eighth Guru of the Sikhs (1661-64); son
   of Har Rai.

HAR RAI. The seventh Guru of the Sikhs (1645-61).

HARSHA. Form of Sanskrit script known as siddha-matrika.

HARSHA CHARITA. Historical record of the reign of Harshavardhana written by Bana.

HARSHA ERA. Era established by Harshavardhana dated from his accession to the throne in 606.

HARSHAVARDHANA (or, Harsha). King of Kanauj and Thaneswar (606-47). He was the brother of Rajyavardhana and the son of Prabhakaravardhana, founder of the Pushyabhuti Dynasty. His reign was marked by incessant wars with Sasanka, the king of Bengal and the Chalukyas. He succeeded in subduing Valabhi, Magadha, Gujarat, and Sind. His empire extended at its zenith from the Himalayas to the Narmada and from Ganjam in the east to Valabhi in the west. He assumed the title of maharajadhiraja or emperor. As a patron of Buddhism he held quinquennial assemblies in which he distributed large treasures. One of these assemblies was attended by the Chinese pilgrim Hiuen Tsang. Harsha was also a poet and dramatist and a patron of letters; the Sanskrit drama Nagananda has been attributed to him.

HARTAL. A complete suspension of work and business as a mode of protest or as a mark of respect; often used as an instrument of civil disobedience.

HARYANA. State of the Indian Union created in 1966, comprising the Hindi-speaking districts of Punjab: Hissar, Mohindergarh, Gurgaon, Rohtak, and Karnal, and parts of Sangrur and Ambala districts. Capital: Chandigarh.

HASAN-UN-NIZAMI. Muslim historian; author of Taj-ul-Ma'asir, a history of the sultanate of Delhi.

HASB-UL-HUKM. Literally, according to order. The initial formula of a state document issued on royal authority. Applied by extension to the document itself.

HASTA. A unit of length in ancient India equivalent to 18 inches.

HASTINGS, Marquis of, Earl of Moira. Full name: Francis

Rawdon.   1754-1826.   Governor general and commander
in chief of India (1813-23).   Consolidated British hegemony over the whole of India through the successful
conduct of three wars: the Napalese War (1814-16),
the Pindari War (1817-19), and the Third Maratha War
(1817-19).   The Treaty of Sagauli which ended the
Nepalese War gained Simla for the British; the Third
Maratha War and the Pindari War led to the extinction
of the Pindaris and the pacification of the Peshwas, the
Bhonslas, and the Sindhias.   Hastings also abolished
the censorship of the press, increased the number of
courts, and introduced the ryotwari system of revenue
collection.   He resigned because of imputations growing
out of his permission to the banking house of Palmer--
with which he was connected--to lend money to the
Nizam.

HASTINGS, WARREN.   1732-1818.   Governor general of
India.   He entered the Company service as a writer at
Calcutta at the age of 18 in 1750; appointed member of
the Bengal Council under Vansittart in 1761; returned
to England in 1764; came back to India as member of
the Madras Council in 1769; appointed governor of Bengal in 1772 and governor general of India in 1774.
Hastings immediately found himself in conflict with his
councilors who insisted on reviewing and reversing all
of his acts.   The fight with the Council was not re-
solved until 1780 when Philip Francis, the leader of the
opposition, was wounded in a duel with Hastings and
forced to return to England.
    Hastings abandoned the dual system set up by Clive
and restructured the judicial and revenue administration.
He created two courts in Calcutta: the Sadr Diwani
Adalat presided over by the governor general in council
for civil cases and the Sadr Nizamat Adalat presided
over by the naib nazim for criminal cases.   He also
transferred the treasury from Murshidabad to Calcutta
and stopped the payment of tribute to the emperor and
halved the allowance paid to the nawab of Bengal.
    His external policy was equally successful.   He de-
posed Chait Singh, the raja of Benares; confiscated the
wealth of the Begums of Oudh, reduced the Rohillas to
submission; broke up the alliance of Haider Ali, Nizam,
and Marathas; captured Bassein and Gwalior; and pacified the Marathas by the Treaty of Salbai (1782).
    Hastings retired in 1785.   Three years later he was
impeached on 20 charges in which the treatment of Chait

Singh and the Begums of Oudh figured largely. He was
acquitted in a famous trial in 1795 in which Edmund
Burke, Richard Sheridan, and Charles Fox were among
the prosecutors.

HAVALDAR. Officer in the Maratha Army, especially the
commandant of a fort. In British Indian Army it de-
signated a sepoy non-commissioned officer corresponding
to a sergeant.

HAVELOCK, General Sir HENRY. 1795-1857. British general during the Sepoy Mutiny; defeated Nana Sahib and
retook Kanpur and Lucknow. He also took part in campaigns in Persia, Afghanistan, and Burma.

HAWKINS, Capt. WILLIAM. Commander of the third voyage
of the Hector to the East Indies; reached Surat in 1608
with a letter from King James I to Emperor Jahangir.
He remained in Jahangir's court until 1611. He returned to England in 1612 and wrote an account of his
experiences.

HAZARI. Commander of a thousand; title of honor granted
at the Mughal court.

HEDIN, SVEN see INDUS

HEMACHANDRA. 1088-1172. Jain monk and scholar patronized by the Solanki king of Gujarat and Kathiawar.
He compiled several dictionaries: a lexicon of Sanskrit
homonyms and synonyms, a botanical glossary, a glossary of provincial words, a biographical dictionary
known as Purusha-charita or Lives of Great Men, and
a manual of politics known as Laghu-arthaniti.

HEMADRI. Jurist under the Yadava kings of Warangal in
the 13th century; author of Chaturvargachintamani.

HEMU. The Hindu chief minister of Adil Shah, the third
ruler of the Sur Dynasty (1554-56). On the death of
Humayun in 1555 Hemu led a large army and captured
Agra, Gwalior, and Delhi. He declared himself an independent sovereign with the title of Raja Bikramajit and
was opposed by Akbar at the Second Battle of Panipat
in 1556. Hemu was defeated, taken prisoner, and beheaded.

HICKY, JAMES AUGUSTUS.   Publisher and editor of first
newspaper in India, the Bengal Gazette (founded 1780).

HIMACHEL PRADESH.   State of the Indian Union that was
constituted as a Union Territory in 1948 comprising 30
former hill states.   The state of Bilaspur was merged
with Himachel Pradesh in 1954.   Under the Punjab Reorganization Act of 1966 certain parts of Punjab were
transferred to Himachel Pradesh: the districts of Simla,
Kulu, Kangra, Lahaul, and Spiti, and parts of Hoshiarpur and Ambala districts.   Capital: Simla.

HIMACHEL SCHOOL   see   PAHARI SCHOOL

HIMALAYAS.   Literally, the abode of snow.   Classical
name: Emodus, Imaus.   Mountain system extending from
the meeting of the borders of USSR, Kashmir, Afghanistan, and Sinkiang, through Nepal, Bhutan, and south
Tibet; contains the highest mountains of the world and
the sources of the Indus, Ganges, and Brahmaputra.
The mountains rise in two parallel ranges: the outer
or southern Himalayas and the inner or northern Himalayas.   The highest peaks are: Everest (29,141 ft.),
K2 (28,250 ft.), Kanchenjunga (28,146 ft.), and
Dhaulagiri (26,492 ft.).

HINAYANA.   Literally, the lower vehicle.   Buddhist sect.
The prevalent form of Buddhism in Ceylon and Burma;
hence also known as Southern Buddhism.   Sometimes
called Theravada from Sanskrit thera, elder.   Its
scriptures are written in Pali.   According to this sect
Gautama Buddha is only a buddha and not a god.   It
offers no prayers or offerings to the Buddha and does
not worship his image.

HINDI [see also MODERN HINDI].   Official language of India; based on Sanskrit and written in Devanagiri script.
It began to be used as a literary language in the 16th
century.   Its two main divisions are: Western and
Eastern.   Western comprises five subdialects: Brajbhasa, Kanauj, Bundeli, Gungaru, and Hindustani.
Eastern has three subdialects: Awadhi, Bagheli, and
Chhattisgarhi.   Awadhi was the language of Tulsi Das
and Hindustani the language of Lalla Lal, the author of
Prem Sagar.   A variant script called Dakhini is used
in the South.

HINDUISM. Religion of India based on the Vedas, the Upanishads, the Bhagavad Gita, the Ramayana, the Mahabharata, and the Sadadarshana or six systems of philosophy. Known as Brahminism in the pre-Buddhist period. It is divided into many sects; three are the Saivas, the Saktas, and the Vaishnavas. Its main tenets include karma, transmigration of souls, mukti or moksha, jajna or sacrificial offerings, and paramatma (supreme soul).

HINDU MAHASABHA. Chauvinist political organization advocating Hindu dominance in Indian Union; founded around 1900 and became a political force under the leadership of Pundit Madan Mohan Malaviya, Lala Lajpat Rai, and V. D. Savarkar.

HINDU-PAD-PADSHAHI. Literally, Hindu empire. Goal of the Hindu rulers who united under Peshwa Baji Rao I to overthrow Muslim rule and establish a Hindu paramountcy in its place.

HINDUSTAN. Literally, land of the Hindus. Loosely used as a synonym for India and more restrictively for India north of the Vindhya Mountains.

HINDUSTANI. Standard vernacular form of both Hindi and Urdu which developed in Rohilkhand. It belongs to the West Hindi group of Hindi languages.

HINDVI see MODERN HINDI

HISAM-UD-DIN A'GHUL BAK, MALIK see OUDH

HITOPADESA. Literally, sound advice. Sanskrit anthology of stories ascribed to Narayana, a Tantrik writer who lived in Bengal in the 13th century.

HIUEN TSANG (or, Yuan Chwang). The most famous of Chinese Buddhist pilgrim-scholars. He came to India in 630 and remained there until 643. He spent eight years (635-43) in the empire of Harshavardhana as his guest and participated in the quinquennial assembly at Allahabad. His observations are recorded in Travels or Records of Western Lands in 12 chuans or books. He also stayed in Nalanda University as a student. He returned to China in 645 bringing with him 657 volumes of manuscripts. He spent the rest of his life translating some of them into Chinese. He died in 664.

HO.   A Kolarian aboriginal tribe related to the Munda.

HOBSON-JOBSON.   (1) A native festival.   The term is a
   corrupt rendering of the Muslim cry, "Ya Hasan! Ya
   Hasan!" during the Muharrum procession.
        (2) (By extension) any corrupt form of native Indian
   words and names used by Europeans.
        (3) Title of an Anglo-Indian dictionary on historical
   principles by Henry Yule and A. C. Burnell.

HOLI.   Major Hindu festival, believed to be once a fertility
   rite of aboriginal origin, celebrated in February-March
   by throwing colored powders and sprinkling colored
   liquids at people.

HOLKAR.   Maratha dynasty and state founded by Malhar
   Rao, a lieutenant of Baji Rao I.   He established himself
   in southwestern Malwa with capital at Indore.   His
   son's widow, the Rani Ahalya Bai, ruled the state with
   great success from 1765 to 1795.   Jaswant Rao I who
   succeeded to the gadi in 1798 was defeated by the British during the Second Maratha War and forced to make
   peace.   His successor Malhar Rao II suffered another
   defeat at the hands of the British during the Third
   Maratha War and was forced to turn over his lands as
   a protected state by the Treaty of Mandasor in 1818.
   The later Holkars were undistinguished rulers.   The
   Holkar Dynasty consisted of ten rulers:
        Malhar Rao (1728)   Hari Rao (1834)
        Ahalya Bai (1765)   Tukoji Rao II (1843)
        Tukoji (1795)   Shivaji Rao (1886)
        Jaswant Rao I (1798)   Tukoji Rao III (1903)
        Malhar Rao II (1811)   Jaswant Rao II (1926)

HOME RULE LEAGUE.   Name of two shortlived nationalist
   organizations, one founded by Bal Gangadhar Tilak in
   Poona in April 1916 and the other by Annie Besant in
   Calcutta in September 1916.

HOOGHLY.   Westernmost river of the Ganges Delta formed
   by the Bhagirathi, Jalangi, and Matabhanga Rivers.
   Length: 150 miles.

HORA-SASTRA see VARAHAMIHIRA

HORI see DHRUPAD

HOWDAH.   Seat for riding on an elephant, often embellished
with expensive trappings and ornaments on royal travels.

HOYSALA.   Dynasty founded by Bittiga or Bittideva in 1111
under the title of Vishnuvardhana.   The Hoysala capital
was Dvarasamudra or the modern Halebid.   The dynasty
was finally overthrown in 1326 by Alauddin Khalji.

HUGHLI.   (1) Westernmost channel of the Ganges, also
called Bhagirathi.
    (2) Town on the Hughli River; site of a Portuguese
settlement in the 16th century that was destroyed by the
Mughals in 1632.

HUMAYUN.   1508-1556.   Second Mughal emperor (1530-40;
1555-56).   He was defeated by the Afghan leader Sher
Khan Sur at the Battle of Chaunsa in 1539 and again in
1540 at the Battle of Kanauj and lost his throne.   He
fled to Persia, gained the support of Shah Tahmasp and
regained Kandahar and Kabul from his brother Kamran.
When the descendants of Sher Shah were in disarray in
1555 Humayun led an invasion of India and regained his
throne by defeating the Afghan forces in the Battle of
Sirhind.   He died six months later.

HUME, ALLAN OCTAVIAN.   1829-1912.   British-born Indian Civil Servant; founder of the Indian National Congress and its secretary for the first 22 years (1885-
1908).

HUN.   A former gold pagoda coin.

HUNA ERA.   Era of the Huns established by Toramana
dated from 448.

HUNS.   Nomadic invaders of India in the fifth century under
Toramana and his son Mihiragula.   They were defeated
in 528 by a confederacy led by Yasodharman, the king
of Malwa, and Narasimha, the Gupta king of Magadha.
They are believed to have later assimilated into Indian
society as Rajputs.

HUSAIN SHAH.   Founder of the Husain Shahi Dynasty of
Bengal who deposed Sultan Sams-ud-din; ruler of Bengal
(1493-1519).

HUSSAIN SHAH SHARQI.   Ruler of Jaunpur (1457-76), last

in the Sharqi line.   He achieved some military suc-
cesses early in his reign with expeditions against Orissa and Gwalior.   But he was defeated and dispossessed
of his kingdom in 1476 by Sultan Bahlol Lodi.   He fled
to Colgong where he spent his later days.   He is
credited with inventing the khyal, a form of romantic
verse.   He died in 1500.

HUVISHKA (also, Huska).   Kushan king who ruled from 162
to 180; son of Kanishka.

HYDASPES, BATTLE OF.   Battle in 325 B.C. between
Alexander the Great and King Poros in which the latter
was defeated.

HYDERABAD.   (1) Formerly, Nizam's Dominions.   State in
the Deccan founded in 1713 by Asaf Jah, subadar who
declared himself independent.   French influence was in
the ascendant in the court of the third and fourth
Nizams, Muzaffar Jang and Salabat Jang.   A treaty of
alliance was made with the British in 1766 and it became a protected state in 1798.   The Nizam refused to
join the Indian Union in 1947 and the state was occupied
by Indian troops in a police action in 1948.   Now part
of Andhra Pradesh.
        (2) City in the Deccan; former capital of Hyderabad
State and present capital of Andhra Pradesh.   It was
founded in 1589 by Muhammad Kuli on the bank of the
Musi River.   Its most important architectural monument
is the Char Minar.

- I -

IBADAT KHANA.   Literally, the house of worship.   Building in Fatehpur Sikri in which discussions on religion
were held.

IBN-BATUTA, ABU ABDULLAH MUHAMMAD.   c1304-c1377.
Arab traveler who visited India from 1333 until 1342
and left a historical account of the reign of Sultan
Muhammad Tughluq.

IBRAHIM ADIL SHAH II.   Sixth sultan of the Adil Shahi
Dynasty of Bijapur (1580-1626).   He was the son of
Chand Bibi, the famous princess of Ahmadnagar.   In
1595 he defeated and killed the sultan of Ahmadnagar and

extended his borders to Mysore. He is best remembered as the patron of Firishta, the historian who faith-
fully chronicled his tolerant reign and his many civil
and revenue reforms.

IBRAHIM LODI.   Third sultan of the Lodi Dynasty and the
last sultan of the Delhi Sultanate (1517-26).   Defeated
and killed by Babur in the First Battle of Panipat in
1526.

IKHTIYAR-UD-DIN MUHAMMAD.   First Muslim conqueror
of Bengal and son of Bakhtiyar Khalji; conquered Bihar
in 1192.   Later he seized Nadia, the capital of the
Sena kings of Bengal and established himself as governor of Bengal with capital at Gaur.   He died in 1206.

ILAHI ERA.   Literally, the Divine Era.   Era established by
Akbar in 1584 and dated from 1556.

ILANGO (also, Ilanko-Adigal).   Chola prince of the seventh
century; author of Silappadigaram, one of the classic
narrative poems in Tamil literature.   A sequel known
as Manimekalai was written by Sattanar.

ILBERT BILL.   Bill sponsored by Sir Courtney Persegrime
Ilbert in 1883 providing that persons of European birth
could be tried by Indian judges.   The bill met with considerable opposition from die-hard Europeans and was
later amended.

ILIYAS SHAH.   Founder of the Iliyas Shahi Dynasty who
ruled Bengal from 1345 to 1490; conquered eastern Bengal in 1352 and subdued Orissa and Tirhut; repulsed an
invasion by Sultan Firoz Shah Tughluq.

ILTUTMISH.   Sultan of Delhi (1211-36).   He was a manu-
mitted slave of Sultan Qutb-ud-din Aibak who rose to
become governor of Badaun and married the sultan's
daughter.   He ascended the throne after defeating Qutb-
ud-din's heir and successor, Aram.   He suppressed a
revolt of Muslim nobles in the provinces; conquered
Malwa and regained Ranthambhor and Gwalior; held off
Chingiz [Genghis] Khan's Mongol hordes; and built the
famous Qutb Minar.

IMAD SHAHI.   Dynasty founded in Berar by Fathullah who
assumed the title of Imad-ul-Mulk. The dynasty ruled

Berar from 1490 until 1574 and consisted of five rulers:
Fatullah (1490), Ala-ud-din (1504), Darya (1529), Burhan (1562), and Tufal (1568).

IMAD-UL-MULK.   Title conferred on highest officials of the
Mughal Empire.

IMPERIAL GAZETTEER OF INDIA.   Monumental work in
26 volumes initiated in 1869 and completed 1907-09 under
William W. Hunter based on a statistical survey of the
topography, ethnology, agriculture, industry, and administration of 240 districts under British and native
rule.   Reissued 1908-1909 in a Provincial Series in 25
volumes.

IMPERIAL LEGISLATIVE COUNCIL.   Legislative body constituted by the Indian Councils Act of 1861.   Its powers
and membership were amended by the Indian Councils
Act of 1892 and the Government of India Act of 1909.
It was renamed Indian Legislative Assembly in 1919 and
the Parliament of India in 1947.

IMPEY, Sir ELIJAH.   1732-1809.   First chief justice of
Bengal (1774-82).   He supported Warren Hastings in his
struggle with the Council; presided at the trial of Nandkumar and sentenced him to death; was recalled in 1783
and threatened with impeachment.

INAM.   Literally, gift or reward.   Rent-free land granted
by the state and held in perpetuity.   The holder of an
inam was known as an inamdar.

INAMDAR   see INAM

INDEPENDENCE DAY.   National day celebrated on August
15 to mark the transfer of power from the British
Crown to the people of India on August 15, 1947.

INDEPENDENCE OF INDIA ACT.   Act of British Parliament
1947 providing for the transfer of sovereign power in
British India to two new dominions, the Union of India
and Pakistan.   It also provided for the lapse of British
paramountcy over native states which became free to
join either dominion.

INDIA.   (1) Geographical region in south Asia; used in ancient times to denote the country of the Indus River and

later extended to cover the entire subcontinent south of the Himalayas, east of Persia, and west of Burma. Also called Hither India or India intra Gangem as distinguished from Further India or India extra Gangem which denoted southeast Asia. From Sanskrit Sindhu, the Indus River.

(2) (also, Bharat). Union of India, a republic established in 1950 with capital at New Delhi. It comprises 21 states and 10 Union Territories:

States

Andhra Pradesh	Manipur
Assam	Meghalaya
Bihar	Nagaland
Gujarat	Orissa
Haryana	Punjab
Himachel Pradesh	Rajasthan
Jammu & Kashmir	Sikkim
Karnataka	Tamil Nadu
Kerala	Tripura
Madhya Pradesh	Uttar Pradesh
Maharashtra	West Bengal
Union	

Union Territories

Andaman & Nicobar	Daman and Diu
Arunachal Pradesh	Goa
Chandigarh	Lakshadweep
Dadra and Nagar Haveli	Mizoram
Delhi	Pondicherry

INDIA COUNCIL (also, Council of India). Body created by the Government of India Act of 1858 to replace the Board of Control. The membership of the Council varied from 12 to 15 and its primary function was to advise the secretary of state for India who was also its president. It was abolished in 1937.

INDIAN ADMINISTRATIVE SERVICE see INDIAN CIVIL SERVICE

INDIAN CIVIL SERVICE. Cadre of superior civil servants and administrators established during the administration of Lord Cornwallis (1786-93) as the "Covenanted Civil Service," because its members had to sign a covenant. Almost all administrative positions above a subcollector were filled by thus covenanted civil

servants.   The Service was described by Lloyd George
as the "steel frame of the empire. "   Under Lord Wellesley the training of civil servants was undertaken by
the College of Fort William at Calcutta and later by
the Haileybury College in England.   From 1853 recruitment was based on competition through public examination; hence members of the Service were nicknamed
competitionwalas.   Indians were not admitted to the
Indian Civil Service until 1864, when Satyendranath
Tagore (brother of Rabindranath) became the first to
pass the competitive examination.   From 1922 examina-
tions were held simultaneously in India and Great
Britain.   The Civil Service was renamed Indian Administrative Service in 1947.

INDIAN CONSTITUENT ASSEMBLY. Body set up in 1946
to draw up a constitution for India.   The assembly
adopted the present Constitution of India in 1949 declaring India to be a federal democratic republic with an
elected president.   The Constitution came into force on
January 20, 1950.

INDIAN COUNCIL FOR CULTURAL RELATIONS. Center
founded in 1950 in New Delhi to strengthen cultural relations between India and other countries; branches in
Bombay, Calcutta, and Madras.   Its activities include
exchange visits between scholars, artists, and persons
of eminence, publications, exhibitions, and lectures,
and work with overseas students.   Publishes Indo-Asian
Culture, Cultural News from India, Thaqafat-ul-Hind,
and ICCR Newsletter.

INDIAN COUNCILS ACTS.   1861: Act of British Parliament
enlarging the powers and membership of the viceroy's
executive council and including nonofficial Indians.   It
also restored to the governments of Bombay and Madras
the right to legislate through executive councils and
created legislative councils in other provinces.
1870: Act of British Parliament empowering governor
general in council to pass ordinances.   It also empow-
ered the governor general to override his council.
1892: Act of British Parliament increasing the powers and membership of the legislative council in the
Center and in the provinces.   The right to discuss bud-
gets and to put interpellations was granted.

INDIAN INSTITUTE OF WORLD CULTURE.   Institute founded

in Bangalore and London to promote exchange between
India and other countries in the field of culture.   Publishes an Annual Report and Transactions.

INDIAN MUSEUM.   Museum established at Calcutta in 1814
to house the zoological, geological, and archaeological
collections of the Asiatic Society of Bengal.   Comprises
six sections: art, anthropology, archaeology, zoology,
geology, and economic botany.

INDIAN NATIONAL CONGRESS.   Indian nationalist organization founded in 1885 on the initiative of an Englishman,
Allan Octavian Hume.   It held its first session in Bombay in 1885 with W. C. Banerjee as president.   At first
a moderate body whose purpose was to voice Indian
grievances it gradually escalated its demands until it
came to espouse, under the leadership of Mahatma
Gandhi, purna swaraj or complete independence.   Its
economic philosophy was based on the promotion of
swadeshi or home industries; its members were expected to wear khaddar or home-spun cloth and its flag
was a tricolor with a charkha or spinning wheel in the
middle.
    The Congress always encompassed extremists and
moderates, socialists and nonsocialists, Hindus and
Muslims within its ranks.   Among the moderates were
G. K. Gokhale, Tej Bahadur Sapru. Motilal Nehru,
Phiroz Shah Mehta, and Dadhabhai Naoroji and among
the extremists Subhas Chandra Bose, Lala Lajpat Rai,
and B. G. Tilak.   It has remained the ruling political
party in India since independence and was for some
time practically coextensive with the state.   In the late
sixties it split into Old and New Congress but the latter
organization under Indira Gandhi was swept into power
in 1970; it is now often referred to as the Congress
Party.

INDIAN PENAL CODE.   Code drawn up by the Indian Law
Commission presided over by Lord Macaulay and enacted in 1860.   The Codes of Civil and Criminal Procedure were enacted in 1861.

INDIAN SOCIETY OF ORIENTAL ART.   Association founded
in 1907 in Calcutta for the promotion of the study of
ancient and contemporary Indian art.   Publishes a
Journal and portfolios and monographs on art.

INDIC.   Branch of the Indo-Iranian group of the Indo-European family of languages whose members include classical Sanskrit, the Prakrits, and the Apabhramsas.

INDO-ARYANS.   Aryans who invaded India about 2000 B. C. and settled in the Indo-Gangetic plain after subduing such autochthonous people as the Dasas.   They were a pastoral people whose religion was based on the Vedas.

INDO-CHINA WAR.   War in 1962 between India and China following border disputes.   In a successful campaign China occupied large areas of Ladakh against an ill-equipped and ill-trained Indian Army.

INDO-GREEKS.   Greek princelings (such as Demetrios, Menander, Antialkidas, and Hermaios) who ruled northern India from the second century B. C. to the first century A. D.

INDO-PAKISTANI WARS.   (1) Armed conflict in 1965 between India and Pakistan over Kashmir.   Ended indecisively with the Tashkent Declaration.
      (2) Armed conflict in 1971 between India and Pakistan over Bangladesh.   In a short and swift campaign the Indian Army liberated the former East Pakistan and helped to establish the independent state of Bangladesh.

INDO-SARACENIC ARCHITECTURE.   Muslim architecture modified by Indian elements characteristic of the Delhi Sultanate period.

INDRA.   A principal deity of the Vedas to whom one fourth of all the hymns are addressed in the Rig Veda.   He is regarded as the god of the firmament and the weather and thus as a dispenser of rain and fertility.

INDRAPRASTHA.   The legendary capital city of the Pandu princes, the protagonists in the Mahabharata; identified with and used for a part of Old Delhi.

INDUS.   Original (Sanskrit) name: Sindhu.   River rising in Tibet and flowing into the Arabian Sea through Kashmir and the Punjab with its many tributaries of which Jhelum, Chinab, Ravi, Vipasa, and the Sutlej are the most important.   It is one of the sacred rivers of the Hindus.   Its source was discovered by Sven Hedin in 1908.

INDUS VALLEY CIVILIZATION. Civilization that flourished
in the valley of the Indus River between 2500 B. C. and
1500 B. C. , evidences of which have been unearthed in
Mohenjo-Daro and Harappa. The excavations revealed
an urban culture with well-laid out towns with public
halls, places of worship, drainage, roads, and public
baths. Their skills included metallurgy, pottery, and
weaving. Their system of writing has not yet been
deciphered.

INSTITUTES OF MANU see MANUSAMHITA

INTERNATIONAL ACADEMY OF INDIAN CULTURE. Organization founded in New Delhi in 1935 to study India's
cultural and historical relations with other Asian countries.

IQBAL, Sir MUHAMMAD. 1876-1938. Muslim poet and
visionary who conceived the idea of a separate Muslim
homeland within the Indian subcontinent; author of Six
Lectures on the Reconstruction of Religious Thought.

IRWIN, Lord; Earl of Halifax. Full name: Edward Frederick Lindley Wood. 1881-1959. Viceroy and governor
general of India (1925-31). His administration was
marked by the appointment of the Simon Commission,
the Civil Disobedience Movement under Mahatma Gandhi, and the Gandhi-Irwin Pact, which was designed to
mollify the Indian nationalists.

ISANAVARMAN see MAUKHARI

ISLAM SHAH SUR. Original name: Jalal Khan; also known
as Salim Shah. Emperor of Delhi (1540-54); son and
successor of Sher Shah; built the fortress of Mankot
in Kashmir.

ITIHASA. Literally, thus indeed it was. A historical epic
about legendary or semilegendary heroes and deeds, as
for example the Mahabharata and Ramayana.

I-TSING (or, I-Ching). Chinese monk and pilgrim who
visited India in 675 and lived at the University of Nalanda until 685; author of A Record of the Buddhist Religion
as Practiced in India and the Malay Archipelago.

IZHAVA. A Panchama class of Malabar also known as
Thiya.

- J -

JAGADDALA. Tantrik seat of learning founded by Rama-
     pala in 1090. It was destroyed in 1207.

JAGANNATH. Literally, the lord of the universe. Name
     of Krishna worshiped as Vishnu at the famous shrine
     at Puri in Orissa. Hobson-Jobsonized as "Juggernaut"
     in modern English.

JAGAT SETH. Literally, world banker. Title conferred
     on Fatehchand, nephew of Manickchand, millionaire
     Bengali banker of the 18th century whose family con-
     trolled the purchase of bullion, regulated the rate of
     exchange, received the land revenue paid by the zamin-
     dars, and remitted the money to the imperial treasury.
     Fatehchand's son, Mahatabchand, played an important
     role in the defeat of Siraj-ud-daulah but the power of
     the family declined after the rise of the Company.

JAGAT SINGH, RANA. Ruler of Mewar, grandson of Rana
     Pratap and son of Rana Amar Singh. He rebuilt the
     famous fort of Chitor. The rebuilt fort was, however,
     demolished in 1654 on the orders of Shah Jahan.

JAI SINGH II. Chief of Amber and Jaipur (1699-1743). On
     the death of Aurangzeb he made an abortive attempt to
     overthrow the Mughal yoke but was later pardoned by
     Bahadur Shah and appointed viceroy of Malwa and Agra.
     He is best remembered as the founder of the city of
     Jaipur and as an astronomer and mathematician who
     built observatories in Jaipur and Delhi.

JAGIR. Land held by a jagirdar and assigned to him by the
     state either conditionally or unconditionally. In the
     former case some public service such as the levy and
     the maintenance of troops was provided for. The as-
     signment was usually for life, lapsing to the state on
     the holder's death, though often renewed to his heir on
     the payment of a nazrana or fine.

JAGJIVANDAS. 1682-1750. Hindi religious poet.

JAHANDAR SHAH. Emperor of India (1712-13); deposed and
     killed by his successor, Farrukhsiyar, with the help of
     the Sayyid brothers.

JAHANGIR.   Original name: Nur-ud-din Muhammad; also,
     Salim.   Fourth Mughal emperor of India (1605-27).
     His consort, Nur Jahan, exercised effective control
     over the administration and her name appeared on the
     coinage.   His rule was troubled by the revolts of his
     sons Khusrav and Khurram and his general, Mahabat
     Khan.   He extended the empire by annexing Ahmadnagar
     in 1616 and Kangra in 1620.   He reduced the Afghan
     barons of Bengal to submission in 1612 and forced Rana
     Amar Singh of Mewar to yield his independence in 1614.

JAI CHAND.   King of Kanauj and Varanasi in the 12th cen-
     tury.   His rival Prithviraj, king of Ajmer and Delhi,
     carried off his daughter and in retaliation Jai Chand
     helped Shihab-ud-din Muhammad Ghori to defeat and
     kill Prithviraj at the Battle of Tarain in 1192.   Jai
     Chand met with the same fate next year at the Battle
     of Chandwar and the kingdom disappeared from the an-
     nals of history.

JAIMINI.   Hindu saint and philosopher, pupil of Vyasa, and
     founder of the Purvamimamsa school of philosophy.

JAINISM.   Religion founded in the sixth century B. C. by
     Vardhamana Mahavira based on the teachings of Pars-
     vanath, both ascetics who are revered as jinas or con-
     querors of passions.   Jainism denies the existence of
     god, though Jinas and Shasanadevis are revered as
     superior and Ganadharas as guardian saints.   Jains re-
     ject also the Vedas, animal sacrifices, and the caste
     system but accept Brahmin priesthood and the doctrine
     of karma.
          They are divided into a clerical body (yatis, or as-
     cetics) and a lay body (shravakas, or listeners).   They
     have two principal sects, Svetambaras (those having
     white garments) and Digambaras (those having the air
     as their garment).   Another division is that into north-
     ern and southern Jains, which, originally geographical,
     has extended to the entire body of canon and traditions.
          Jainism holds that salvation can be attained only
     through tri-ratna--right faith, right conduct, and right
     knowledge--and ahimsa, or nonviolence, is regarded as
     an essential requisite for achieving tri-ratna.   No Hindu
     sect is more rigorous in respect for everything that has
     life because Jains believe--unlike Buddhists--that souls
     are eternal.   The Jain canons include purvas, angas,
     upanga, mula sutra; the Svetambara scriptures are

comprised of 45 works in six groups, called agamas, written in Ardhamagadhi; those of the Digambaras are written in Sanskrit.

JAINTIA. Kingdom that formerly occupied the territory between Jaintia Hills and the Barak River; founded about 1500 by Parbat Ray with capital at Jaintiapur. It was often at war with neighboring Cooch Behar and the Ahoms. The state was annexed by the British in 1835. Its people are related to the Khasis.

JAIPAL (also, Jayapala). Shahiya king of Waihand (Udabhandapur) who ruled over a large kingdom extending from Kangra to Laghman in Afghanistan. He was defeated twice by the Muslim rulers of Ghazni--Amir Sabuktigin and his son, Sultan Mahmud.

JAIPUR. (1) State in Rajasthan; founded in 1128 by Dulha Rai, a Kachhwaha Rajput; allies of the Mughals under Akbar; later secured British protection by the Treaty of Jaipur in 1817.
     (2) City in Rajasthan; capital of former Jaipur state and present-day Rajasthan; founded in 1728 by Maharaja Jai Singh II who also built an astronomical observatory there.

JAI SINGH. Chief of Amber (Jaipur); commander of the Mughal Army under Aurangzeb; defeated Prince Shuja and Prince Dara in the war of succession; forced Shivaji to conclude the Treaty of Purandahar ceding 23 forts to the Emperor at Delhi and acknowledging his suzerainty.

JAJATI see KESARI

JAJNAGAR. Name by which Orissa was known to the Muslims.

JALAL-UD-DIN KHALJI. Original name: Firuz Shah Khalji. Founder of the Khalji Dynasty and sultan of Delhi (1290-96). Repulsed a Mongol invasion in 1292. Murdered by Alauddin, his nephew and son-in-law, in 1296.

JALLIANWALLA BAGH. Public square in Amritsar; scene in 1919 of the infamous massacre on the orders of General Reginald Dyer of 379 anti-British demonstrators. A commission of inquiry into the shooting censured the general, who was permitted to resign.

JAM. Title borne by certain chiefs in Kutch, Kathiawar, and lower Indus.

JAMABANDI. The determination of the amount of land revenue due for a year or a period of years from an estate or village. Also applied to the annual rent-roll giving details of the holding of each cultivator.

JAMADAR. (In the modern Indian Army) officer of a company of sepoys ranking below a subadar.

JAMDAD. A type of dagger, broad at the base and slightly curved, with a cross grip.

JAMMU AND KASHMIR. (1) Former native state ruled by a dynasty of Dogra rulers founded by Golab Singh who obtained Jammu from Ranjit Singh in 1820 and Kashmir from the British in 1846. In 1947 the maharaja Hari Singh acceded to the Dominion of India. This led to an invasion of the state by Pakistani forces under the name of Azad Kashmir. The hostilities were ended by a ceasefire in 1949. War erupted again in 1966 and was concluded by the Tashkent Declaration confirming the 1949 ceasefire and leaving Pakistan in possession of 84,000 square kilometers. The monarchy was abolished in 1952.
(2) State of the Indian Union comprising four districts in the Kashmir province and six districts in the Jammu province governed by a permanent constitution that came into force in 1957. Summer capital: Srinagar; winter capital: Jammu.

JAMRUD, BATTLE OF. Battle in 1803 between Maharaja Ranjit Singh and Dost Muhammad, Amir of Afghanistan, in which the amir was defeated and compelled to surrender Peshawar.

JAMUNA. Name of the Brahmaputra River in Bangladesh.

JANA GANA MANA. National anthem of India composed by Rabindranath Tagore.

JANAKA-MELA SYSTEM see VENKATAMAKHIN

JANGAMA. A priest of the Lingayet sect.

JANMASHTAMI. Also called Gokulashtami, after Gokula, the

birthplace of Krishna.   Festival celebrating the birth of
Krishna in August-September.

JANPAN.   A type of sedan or portable chair used in the hill
   stations of North India carried by two pairs of men.

JAN SANGH.   Hindu militant political party; offshoot of
   Hindu Mahasabha.

JARIPATKA.   The pennon of the peshwa's standard; also
   the golden sash presented by the peshwa to officers in
   his service.

JASWANT SINGH.   Raja of Marwar with capital at Jodhpur;
   commander in the service of Shah Jahan and later
   Aurangzeb; died in Jamrud in 1678.

JAT.   Martial race living in the region around Agra and
   Mathura.   They rose against Aurangzeb and under
   Churaman Singh attempted to throw off the Mughal
   yoke.   His successors Badan Singh and Suraj Mal united
   the Jat people and created the state of Bharatpur.   In
   1826 the British captured the fort of Bharatpur and it
   became a protected state.

JATAKAS.   One of the sacred books of the Buddhists, a
   division of the Khuddakanikaya or collection of short
   treatises in the Suttapitaka, compiled in its present form
   in the fifth century.   It contains 547 stories, legends,
   fables, and maxims.   They deal with the lives of the
   Buddha in previous births.

JAUHAR.   Rajput martial ritual of self-immolation after
   putting wives and children to death when faced with defeat and capture.

JAUNPUR.   (1) City in Uttar Pradesh founded by Sultan Firoz
   Shah in honor of Muhammad Tughluq whose original name
   was Jauna Khan.   It was situated on the Gumti River
   and was the capital of Jaunpur state.
      (2) Independent kingdom founded by Khwaja Jahan,
   founder of the Sharqi Dynasty, during the time of Timur's invasion.   Noted for architectural monuments most
   of which date to the Sharqi rule.

JAUNSARI.   A western Pahari dialect.

JAYACHANDRA   see   GAHADVALA

JAYADEVA. Bengali poet of the 11th or 12th century in the
   court of Lakshmana, the Sena king; author of Gita
   Govinda, one of the classic Hindu dramas.

JAYANANDA   see   CHAITANYA

JAYASTAMBHA. Also known as kirttistambha. Literally,
   tower of fame. Tower built in Chitor in the 15th century by Rana Kumbha (1431-69) in celebration of a victory over the Muslims.

JEJAKABHUKTI (also, Jijhoti). Land between the Yamuna
   and the Narmada; modern Bundelkhand ruled for a
   period by the Chandellas.

JEWS OF COCHIN. Small Jewish community in Cochin believed to be descendants of immigrants who came to
   Malabar after the destruction of the Temple in 70.
   They became a flourishing community within a few centuries and in 750 their leader Joseph Rabban was
   granted feudatory rights by Cheraman Perumal. Marco
   Polo found them to be a mixed community of white and
   black Jews. In the 16th century they were almost wiped
   out by the Muslims. The Cochin synagogue was built
   in 1568, burned down by the Portuguese in 1662, and
   rebuilt in 1668.

JHALLARI. Cymbal played with two hands.

JHANSI. State in Bundelkhand; a Maratha dependency until
   1819 when it became a British protectorate. In 1853
   Lord Dalhousie annexed it to the British Empire on the
   strength of the Doctrine of Lapse. The disaffected
   dowager Rani Lakshmi Bai lent her support to the
   mutineers during the Sepoy Mutiny. It was recaptured
   by the British in 1858 and ceded to Gwalior in 1861.

JHELUM. Ancient name: Hydaspes. River in the Punjab
   rising in Kashmir and joining the Chinab northeast of
   Multan. On its banks Alexander the Great defeated
   Porus in 326 B. C.

JHOOM. Type of cultivation practiced in the hill forests of
   India under which a tract is cleared by fire, cultivated
   for a few years, and then abandoned for another area
   where the process is repeated.

JIMUTAVAHANA   see   DAYABHAGA

JINA (In Jainism) conqueror of passions.   Title of saints.

JINNAH, MUHAMMAD ALI.   1876-1948.   Muslim statesman
    who advocated the creation of Pakistan and served
    (1947-48) as its first governor general.   He was presi-
    dent (1916; 1920; 1934-48) of the All-India Muslim
    League and cooperated actively with the Indian National
    Congress from 1916 to 1921.   For his role in the cre-
    ation of Pakistan he was given the title of Qaid-i-Azam.

JITAL.   Ancient copper coin worth 1/64 of the silver tanka,
    corresponding to the pice of British India.

JIZIYA.   Poll tax levied on non-Muslims; first levied by
    Muhammad bin Kasim, the Muslim conqueror of Sind in
    712; briefly abolished under Akbar and reimposed by
    Aurangzeb; discontinued from the time of Emperor
    Muhammad Shah (1719-48).

JNANADEVA.   1275-96.   Marathi religious writer; author
    of Jnaneswari in Old Marathi.

JODHPUR.   (1) City in Rajasthan founded in 1459 by Rao
    Jodha, a descendant of Raja Jai Chand of Kanauj.
        (2) State in Rajasthan founded by Rao Chand.   En-
    tered into alliance with the Mughals and its raja Jaswant
    Singh was a commander in the army of Aurangzeb.   Af-
    ter his death Aurangzeb plotted to convert his son Ajit
    Singh to Islam.   This led to the alliance of Jodhpur,
    Jaipur, and Udaipur in the Rajput War against further
    Muslim inroads.   In 1818 Jodhpur became a British
    protectorate.

"JOHN COMPANY."   Personification of the East India Com-
    pany; believed to be a corruption of Company Jahan
    (on the model of Shah Jahan and other royal names end-
    ing with Jahan).

JOINT FAMILY.   Hindu social institution by which sons re-
    main even after marriage under the parental roof, the
    income of all members being held in common and the
    needs of each member met from the common pool.

JONES, Sir WILLIAM.   1746-94.   British Orientalist and
    jurist; appointed judge of the Supreme Court in Calcutta

in 1783; founded the Asiatic Society of Bengal in 1784; translated Kalidasa's Sakuntala, Hitopadesa, Manusamhita, and other Sanskrit works into English.   His legal works include Mohammedan Law of Inheritance and Mohammedan Law of Succession.

JONG.   Residence of a feudal chief or penlop of Bhutan.

JULLUNDER (also, Jalandhar).   (1) The doab between the Bias and the Sutlej; (2) Town and district in the Punjab.

JUMLADAR.   Officer in the Maratha Army under Shivaji and his successors.

JUMMA.   The total assessment of land revenue from any particular mahal or estate.

JUMMA MASJID.   Large mosque for congregational worship; largest of which is the one at Delhi built 1644-58.

JUMNA see YAMUNA

JUNIOR MERCHANT.   Designation of the senior category of East India Company's civil service during the period from the ninth to the eleventh year of service.

JUTKA.   Literally, quick.   Horse-drawn cab of Tamil Nadu resembling a box with open ends.

- K -

KABIR.   1488-1512.   Hindu religious reformer of Muslim birth who lived in Varanasi.   He became a disciple of Ramanand and taught a form of monotheistic Vaishnavism.   He rejected every distinction of caste, religion, and sect.   Kabir's aim was to found a religion that would unite the Hindus and Muslims.   His teachings exercised an important influence in northern India in the 15th and 16th centuries and his followers came to be known as Kabirpanthis.

KABUL.   Ancient name: Ortospana.   Capital of Afghanistan on the Kabul River.   It was part of the Indian empire under the Mauryas, the Kushans, and the Mughals.   The British captured it twice during the First Afghan War and again during the Second Afghan War.

KACHARI. Assamese tribe, the earliest known inhabitants of the Brahmaputra Valley, from whom the name of Cachar is derived. A kingdom of the Kacharis flourished from the 13th century with capital at Dimapur. Following the Ahom conquest of Assam, the Kacharis abandoned their state and founded a new kingdom with Maibong as the capital. Here they faced opposition from the Ahoms, the Burmese, and the Manipuris. The state was annexed to the British Empire in 1832.

KACHHWAHA. A Rajput tribe of Jaipur and Amber.

KADAMBA. Dynasty founded by Mayurasarman (fl. fourth century) that ruled over north and south Canara and western Mysore with its capital at Vanavasi, or Vaijayanti.

KADAMBARI see BANA

KADAR. Food-gathering forest tribe of Cochin.

KADPHISES I. Full name: Kujala Kara Kadphises. Founder of the Kushan Dynasty who ruled, from 40 to 77, a vast empire that extended beyond the Indus into Afghanistan.

KAFUR. Hindu eunuch who rose high in the service of Sultan Alauddin Khalji and became Malik-Naib in 1307. He commanded expeditions to Devagiri, Warangal, Dvarasamudra, Ma'bar, and Madurai and extended the sultan's dominions to Rameswaram. After the death of Alauddin, Kafur declared himself sultan after removing all rivals but was murdered after only 35 days on the throne.

KAIMAL. Title of a Nair chief.

KAIQUBAD. Sultan of Delhi (1287-90); a dissolute monarch who ascended the throne at the age of 17 and was overthrown and killed--thus ending the Slave Dynasty.

KAITHAL, BATTLE OF. Battle in 1240 between Sultana Raziya and her husband Altuniya on one side and her brother Bahram on the other which ended in a victory for Bahram, who was declared sultan and ruled as Muizz-ud-din Bahram from 1240 to 1242.

KAKALI. An airblown musical instrument with a soft and gentle note.

KAKATIYA. Dynasty of the kingdom of Warangal; rose to
power about 1200 after the fall of the Chalukyas of
Kalyani; defeated by the armies of Alauddin Khalji and
Ghiyas-ud-din Tughluq about 1310 and disappeared from
the annals of history when the kingdom was annexed
by Tughluq in 1320.

KALACHURIS (also, Haihayas).   People who lived in Malwa
and northern Maharashtra.   They established the Chedi
kingdom which reached its zenith under Gangeyadeva
Kalachuri (1015-40) and Karnadeva (1040-70).   The kingdom declined in power after being defeated by Kirttivarman Chandella.

KALAKSHETRA.   Center founded in Madras in 1936 for the
promotion of classical music, dancing, theatrical art,
painting, and handicraft; maintains a weaving center for
the production of silk and cotton costumes in traditional
design; publishes Kalakshetra.

KALANJAR. Strong fort in Banda district in Uttar Pradesh;
fell to Shihab-ud-din Muhammad Ghori in 1203, to Sher
Shah in 1545, and to Akbar in 1569.

KALAT.   Former British protectorate in Baluchistan ruled
by a khan. It was captured by the British in 1839-40
and annexed to the Empire in 1888.

KALHANA. Sanskrit historian; author of Rajatarangini, a
chronicle of the kings of Kashmir, written in the 12th
century.

KALI. Hindu goddess of aboriginal origin worshiped widely
in Bengal; wife of Siva and personification of the terrible
aspect of Sakti or cosmic energy. The Thugs killed
their victims in her honor. Often identified as Durga.

KALIDAS.   Sanskrit poet and dramatist of the fifth century;
one of the "nine gems" of the court of Vikramaditya.
He is the undisputed author of two dramas, Sakuntala
and Vikramorvasi and the probable author of Malavikagnimitra, Raghuvamsa, Kumarasambhava, Meghaduta, and
Ritusamhara.

KALINGA. Region on the east coast between the Mahanadi
and the Godavari Rivers; scene of a fierce and bloody
war that caused Asoka to abjure violence and embrace
Buddhism.

KALI YUGA (also, Yudhisthira Era).   Hindu era dated from
    3102 B. C.   See YUGA.

KALPASUTRA   see   MAHAVIRA

KALSI.   Unit of weight equal to about 640 lbs.

KALYANI.   City in Andhra Pradesh; capital of the Chalukya
    kingdom (973-1190).

KAMARUPA   see   ASSAM

KAMARUPA ANUSANDHAN SAMITI.   Historical research
    society founded in Gauhati, Assam, in 1912.   Publishes
    the Journal of Assam Research Society.

KAMATA   see   ASSAM

KAMBOJA.   (1) Region including southwest Kashmir in Aso-
    kan times; (2) People of Kamboja.

KANARA   see   CANARA

KANARESE.   Dravidian language spoken mainly in Karnataka.
    It received royal patronage under the Rashtrakutas of
    Malkhed and the Gangas of Talkad.   During the period
    from the 10th to the 12th century a number of Jain writ-
    ers contributed to its literature among whom was Nemi-
    chandra.   During the same period Pampa, Ponna, and
    Ranna, known as the Three Gems, wrote classic reli-
    gious works based on Jain and Hindu scriptures.   Two
    more Jain writers appeared in the 12th century: Naga-
    chandra, also called Abhinava-Pampa, and Vritta-Vilasa.
    In the 17th century Lakshmisa wrote the Jaimini Bharata
    and Shadaksharadeva wrote Rajesekhara.   The most
    famous Kanarese poet of the modern period is Govinda
    Pai.

KANAUJ.   Ancient name: Kanya Kubja; classical name:
    Canogyza.   Ancient city referred to in the Mahabharata;
    gained in importance as the capital of Harshavardhana;
    described as a prosperous fortified city four miles in
    length with numerous tanks and gardens by Hiuen Tsang
    who visited it in 636.   It was also known at this period
    as Mahodaya Sree.
        It became the capital of the Pratihara kings (816-1090).
    After the decline of the Pratihara power it came under

the rule of Gahadvala Rajputs or Rathors in the 12th century. After the defeat of Jai Chand, the last Rathor king, by Shihab-ud-din Muhammad Ghori in 1194 the city passed into oblivion and was razed to the ground by Sher Shah Sur. Its ruins are said to occupy an area greater than that of modern London.

KANCHIPURAM (or, Kanchi). City of temples in Tamil Nadu; one of the seven sacred Hindu cities; capital of Pallavas; visited by Hiuen Tsang about 640; noted as the birthplace of the Buddhist philosopher Dharmapala and the place where the Hindu philosopher Ramanuja taught for many years.

KANDA. (In Sanskrit literature) division of a larger work dealing with the same episode or theme.

KANGRA. Fort near Hardwar in Uttar Pradesh; conquered by Jahangir in 1620; the territory it commanded became a part of Ranjit Singh's dominions in 1811; annexed to the British Empire in 1848; famous for its school of painting developed under Mughal patronage [see next entry].

KANGRA VALLEY SCHOOL. School of painting which flourished in the mid-18th century in the hill states of northern India. It represented a fusion of Rajput and Mughal styles.

KANHOJI ANGIRA, fl. 18th century. Maratha pirate who terrorized the western coast of India from his strongholds at Gheria and Suvarnadrug.

KANI. (1) Coin equal to 1/64 of a monetary unit, as the jital (1/64 of a tanka) or the pice (1/64 of a rupee).
(2) Unit of land measurement in Tamil Nadu equal to 24 manais or 1.322 acres.

KANISHKA. Kushan king who is believed to have begun his reign either in 78 or in 120. He ruled for about 24 years from a capital at Peshawar and his dominions extended over Kashmir, Afghanistan, the Indo-Gangetic plain, Khotan, Yarkand, and Kashgar. The Fourth Buddhist Council was held under his auspices. He was also a great builder and is reputed to have built the tower at Peshawar, an eponymous city in Kashmir, and many monuments in Mathura, Sarnath, Taxila, and

Amaravati.   He also patronized artists of the Gandhara
School.

KANPUR.   City on the Ganges in Uttar Pradesh; former
garrison town.   It fell twice to the mutineers during the
Sepoy Mutiny and is the site of a massacre of the
British residents in 1857.

KANUNGO.   The accountant and registrar of a pargana whose
duties included the interpretation of Hindu customs to
Muslim rulers.

KANVA (or, Kanvayana).   Dynasty founded by Vasudeva in
73 B. C. in Magadha.   It lasted for 45 years.

KAPAYA NAYAKA.   Hindu chieftain of Telengana who in the
14th century joined Harihara and Bukka in overthrowing
Muslim power in the south.

KAPILA.   Sage and founder, in the sixth century B. C. , of
Samkhya, the oldest of the six orthodox systems of
Hindu philosophy.   Author of Samkhya Pravacana Sutra.

KAPILAVASTU.   Town, near the modern village of Paderia
in the Nepali Tarai (the belt of marshes and jungles that
runs along the foot of the Himalayas straddling both
Nepal and India); birthplace of Gautama Buddha and
capital of the Sakya principality.

KAPILENDRA (also, Kapileswara).   Founder of a dynasty
of Oriyan kings who ruled from 1453 to 1470.   He overthrew the Ganga Dynasty and his last descendant was
overthrown by the Bhoi Dynasty.

KAPU.   A Kshattriya subcaste of Andhra Pradesh related
to the Reddis of Andhra and the Rathors of Rajasthan;
now primarily agriculturists.

KAPUR SINGH.   Sikh leader of the 18th century who took a
leading part in developing the Khalsa.

KARDAMAKA.   Saka satrapal dynasty (77-398) founded by
Chasthana; so called after the Kardama River in Bactria.
The greatest king of this line was Rudradaman (130-158)
who built the Girnar Prasasti at Junagadh in Kathiawar.
His capital Ujjain was a center of Sanskrit culture.
His sway extended over Malwa, Kathiawar, Saurashtra,
Rajasthan, Kutch, lower Indus, Gujarat, and Konkan.

KARIKKAL   see   CHOLAS

KARKOTA.   Kashmirian dynasty founded in the seventh century by Durlabhavardhana.   It ruled until 855 when it was overthrown by the Utpalas.

KARMA-MIMAMSA   see   MIMAMSA

KARNADEVA.   Second king of the Kalachuri Dynasty of Chedi (1040-1070); son of Gangeyadeva Kalachuri.   He extended the Chedi power by inflicting a crushing defeat on Bhoja, king of Malwa in 1060.   Toward the end of his reign he suffered a defeat at the hands of Kirttivarman Chandella and this defeat is believed to mark the beginning of the decline of Chedi kingdon.

KARNAL, BATTLE OF.   Battle in 1739 between Nadir Shah and Muhammad Shah, the Mughal emperor, in which the latter was defeated.

KARNAM.   Village accountant or town clerk in Andhra Pradesh.

KARNATA   see   ARAVIDU

KARNATAKA.   State of the Indian Union constituted under the States Reorganization Act of 1956 comprising the old native states of Mysore and Coorg, Bijapur, Canara, and Dharwar districts and part of Belgaum district of the former Bombay state, parts of Gulbarga, Raichur, and Bidar districts of the former state of Hyderabad and part of South Canara district and Kollegal taluk of Coimbatore district of former Madras state.   Capital: Bangalore.

KARPURA-MANJARI.   Prakrit drama by Rajasekhara who was also the author of three Sanskrit dramas: Balaramayana, Prachandapandava, and Viddhashalabhanjika.

KARSHAPANA.   A copper coin of ancient India equal to 80 rattis.

KASHMIR.   (1) Region in northern India bounded by Afghanistan, Tibet, Sinkiang, and the Punjab.   It was a part of the Kushan Empire in the second century.   Buddhism was introduced by Asoka and flourished for a period. Later it was ruled by a succession of Hindu dynasties:

Karkota, Utpala, Yassakara, and Parvagupta. In 1346
a Muslim soldier of fortune usurped the throne under
the name of Sams-ud-din. His descendants ruled Kashmir until 1586 when it was annexed by Akbar. It was
under the Afghan Durranis from 1757 to 1819 when they
ceded it to Ranjit Singh.

Following the First Sikh War Kashmir was sold to
Golab Singh of Jammu for ten million rupees. Golab
Singh later entered into a treaty with the British by
which he was recognized as the maharaja of Jammu and
Kashmir. Golab Singh's dynasty ruled Kashmir until
independence when the state acceded to the Indian Union.
In the ensuing conflict between India and Pakistan,
Pakistani and Azad Kashmir forces occupied the north-
west portion of the state.

(2) See Jammu and Kashmir.

KASHMIRI. A Dardic language related to Prakrit used in
Kashmir.

KASHYAPA MATANGA. Indian Buddhist monk who along
with Dharmaratna went to China in 65 and translated
Buddhist scriptures from Pali and Sanskrit into Chinese.

KASI see VARANASI

KASIMBAZAR. Town near Murshidabad in West Bengal;
capital of the Nawabs of Bengal in the 18th century.

KASU. Ancient copper coin of low value derived from
karshapana.

KATAR. A type of dagger with a solid blade of about 24
inches, the handle of which consisted of two parallel
bars with a cross piece joining them.

KATHA. A type of entertainment in Maharashtra consisting
of a narrative recitation interspersed with music and
singing.

KATHAIOI. Ancient tribe that inhabited the territory between
the Chinab and the Ravi with capital at Sangala and
which submitted to Alexander the Great during his invasion.

KATHAK. Semiclassical story-dance originating in northern
India in the 15th and 16th centuries depicting incidents

in the life of Krishna or based on stories from the
Epics. The dance is marked by angika (posture),
mudra (hand movement), abhinaya (mime), gati (gliding
movement), chakra (spinning movement) and tatkar (foot
movement).

KATHAKALI. Mimetic all-male dance-drama of Kerala
originating in the 14th century as folk pantomime. The
stylized postures and gestures of the dancers are ac-
centuated by grotesque masks. It is generally played
al fresco with minimum stage settings and often extends
from sunset to dawn. It is accompanied by orchestral
instruments as the maddalam (cylindrical drum), chenda
(round drum) and other cymbals and stringed instruments.

KATHASARITSAGARA. Literally, the ocean of stories. A
collection of stories written in the 11th century by
Somadeva-bhatta of Kashmir; drawn from a larger work,
the Brihatkatha.

KATHIAWAR. Peninsula between the Gulf of Kutch and the
Gulf of Cambay on the west coast, also known as Saurashtra. It was under Maurya, Saka, and Gupta rule
until the seventh century when it broke up into small
Hindu principalities. The region passed into the control of Muslim rulers after the 11th century. It was
joined to the Bombay Presidency after the Third Maratha War.

KATHOPATHAKAN see CAREY, WILLIAM

KATTHA. A unit of land measurement used in Bengal and
Bihar equal to 1/20 of a smaller bigha (the "kutcha
bigha"), or 80 square yards.

KATYAYANA. Sanskrit grammarian of the second century;
author of Vartikka, a supplement to Panini's grammar,
Ashtadhyayi.

KAUTILYA (also, Chanakya, Vishnugupta). Chief minister
of Chandragupta Maurya; took a leading part in the overthrow of the Nanda Dynasty and the elevation of Chandragupta to the throne; author of Arthasastra (or Chanak-
yasutra). He is the chief character in the drama,
Mudrarakshasa.

KAVARATTI ISLAND   see   LAKSHADWEEP

KAVYA. Any of several extended poetical compositions in
    Sanskrit embellished with ornate descriptions of nature
    or heroic and romantic deeds.   Longer poems are
    known as maha kavyas.   There are six maha kavyas in
    Sanskrit literature: Raghuvamsa and Kumarasambhava
    by Kalidas, Kiratarjuniya by Bharavi, Bhattikavya by
    Bhartrihari, Sisupalavadha by Magha, Janaki-harana by
    Kumaradasa, and Naishadha-charita by Sri Harsha.

KAVYADARSA see 2DANDIN

KAYAL. City and port on the Tamraparni River in south
    India; visited by Marco Polo in 1288 and 1299.

KAYASTH. An important Hindu subcaste of northern India
    consisting of scribes, clerks, and officials.

KEDDAH. Mode of capturing elephants by making a trench
    round an area and enticing the wild animals by means
    of tame decoys.

KEDLESTON, Marquess of see CURZON

KERALA. State created under the States Reorganization
    Act of 1956 consisting of the old native states of Tra-
    vancore and Cochin (excepting four taluks of Trivandrum
    district and part of the Shencottah taluk of Quilon dis-
    trict), Malabar district and the Kasargod taluk of South
    Canara. Capital: Trivandrum.

KERALAPUTRAS. People believed to have inhabited the
    Malabar coast in Asokan times; mentioned in the Rock
    Edict II of Asoka.

KESARI. Dynasty of kings of Orissa, founded by Jajati,
    that ruled from 474 to 950. Jajati himself ruled for
    nearly 52 years from 474 until 526. Their first capital
    was Jajpur (or Jajnagar); later it was shifted to Bhuba-
    neswar; and finally to Katak (the modern Cuttack). The
    dynasty was overthrown by the Cholas in the tenth cen-
    tury.

KHADI (also, khaddar). Cloth handspun on a charkha; popu-
    larized by Mahatma Gandhi to symbolize freedom from
    foreign textiles.

KHAFI KHAN.   Nom de plume of Muhammad Hashim of Kwaf,
   author of Muntakhab-ul-Lubab, a history of the reign of
   Aurangzeb and his successors up to the time of his
   patron, Muhammad Shah.

KHAJURAHO.   Chandella city in Bundelkhand, built in the
   10th and 11th centuries; famous for its temples and
   erotic sculptures.

KHAJWAH, BATTLE OF.   Battle in 1659 between Prince
   Aurangzeb and Prince Shuja in which Shuja was defeated.

KHALISA.   (1) The public exchequer in which the revenue
   business was transacted under the Mughal administration.
      (2) Lands owned by the state as distinguished from
   jagirs and inams.

KHALJI.   (1) Dynasty of Turkish origin founded by Jalal-ud-
   din Firuz Shah in 1290.   It ruled the Delhi Sultanate
   until 1320.   The dynasty consisted of six kings:
      Jalal-ud-din Firuz Shah (1290)
      Rukn-ud-din Ibrahim (1296)
      Alauddin Sikander Sani Muhammad Shah (1296)
      Shihab-ud-din Umar (1316)
      Qutb-ud-din Mubarak (1316)
      Nasir-ud-din Khusrav (1320)
         (2) Dynasty of Malwa founded by Mahmud Khalji in
   1436.   It consisted of four rulers: Mahmud I (1436),
   Ghiyas (1469), Nasir (1500), and Mahmud II (1510).

KHALSA.   (1) Crown land in the Delhi Sultanate.
      (2) The exchequer or the office in which the business
   of the revenue department was transacted in Mughal
   times.   This office was retained by the East India Company for a time.
      (3) (with capital) Brotherhood of the Sikhs into which
   members are initiated through the ceremony of Pahul or
   baptism which consists of sweet buttered flour.   All
   members of the Khalsa are entitled to the title of Singh.

KHAM.   Tax in Indo-Muslim times, amounting to one-fifth
   of the spoils of war and the produce of mines.

KHAN.   Title of a Muslim lord or prince introduced by
   the Mughals.   A superior khan was known as khan
   khanam.

KHANDESI. A modern Indian vernacular spoken in Khandesh.

KHANI, A'AAZ-UD-DIN KHALID   see DALA'IL-I FIRUZ SHAHI

KHAN KHANAN. A military title in the Mughal Empire.

KHANUA, BATTLE OF. Battle in 1527 between Emperor Babur and Rana Sanga of Mewar in which the Rana was defeated.

KHARAJ. Tax or tribute levied by Muslim rulers on conquered infidels. (Also, Khiraj).

KHARDA, BATTLE OF. Battle in 1795 between the Nizam and the Marathas in which the Nizam was defeated.

KHARIF. Crop sown at the beginning of the rainy season (April-May) and harvested after it--such as rice, millets, maize, cotton, rape, etc.

KHAROSTHI. Ancient Indian script written from right to left; used in Asokan Rock Edicts of Mansera and Shahbazghari.

KHAS. Collective name applied to the chief officers and nobles of the Mughal court.

KHATRI   see SAURASHTRA (2)

KHATTRI. A subcaste of the Kayasthas found in Punjab and Uttar Pradesh.

KHAZANA. Public treasury in the charge of a khazanchi, or treasurer.

KHEN. Tribe that established a kingdom with Kamatapur as capital near Cooch Behar. The state was overrun by Alauddin Husain Shah about 1498.

KHERWARI. A Kolarian language spoken in central India.

KHILAFAT MOVEMENT. Politico-religious Muslim movement led by two brothers, Shaukat Ali and Muhammad Ali, supporting the role of the Sultan of Turkey as the Caliph of Islam and expressing ethnic solidarity with the Turks after World War I.

KHILAT.   A dress of honor presented by a superior on
ceremonial occasion.   There were among the later
Mughals five degrees of khilat, which sometimes consisted, as a special mark of favor, of clothes that the
emperor had actually worn.

KHIRAJ.   Tribute levied by Muslim rulers on conquered infidels. (Also, Kharaj).

KHIZR KHAN SAYYID.   Founder of the Sayyid Dynasty of
the Delhi Sultanate; governor of Multan under Timur;
defeated the last Tughluq sultan and proclaimed himself
sultan in 1414.

KHOL.   Indian musical instrument.

KHOND (also, Kand or Kui).   A Kolarian aboriginal tribe
living in Central India.

KHOT.   System of land tenure in Maharashtra under which
the land was legally held by petty zamindars called
khotis, who were partly hereditary officials and partly
landowners with proprietary rights.

KHUDAI KHIDMATGAR.   Literally, servant of god.   Former
nationalist organization of Pathans in the North-West
Frontier Province allied with the Indian National Congress.

KHUDDAKANIKAYA   see   JATAKAS

KHUSRAV, AMIR.   1255-1325.   Celebrated Persian-born
musician at the Khalji court who invented the sitar.
Khusrav was also a historian, linguist, lexicographer,
and poet who wrote in Persian, Urdu, and Hindi.   His
extant works include historical masnavis, poems, and
two histories: Tughluqnamah and Tarikh-i-Alai.

KHUSRAV, Prince.   Eldest son of Jahangir; an attempt to
enthrone him as successor to Akbar brought him into
conflict with his father who kept him in confinement.
He led two more unsuccessful revolts against his father
and ended his days blind in prison.

KHUSRAV KHAN.   Chief minister and favorite of Sultan
Mubarak Khalji; murdered his master and usurped the
throne in 1320 but was himself murdered five

months later.

KHYAL.   Love song invented by Sultan Hussain Shah Sharqi
    of Jaunpur.   A variant is the tappa developed by Shori
    in the 18th century.

KHYBER PASS.   Mountain pass in East Afghanistan south
    of the Kabul River leading from Fort Jumrud to Dakka
    and commanding the route from Peshawar to Kabul; his-
    toric route traversed by all invaders of India from the
    time of Alexander the Great.

KIRAT-ARJUNIYA see BHARAVI

KIRKEE, BATTLE OF.   Battle in 1817 between the British
    force, led by Mountstuart Elphinstone, and Peshwa
    Baji Rao in which the Peshwa was defeated.

KIRTAN see BHAJAN

KIRTTIVARMAN.   Chandella ruler of Bundelkhand (1049-
    1100) whose greatest exploit was his defeat of Karna-
    deva, the Kalachuri king of Chedi.   He built the arti-
    ficial lake known as Kirat Sagar near Mahoba.   Sri
    Krishna Misra, author of Probodhachandrodaya, was
    one of the many scholars and writers whom he patron-
    ized.

KIST.   Any of the installments in which land revenue is
    paid into the treasury.

KODAGA.   A Kshattriya subcaste of Coorg.

KODAGU.   A Dravidian language spoken by the Khonds of
    Bihar and Orissa.

KOH-I-NOOR.   Literally, mountain of light.   Fabulous dia-
    mond that once adorned the Mughal crown; part of
    Nadir Shah's loot carried back to Persia after the sack
    of Delhi in 1739; later passed into the hands of Ahmad
    Shah Abdali and Shah Shuja who yielded it to Ranjit
    Singh; acquired by Queen Victoria in 1850 and now set
    in the British crown.   It once weighed 186 carats but
    has been recut and is now considerably smaller.

KOL.   (1) A Kolarian aboriginal tribe of Chota Nagpur; (2)
    language of this tribe.

KOLAMI. A Dravidian language of the Gondi group spoken in central India.

KOLARIAN. Family of aboriginal tribes who live in Central India. They are dark, short of stature, with thick lips and broad noses.

KOLHAPUR. City and former state in the Deccan ruled until 1947 by the descendants of Shivaji; it became a British protectorate after the end of the Third Maratha War.

KOLLAM (or, Malabar Era). Era used by the Chera kings of Kerala dated from 824.

KONKAN. Maritime region extending along the Arabian Sea from Daman to Goa including the districts of Bombay, Thana, Kolaba, Ratnagiri, Janjira, Savantvadi, and Goa.

KONKANI. A dialect of Marathi spoken on the west coast of Maharashtra.

KOPPAM, BATTLE OF. Battle in 1152 or 1153 between Someswara, the Chalukya king of Kalyani, and Rajadhiraja, the Chola king, in which the latter was defeated.

KORAGA. A Panchama class of South Canara primarily engaged as basket weavers.

KORIGAON, BATTLE OF. Battle in 1818 between the British and Peshwa Baji Rao II in which the Peshwa was defeated.

KOS. A unit of distance in ancient and medieval India, defined in the Ain-i-Akbari as 2 miles, 4 furlongs, and 183 1/2 yards.

KOSHALA. (1) Ancient kingdom with capital at Ayodhya whose king Dasaratha and son Rama are the heroes of the epic Ramayana. It was one of the 16 mahajanapadas or major states of the sixth century B. C. Much of its history consists of conflicts with Magadha for supremacy. In the event it was absorbed by Magadha in the reign of Ajatasatru (494-467 B. C.)
    (2) Kingdom in south India in the upper Mahanadi

Valley comprising modern Bilaspur, Raipur, and Sambalpur with capital at Sripura (Sripur).

KOTAH. (1) City on the Chambal River in Rajasthan. (2) Former native state created by Shah Jahan in 1625.

KOTAH, BATTLE OF. Battle in 1804 between Holkar's army and a small force of the East India Company led by Col. Monson in which the latter was defeated.

KOTWAL. Title of the superintendent of police of a town in Mughal times. The office was abolished in 1862.

KOZHIKODE. Former name: Calicut. Port in Kerala on the west coast. Capital of a former principality ruled by the zamorins. In 1498 Vasco da Gama arrived here, thus opening the era of European settlements in India.

KRISHNA. (1) Hindu god, the eighth avatar of Vishnu; son of Vasudeva and Devaki, the last of the Yadavas. He became king of the Yadavas and took part in the war of the sons of Pandu against those of Dhritarashtra. His legends are developed in the Mahabharata, the Puranas, and the Bhagavad-Gita.
    (2) River in the Deccan rising in the Western Ghats and flowing into the Bay of Bengal.

KRISHNADAS, KAVIRAJ see CHAITANYA

KRISHNADEVA RAYA. Great monarch of Vijayanagar who ruled from 1509 to 1529; third king of the Tuluva Dynasty. He defeated Yusuf Adil Shah, the sultan of Bijapur, and recovered the fortress of Raichur. He extended his frontiers to Orissa in the north and to Seringapatam in the south. He was also a patron of the arts, letters, and religion.

KSHAHARATA. Satrapal dynasty by Bhumaka with capital at Nasik. The most famous king of this line was Nahapana who ruled in the second century over the northern part of Maharashtra, Malwa, Kathiawar, and southern Rajasthan.

KSHATTRIYA (also, Rajanya). The second among the four Hindu castes comprising the warrior and ruling classes. From Sanskrit kshatra, rule or authority.

KSHUDRAKAS. Tribe, called by classical historians Oxy-drakoi, who inhabited the region between the Jhelum and the Chinab; they submitted to Alexander the Great during his invasion of India.

KUBJA VISHNUVARDHANA. Younger brother of the Chal-ukya king Pulakeshin II appointed in 611 as governor of Vengi. In 615 he declared his independence and founded the dynasty of Eastern Chalukyas with his capital at Pishtapura (modern Pithapuram).

KUCHIPUDI. A religious dance-drama named after a small village in Andhra Pradesh. It is performed by male dancers only. The dance is preceded by daru, an elaborate pattern of postures and gestures.

KUI. A Dravidian language spoken in Orissa.

KUI-GONDI. A branch of the Dravidian family of languages including Kui, Gondi, Bhili, Kolimi, and Naiki.

KULINISM. System of elitism intended to perpetuate the exclusiveness and genetic purity of Brahmin classes in Bengal introduced by the Sena kings Vallalasena and Lakshmanasena. It limited intermarriages to certain social groups.

KULIN-KULA-SARBBASVA see RAMNARAYAN

KULKARNI. Title of the village accountant in central and western India.

KULLUKA. Bengali Sanskrit scholar of the 14th century; author of a commentary on Manusamhita (the Institutes of Manu).

KULOTTUNGA I (also, Rajendra III). Founder of the Cha-lukya-Chola Dynasty who ruled from 1070 to 1122. He was the son of a Chola princess and an Eastern Cha-lukya king. Remembered for a revenue survey of the Chola kingdom.

KULUI. Western Pahari dialect spoken in Kulu Valley in the Punjab.

KUMARAGHOSHA. Bengali Buddhist monk, guru of the Sailendra kings of Java.

KUMARAMATYA.   Title of a high official in the Gupta Empire.

KUMBAKONAM.   Town in Tamil Nadu; former capital of the Chola Empire and site of a famous temple.

KUMBHA.   Rana of Mewar (1431-69); fought incessant wars with his neighbors, the Muslim rulers of Malwa and Gujarat.   He was also a great builder who built 32 fortresses and the tower known as Kirttistambha or Jayastambha.

KUMBH MELA.   Literally, pot festival.   The largest of the religious Hindu gatherings held periodically in northern India; every three years at Hardwar, Nasik, and Ujjain and every 12 years at Allahabad.

KUMBI.   A Kshattriya subcaste now primarily engaged in agriculture.

KUNIKA   see   AJATASATRU

KUNJAN NAMBIAR   see   MALAYALAM

KUPPUSWAMI SASTRI RESEARCH INSTITUTE.   Institution founded in Madras in 1944 at the Sanskrit College, Madras, for the promotion of Indological studies.   Publishes Journal of Oriental Research.

KURAL (also, Tirukkural).   Collection of brief metrical proverbs on various aspects of life and religion composed probably in the fourth or fifth century and traditionally attributed to Tiruvalluvar; a classic work embodying the moral and ethical ideas of the Tamil people.

KURNOOL.   Town in Andhra Pradesh at the junction of the Tungabhadra and Kunderu Rivers; former principality ruled by a Nawab until it was annexed by Lord Auckland.

KURRAM (also, kottam).   Administrative unit of the Chola Empire consisting of a group of villages vested with extensive powers of self-government in matters of taxation.   It also dispensed justice and maintained peace within its limits.   It managed its affairs through an elected assembly called mahasabha.

KURUKH (also, Oraon).   A Davidian language spoken in parts of West Bengal and Madhya Pradesh.

KURUKSHETRA. (In the Mahabharata) battlefield where the
   Kurus or Kauravas and the Pandavas fought a fierce
   battle for 18 days; traditionally believed to be in the
   Punjab near Delhi.

KURUS.   The 100 sons of Dhritarashtra, king of Indraprastha, whose conflict with the Pandavas forms the theme
   of the epic Mahabharata.

KUSHANA. Script used in the Kushan Empire in the first
   and second century based on the Mauryan and Sungan
   forms of Brahmi.

KUSHANS.   A branch of the Yueh-chi horde who under Kujala Kara Kadphises established the Kushan Dynasty
   that ruled over NW India from 48 until 220.

KUSINAGRA.   Town in Uttar Pradesh east of Gorakhpur;
   believed to be the place where Gautama Buddha attained
   parinirvana.

KUTCH.   Former state in western India adjoining Sind with
   capital at Bhuj; now part of Gujarat.

KUTCH, RANN OF.   Salt morass, flooded at times, in
   Gujarat adjoining Sind.   In ancient times it was a shal-
   low arm of the Arabian Sea but was later filled in by
   sediment from the Indus which has since changed its
   course westward.   Its northwest and southeast parts are
   known respectively as the Great and the Little Rann of
   Kutch.

KUTILA.   Script from which Bengali, Maithili, Oriya,
   Gujarati, and Manipuri evolved.   Kaithi is a cursive
   form used in Bihar, Uttar Pradesh, and Nepal.

- L -

LADAKH.   District in East Kashmir in the Karakorum
   range conquered and annexed by Kashmir in a campaign
   that lasted from 1834 to 1842.   Capital: Leh.

LAGHU-ARTHANITI see   HEMACHANDRA

LAHNDA.   Western Punjabi or Hindvi spoken in Hazara district in northwest India.

LAHORI, ABDUL HAMID   see   PADSHAH-NAMA

LAIHAROBA   see   MANIPURI (1)

LAJPAT RAI, LALA.   1856-1928.   Indian nationalist lead-
    er; president of the Indian National Congress in 1919;
    espoused extremist views and was deported to Burma;
    organized the boycott of the Simon Commission in 1928;
    founded the Anglo-Vedic College at Lahore and the
    journal The Punjabee; author of England's Debt to India,
    Unhappy India, and other works.

LAKH.   (also, lac).   The number 100,000.   See also
    Crore.

LAKSHADWEEP.   A Union Territory of the Indian Union
    constituted in 1956 comprising a group of 24 islands in
    the Arabian Sea near Kerala, the northern group of
    which is called the Amindivis and the southern the Lac-
    cadives.   Minicoy is the largest island.   Headquarters:
    Kavaratti Island.

LAKSHMANA.   (In the Ramayana) son of Dasharatha by
    Sumitra and half brother of Rama, who accompanied him
    on his exile for 14 years.

LAKSHMANA SENA.   Sena king of Bengal (1178/9-1199/
    1202).   Extended the Sena borders by conquering Kam-
    arupa and Varanasi.   He was also a patron of many
    poets, such as Jayadeva and Dhoyi, and the jurist
    Halayudha.

LAKSHMANA SENA ERA.   Era established by Lakshmana
    Sena in 1190.

LAKSHMI BAI.   The dowager rani of Jhansi whose husband's
    state had been annexed by Lord Dalhousie in 1853
    through the application of the Doctrine of Lapse.   On
    the outbreak of the Sepoy Mutiny the rani joined the
    malcontents, led the sepoys in a successful attack on
    Gwalior but was defeated in the Battles of Marar and
    Kotah and killed.

LAKSHMISA   see   KANARESE

LALDAS.   d1648.   Hindi poet and disciple of Kabir who be-
    longed to the Meos tribe and came from Alwar.   He

founded the sect of Laldasis, a minor Vaishnava sect that stressed bhajan, or devotional worship. They practiced a form of monotheism that had much in common with that of Kabir.

LALIT KALA AKADEMI. Organization founded at New Delhi in 1954 under the auspices of the government of India to promote the development of painting, sculpture, architecture, and the applied arts and to coordinate the activities of state academies and art associations. Publishes Lalit Kala and Lalit Kala Contemporary.

LALLA LAL. 1763-1825. Hindi poet. Born in a Brahmin family in Gujarat but settled in North India. His principal works include a translation of the Hitopadesa into Hindi and a verse-epic entitled Premasagara based on the Bhagavata Purana.

LALSONT, BATTLE OF. Battle in 1787 between the Mughal Army and Mahadaji Sindhia in which Sindhia was defeated.

LAMBARA. Wandering tribe of dealers in grain and salt, better known as Banjara.

LANSDOWNE, Marquis of. Full name: Henry Charles Keith Petty-Fitzmaurice. 1845-1927. Viceroy and governor general of India (1888-93). He stablized the Indian rupee by closing the mints to free coinage. He caused the demarcation of the NW frontier of India known as the Durand Line, brought Sikkim under British protection, and suppressed a revolt in Manipur.

LASCAR. (1) An inferior artilleryman; (2) sailor. From Persian lashkar, army, camp.

LASWARI, BATTLE OF. Battle in 1803 between the British Army under Lord Wellesley and the Marathas under Sindhia in which the Marathas were defeated.

LATHI. A stick or bludgeon bound with iron rings used by the police as a weapon.

LAWRENCE, Sir HENRY MONTGOMERY. 1806-1857. English administrator and general; British resident at Lahore (1847), governor general's agent in Rajputana (1853) and chief commissioner of Oudh (1857). He died in the defense of Lucknow against the mutineers in 1857.

LAWRENCE, Lord JOHN. 1811-79. Viceroy and governor general of India (1864-69); brother of Sir Henry Lawrence. As chief commissioner of the Punjab he reformed the land tenancy system and introduced an efficient administrative system. The leading part he played in suppressing the Mutiny with the help of the loyal Sikh regiments earned him the title of "Savior of India." As viceroy he opposed the "forward" frontier policy and supported the extension of education.

LEGISLATIVE ASSEMBLY. The principal lawmaking body in India from 1919 until 1950 and the principal lawmaking body in the states of the Indian Union from 1950.

LEGISLATIVE COUNCIL. The legislature of the Central and Provincial governments from 1861 until 1919; the legislatures of the provinces from 1919 until 1950; and the upper house of a bicameral state legislature from 1950.

LEPCHA (also, Rong). Language of Sikkim; member of the Tibeto-Himalayan branch of the Sino-Tibetan family.

LICHCHHAVI ERA. Era of the Lichchhavi tribe dated from 111.

LICHCHHAVIS. A Kshattriya tribe who lived in Bihar with their capital at Vaisali from the sixth century B.C. to the fourth century A.D. They had a republican form of government.

LINGAYET. Hindu sect founded by Basava in the 12th century. They worshiped Siva in his phallic form; denied the doctrine of rebirth and the Vedas; and rejected Brahminical authority. The sect flourished primarily in the Canara region.

LINGUISTIC SURVEY OF INDIA. Survey of Indian languages by Sir George A. Grierson on behalf of the government of India; published 1903-1928 in 11 volumes.

LINLITHGOW, Lord; Earl of Hopetoun. Full name: Victor Alexander John Hope. 1887-1951. Viceroy and governor general of India (1936-43). He was chairman of the Joint Select Committee on Indian constitutional reform which prepared the Linlithgow Report. His viceroyalty was marked by the implementation of the

Government of India Act of 1935 in the provinces, the Second World War, and the Famine of 1943.

LION PILLAR. Stone pillar erected by Asoka at Sarnath, near Varanasi, to commemorate the first sermon of Gautama Buddha delivered here. The pillar is surmounted by a lion capital. The wheel or chakra motif which appears on the pillar has been adopted as the symbol of the Republic of India.

LODHA. A Kshattriya subcaste of Uttar Pradesh and Rajasthan now primarily engaged in agriculture.

LODI. Dynasty founded in 1451 by Bahlol Lodi which ruled the Delhi Sultanate until 1526. It consisted of three rulers: Bahlol Lodi (1451), Nizam Khan Sikandar Lodi (1489), and Ibrahim Lodi (1517).

LOHANI. Afghan tribe that settled in Bihar under Dariya Khan Lohani; rose against the harsh rule of Ibrahim Lodi and set up an independent kingdom; again forced to submit to Delhi by Babur at the Battle of Gogra in 1529.

LOHAR. Member of a nomadic caste of Hindus employed as craftsmen in wood or metal.

LOHARA. Kashmiri dynasty founded by Sangramaraja in 1003 that lasted until 1315, when it was overthrown by a Muslim soldier of fortune named Shah Mirza.

LOK SABHA. Literally, House of the People; lower house of the Indian Parliament.

LUBBAI. Member of a Tamil-speaking Muslim community, believed to be descendants of Arab traders.

LUCKNOW. City on the Gumti River; capital of Uttar Pradesh and former capital of Oudh from 1775 until 1856. The capture of Lucknow by the mutineers in 1857 and its later recovery by Colin Campbell's forces was a turning point in the Sepoy Mutiny. The city is also noted for the Imambara mausoleum dating from the middle of the 18th century.

LUMBERDAR. The registered representative of a community in which land is held in common who is responsible for the payment of taxes.

¹LYTTON, Lord. Full name: Edward Robert Bulwer-Lyt-
    ton; pseudonym: Owen Meredith. 1831-1891. Viceroy
    and governor general of India (1876-1880). During his
    tenure Queen Victoria was crowned Empress of India.
    His administration was marked by the Famine Code,
    the passing of the Vernacular Press Act, and the intro-
    duction of the salt tax. During the Second Afghan War
    (1878-79) he removed Sher Ali from the amirship of
    Afghanistan.

²LYTTON, Lord. Full name: Victor Alexander George
    Robert. 1876-1947. Officiating viceroy and governor
    general of India (10 April to 7 August 1925). Son of
    Edward Robert Bulwer-Lytton.

- M -

MAASIR-I-ALAMGIRI. A history of the reign of Aurangzeb
    Alamgir, written by Muhammad Saqi.

MA'BAR. Name given by Muslim historians to the Coro-
    mandel coast. It was conquered and annexed to the
    Delhi Sultanate by Alauddin Khalji but became independent
    in 1334 under Ahsan Shah.

MACAULAY, Lord. Full name: Thomas Babington Macau-
    lay. 1800-1859. He served (1834-38) as Law Member
    of the governor general's executive council and was
    responsible for the drawing up of the Indian Penal Code
    which was adopted in 1860. He is also remembered as
    an advocate of the introduction of the English language
    as the medium of instruction in India.

MACHILIPATNAM. Former name: Masulipattam; also,
    Bandar. Town and seaport on the Bay of Bengal in
    Andhra Pradesh; site of an English settlement in 1611
    and a French settlement in 1669. It has never regained
    prosperity since a tidal wave inundated it in 1864 with
    a loss of 30,000 lives.

MACMAHON LINE. Boundary line between India and Tibet
    drawn up by Sir Henry MacMahon.

MACPHERSON, Sir JOHN. 1745-1821. Governor general
    of India (1785-86). Entered the Company's service in
    Madras as a writer in 1770 and served on the Council

at Calcutta in 1781. Succeeded Warren Hastings as
governor general in 1785.

[1]MADHAVA (also, Vidyaranya). Prime minister of Bukka,
one of the founders of the Vijayanagar Empire; an authority on Hindu medicine, especially in the field of
nidana or diagnosis.

[2]MADHAVA. 1197-1280. Founder of a dualistic school of
philosophy whose teachings show traces of Christian
influence. He was called by his followers Ananda-
tirtha.

MADHAVA RAO. 1744-1772. Fourth Peshwa (1761-72).
His military exploits included the defeat of the Nizam,
Haider Ali, and Bhonsla Raja. In 1771 he occupied
Malwa and Bundelkhand, reduced the Rajputs, Jats,
and Rohillas to submission, entered Delhi and with the
help of Mahadaji Sindhia restored Shah Alam II to the
throne. He died at the age of 28 in 1772. Do not con-
fuse with Mahadaji Sindhia (q.v.), who bore the same
name formally and whose history is intertwined with the
Peshwa's.

MADHYA BHARAT. Erstwhile state in the Union of India
formed in 1948 by the merger of 25 former native
states of which the principal ones were Gwalior and
Indore. Now part of Madhya Pradesh.

MADHYAMIKA. Ancient town near Chitor in Rajasthan, now
called Nagari. Two Sunga inscriptions here record
asvamedha and vajapeya sacrifices. See also VAJA-
PEYA.

MADHYAMIKA SASTRA see [1]NAGARJUNA

MADHYA PRADESH. State in the Indian Union formed in
1956 comprising 17 districts of the state of the same
name formed in 1947, the former state of Madhya
Bharat, the former states of Bhopal and Vindhya Pradesh and the Sironj subdivision of Kotah district. Capital: Bhopal.

MADOL. Drum used on religious occasions in Bengal.

MADRAS. (1) Former presidency and state, now renamed
Tamil Nadu.

(2) City on the east coast built around Fort St.
George, an East India Company settlement founded in
1640 by Francis Day on a site granted by the raja of
Chandragiri.   In 1642 Madras displaced Masulipattam
(now Machilipatnam) as the principal factory on the east
coast.   It later became capital of the Madras Presidency
which extended from Orissa to Tirunelvely district.   The
Apostle St. Thomas was martyred in Mylapore, a suburb
of Madras.

MADURAI.   City in Tamil Nadu.   It was the capital of the
Pandyan kingdom from the 5th century until the invasion
of Alauddin Khalji in 1311.   Later it became the seat of
the Ma'bar kingdom established by Ahsan Shah in 1334
and was annexed by Vijayanagar in 1377-78.   After the
fall of Vijayanagar it was ruled by petty chiefs called
Nayaks.   The great temple of Madurai was built for the
most part in the 17th century.

MAGADHA.   Ancient kingdom in NE India whose history goes
back to Vedic times.   It corresponds to the Patna and
Gaya districts in modern Bihar.   The first great historical king of Magadha was Bimbisara, a contemporary
of Gautama Buddha and Vardhamana Mahavira, who enlarged the kingdom by annexing Anga or East Bihar.
Bimbisara's son Ajatasatru built the fort of Pataligrama
which became the nucleus of the city of Pataliputra.
Pataliputra was the capital of the Nanda Dynasty which
overthrew the Bimbisara line.
    Mahapadma Nanda extended the Magadhan Empire
from Kalinga to the Beas River.   Chandragupta Maurya
who supplanted the Nandas ruled over one of the largest
empires in Indian history.   His grandson Asoka employed the imperial resources for the promotion of Buddhism.   The last descendant of Asoka, Brihadratha, was
overthrown by his own commander-in-chief Pushyamitra
about 187 B. C.
    The Magadhan power declined under the Sungas and
the Kanvas but was resuscitated under the imperial
Guptas whose empire extended south as far as Kanchipuram.   After the fall of the Guptas Magadha slid into
obscurity and the final coup de grace was administered
by the Muslim invasions in the 12th and 13th centuries.

MAGADHI.   A Prakrit language related to Pali and spoken
in Magadha.   Forms of Magadhi were: Chandali,
Sakari, Odra, the parent of Oriya, and Prachya, the
parent of modern Bengali and Assamese.

MAHABALIPURAM.   Ancient Pallava town on the Bay of
    Bengal founded by king Narasimha Varman, noted for
    seven monolithic temples carved in the shape of a
    ratha or chariot from a single boulder of granite.

MAHABAT KHAN.   Real name: Zamana Beg. Mughal gen-
    eral under Jahangir and Shah Jahan; reduced Rana Amar
    Singh of Mewar to submission; opposed by Nur Jahan;
    led a coup against the emperor in 1626 and held Jahan-
    gir as a prisoner for a while; joined Prince Khurram
    in his revolt against his father; rewarded by him when
    he became emperor as Shah Jahan with imperial com-
    mand; captured Daulatabad and Ahmadnagar; foiled in
    attempt to take Bijapur and died in disgrace in 1634.

MAHABHARATA.   One of the two great epics of ancient
    India attributed to the sage Vyasa.   It contains over
    100,000 distichs, divided into 18 parvans and includes
    the religious poem Bhagavad-Gita.   It is believed to
    have been composed between 200 B. C. and A. D. 200.
    The theme of the epic is the great war between the
    Kurus and the Pandavas for the possession of a kingdom
    occupying the region around modern Delhi.

MAHABHASYA.   Literally, Great Commentary. Patanjali's
    Sanskrit commentary on the grammatical sutras of
    Panini, written sometime between 140 B. C. and A. D.
    60.

MAHA BODHI SOCIETY.   Buddhist organization founded in
    1891 at Calcutta with branches in 11 other cities.   Pub-
    lishes Mahabodhi Journal and Dharmaduta.

MAHADAJI SINDHIA.   Real name: Madhava Rao.   Illegiti-
    mate son and successor (ruled 1761-94) of Ranoji Sindhia
    (q. v.) of the Maratha Confederacy.   He succeeded to
    the gadi (throne) of the Sindhias in 1761, the same year
    that Madhava Rao (q. v.), son of Peshwa Balaji Baji
    Rao, succeeded to the peshwaship.   The two, named
    identically, should not be confused.   In 1771 he became
    the protector of, and helped Peshwa Madhava Rao to
    reinstate to the throne of Delhi, Emperor Shah Alam II.
    He mediated the Treaty of Salbai which concluded the
    First Maratha War (1775-82).   He modernized his army
    with the help of Count de Boigne and equipped it with
    artillery.

MAHADANDANAYAKA.   Title of the military commander in
the Gupta Empire.

MAHAKSHATRAPAS see   GREAT SATRAPS

MAHAL.   (1) An estate considered as a unit of land tenure.
   (2) Edifice or building, especially a palace set apart
for royal consorts.

MAHALLA.   Village, especially considered as a unit of administration or local self-government.

MAHALWARI.   System of land tenure in Uttar Pradesh under
which the government recognized mahals or village communities as owners of land liable for the payment of
revenue.   The elders of the mahal divided the assessment among the cultivators in proportion to their holdings.

MAHANADI.   River rising in Madhya Pradesh and flowing
east through a delta into the Bay of Bengal near Cuttack.

MAHANT.   An abbot of a math, or Hindu monastery.

MAHAPADMA.   Founder of the Nanda Dynasty of Magadha;
an empire builder who lived in the first half of the
fourth century B. C.

MAHAPURANAS.   The Vishnu Purana and the Bhagavata
Purana, considered as the great puranas of Sanskrit
literature.

MAHARAJA.   Title of a sovereign prince of a large state.

MAHARAJADHIRAJA.   King of kings or emperor; title assumed by Hindu rulers who held sway over a large
empire.

MAHARANI.   Queen of a maharaja.

MAHARASHTRA.   (1) Region in west India east of Warda
River consisting of three divisions: Konkan, Maval,
and Desh.   Ruled from early times by Sakas, Guptas,
Chalukyas, Rashtrakutas, Yadavas, Bahmanis, and the
Marathas.
   (2) State in the Union of India created in 1960

comprising Marathi-speaking areas of the former Bombay Presidency, Hyderabad state (also known as Marathwada), and Madhya Pradesh (also known as Vidarbha). Capital: Bombay.

MAHARASHTRI.   Old Marathi language spoken in Berar from which modern Marathi is derived.   This is the form of Prakrit in which Sattasai by Hala, Setubandham by Pravarasena, and the later scriptures of the Jain Svetambaras are written.

MAHASABHA.   (1) A large assembly.
     (2) Assembly which managed the affairs of a kurram, the administrative unit of the Chola Empire.

MAHA-SIVARATHRI.   Literally, the great night of Siva. Hindu festival observed on the 13th day in the dark half of Magha (January-February) or Phalguna (February-March).

MAHATMA.   Literally, great soul; title applied to a social and religious leader regarded as an extraordinary or holy person--Mohandas K. Gandhi notably.

MAHAVAMSA   see   MAHENDRA

MAHAVIBHASA SASTRA   see   VASUMITRA

MAHAVIRA, VARDHAMANA.   Also known by the titles of Kevalin (omniscient) and Nirgrantha (one who is free from bondage).   Founder of Jainism and the 24th and last Jina or conqueror who lived about 500 B.C.   Born in a noble family in the time of Bimbisara; renounced the world at the age of 30; practiced severe ascetic penances and gained perfect knowledge at the age of 42; preached for 30 years and died in the time of Ajatasatru at Pava in Patna district in Bihar.   His legendary history is given in the Kalpasutra and Mahaviracharita.

MAHAVIRACHARITA   see   BHAVABHUTI; MAHAVIRA

MAHAYANA.   Literally, the higher vehicle.   Buddhist sect. The prevalent form of Buddhism in Nepal, China, Tibet, Mongolia, Korea, and Japan; hence also known as Northern Buddhism.   Its scriptures are written in Sanskrit.   Mahayanism regards Buddha as one of an infinite number of buddhas who are gods of supernatural power and who should therefore be adored and to whom prayers and offerings should be made. The goal of Mahayanism is not merely the individual nirvana but the good of human community.

MAHE. Seaport and small French settlement on the east coast near Tellicherry; merged with the Indian Union in 1950.

MAHENDRA. Son or brother of Asoka; Buddhist missionary who went along with his sister Sanghamitra to Ceylon in 251 B. C. and converted King Tissa; his work is recorded in Dipavamsa and Mahavamsa. He died about 204 B. C.

MAHI. River flowing into the upper part of the Gulf of Cambay; noted for its fierce floods and deep gullies.

MAHIPALA I. 978-1030. Ninth king of the Pala Dynasty, noted for his many public works. He lost much of his territory to the Senas, Chandras, Cholas, and the Kalachuris.

MAHL. A language spoken in Minicoy in the Laccadives.

MAHMUD BEGARA. Sixth and greatest sultan of Gujarat (1459-1511). He conquered Junagarh, Champaner, and Oudh and defeated the sultan of Ahmadnagar and the Portuguese.

MAHMUD GAWAN, Khwaja. Persian-born adviser and minister to three Bahmani sultans: Humayun (1457-61), Nizam (1461-63), and Muhammad (1463-82). He was a patron of arts, letters, and architecture. Murdered by the Sultan on the instigation of Deccani nobles in 1481.

MAHMUD KHALJI. Founder of the Khalji Dynasty of Malwa; minister of Mahmud Ghuri who usurped the throne after murdering his sovereign in 1436. He ruled for 33 years until 1469.

MAHMUD OF GHAZNI. 971-1030. Sultan of Ghazni (997-1030). He was an ardent Muslim who spent his career attempting to carry Islam into India; made 17 plundering raids subduing Punjab, Thaneswar, Kanauj, Gwalior, Kalanjar, Kathiawar, and Multan. His famous expedition against Somnath in 1026 led to the sack of its

temple reputed to have been filled with untold wealth.
Mahmud was also a patron of arts and letters and he
made Ghazni one of the most important centers of the
Islamic world.

MAHMUD TUGHLUQ.   Last Tughluq sultan of Delhi (1394-
1413).   His rule was marked by the disintegration of
Delhi Empire with Jaunpur, Gujarat, Malwa, and
Khandesh breaking away as independent kingdoms.   The
invasion of Timur and his sack of Delhi dealt the final
coup de grâce to his rule.

MAHOBA.   Town in Hamirpur district in Uttar Pradesh;
capital of the Chandel Dynasty from the ninth to the
13th centuries; noted for its temples and architecture.

MAHRATTA DITCH.   An excavation made in 1742 on the
landward side of Calcutta to protect the settlement from
Maratha depradations.

MAHSUD.   Warlike Afghan tribe who lived near the Durand
Line and proved a source of constant irritation to the
British.

MAITHILI (also, Tirhutia).   A dialect of Bihari spoken in
Tirhut, Champaran, eastern Monghyr, Bhagalpur, and
western Purnea in Bihar.

MAITRAKA.   Rajput dynasty founded by Bhatarka at Valabhi
in eastern Saurashtra in the fifth century; in power until
the Muslim invasions of the eighth century.   A branch
of this dynasty established itself in western Malwa in
the sixth century.

MAJUMDAR.   A revenue accountant who kept the account of
the jama or revenue collections.

MALABAR.   (1) Western coastal region of South India corresponding roughly to modern Kerala state.
(2) District in Kerala with Kozhikode as headquarters.

MALABAR RITES.   Pseudo-Hindu rites and practices promoted by Father Roberto de Nobili among the Catholics
of South India.   They included the observance of caste,
the investiture of a sacred thread, the use of Hindu
names, child marriages, the use of tali or marriage
thread, the practice of divination and auguries, the

exclusion of women from churches during certain periods, the use of cowdung ashes for smearing the body, and ceremonial bathing. All these rites were banned by Pope Gregory XV in 1623 and Cardinal de Tournon in 1704.

MALATIMADHAVA   see   BHAVABHUTI

MALAVIKAGNIMITRA.   Sanskrit historical drama written by Kalidas in the fifth century; the first Sunga king Pushyamitra and his son Agnimitra, lover of Malavi, are the main protagonists.

MALAVIYA, Pundit MADAN MOHAN.   1861-1946.   Hindu nationalist leader; twice president of the Indian National Congress and thrice president of the Hindu Mahasabha; founded the Benares Hindu University in 1915.

MALAYALAM.   A Dravidian language with strong Sanskrit affinity spoken in Kerala.   Its greatest writers were Cherusseri (fl. 1570), Ezhuttachan (fl. 1650), and Kunjan Nambiar (fl. 1740).   Kunjan Nambiar is associated with a form of narrative poetry known as tullal.

MALHAR RAO HOLKAR.   Founder of the Holkar Dynasty and ruler of Indore from 1728 to 1765.   He was a lieutenant of Peshwa Baji Rao I and a member of the Maratha confederacy.

MALIK AHMAD.   Founder of the Nizam Shahi Dynasty of Ahmadnagar; governor of Junnar under the Bahmani sultan Mahmud; proclaimed independence in 1490 under the title Ahmad Nizam Shah (q. v.).   He conquered and annexed Deogiri or Daulatabad in 1499.   He died in 1508.

MALIK AMBER.   Abyssinian slave who rose in 1601 to become chief minister of Ahmadnagar; repulsed Mughal attempts to conquer the Deccani kingdom and introduced an efficient system of administration.

MALIK GHAZI SHAHNA.   Court architect of Sultan Firoz Shah Tughluq who built the cities of Firuzabad and Jaunpur as well as the Yamuna Canal.

MALIK SARVAR   see   SHARQI

MALLAS.   Tribe who inhabited Pava and Kusinagara in
Buddhist times.

MALTO.   A dialect of Kurukh spoken in Rajmahal district
in Bengal.

MALUKDAS.   1574-1682.   Hindi poet and disciple of Kabir
whose writings show traces of Persian influence.

MALWA.   Region inhabited by the Malavas, the tribe known
to classical historians as Malloi who were defeated by
Alexander the Great.   Later they moved from the region of the Ravi River to Avanti and founded a kingdom
with capital at Ujjain.   They were successively under
the Sakas, Guptas, Huns, Chalukyas, Gurjara-Pratiharas, the Delhi Sultanate, the kingdom of Gujarat, the
Mughals, and the Marathas.   An independent kingdom
ruled by two Muslim dynasties, the Ghuris and the
Khaljis, flourished here from 1392 to 1531.   The reign
of king Yasodharman, who defeated the Hun Mihiragula
in 528, is considered the period of Malwa's greatest
power and prosperity.

MAMLATDAR.   Title of an official in charge of a taluk in
western India.

MAMLATDARI.   System of land tenure in Gujarat and
Maharashtra under which local officials known as mam-
latdars settled the assessment and collected the revenue
by bargaining with the heads of villages.

MANAI.   Unit of land measurement in Tamil Nadu equal to
100 square feet.

MANAVA-DHARMA-SHASTRA   see   BHRIGU

MANCHI.   Large cargo-boat with a single mast and square
sail plying the Malabar coast.

MANCHIL.   A type of litter used in SW India.

MANDALA.   (1) A province of the Chola kingdom made up
of a number of nadus or districts.
           (2) (In Sanskrit literature) division of a large work.

MANDASOR.   Ancient town in Malwa; capital of King Yasodharman and home of the poet Kalidas.

MANDIALI.   A dialect of Pahari spoken in Mandi.

MANDU.   City in Malwa; capital of the Ghuri Dynasty; noted
    for fine buildings including the palace of Baz Bahadur
    and Rupmati.

MANDUKYA KARIKA   see   ADVAITA

MANGALORE.   Seaport and headquarters of south Canara
    district.   The Portuguese established a factory here in
    1554.   It was destroyed by the Arabs in 1596.   In 1763
    the town was captured by the sultan of Mysore.   It
    came under British control in 1799.

MANGALORE, TREATY OF.   Treaty in 1784 concluding the
    Second Mysore War between the East India Company and
    Tipu Sultan.   The treaty provided for the mutual re-
    storation of conquered areas.

MANGO TRICK.   Act of legerdemain attributed to Indian
    jugglers by which the stone of the mango fruit is shown
    to grow into a tree and bear leaves and fruits within
    the space of minutes.   The Autobiography of Emperor
    Jahangir contains a description of a mango trick which
    he witnessed.

MANIKKAVASAGAR.   Saiva mystic and Tamil poet of the
    tenth century.

MANIMEKALAI.   Tamil epic poem of the fifth century by
    Sattanar.

MANIPUR.   (1) Former state and chief commissionership in
    NE India.   In 1714 a Hindu chieftain, Gharib Nawaz,
    seized the territory and set up an independent kingdom.
    After the Anglo-Burmese War the kingdom was recog-
    nized as a protectorate by the British.   In 1890 the
    legitimate king was overthrown and a puppet was set up
    by the commander-in-chief, Tikendrjit.   British attempts
    to interfere led to a serious uprising in which the chief
    commissioner was murdered.   The British Army there-
    upon overran the state, deposed the usurper, and ap-
    pointed a minor as the new raja with a British political
    agent as administrator.
        (2) State in the Union of India inhabited by over 40
    tribes and subtribes belonging to the two main groups
    of Nagas and Kukis.   Capital: Imphal.

MANIPURI. (1) Colorful dance originating in the hill region
of Manipur danced by both men and women either accompanied by a chorus of singers or providing their
own vocal accompaniment. One form known as Laiharoba or the merrymaking of the gods is especially popular.
(2) (also, Meithei). Language spoken in Manipur;
member of the Arakan-Burmese branch of the Sino-
Tibetan family.

MANJADI. Unit of weight used in South India for precious
stones.

MANRIQUE, SEBASTIAN. Spanish friar and traveler who
has left an interesting account of the siege of Hughli
by the army of Shah Jahan in 1632.

MANSABDAR. Holder of a mansab or military title conferred by the Mughals required to supply and maintain
a certain number of troops for imperial service; divided
into 33 grades ranging from mansabdars of ten to mansabdars of 10,000; they were also expected to furnish
elephants and other animals. Their salaries were
sometimes paid in cash and sometimes by assignment
of jagirs depending on the rank and strength of the
contingent.

MAN SINGH. Tonwar king of Gwalior (1486-1517). Man
Singh successfully preserved the independence of Gwalior
against the inroads of the Mughals and the Muslim rulers of Jaunpur and Malwa. He also developed Gwalior
into a center of fine arts and music and built the famous
palace in the city.

MAN SINGH, KUNWAR. Raja of Amber; shone as a great
general under Akbar and led the Mughal army to victory
in the Deccan, Kabul, and Bengal.

MANTRI. Cabinet minister or royal adviser in a Hindu
state.

MANTRI-PARISHAD. (In ancient India) council of ministers
headed by the mahamantrin or chief minister.

MANU, INSTITUTES OF see MANUSAMHITA

MANUCCI, NICCOLO. Venetian traveler who came to India

as a youth in 1653 and managed to survive more than
50 years of colorful adventures which he recounted,
embroidered with gossip, in four volumes of Storia do
Mogor.

MANUCHARITA   see   PEDDANA

MANUSAMHITA (also, Institutes [or, Laws] of Manu).   The
most important of the Dharmasastras, said to be written by the sage Manu.   It spells out the domestic, religious, and social duties of the Hindu householder.   It
is ascribed sometimes to the sage Bhrigu, who is believed to have lived in the early part of the Christian
Era.

MANYAKHETA.   Town in Andhra Pradesh near Malkhed;
capital of the Rashtrakuta kingdom.

MARAKKAL.   Unit of grain measurement formerly in use
in Madras; generally 12 sers of grain (or 24 3/4 lbs.).

MARAMAT.   Department of civil public works in Madras.

MARATHA CONFEDERACY.   The five leaders of the Maratha nation--Peshwa Baji Rao I, Raghuji Bhonsla, Ranoji
Sindhia, Malhar Rao Holkar, and Damaji Gaekwad--who
carved up the Maratha dominions while owing nominal
allegiance to the Satara throne.

MARATHA WARS.   First Maratha War (1775-82).   Caused
by British support for Raghoba, opponent of Peshwa
Madhav Rao Narayan.   The course of the war was
marked by the surrender of the British forces in 1779
at Wargaon; the repudiation of the Convention of Wargaon by Warren Hastings; and the capture of Gwalior by
Major Popham in 1780.   Concluded by the Treaty of
Salbai by which the Company gained Salsette.
    Second Maratha War (1803-05).   Caused by the Treaty
of Bassein between Peshwa Baji Rao II and the East India Company under which the British undertook to restore the peshwa to the throne at Poona from which he
had been displaced by Sindhia and Holkar.   In return
the peshwa accepted the protection of the Company.
The treaty was repudiated by the three Maratha chieftains, Holkar, Sindhia, and Bhonsla.   The British defeated Sindhia and Bhonsla at the Battle of Assaye in
1803 and the Bhonsla forces again at the battle of Argaon

in 1804. Bhonsla was compelled to accept protected status and cede Cuttack. Lord Lake defeated Sindhia at the Battle of Laswari and forced him by the Treaty of Surji Arjangaon to cede all territories between the Ganges and the Yamuna in 1803. Holkar was defeated in the Battle of Deeg in 1804 and made to yield all territories north of the Chambal River.

Third Maratha War (1817-19). The Maratha power led by Peshwa Baji Rao II was permanently destroyed in six battles. The Bhonsla forces were defeated at the Battles of Sitabaldi and Nagpur (1817), Holkar at Mahidpur (1817), the peshwa at Kirkee (1817), Korigaon (1818), and Ashti (1818). The peshwa surrendered to the British and was exiled to Kanpur and the peshwaship was abolished. The Bhonsla Raja became a subsidiary prince ceding all territories north of the Narmada while Holkar gained the same status by ceding all territories south of the Narmada.

MARATHI. Indo-Aryan language derived from the Prakrit Maharashtri spoken mainly in Maharashtra. It developed into a major language through the patronage of the Yadava rulers. Its greatest writers in the middle ages were Hindu mystics: Jnanadeva (1275-96); Namdev (1270-1350); Ekanath (fl. 1560); Tukaram (1607-49); and Ramdas (1608-81). In the early modern period three writers stand out: Thomas Stephens (who translated the Bible into Marathi), Muktesvar, and Shaikh Muhammad. The best-known among modern Marathi writers are Baba Padamanji, Chiplunkar, and Agarkar. Baba Padamanji is the author of the first Marathi novel.

MARWARI (also, Sowcar). Caste of money lenders of Rajasthan and Marwar. Members of this caste, most of whom are Jains by religion, are found in all parts of India wielding considerable financial power.

MASNAD. Large cushion used by Indian princes in place of a throne.

MASNAVI. In Urdu and Persian literature a long poem based on historical events.

MASULA. Surf boat used on the Coromandel coast formed of planks sewn together with coir twine.

MASULIPATTAM see MACHILIPATNAM

MATH.   Hindu monastery, especially regarded as the center
of a sect or school of philosophy.

MATHURA.   Ancient city on the Yamuna in Uttar Pradesh
regarded as the birthplace of Krishna.   It was a Buddhist and Jain center in the time of Fa-Hien.   The
town was plundered and devastated by the Muslims in
1017, 1500, and 1757.   It was for a while the capital of
the Jat king Suraj Mal.

MATSYA.   Ancient kingdom in Rajputana with capital at
Viratanagara (or, Bairat) which formed one of the constituent units of the Magadha Empire and is mentioned
in the Mahabharata and the Vedas.

MATSYA PURANA.   One of the 18 puranas containing lists
of dynasties and kings.

MAUKHARI.   Dynasty founded in 554 by Isanavarman who
assumed the title Maharajadhiraja and ruled over an empire comprising Uttar Pradesh and parts of Bihar.   The
dynasty lasted until 606 when it was displaced by Harshavardhana.

MAULANA.   Title of a Muslim theologian or scholar.

MAULAVI.   Title of a Muslim judge or doctor of law.

MAUND (also, man).   Unit of weight of great antiquity,
identified with the Egyptian men, the Hebrew maneh,
and the Roman mina.   The standard maund is equal to
40 sers or 82 1/3 lbs.   The weights of local maunds
varied considerably from 18 lbs. in Travancore to
163 1/4 lbs. in Ahmadnagar.

MAURYA.   Dynasty founded in 322 B. C. by Chandragupta
Maurya who ruled over an extensive empire with capital
at Pataliputra.   He expelled the Greeks from the Punjab
and Taxila and forced Seleucus to divest himself of all
his Indian territories.   The third king of this dynasty
was Asoka who ruled from 273 B. C. to 232 B. C.   The
successors of Asoka were weak and the last Maurya
king Brihadratha was overthrown about 185 B. C. by
Pushyamitra, the founder of the Sunga Dynasty.
     According to some authorities there were ten rulers
in this line but no certain dates have been assigned to
Asoka's successors:

Chandragupta (324 B. C.)   Samprati
Bindusara (302 B. C.)   Shalishuka
Asoka (273 B. C.)   Devavarman
Kunala   Statadhanus
Bandhupalita or Dasharatha   Brihadratha

MAVAL.   Region in Maharashtra 20 miles in breadth to the
east of the Western Ghats.

MAWALI.   A hill tribe of the Western Ghats.

MAYO, Lord.   Full name: Richard Southwell Bourke.
Viceroy and governor general of India (1869-72).   He
improved the financial administration of the government
of India and organized the first census and statistical
survey of the country.

MAYURASARMAN.   Founder of the Kadamba (q. v.) Dynasty
of Mysore in the fourth century.

MEERUT.   Town in Uttar Pradesh; scene of the outbreak
of the Sepoy Mutiny on May 10, 1857.

MEGASTHENES.   Greek writer and ambassador of the Syrian ruler Seleucus Nikator at the court of Chandragupta
Maurya; author of Indica.

MEGHADUTA.   Literally, the cloud messenger.   Sanskrit
poem by Kalidas.

MEGHALAYA.   State of the Union of India comprising the
Garo, Kasi, and Jaintia Hills region.   Capital: Shillong.

MENANDER.   Indo-Greek king of the Punjab (160-140 B. C.)
who embraced Buddhism.   The Buddhist text Milindapanha (Questions [or Dialogues] of Milinda), dated 140
B. C. by Buddhist historians is a record of his theologi-
cal discussions with the monk Nagasena.

MEOS.   Hindu tribe inhabiting the Delhi region who were
slaughtered to the last person by Balban in 1260.

METCALFE, Lord CHARLES.   1785-1846.   Officiating governor general of India (1835-36).   Negotiated the Treaty
of Amritsar with Ranjit Singh in 1809; served as resident in Gwalior, Hyderabad, and Delhi, and governor of
Agra, North West Province (later United Provinces) and

Madras.   As governor general his most important act
was to remove all restrictions on the press.

MEWAR.   Kingdom in Rajasthan later known as Udaipur
ruled by a dynasty of ranas established by Hamir in the
14th century.   The line consisted of 33 kings in an un-
broken succession:

Hamir	Raja Simha I (1652)
Kshetra Simha (1364)	Jay Simha (1680)
Laksha (1382)	Amara Simha II (1699)
Mokala (1418)	Sangrama Simha II (1711)
Kumbha (1430)	Jagat Simha II (1734)
Udaya Karan (1469)	Pratapa Simha II (1752)
Rayamalla (1474)	Raja Simha II (1754)
Sangrama (1509)	Ari Simha II (1761)
Ratna Simha (1527)	Hamir II (1773)
Bikramajit (1532)	Bhim Simha (1778)
Ranbir (1535)	Jawan Simha (1828)
Udaya Simha (1537)	Sardar Simha (1838)
Pratapa Simha (1572)	Sarup Simha (1842)
Amara Simha (1597)	Shambhu (1861)
Karan (1620)	Sujan Simha (1874)
Jagat Simha (1628)	Fateh Simha (1884)
	Bhopal Simha (1930)

MIANI, BATTLE OF.   Battle in 1843 between East India
Company forces led by Sir Charles Napier and the
Amirs of Sind in which the Amirs were defeated.

MIHIRAGULA.   Hun king, successor of Toramana, who ascended the throne in 500 with capital at Sakala or Sial-
kot.   His rule was marked by the persecution of Buddhists.   In 528 a confederacy led by Baladitya, king of
Magadha, and Yasodharman, king of Mandasor, defeated
him and forced him to flee to Kashmir where he ruled
until his death.

MILINDAPANHA.   Literally, the Questions of Milinda.   A
Buddhist text in Socratic form in which Milinda (i. e. ,
Menander) discusses Buddhist doctrines with the sage
Nagasena; dated 140 B. C. third century by Buddhist
historians.

MIMAMSA.   One of the six orthodox systems of Hindu philosophy founded by Jaimini dealing with Vedic rituals
and ceremonies through an elaborate system of rules
(vidhi) and prohibitions (nisheda).   Divided into Purva

(early) and Uttara (later). Also known as Karma-Mimamsa because it emphasizes action and Vakya-sastra
or the study of words.

MINHAJ-I-SIRAJ (also, Minhaj-ud-din Siraj). Court historian of Sultan Nasir-ud-din; author of Tabaqat-i-Nasiri.

[1]MINTO, Earl of. Full name: Sir Gilbert Elliot-Murray-
Kynynmond. 1751-1814. Governor general of India
(1807-13). His administration was marked by the
Treaty of Amritsar with Ranjit Singh.

[2]MINTO, Earl of. Full name: Gilbert John Elliot-Murray-
Kynynmond. 1845-1914. Viceroy and governor general
of India (1905-10). Associated with Lord Morley in
formulating the Constitutional Reforms embodied in the
Government of India Act of 1909; suppressed the rising
tide of terrorism that followed in the wake of the Partition of Bengal; and gave official recognition to the principle of communal representation for religious and racial minorities.

MIR. Designation of the head of department in the Mughal
administration.

MIRABAI. c1450-c1547. Hindi poet and disciple of Raidas.
Her poems are written in the Braj dialect of Western
Hindi.

MIRANPUR KATRA, BATTLE OF. Battle in 1774 between
Nawab Shuja-ud-daulah of Oudh and the Rohillas in which
the Rohillas were defeated.

MIR BAKSHI. Title of the head of the military department
in the Mughal administration.

MIR JAFAR. Nawab of Bengal (1757-60; 1763-65). Con-
spired and entered into a treaty with the British for
help in deposing his rival Nawab Siraj-ud-daulah and
obtaining his throne; installed in 1757 as Nawab of Bengal following the defeat and death of Siraj-ud-daulah at
the Battle of Plassey; in return granted the Company
the 24 Parganas and paid 28,950,000 rupees to the
Company's servants including Robert Clive as compen-
sation and gratuity.
    The Nawab was rendered bankrupt as a result of these
largesses and began to conspire with the Dutch to oust

the British; deposed in favor of Mir Qasim in 1760 but
was restored to the throne in 1763 on the outbreak of
a war between Mir Qasim and the British.   The Company imposed harsher terms for his reinstatement.   He
was required to pay 72,50,000 rupees to Fort William,
to levy a duty of only 2% on English trade in salt, and
to accept a British resident at Murshidabad.   Mir Jafar
died in 1765.

MIR JUMLA.   Persian-born adventurer who rose to become
chief minister of Sultan Abdullah Qutb Shah of Golkonda.
Shifted loyalty to the Mughals in 1656 and became chief
minister of Shah Jahan; supported Aurangzeb in the war
of succession and was rewarded in 1660 with the gov-
ernorship of Bengal; led an expedition to Assam in 1662
which overran the country and forced the Ahoms to cede
large areas to the Mughals and to pay a heavy indemnity; worn out by these exertions, he died in 1663.

MIR QASIM.   Son-in-law of Mir Jafar installed by the British as the Nawab of Bengal in 1760 in return for the
cession of Burdwan, Chittagong, and Midnapore in addition to a grant of two million rupees.   Once in power
he tried to throw off the Company's yoke and to be
master in his own house.   He moved the capital from
Murshidabad to Monghyr so as to escape the proximity
of Calcutta.   His efforts to correct the abuses of free
private trade by the Company's servants earned him
their hostility and soon led to war.   He was defeated
by the British at the Battles of Katwa, Gheria, and
Udhuanala and forced to flee to Oudh where he joined
forces with Shuja-ud-daulah, the Nawab of Oudh, and
Emperor Shah Alam II; the defeat of the combined army
at the Battle of Buxar in 1764 marked the end of the
road for Mir Qasim.

MIR SAMAN.   Title of the minister in charge of factories
and stores in the Mughal administration.

MIRZA.   A Persian title of honor, generally applied to persons of noble birth.

MIRZA [or Mir] SHAH.   The first Muslim sultan of Kashmir; usurped the throne in 1346 under the name of
Sams-ud-din and founded a dynasty that ruled until 1541.

MISHRA, VACASPATI see ADVAITA

MISL.   One of the 12 units into which the Sikh confederacy was divided: Ahluwalia, Bhangi, Dalewalia, Fyzulla-puria, Kanheya, Karora Singhia, Nakai, Nihang, Nishan-wala, Phulkia, Ramgarhia, and Sukerchakia.

MISRA, SRI KRISHNA   see   KIRTTIVARMAN

MITAKSHARA.   Sanskrit legal classic written by Vijnanes-wara, a native of Kalyani, during the reign of Vikra-maditya Chalukya (1076-1126); basis of Hindu law throughout India except Bengal and Assam.

MITHILA.   Seat of learning, famous for its school of logic, that flourished from the 12th to the 15th century. Among its scholars were Gangesa, Vardhamana, Sarvabhauma, and Vidyapati.

MIYANA.   Type of litter or palanquin suspended under a straight bamboo pole by which it is carried and shaded by a frame covered with cloth.

MIZORAM.   A Union Territory of the Indian Union comprising the Mizo Hill region.

MLECHCHHA.   Literally, barbarian.   Term applied by Hindus to all persons outside the caste system, especially foreigners.

MODERN HINDI.   Language derived from Hindvi, a dialect spoken in Delhi and Meerut in Mughal times.   Under the influence of Urdu it became Khariboli or pure speech.   Its emergence as a modern language is due to the influence of John Gilchrist, Harischandra, and Mahavir Prasad Dvivedi.

MOFUSSIL.   The rural localities of a district as distinguished from the chief station.

MOGHUL   see   MUGHAL

MOHENJO-DARO.   Archaeological site in Larkana district in Sind where evidences of the Indus Valley civilization have been found.   Excavations revealed large well-laid-out cities with brick houses and a sewage system.   Remains of a prehistoric embankment point to efforts at primitive flood control.

MOHUR.   Formerly the chief gold coin of British India.   It
was introduced by the Delhi Sultanate and tended to a
standard weights of 100 rattis of pure gold, or about
175 grains.   It was made legal tender by the East India
Company in 1793 for 16 sicca (q. v.) rupees.   The
Company's gold mohur weighed 180 grams troy and contained 165 grams of pure gold.

MONTAGUE-CHELMSFORD REPORT.   Report on Indian
constitutional reforms prepared by Edwin Montague and
Lord Chelmsford which formed the basis of the Government of India Act of 1919 directed to "the progressive
realization of responsible government in India."

MOPLAHS.   The Muslim community of Malabar believed to
be descendants of Arab traders; led an uprising against
the British in 1925.

MOUNTBATTEN, Lord LOUIS.   Real name: Prince Louis
Francis Albert Victor Nicholas of Battenberg [name officially changed to Mountbattan as of World War I];
titles: Earl Mountbatten of Burma; Baron Romsey.
1900-   .   Last governor general of British India
(March-August 1947) and first governor general of the
Dominion of India (1947-48).   Presided over the historic
transfer of power from the Crown to the people of India.

MRICHCHHAKATIKA.   Literally, the Little Clay Cart.
Sanskrit drama written in the first or second century
though some authorities place it in the fifth or sixth
century.   Its authorship is variously attributed to
Sudraka, Bhasa, or Dandin.   The drama relates the
story of Charudatta, a virtuous Brahmin, and Vasanta-
sena, a beautiful and wealthy courtesan.

MRIDANGA.   Literally, clay body.   Barrel-shaped drum
beaten at both ends used in classical music and as an
accompaniment to Bharata Natyam.

MUDA.   A unit of grain measurement used in Maharashtra
and Gujarat equal to a little over one cubic foot.

MUDALIAR.   Title assumed by members of a Sudra caste
in Tamil Nadu.

MUDKI, BATTLE OF.   Battle in 1845 between the English
and the Sikhs in which the Sikhs were defeated.

MUDRA.   Literally, gesture.   A position of hands and
fingers used in dancing and rituals to convey a sym-
bolic meaning.   Manuals describe over a thousand mud-
ras including 32 major hand positions, 12 hand movements, and 24 combined positions.

MUDRARAKSHASA.   Literally, the Ogre and the Signet Ring.
Classical Sanskrit political drama in seven acts by
Visakhadatta; assigned to the Gupta period.

MUFTI.   Muslim law officer who expounded the law and
delivered the fatwa.   Properly the mufti was superior
to the qasi who executed the judgment.

MUGDHABODHA   see   BOPADEVA

MUGHAL.   Dynasty founded in 1526 by Babur which ruled
India effectively until the death of Aurangzeb in 1707 and
nominally from 1707 until 1857 when the last Mughal
emperor was exiled from India for taking part in the
Sepoy Mutiny.   The line consisted of 26 sovereigns,
though only 19 sat on the throne; Babur, Humayun,
Akbar, Jahangir, Shah Jahan, and Aurangzeb are known
as the Great Mughals while the descendants of Aurangzeb are known as the Later Mughals.   At its zenith the
dynasty ruled over the whole Indian subcontinent with
the exception of Assam and pockets of South India.   Its
power was weakened in the 18th century by wars of
succession, the alienation of Hindus and Sikhs, the rise
of European power, and by the successive depradations
of Nadir Shah and Ahmad Shah Abdali.
    Zahir-ud-din Babur (1526)
    Muhammad Humayun (1530)
    Jalal-ud-din Akbar (1556)
    Nur-ud-din Muhammad Jahangir (1605)
    Davar Bakhsh (1627)
    Khurram Shihab-ud-din Muhammad Shah Jahan (1628)
    Murad Bakhsh (1657)
    Shah Shuja (1657)
    Muhyi-ud-din Muhammad Aurangzeb Alamgir (1658)
    Azam Shah (1707)
    Kam Bak'sh (1707)
    Mu'azzam Shah Alam I Bahadur Shah I (1707)
    Azim-ush-Shan (1712)
    Mu'izz-ud-din Jahandar Shah (1712)
    Muhammad Farrukhsiyar (1713)
    Rafi-ud-darajat (1719)

Rafi-ud-daulah Shah Jahan II (1719)
Muhammad Shah (1719)
Muhammad Ibrahim (1720)
Ahmad Shah (1748)
Aziz-ud-din Alamgir II (1754)
Shah Jahan III (1759)
Mirza Abdullah Ali Gohar Shah Alam II (1759)
Bidar Bakht (1788)
Akbar Shah II (1806)
Bahadur Shah II (1837)

MUGHAL SCHOOL.   School of miniature painting which
  flourished under the patronage of Mughal emperors.
  Sayyid Ali Abdus Samad and Daswanath are the best
  representatives of this school.

MUHAMMAD BIN-TUGHLUQ.   Sultan of Delhi (1325-1351).
  He extended the Sultanate by conquering Warangal,
  Ma'bar, and Dvarasamudra.   He is remembered as an
  eccentric monarch whose best schemes failed because
  they were unsuited to the times.   In 1327 he transferred
  the capital from Delhi to Devagiri (renamed Daulatabad)
  and insisted on a massive transfer of population.   Three
  years later he issued token currency in lieu of gold
  and caused great confusion because the new copper
  tokens were easily counterfeited.   His proposed expeditions against Persia and Kumaon were abandoned after
  the loss of men and money.   Famines, heavy taxes,
  and tyranny combined to goad various provinces to revolt and in suppressing one of these in Sind he died in
  1351.

MUHAMMAD GHORI [or Ghuri], SHIHAB-UD-DIN (or, Muiz-
  ud-din).   Founder of Muslim rule in India and of the
  Delhi Sultanate.   A born warrior and empire builder,
  he conquered Multan in 1175 and Punjab in 1186.   In
  1192 in the Second Battle of Tarain he defeated the
  Rajput confederacy led by Prithviraj, the Chauhan king
  of Ajmer and Delhi.   This victory opened the gates of
  Hindustan to the Muslim tide and Delhi fell to Shihab-
  ud-din's lieutenant Qutb-ud-din in 1193.   Next year he
  routed and killed Raja Jai Chand of Kanauj at the Battle
  of Chandwar.   By 1206 when he died he was the master
  of northern India including Bihar and Bengal.

MUHAMMAD IBN-KASIM.   General of Al-Hajjaj, governor
  of Iraq, who invaded Sind in 712.   He crossed the Indus,

defeated and killed king Dahir at the Battle of Raor,
occupied Multan and Alor, and established Muslim rule
in the Indian subcontinent. Later he incurred the wrath
of Caliph Sulaiman who had him tortured to death.

MUHAMMAD KULI. Sultan of Golkonda (1580-1612), fifth
in the Qutb Shahi line. His reign was marked by incessant wars in Orissa and the Carnatic. He is best
remembered as the founder of the city of Hyderabad in
1589.

MUHAMMAD RUHELA ALI. Founder of the Ruhela Dynasty
of Rampur in Rohilkhand.

MUHAMMAD SHAH. 18th Mughal emperor of Delhi (1719-
48). He ended the stranglehold of the Sayyid Brothers
on the throne by executing them. His rule was marked
by the progressive breakup of the empire. Deccan,
Oudh, Rohilkhand, and Bengal seceded from the Mughal
dominion. He was also forced to relinquish Malwa to
Peshwa Baji Rao I in 1737. A more serious blow was
the invasion of Nadir Shah in 1739 which left the country bleeding. Sometime before his death he staved off
an invasion by Ahmad Shah Abdali.

MUHARRUM. (1) First month of the Muslim year. (2)
Religious festival of Shiite Muslims held during the
month of Muharrum to mark the death of Hasan, grandson of the Prophet Muhammad.

MUHTARAFA. Collective name applied in Bombay and
Madras Presidencies for a variety of imposts and taxes
other than land revenue; corresponds to sayer in Bengal.

MUKKADDAM. Headman of a village, caste, or guild.

MUKTESVAR see MARATHI

MULARAJA. Founder of the Solanki Dynasty of the Anhilwara kingdom in Gujarat. He ruled from 942 to 997.

MULA SUTRA. Literally, cardinal principles. Sourcebook
of Jain doctrines, written in Ardha Magadhi, often
cited in canonical literature.

MULKI. A native Hyderabadi, especially one who served in
the administration of the former Nizams of Hyderabad.

MUNDA. (1) A Kolarian aboriginal tribe of Central India.
They are sometimes identified with the Murunda of the
Puranas.
(2) (also, Kolarian or Kol). Austric language con-
sisting of a large number of dialects spoken in Chota
Nagpur and Himalayan regions. Divided into Southern
Munda and Northern Munda.

MUNDARI. Kolarian language spoken by the Mundas.

MUNDY, PETER. An employee of the East India Company
who traveled in northern India from 1628 to 1634. His
work, The Travels of Peter Mundy, in five volumes,
gives an accurate description of the country under Shah
Jahan including the famine of 1630 and the destruction
of the Hindu temples of Benares.

MUNI. Anchorite who has taken the vow of mouna or silence
and is credited with preternatural powers.

[1]MUNIM KHAN. Son of Sultan Beg. Munim Khan was instrumental in enabling Prince Muazzam, son of Aurangzeb, to proclaim himself emperor at Agra shortly after
the death of his father. In reward Munim Khan was
appointed revenue minister under the new emperor
Bahadur Shah. He also distinguished himself in the
field, defeating the forces of Kam Baksh in 1707 and
the Sikh leader Banda in 1710.

[2]MUNIM KHAN. Mughal commander of Kabul under Humayun and Akbar. On the dismissal of Bairam Khan he
was appointed Khan Khanan or supreme commander. He
led the Mughal expedition to Bengal which defeated
Daud, the Afghan ruler of Bengal, in the Battle of
Tukaroi in 1575.

MUNRO, Sir THOMAS. 1761-1827. Governor of Madras
(1820-27). Remembered for the introduction of ryotwari
system of land tenure in Madras Presidency.

MUNSHI. A teacher of native languages; formerly a secretary employed by a European as an interpreter and
linguist.

MUNSIF. Title of a civil judge of the lowest grade. The
office was first established in 1793.

MUNTAKHAB-UL-LUBAB see KHAFI KHAN

MUNTAKHABU-T-TAWARIK see BADAONI

MURALI see BANSRI

MURSHID QULI JAFAR KHAN. Persian-born Mughal official who was appointed Diwan of the Deccan by Aurangzeb in 1656. His efficient administration led to his
appointment in 1701 as Diwan of Bengal independent of
the viceroy. He transferred the revenue offices from
Dacca to a new city named after him as Murshidabad.
After the death of Aurangzeb he became viceroy of Bengal, Bihar, and Orissa, a post he held until his death
in 1726.

MUSLIM LEAGUE. Communal organization of Indian Muslims founded in 1906 through the initiative of Nawab
Salim-ul-lah of Dacca. Its goal was to protect and up-
hold Muslim interests especially vis-à-vis the Hindus,
who formed the majority in the Indian National Congress. In the thirties it began to sponsor the demand
for an independent state called Pakistan comprising areas in NW and NE India with a Muslim majority. Under Muhammad Ali Jinnah, its president for many
years, this demand was pressed forcefully and finally
granted in 1947.

MUZAFFAR JANG. Nizam of Hyderabad (1750-51), and
grandson of the first Nizam-ul-Mulk Chin Qilich Khan
Asaf Jah. On the death of Asaf Jah in 1748, Muzaffar
Jang found his claims to the throne opposed by his
uncle Nasir Jang. In the war of succession that followed Muzaffar Jang obtained the military assistance of
the French and of Chanda Sahib, pretender to the throne
of Arcot. Their combined army was, however, defeated by Nasir Jang at Veludavur in 1750 and Muzaffar
Jang was forced to surrender. A few months later
Nasir Jang was ambushed and killed and Muzaffar Jang
was proclaimed the Nizam. A year later Muzaffar Jang
was himself killed in a skirmish.

MYSORE. (1) Region in the Deccan ruled in ancient times
by the Kadambas. In the 12th century it passed into
the hands of the Hoysalas. It was for a time part of
the dominions of Alauddin Khalji and later of Vijayanagar.
After the fall of Vijayanagar the kingdom was ruled by a

petty dynasty the last king of which was displaced by
Haider Ali. After the defeat and death of Haider's son
Tipu Sultan the kingdom reverted to the rule of the
Hindu kings of the Wadyar line.

(2) City in Karnataka state; former capital of Mysore
state.

MYSORE WARS.   First Mysore War (1767-69).   Caused by
English support for the Nizam.   Concluded by a treaty
favorable to Haider Ali.

Second Mysore War (1780-84). Caused by the refusal
of the British to help Haider Ali against the Marathas
according to the terms of the treaty of 1769 and by the
English attack on Mahe in Haider's dominions.   Haider
Ali joined the Nizam and the Marathas in a triple alliance against the British but had to carry on the war
alone when the Company lured the Nizam away and
pacified the Marathas by the Treaty of Salbai.   Haider
Ali was defeated thrice in 1781--at Porto Novo, Pollilore, and Sholinghur--and died in 1782.   His son Tipu
Sultan besieged Mangalore and forced the British Army
to capitulate at Thanjavur.   Concluded by the Treaty of
Mangalore in 1784 by which both sides agreed to relinquish their conquests.

Third Mysore War (1790-92).   Caused by Tipu Sultan's invasion of Travancore, a British ally.   Lord
Cornwallis himself led the campaign, besieged Seringapatam, and forced Tipu to submit on humiliating terms.
He was forced to surrender two of his sons as hostages,
to pay an indemnity of 30 million rupees, and to cede
half his kingdom--of which Dindigul, Baramahal, Coorg,
and Malabar went to the British, the territory between
the Wardha and Krishna Rivers went to the Marathas,
and that between Krishna and Pennar went to the Nizam.

Fourth Mysore War (March-May 1799).   Caused by
Tipu's refusal to accept subsidiary alliance under British paramountcy.   The Company's army led by Arthur
Wellesley (future Duke of Wellington) defeated Tipu in
two pitched battles and drove him into the Seringapatam
fort which was taken by assault.   Tipu died in the fight-
ing.   Mysore proper was restored to Krishnaraja, a
scion of the old Hindu line of rulers.   Canara, Coimbatore, and Seringapatam were annexed to British dominions.

- N -

NABHADAS. Hindi poet in the time of Jahangir; author of
    Bhakta mala in Braj dialect, a compendium of the lives
    of 200 Vaishnavite saints.

NABOB.   Term applied in England in the 18th century to
    East India Company servants who had amassed a for-
    tune in India.

NADIR SHAH (also, Tahmasp Quli Khan).   c1688-1747.
    Shah of Persia (1736-1747).   Invaded India in 1739;
    sacked Delhi and left with a priceless booty that in-
    cluded the Peacock Throne and the Koh-i-noor diamond.

NADU.   A district comprised of kurrams in the Chola king-
    dom.

NAGA.   (1) A hill people of Scythian origin associated with
    naga or serpent worship.   Their name may also have
    been derived from the Sanskrit word naga, highland.
    Nagas were highly civilized people whose mode of writ-
    ing was adapted in the nagari script.   In historical
    times the Nagas founded many dynasties as Haryanka,
    Sisunaga, Lichchhavi, Bharasiva, and Padmavati.
    Several other dynasties were either linked with Nagas
    or claimed descent from them.
        (2) A hill tribe of Assam of Mongoloid origin whose
    name is derived from the Sanskrit word nagna, nude.
    They were formerly head-hunting aboriginals but the
    majority are now Christians.   The chief tribes in num-
    erical order are: Angami, Ao, Sema, Konyak, Chakhe-
    sang, Lotha, Phom, Khiemnungam, Chang, Yimchunger,
    Zeliang-kuki, Rengma, and Sangtan.   They practice a
    traditional form of cultivation called jhumming.
        (3) Language spoken by the Nagas (of definition no.
    2) belonging to the Tibeto-Burman group of the Sino-
    Tibetan family of languages.

NAGABHATA I.   Founder of the Gurjara-Pratihara Dynasty
    of the eighth century.

NAGALAND.   State of the Indian Union comprising the for-
    mer Naga Hills district of Assam and the former
    Tuensang Frontier division of the North-East Frontier
    Agency.   Capital: Kohima.

NAGANANDA. Sanskrit drama attributed to Harshavardhana
and assigned to the seventh century.

NAGAPPATTINAM. Town in Tamil Nadu; site of an early
Dutch settlement.

NAGARAKA. (In ancient India) head of a district.

NAGARI see DEVANAGIRI

[1]NAGARJUNA. Buddhist philosopher born in South India;
founder of the Madhyamika school of Mahayana philosophy and first patriarch of the Buddhist church.   Three
treatises are attributed to him: Madhyamika Sastra,
Dvadasa Sastra, and Sata Sastra. He is believed to
have ended his life by his own hand.

[2]NAGARJUNA. Hindu chemist of the seventh or eighth century; author of Rasaratnakara.

NAGARJUNIKONDA. Place near the Krishna River in Andhra Pradesh now submerged; center of Buddhist art and
architecture noted for its sculptures.

NAGASENA. Buddhist sage who figures as the locutor ex-
pounding Buddhist doctrines to Menander in Milindapanha.

NAGASWARA. Literally, snake-note. The South Indian fife.

NAGPUR. City in Maharashtra and center of Vidharba region; seat of the Maratha Bhonslas; annexed to the
British Raj in 1854 under the Doctrine of Lapse and
made capital of Central Provinces.

NAHAPANA. Satrap of the Kshaharata line of the Sakas
which ruled over a large empire comprising Maharashtra, Konkan, Kathiawar, Malwa, and Ajmer in the
second century with capital at Nasik.

NAIB. A deputy or lieutenant, as naib-nazim.

NAIK. (1) Title of honor applied to the kings of Vijayanagar
and the petty rulers of Madurai.
(2) Title of the headman of a camp of Banjaras.

NAIK-GOPAL. Court musician of the Khalji sultans and exponent of the ragas of Hindustani music.

NAIKI.   A Dravidian language of the Gondi group spoken in
central India.

NAIR.   A group of declassed Malabar Kshattriyas including
the Menon, Kurup, Nambiar, Panikkar clans.   By tradition this group is polyandrous and matriarchal and their
social system is marked by marumakkathayam or matri-
lineal line of succession.   The social unit is an extended family called the tarvad of which the eldest
woman is the head and the eldest man only the karnavan
or manager.

NALANDA.   Seat of a Buddhist university from the first to
the twelfth century in Bihar.   Hiuen Tsang recorded in
635 that 300 lecture rooms and a library that occupied
three buildings served 150 teachers and 3000 students
from all over Asia.   No fees were charged and clothes,
food, and medicine were supplied free by the university
which was maintained through the revenue of 200 villages
assigned for its upkeep.   The university flourished under the Pala kings who ruled from the 8th to the 12th
century but was destroyed by the early Muslim invaders.

NALANDA PALI INSTITUTE.   Institution founded in Nalanda,
Bihar, in 1951 for research in Pali language and literature.   Publishes Nava Nalanda Mahavihara Research.

NAMBUDIRI.   An orthodox class of Brahmins of Malabar,
noted for their strict adherence to rituals and proficiency
in the Vedas.

NAMDEV see MARATHI

NAMMALVAR see ALVAR

NANA FADNAVIS.   Maratha Brahmin chief minister of Peshwa Madhav Rao and the undisputed power behind the
throne from 1774 until 1800.   He led the Maratha
forces in the First Maratha War and wars with Tipu
Sultan and the Nizam.   Nana's power was diminished
when the peshwa committed suicide and was succeeded
by the son of his old rival Raghaba, Baji Rao II.   He,
however, managed to hold on to his power until his
death in 1800.

NANAK.   1469-1539.   Founder of Sikhism and its first Guru

whose sayings and hymns comprise the Adi Granth, the
bible of the Sikhs. Born in a Khatri family near Lahore, Nanak was greatly influenced by Kabir and made
pilgrimage to Mecca and Medina. Nanak tried to fuse
the more acceptable elements of Hinduism and Islam in
his new religion which gained an impressive following
in the Punjab and changed the religious map of India.

NANA SAHIB (also, Dandu Pant). c1825–c1860. Adopted
son of the exiled Peshwa Baji Rao II who was disin-
herited of his title and deprived of his allowance by
Lord Dalhousie; led the mutineers at Kanpur at the outbreak of the Sepoy Mutiny and directed the massacre
of British soldiers and citizens; declared peshwa at
Gwalior by Tantia Topi in 1858; defeated and forced to
flee; died in unknown circumstances.

NANDA. Dynasty founded in 362 B. C. by Mahapadma Nanda
in Magadha. The dynasty consisted of nine kings and
were described in classical accounts as immensely
wealthy and powerful. It was overthrown by Chandragupta Maurya in 322 B. C.

NANDKUMAR. A Brahmin official under the Nawab of Bengal who played a prominent role in the early history of
the British in Bengal. As faujdar of Hughli he helped
the English capture Chandernagore. After the Battle of
Plassey in 1757 he rose in power and influence and was
granted the title of maharaja by the Emperor Shah Alam
II in 1764. Next year he was appointed naib or deputy
collector of the subah of Bengal. Soon he fell from
favor and was dismissed from his post. Growing es-
trangement between Nandkumar and Warren Hastings
culminated in the submission of grave charges of corruption against Hastings before the Executive Council
by Nandkumar in 1775. Friends of Warren Hastings,
such as Richard Barwell, countered by bringing a charge
of conspiracy against Nandkumar to which was later
added a charge of forgery. The trial of Nandkumar on
both these charges was presided over by Sir Elijah Impey (a friend of Warren Hastings) who, after a summary
trial, found Nandkumar guilty and sentenced him to
death. The trial and execution of Nandkumar soon became a cause célèbre and constituted one of the principal
charges against Warren Hastings at the time of his impeachment.

NANNIAH see TELUGU

NAPIER, Sir CHARLES JAMES. 1782-1853. British general who commanded the Company's victorious army in the war which finally destroyed the Amirs of Sind and led to the annexation of the province. He wired the news of his victory to the Board in a single cryptic Latin word: peccavi, a pun meaning "I have Sin(ne)d. "

NARA NARAYAN. King of Cooch Behar (1540-1584). He was the son and successor of Biswa Singh, founder of the state of Cooch Behar. Through successful military expeditions he enlarged his kingdom to include a large area of Assam and Rangpur. As the patron of Sankaradeva, the Vaishnavite reformer, he did much to advance the cause of Vaishnavism in Assam.

NARASIMHA see HUNS

NARASIMHA MEHTO. 1414-80. Gujarati poet generally regarded as the father of Gujarati poetry.

NARASIMHA VARMAN (also, Rajasimha). The greatest of the Pallava kings (625-45). In 642 he defeated and killed Pulakeshin II, the Chalukya king, and took his capital Vatapi. He was also a great temple builder.

NARAYAN, JAYAPRAKASH. 1901- . Indian socialist and Sarvodaya leader; organized in 1933 the first session of the Congress Socialist Bloc; took an active part in the civil disobedience movement; left the Congress after independence to found the Sarvodaya movement.

NARAYANA see HITOPADESA

NARMADA. River in central and western India rising in north Madhya Pradesh and flowing west through the Vindhya and Satpura ranges to the Gulf of Cambay. Length, 800 miles.

NASIK. Town in Maharashtra near the source of the Godavari noted as one of the seven sacred cities of Hindus and as the site of a Kumbh mela. It figures in the Ramayana; later it was the capital of the Kshaharata in the first century, of the Vakatakas in the third century, and of the Chalukyas in the seventh century.

NASIR-UD-DIN MAHMUD. Sultan of Delhi (1246-1266); son-
in-law of Ulugh Khan who later became Ghiyas-ud-din
Balban. An account of his reign survives in Tabaqat-i-
Nasiri by Minhaj-i-Siraj.

NATAKA. (In Sanskrit drama) a heroic or classic drama.

NATARAJA. A form of the Hindu god Siva as the lord of
dance.

NATIONAL ARCHIVES OF INDIA. Public record office of
India containing over 100,000 historical documents; established in 1891 in New Delhi. Publishes Indian Archives.

NATIONAL BOOK TRUST. Autonomous body set up by the
government of India to produce and encourage the production of good literature and to make such literature
available at moderate prices to the public. The Trust
also arranges national and regional book exhibitions.

NATIONAL LIBRARY. Central library established at Cal-
cutta in 1902 by the amalgamation of the Calcutta Public
Library and the Imperial Library. Publishes Indian
National Bibliography (1957-) and A Bibliography of
Indology, Enumerating Basic Publications on All Aspects
of Indian Culture (1960-).

NATIONAL MUSEUM OF INDIA. Museum established at New
Delhi in 1949 with nine departments: art, archeology,
anthropology, model-making, presentation, preservation,
publication, library, and photography. It contains prehistoric tools and artifacts, illustrated manuscripts and
miniatures, murals, decorative arts, textiles, coins,
and armor.

NATYA-SASTRA see BHARATA

NAUROZ. The vernal equinox celebrated as the Parsi New
Year's Day.

NAVARATHRI. Major Hindu festival marking the autumnal
equinox in September-October; called Durga Puja in
Bengal. The tenth day of this festival is Dassara or
Dussehra which commemorates the victory of Rama or
Ravana and is therefore also called Vijaya-dasami.

NAVA RATNA. Literally, nine gems. Term applied to the
    nine worthies who were patronized by Vikramaditya, the
    legendary king of Ujjain. They were: (1) Dhanvantari
    the physician, (2) Kshapanaka the poet, (3) Sanku the
    poet, (4) Vetalabhatta the poet, (5) Amarasimha the
    lexicographer, (6) Kalidas the poet, (7) Varahamihira
    the astronomer, (8) Ghatakarpara the poet, and (9)
    Vararuchi the dramatist, grammarian, and astronomer.

NAWAB. Title of the governor or viceroy of a Mughal pro-
    vince; later adopted as the title of the independent rul-
    ers of Arcot, Oudh, and Bengal.

NAWARA. A large barge; also applied to a flotilla of boats.

NAYYAKA. Hindu dynasty (1420-1736), originally feudatory
    rulers of Vijayanagar (q. v.) and later independent rul-
    ers of Madurai, founded by Visvanatha. Tirumalai
    (1623-60) was the most famous ruler of this line. The
    Nayyakas were great builders of temples, including
    those at Madurai and Srirangam.

NAZIM. Title of the governor or viceroy of a Mughal pro-
    vince.

NAZR. Literally, votive offering. Ceremonial present from
    an inferior to a superior.

NEDUM-CHEZHIYAN see PANDYA

NEHRU, JAWAHARLAL. 1889-1964. Indian nationalist
    leader and first prime minister of India; son of Motilal
    Nehru and father of Indira Gandhi. Educated at Harrow
    and Cambridge he returned to India and joined the non-
    cooperation movement in 1920 and became an associate
    of Gandhi. He headed the left wing of the Indian Na-
    tional Congress and advocated socialism at home and
    an anti-imperialist stand abroad. He was president of
    the Indian National Congress four times (1929, 1936,
    1946, 1951-54) and its general secretary for ten years
    (1929-39).
        Became prime minister in 1947 and remained in that
    office until his death in 1964. His greatest successes
    were in the field of foreign affairs where he formulated
    the principle of nonalignment and was generally acknowl-
    edged as the leader of the Third World. He set India
    on a course of moderate socialism and secularism in

domestic affairs.   Author of Autobiography, Glimpses
of World History, A Bunch of Old Letters, and Discovery of India.

NEHRU, Pandit MOTILAL.   1861-1931.   Indian nationalist
    leader; father of Jawaharlal Nehru.   He left a flourish-
    ing law practice to join the nationalist movement and
    launched the journal called The Independent; joined the
    noncooperation movement in 1920; formed the Swaraj
    Party within the Congress along with C. R. Das and
    became its principal spokesman; twice president of the
    Indian National Congress (1919; 1928); author of the
    Nehru Report advocating dominion status for India.
    Rejection of this report by the British government led
    him to join the civil disobedience movement in 1930 and
    to court imprisonment.   He died a year later.

NEPALESE ERA.   Era used in Nepal dated from 879.

NEW DELHI.   Capital of India since 1912; situated on the
    west bank of the Yamuna southeast of Old Delhi.   The
    entire city was designed by Sir Edwin Lutyens, the
    famous British architect.

NICOBARI.   A Kolarian language spoken in the Andaman and
    Nicobar Islands.

NIKITIN, ATHANASIUS.   Russian merchant and traveler who
    visited India from 1470 to 1474 and left an account of
    his travels.

NILGIRI.   Mountain ranges at the southern end of the My-
    sore tableland containing the hill stations of Ootacamund
    and Coonoor.   Highest peak: Doda Betta (8,640 ft).

NIRGRANTHA.   Literally, without knots.   A Jain ascetic of
    the nudist sect.

NIRKH.   A tariff rate or price current, especially one pub-
    lished by authority.

NIRVANA.   Properly: nibbana.   Literally, blown out, as a
    candle.   Nonexistence considered as the goal of a
    bodhisattva.

NISHKA.   A gold coin of ancient India equal to 320 rattis.

NIZAMAT ADALAT. The supreme court of criminal justice under the Muslim rulers. It was presided over by the nazim or the viceroy of the province.

NIZAM SHAHI. Dynasty founded by Malik Ahmad in 1490 at Junnar which ruled Ahmadnagar until its annexation to the Mughal Empire in 1637. Malik Ahmad assumed the title of Nizam Shah and later transferred the capital to Ahmadnagar. The line consisted of 12 kings:

Malik Ahmad (1490)	Burhan II (1591)
Burham (1509)	Ibrahim (1595)
Husain (1553)	Bahadur (1596)
Murtaza Shah (1565)	Ahmad II (1596)
Miran Husain (1586)	Murtaza Shah II (1603)
Ismail (1589)	Husain Shah II (1630)

NIZAM-UD-DIN. Court historian in the time of Akbar; author of Tabaqat-i-Akbari.

NIZAM-UL-MULK. Literally, deputy for the whole empire. Title conferred on Chin Qilich Khan by Emperor Muhammad Shah and assumed by his descendants who ruled Hyderabad until 1948.

NOBILI, ROBERTO DE see MALABAR RITES

NONCOOPERATION MOVEMENT. Mass movement launched by Mahatma Gandhi in 1919-20 which brought Hindus and Muslims in a common cause against the British. The movement collapsed in 1924 when the Muslims drifted away and the moderates led by Motilal Nehru and C. R. Das withdrew in favor of more conventional and constitutional means of opposition.

NORTHBROOK, Earl of. Full name: Thomas George Baring. 1826-1904. Viceroy and governor general of India (1872-76). Administration marked by the reduction of import duties and abolition of export duties. Resigned over differences with Lord Salisbury, secretary of state for India, on policies toward Afghanistan.

NORTHERN CIRCARS. District in Andhra Pradesh occupied by Nizam, the French, and eventually the English in the 18th century.

NORTH-WEST FRONTIER PROVINCE. Province of British India created by Lord Curzon in 1901 comprising the four trans-Indus districts of Peshawar, Kohat, Bannu, and Dera Ismail Khan, parts of the Hazara district, and the political agencies of Kurram, Malakand, Khyber, Tochi, Gomal, and Shirani; administered until 1932 by a chief commissioner and since then by a governor; now part of Pakistan.

NUNIZ, FERNÃO. A Portuguese horse trader who resided in the kingdom of Vijayanagar from 1535 to 37. His chronicle of the Vijayanagar rulers is a primary source for the history of that kingdom.

NUR JAHAN (or, Nur Mahal). Original name: Mihr-un-nisa. Literally, light of the world. Consort of Jahangir. Played a dominant role in suppressing a coup of Mahabat Khan. Became virtual ruler of the empire toward the end of Jahangir's reign and her name appeared on coins along with that of the emperor.

NUSHKA-I-DILKUSHA   see   BHIMSEN

NUSRAT SHAH.   Eighth Tughluq sultan (1395-1398/9).

NYAYA. One of the six orthodox systems of Hindu philosophy codified by Gautama in Nyaya-sutra. Gautama is regarded as the father of Indian logic and as the Indian Aristotle. Nyaya deals with epistemology and the laws of analysis and discussion. It is therefore also called tarka-vidya (science of reason) and vada-vidya (science of discussion).

NYAYAKANDALI   see   VAISESHIKA

- O -

ODANTAPURA (also, Udantapura). Medieval university founded by Gopala, the Pala king in 745. It was destroyed by Ikhtiar Khalji in 1198.

OLA BOOK. A book made from strips of Palmyra palm leaves. After soaking in hot water the leaves are pressed smooth and cut into strips three inches wide and one to three feet long. Through a hole pierced at each end a cord is passed so as to secure the leaves between two lacquered wooden boards. Writing is done with an iron stylus and the incisions are made visible by rubbing in a mixture of charcoal and oil.

ORAON (also, Uraon). (1) A Kolarian aboriginal tribe living in Chota Nagpur; (2) language of this tribe.

ORIENTAL INSTITUTE. Institution founded in Bardoa in 1915. Its library contains 25,000 rare manuscripts. Publishes Gaekwad's Oriental Series, SRG Lecture Series, MS University Oriental Series, Archaeology Series, Prachina Gurjara Granthamala Journal, Svadhryayo, and Critical and Illustrated Edition of Valmiki Ramayana.

ORISSA. (1) Region known in ancient times as Kalinga and in Muslim times as Jajnagar. It formed part of the Magadhan and Maurya Empires in pre-Christian times. After the fall of the Mauryas it became independent under the Cheta Dynasty and flourished under king Kharavela. It was under the Bhanja Dynasty from the 9th to the 11th century and under the Eastern Ganga Dynasty from the 11th to the 14th century. It was overrun by the Muslims under Alauddin Khalji and Firoz Tughluq. In 1572 it was annexed to the Mughal Empire by Akbar and constituted as part of the suba of Bengal. In 1765 the Company was granted the diwani of part of this region while the other part had been ceded by Nawab Alivardi Khan to the Marathas. The Maratha portion also came into the hands of the Company under the Treaty of Deogaon in 1803. It was part of the Bengal Presidency until 1912 when it was separated and joined to Bihar. It became a separate province in 1936.

(2) State in the Union of India. Capital: Bhubaneswar.

ORIYA (or Odiya). An Indic language spoken in Orissa. Sarala Das in the 14th century was the first noted name in Oriya literature. He was followed in the 15th century by Balaram Das and Jagannath Das, two of a group known as Five Friends; in the 17th century by the poet Upendra Bhanja; in the 18th century by Brajnath Badajena, author of the historical poem Samar Taranga; in the 19th century by Bhaktacharan, the Vaishnava poet; Gopalkrishna, lyric poet; and Bhima Bhoi, Buddhist poet; and in the 20th century by Fakirmohan, regarded as the Father of Oriya Prose; Radhanath, poet laureate; and Madhusudhan Rao, mystic and poet.

OSTEND COMPANY. Belgian East India Company founded in 1722.

OUDH.   Region in Uttar Pradesh.   In the age of Ramayana
   it was the kingdom of Koshala ruled by Dasaratha,
   father of Rama, with its capital at Ayodhya from which
   the name Oudh is derived.   In historical times it was
   one of the 16 large states, with its capital at Sravasti.
   It later became part of the Magadhan, Gupta, and Gurjara-Pratihara Empires.   It was conquered for the
   Delhi Sultanate by Malik Hisam-ud-din A'ghul Bak and
   was eventually annexed to the Mughal Empire.   It was
   one of the subas into which the Mughal Empire was
   divided.   In 1724 the Mughal governor Saadat Khan
   made himself independent and founded the line of the
   nawabs of Oudh.   In 1798 the British imposed their own
   nominee Saadat Ali as the Nawab, making Oudh a feudatory state under the Company.   In 1801 Oudh surrendered
   Rohilkhand and the lower Doab to the British.   The later
   nawabs of Oudh were debauched and effeminate despots
   and the British rescued the state from their misgov-
   ernment in 1856.

Saadat Khan (1724)	Ghazi-ud-din Haider (1814)
Safdar Jang (1739)	Nasir-ud-din Haider (1827)
Shuja-ud-daula (1754)	Ali Shah (1837)
Asaf-ud-daula (1775)	Amjad Ali Shah (1842)
Wazir Ali (1797)	Wajid Ali Shah (1847)
Saadat Ali (1798)	

- P -

PADA.   Devotional song based on religious themes.   Called
   abhanga in Maharashtra.

PADAMANJI, BABA   see   MARATHI

PADARTHADHARMASAMGRAHA   see   VAISESHIKA

PADMABHUSANA.   National civil award, third in degree of
   honor, conferred on Indian citizens by the government
   of India.

PADMASAMBHAVA.   Indian monk of the eighth century who
   went to Tibet and founded the Red Hat sect of Buddhism.

PADMA SRI.   National civil award, fourth in degree of
   honor, conferred on Indian citizens by the government
   of India.

PADMAVIBHUSANA. National civil award, second in degree of honor, conferred on Indian citizens by the government of India.

PADSHAHNAMA. History of the reign (mid-17th century) of Shah Jahan by Abdul Hamid Lahori.

PAES, DOMINGO. Portuguese traveler who visited Vijayanagar in 1552 and wrote an account of the kingdom under Krishnadeva Raya.

PAGODA. (1) A South Indian temple. From Sanskrit bhagavatam, goddess.
(2) Former gold coin of India worth 42 fanams. Accounts in Madras Presidency were kept in pagodas, fanams, and kasu until 1818 when the rupee was made the standard legal tender.

PAHARI. A modern Indian vernacular consisting of many dialects, such as Jaunsari, Kului, Chambiali, Mandiali, Suketi, and Sirmauri.

PAHARI SCHOOL. School of painting, also called Himachel school, which flourished in Jammu and Kashmir and north-east Punjab in the 18th and 19th centuries.

PAHLAVA. Hindu term for Parthian.

PAISA. Plural: paise. Modern monetary unit of India worth 1/100 of a rupee.

PAISACHI. A lesser Prakrit spoken by the Abhiras of the northwest.

PAITHAN (also, Pratisthana). Town on the upper Godavari Valley; capital of the early Andhra kings.

PAKHWAJ. Drum resembling the mridanga introduced by the Muslims.

PAKISTAN. State founded in 1947 through the division of British India into the dominions of India and Pakistan. It comprised the old provinces of Sind, North West Frontier Province, Eastern Bengal, Western Punjab, part of Sylhet, and Baluchistan. It also gained control of between one-third and one-half of Kashmir known as Azad Kashmir. In 1971 East Bengal (also called East

Pakistan) broke away after an armed struggle and established itself as an independent republic.

Pakistan is an Islamic Republic with a modified parliamentary system of government. It was under military rule from 1955 to 1972. It was a member of the Commonwealth of Nations from 1947 to 1972. Capital: Islamabad.

Pakistan was first conceived in 1930 by the poet Sir Muhammad Iqbal as a loose federation of provinces with a Muslim majority within the Indian Union. The idea was vigorously articulated by Choudhri Rahmat Ali who coined the term Pakistan in 1933 as a blend of pak (pure) and stan (land). It was adopted by the Muslim League in 1940 under M. A. Jinnah as its official goal. The demand was accepted by the Indian National Congress in 1947 on the eve of the transfer of power.

PALA. (1) Bengali dynasty established about 750 by Gopala; ruled Bengal until 1155 and Bihar until 1199. The second Pala king Dharmapala was the greatest of the line and his successor Devapala moved the capital from Monghyr to Pataliputra. The Palas were patrons of Buddhism and Buddhist centers of learning as Nalanda and Vikramasila. The dynasty consisted of 17 rulers:

Gopala	Nayapala
Dharmapala (752)	Vigrahapala III (1074)
Devapala	Mahipala II
Vigrahapala	Shurapala II
Narayanapala (875)	Ramapala
Rajyapala	Kumarapala (1142)
Gopala II	Gopala III
Vigrahapala II	Madanapala
Mahipala I (1026)	

(2) Dynasty of Kamarupa (Assam) founded in 1000 by Brahamapala consisting of seven kings who ruled until the middle of the 12th century when the last king was overthrown by the Palas of Bengal:

Brahmapala	Harsapala
Ratnapala	Dharmapala
Indrapala	Jayapala
Gopala	

PALANQUIN. A boxlike litter with a pole projecting before and behind which is borne on the shoulders of four or six men.

PALA SCHOOL. School of miniature painting which flourished

from 750 until 1250 of which Dhiman and his son Bhitpalo
are the most famous.

PALI.   A Prakrit language that developed into the sacred
language of Buddhism.   It is the parent of Sinhalese.

PALIYA.   A Panchama class of food-gatherers and hunters
of Madurai.

PALLAVA.   Dynasty founded in south India in unrecorded
times; the earliest known king is Vishnugopa of Kanchi.
They ruled over a region comprising modern Arcot,
Madras, Tiruchirapally, and Thanjavur with capital at
Kanchi.   Their golden age lasted for two centuries from
the sixth to the eighth.   Their history was marked by
intermittent wars with the Rashtrakutas and the Chalukyas of Vatapi.   The Pallava decline began with the
capture of Kanchi by the Chalukya king Vikramaditya I
in 655 and again by Vikramaditya II in 740.   The last
of the line, Aparajita Pallava, was defeated by the
Chola king Aditya I in the ninth century and the Pallavas
disappeared from the annals of history.
   The kings of this dynasty were great builders and
founded the city of Mahabalipuram and built the temple
at Kanchi.   There are great gaps in our knowledge of
Pallava rule and the names of only 11 rulers are known
with certainty:

Simhavarman IV (436)   Parameshvaravarman I
Vishnugopa (450)   (674)
Simhavishnu   Narasimhavarman II
Mahendravarman I   Parameshvaravarman II
Narasimhavarman I (642)   Mahendravarman III
Mahendravarman II   Nandivarman II (717)

PALPA, BATTLE OF.   Battle in the course of the Gurkha
War (1814-16) between the British and the Gurkhas in
which the former suffered a reverse.

PALWAR.   A large boat used in Bengal carrying up to 15
tons.

PANCHAMA.   Literally, fifth.   Hindus who fall outside the
four castes.   Also called Untouchables, Depressed
Castes, Scheduled Castes, Harijan, Adivasis, or Avarna
or "casteless."   Panchama includes Ullalah, Pulaiyan,
Paraiyan, and Izhavan.

PANCHANGA. Literally, five limbs. Hindu calendar so
named from its five divisions: (1) solar days, (2) lunar
days, (3) nakshatras or lunar asterisms, (4) yoga or
the conjunction of planets, and (5) karana or one of 11
divisions of the day.

PANCHATANTRA. Literally, five books. Classic Sanskrit
anthology of animal fables of unknown authorship dating
from the third century.

PANCHAYAT. Village meeting presided over by a committee of five (pancha) including the headman.

PANCH SHILA. Literally, the five principles. The guiding
principles of Indian foreign policy enunciated by Jawaharlal Nehru, prime minister of India (1947-64). The
cardinal principle in this group was nonalignment.

PANDA. Hindu temple priest who guides pilgrims and per-
forms rituals on their behalf.

PANDARAM. A Hindu ascetic or mendicant of the Sudra
caste in South India.

PANDAVAS. (In the Mahabharata) the five sons of Pandu:
Yudhishthira, Bhima, and Arjuna by Kunti and Nakula
and Sahadeva by Madri.

PANDIT. A Hindu scholar who is learned enough in the
scriptures to interpret and expound them.

PANDIT RAO. One of the ashtapradhan or eight chiefs of
the Maratha administration in charge of religious affairs. He also functioned as the royal chaplain.

PANDYA. Ancient kingdom in south India noticed in the
classical accounts of Periplus, Ptolemy, Megasthenes,
and Marco Polo. It occupied the region comprising
modern districts of Madurai and Tirunelvely, with its
capital at Madurai. The earliest known Pandya king
was Nedum-Chezhiyan in the second century. By the
ninth century the Pandyas were subordinate to the Pallavas and from the 10th to the 13th to the Cholas. 17
Pandya rajas ruled the kingdom from 1100 to 1567 of
whom the most important was Jadavarman Sundara
(1251-71). In 1310 the kingdom fell to Malik Kafur,
general of Alauddin Khalji. During the time of the

Sultanate it was known as Ma'bar. An independent
Muslim dynasty founded by Jalal-ud-din Ahsan Shah
ruled the region from 1335 until 1378 when it was absorbed by Vijayanagar. Petty rulers known as polygars
continued to flourish in the Pandya land in times of un-
identified sovereignty.

PANGUL, BATTLE OF. Battle in 1420 between the Bahmani
sultan Firuz Shah and Deva Raya, the king of Vijayanagar, in which the former was defeated.

PANINI. Sanskrit grammarian of the second or fourth century B. C. He is said to have been born at Shalatura
in Gandhara. His famous grammar, Ashtadhyayi, consists, as the name indicates, of eight chapters, each
divided into four subchapters, with these again divided
into a number of sutras or aphorisms, nearly 4,000 in
number. It describes in minute detail every syntactic
usage, inflection, and derivation of Sanskrit in Vedic
times. The key to Panini's grammar lies in the alge-
braic symbols which he invented to denote precisely all
parts of speech and inflections. It is perhaps the
world's first treatise on language and the earliest work
on descriptive linguistics.

PANIPAT, BATTLE OF. (1) First Battle of Panipat. Bat-
tle in 1526 between Babur and Ibrahim Lodi, sultan of
Delhi, in which the sultan was defeated. Marked the
beginning of Mughal rule in India.
      (2) Second Battle of Panipat. Battle in 1556 between
Hemu, general of Adil Shah Sur, and Akbar in which
Hemu was defeated and slain.
      (3) Third Battle of Panipat. Battle in 1761 between
Ahmad Shah Abdali and the combined armies of Shah
Alam II and the Marathas under Sadasiva Rao Bhao in
which the allies were defeated.

PANJHAZARI. Officer in the Maratha Army.

PANT, DANDU see NANA SAHIB

PANT PRATINIDHI. Maratha administrative officer originally superior to the peshwa. The post declined in im-
portance with the ascendancy of the peshwas.

PARAIYA. Tamil Panchama caste of field laborers so called
because they carried a small drum or parai to warn
wayfarers of their polluting presence.

PARAMA-HAMSA.   Literally, supreme swan.   An ascetic
who has reached the highest degree of renunciation of
the world and union with the infinite.

PARAMARA (also, Pawar).   Dynasty founded in Malwa by
Upendra or Krishnaraja early in the ninth century with
capital at Dhara.   The line consisted of eight kings
whose reigns were marked by intermittent wars with
their neighbors, especially the Chalukyas.

PARAMARTHA.   499-569.   Buddhist monk and scholar; author of Life of Vasubandhu.

PARAMATMAN see BRAHMAN

PARAMOUNT POWER.   Term applied to the British Crown
in its role as suzerain and protector of Indian native
states.   It was particularly used in treaties between
the British government and Indian rulers.

PARDAO.   A gold coin worth half a pagoda which gained
early currency in Goa; believed to be a corrupt form
of Pratapa, the name of a Raja of Ikkeri.

PARDHAN (also, patari).   Traditional bard of the Gond tribe
in Madhya Pradesh.

PARGANA.   A subdivision of a Mughal suba.

PARINIRVANA.   Literally, holy nirvana; applied to the nirvana of Gautama Buddha to distinguish that important
event from the nirvana of lesser mortals.

PARISHAD.   Assembly of men learned in the law.

PARSIS.   Persians of the Zoroastrian faith who emigrated
to India in the seventh and eighth centuries to escape
Muslim persecutions.   Their earliest settlement was at
Sanjan on the west coast in Gujarat and they later
moved to Bombay where they became a rich and influ-
ential community.

PARSVANATH.   23rd tirthankara or step-maker of the Jains
who lived two centuries before Mahavira.   He is believed to have established the doctrinal framework of
Jainism.

PARTITION OF BENGAL.   (1) Partition of the Bengal Presidency in 1905 by Lord Curzon by which 15 districts
of eastern Bengal and northern Bengal in the Rajshahi,
Dacca, and Chittagong divisions were merged with Assam in a new unit called Eastern Bengal and Assam.
This step led to massive public agitation and was re-
scinded in 1911.
    (2) Partition of Bengal Presidency in 1947 into East
Bengal, a state of Pakistan, and West Bengal, a state
of India.   East Bengal became Bangladesh in 1972.

PARTITION OF INDIA.   Partition of the Indian Empire into
two dominions in 1947: India and Pakistan.   Under this
division provinces with Muslim majorities were constituted into an Islamic state.   Punjab and Bengal were
divided on communal lines under the Radcliffe Award
and West Punjab and East Bengal were added to Baluchistan, Sind, and North-West Frontier Province to
form Pakistan.

PARVA.   (In Sanskrit literature) section of a work dealing
with one episode.

PARWANA.   An order or grant under royal seal; a letter
of authority from an official to a subordinate; a license
or pass.

PATALIPUTRA.   Fabled city at the confluence of the Son
and the Ganges, near modern Patna.   The fort was
built by king Ajatasatru and his grandson Udaya built the
nearby city of Kusumapura in the fifth century B. C.
Under Chandragupta Maurya the town became the imperial capital, a position it continued to hold under the
Sungas, the Kanvas, and the Guptas.

PATAN see ANHILWARA

PATANJALI.   (1) Sanskrit grammarian of the second century B. C.; author of Mahabhasya, a commentary on
Panini's Ashtadhyayi.   He is believed to have lived in
Kashmir.
    (2) Brahmin philosopher of the fourth century; author
of Yoga Sutra.

PATANULI see SAURASHTRA (2)

PATEL.   Hereditary head of a village in Maharashtra and
Gujarat.

PATEL, VALLABHAI JAHVERBHAI. 1875-1950. Indian
   nationalist leader and statesman; deputy prime minister
   of India (1947-50).   Entered politics in 1916 and became
   a close associate of Mahatma Gandhi; took a prominent
   part in the Bardoli satyagraha; president of the Indian
   National Congress (1931); as deputy prime minister successfully integrated more than 500 native states into the
   Indian Union.

PATELA.   A large flat-bottomed boat on the Ganges.

PATHAN.   Pushtu-speaking tribesmen of North-West Frontier
   Province divided into numerous subtribes, such as
   Yusufzai, Orakzai, Mohmand, Afridi, Mahsud, and
   Waziri.   The Lodi, Khalji, and Sur rulers of India
   were of Pathan stock.

PATIALA.   (1) City in the Punjab; former capital of Patiala
   state and Patiala and East Punjab States Union.
       (2) Former princely state founded in 1763 by a chief
   of the Phulkian misl of the Sikhs.   It became a protected state in 1809.

PATNA.   City on the Ganges near the junction of the Gandak
   and Son Rivers; capital of Bihar state; site of an early
   English factory.

PATNI.   A type of land tenure in Bengal under which a
   patni or subdivision of a zamindari was held by a pat-
   nidar in perpetuity with the right of hereditary succession and of selling or subletting the whole or part of
   the estate.

PATTA.   (1) A deed of lease, especially a document given
   by the collector to a zamindar specifying the conditions
   under which the land is held.
       (2) A primitive style of Hindu painting so called from
   the patta (a scroll, board, tablet, or plaque) on which
   religious scenes were depicted.

PATTAMAR.   A swift lateen-rigged sailing vessel with one,
   two, or three masts, common on the west coast.

PATTIDARI.   System of land tenure in northern India in
   which the revenue unit is a coparcenary village or estate
   comprising many villages or the subdivision of a mahal.

PATWAR.   Village accountant whose duty was to keep all
    accounts relating to land.

PAYAR.   (In Sanskrit) a heroic couplet.

PEACOCK THRONE.   Throne studded with precious gems
    and stones made by Bebadal Khan for Shah Jahan.   The
    throne was carried away to Persia by Nadir Shah after
    his sack of Delhi in 1739.

PEDDANA.   16th-century poet laureate and Father of Telugu
    poetry; author of Manucharita.   Peddana was court poet
    to Krishnadevaraya of Vijayanagar.

PENLOP.   Title of the feudal aristocracy of Bhutan.

PEPSU [acronym].   Patiala and East Punjab States Union,
    a state of the Indian Union from 1948 until 1956 com-
    prising Patiala and other cis-Sutlej states.

PERIPLUS OF THE ERYTHRAEN SEA.   An account of India
    and the Indian Ocean by an unknown Greek merchant of
    the first century.

PERMANENT SETTLEMENT.   System of land tenure and
    revenue collection introduced by Lord Cornwallis in
    Bengal, Bihar, and Orissa in 1793.   Under this system
    the zamindars became owners of the land on condition
    that they pay into the treasury annually 90 percent of the
    estimated revenue.

PERUMAL.   Dynasty which ruled over Chera or Kerala from
    400 to 826.   The last Perumal king was Cheraman Peru-
    mal who is believed to have converted to Islam.

PESHAWAR.   City in North-West Frontier Province known
    in ancient times as Purushapur; capital of the Kushan
    Empire.   It was under Afghan rule from the tenth cen-
    tury except for a brief period from 1834 to 1848 when
    it was part of Ranjit Singh's dominions.

PESHCUSH.   Literally, first fruits.   Present or gift given
    to a superior on certain occasions; also applied to the
    quit rent paid for lands formerly rent-free or in sub-
    stitution for service no longer exacted.

PESHKUBZ.   A form of dagger, the blade of which has a

straight thick back while the edges curve inward from
a broad base to a sharp point.

PESHWA. Originally the mukhya pradhan or chief minister
in Shivaji's cabinet.   During the reign of Raja Shahu,
Peshwa Balaji Viswanath began to wield absolute power
as the virtual ruler and he made the peshwaship hereditary in his family.   Under Baji Rao I the peshwa became the leader of the Maratha confederacy.   He also
transferred the capital to Satara.   The Third Battle of
Panipat (1761), in which Ahmad Shah Abdali inflicted a
decisive defeat on Maratha forces, marked the beginning
of the decline of Peshwa power, a process hastened by
the three Anglo-Maratha Wars.
    The peshwa throne regained some of its influence under
Nana Fadnavis, chief minister of Peshwa Madhav Rao Narain.   The office was abolished in 1819 and the last peshwa
Baji Rao II was exiled to Kanpur.   The Peshwa line consisted of eight rulers:

Balaji Viswanath (1714)	Narayan Rao (1772)
Baji Rao I (1720)	Raghunath Rao (Raghoba)
Balaji Baji Rao (1740)	(1773)
Madhava Rao Ballal	Madhav Rao Narayan
(1761)	(1774)
	Baji Rao II (1796)

PICE. A small copper coin in the British-Indian system of
currency worth 1/4 of an anna and 1/64 of a rupee.

PIE. The smallest copper coin in the British-Indian system
of currency worth 1/12 of an anna and 1/192 of a
rupee.

PILLAI. Title bestowed by Tamil sovereigns on members
of a higher class of Sudras.   Bearers of this title were
exempted from customary manual labor.

PINDARI. Literally, plunderers.   Horde of mounted soldiers
of fortune, notorious for their rapacity, who plundered
and terrorized central India under the shelter of Maratha power in the 18th century.   They were effectively
suppressed by Lord Hastings after the Third Maratha War.

PINJRAPOL. Jain and Hindu institution for the care of animals, birds, and insects.

PIR. A Muslim saint; applied by extension to the tomb of
a holy man considered as a place of pilgrimage.

PITAKAS. Literally, baskets. One of three groups of writings that constitute the Tripitaka: Sutta Pitaka, Vinaya Pitaka, and Abhidhamma Pitaka.

PITINIKAS. Tribe on the western border of Asoka's empire mentioned in his rock edicts V and VIII.

PITT'S INDIA ACT. Act of British Parliament 1784 sponsored by William Pitt the Younger which strengthened Crown authority over British territory in India. It set up a Board of Control with supervisory powers over the Court of Directors. The approval of the Board was required for all dispatches sent to Indian agents. It was vested with powers to recall governors and governors general. The presidency council members were reduced in number from four to three and the governor general in council was given powers over presidency governors in matters of revenue, war, and diplomacy. The governor general in council was forbidden to declare war or conclude treaties without the sanction of the Board. The governor general was also given power to override the council in certain situations.

PLASSEY, BATTLE OF. Battle in 1757 between the East India Company forces led by Robert Clive and Nawab Siraj-ud-daulah in which the nawab was defeated. This battle marked the beginning of British rule in India.

PODDAR. A keeper of cash attached to a treasury whose business was to weigh money and bullion and appraise the value of coins.

POLIGAR. Properly: palaiyakkaran, the holder of a palaiyam or feudal estate. Petty feudal chief in Tamil Nadu some of whom opposed the British in the Poligar Wars of the 18th century.

POLLILORE, BATTLE OF. Battle in 1781 between Haider Ali and the East India Company forces led by Sir Eyre Coote in which the former was defeated.

PONDICHERRY. (1) Indian name: Pudicherry. Port and town on the Coromandel coast; site of a French settlement founded in 1674 by François Martin. It was conquered and held by the British several times in the 17th century but was finally restored to the French in 1816. Capital of French territories in India until 1950 when the French relinquished possession.

(2) A Union Territory of the Indian Union constituted in 1962 comprising the former French settlements of Pondicherry, Mahe, and Yanaon.

PONGAL.   South Indian festival marking the beginning of the Tamil New Year.

POONA.   City in Maharashtra on the Muta River near the crest of the Western Ghats and commanding one of the passes to Bombay; capital of Marathas under Shivaji and Shambuji and from 1749 until 1817 when it fell to the British.

POONA, TREATY OF.   Treaty in 1817 between Peshwa Baji Rao II and the British under which the peshwa severed himself from the Maratha confederacy and accepted a British contingent at Poona.

POROS.   Indian king whose kingdom was bounded by the Jhelum and the Chinab at the time of the invasion of India by Alexander the Great.   He was defeated in battle by Alexander who was so impressed by his bravery that his lands were restored to him.

PORTO NOVO, BATTLE OF.   Battle in 1781 between Haider Ali and the East India Company forces led by Sir Eyre Coote in which the former was defeated.

PRABHU.   The writer caste in western India; also an honorific title assumed by the Kayastha caste.

PRACHANDAPANDAVA   see RAJASEKHARA

PRADHAN.   Head of department under the Peshwa in the Maratha administration.

PRAGJYOTISHA.   (In the Mahabharata) ancient variant name (along with Kamarupa) for Assam with its capital at Pragjyotishapura; identified with Gauhati.

PRAHASANA.   (In Sanskrit drama) one-act farce.

PRAKARANA.   (In Sanskrit drama) social comedy of manners.

PRAKRIT.   Demotic form of Sanskrit which forms the

connecting link between Sanskrit and modern Indic languages. In the time of Alexander the Great Prakrit
was the spoken dialect of the people and Pali became
the sacred language of the Buddhists because as a form
of Prakrit it would be easily understood by all classes.
The oldest Prakrit grammarian, Vararuchi, distinguishes
four dialects of Prakrit, while Sahityadarpana enumer-
ates 14--the most important of them being Pali, Gatha,
Sauraseni, Magadhi, Ardha Magadhi, Maharashtri,
Paisachi, Saurashtri, Gaurjari or Old Gujarati, and
Vrachadi.

PRANTH. One of the divisions into which an empire or
state is divided for administrative or racial reasons.

PRARTHANA SAMAJ see BRAHMA SAMAJ

PRASAD, RAJENDRA. 1884-1963. First president or rashtrapati of India (1950-62). A leading figure in the nationalist movement since 1920; four times president of
the Indian National Congress (1932, 1934, 1939, 1947);
presided over the drafting of the Indian Constitution
(1948-50).

PRASASTAPADA see VAISESHIKA

PRASASTI. A panegyric in verse narrating the exploits of
a Hindu ruler. They were sometimes engraved on
rocks and pillars or inscribed on copper plates.

PRATAP SINHA, Rana. Valiant Rajput ruler of Mewar
(1572-97) who fought with Akbar all his life and, though
successively defeated, successfully maintained a pre-
carious independence until death.

PRATIHARA see GURJARA-PRATIHARA

PRAVARASENA I see VAKATAKA

PREMANAND. 1636-1734. Gujarati poet.

PREMASAGARA see LALLA LAL

PREMCHAND. 1880-1936. Greatest and best known modern Hindi writer; pioneer of the Hindi novel.

PRITHVIRAJ CHAUHAN (also, Rai Pithora). King of
Sambhar, Ajmer, and Delhi, famed in legend as the ab-
ductor of Sanjukta, daughter of his rival Raja Jayachan-

dra. A great warrior, he defeated the Chandella king Parmal and Shihab-ud-din Muhammad Ghori in the First Battle of Tarain in 1191. He was defeated and slain on the same battlefield a year later by the Afghan forces. His deeds are recorded by Chand Bardai in Chand Raisa.

PROBODHACHANDRODAYA   see   KIRTTIVARMAN

PUGA. (In ancient India) a meeting of a group of traders.

PUJARI. A Brahmin who conducts puja or ritual worship.

PULAKESHIN I. Founder of the Chalukya Dynasty of Vatapi in the sixth century.

PULAKESHIN II. Chalukya king (609-655) who carried his arms into Gujarat, Rajputana, and Malwa and conquered Vengi. He repulsed Harshavardhana in 620 and defeated the Pallava king Mahendravarman in 609. His court at Vatapi was visited by the Chinese pilgrim Hiuen Tsang and an embassy from the Persian emperor Khusru II. He was defeated and slain in 642 by the Pallava king Narasimha Varman.

PULAYA. A Panchama class of Kerala who were until recent times tree dwellers.

PULICAT. Town in Tamil Nadu; seat of a former Dutch factory.

PUNDIT see PANDIT

PUNJAB. (1) Literally, land of the five rivers. Region in NW India between the Indus and the Sutlej. Site of the Indus Valley Civilization in prehistoric times; invaded by Alexander the Great in 326 B. C. and, in succeeding waves, by the Graeco-Bactrians, Sakas, Kushans, and Huns; part of the Delhi Sultanate and the Mughal Empire from 1206. Sikhism was born here and developed into a dominant force in the 18th and 19th centuries. Divided into West Punjab and East Punjab on communal lines on the eve of independence in 1947.
    (2) State in the Union of India created in 1966 comprising Punjabi-speaking districts of Gurdaspur (excluding Dalhousie), Amritsar, Kapurthala, Jullunder, Ferozepur, Bhatinda, Patiala, Ludhiana and parts of Sangrur, Hoshiarpur, Ambala, and Kharar. Capital: Chandigarh.

PUNJABI. Language spoken in the Punjab derived from Sauraseni Prakrit. A mixture of Punjabi and Old Braj is known
as Pingala or Bangaru.

PUNKAH. (1) A portable hand-fan made from a palmyra
leaf.
(2) A large, fixed, and swinging fan formed of cloth
stretched on a rectangular frame and suspended from
the ceiling, used to agitate the air in hot weather with
the aid of a rope and pulley.

PURAMDARADASA. c1555. Celebrated Canarese classical
singer at the Vijayanagar court who systematized Karnataka music.

✟ PURANAS. Any of a class of ancient sacred Hindu writings
composed in epic couplets and consisting partly of legendary histories and party of speculative cosmogony including genealogies of gods and heroes. They are 18 in
number:

Vayu	Naradiya	Varaha
Vishnu	Markandeya	Skanda
Brahmmanda	Agneya	Vamana
Bhagvata	Bhavishya	Karuma
Brahma	Brahmavaivarta	Goduda
Padma	Lainga	Matsya

PURANDAHAR, TREATY OF. Treaty in 1776 between the
Marathas and the Company by which the latter was
granted Salsette in return for disavowing Raghoba.

PURDAH. Curtain serving to screen women from the sight
of strangers or men; applied by extension to the condition of women so hidden.

PURI. City in Orissa; place of Hindu pilgrimage containing
the temple of Jagannath built by Anantavarman Choda
Ganga (1076-1147).

PURNA SWARAJ. Literally, complete independence. Goal
of Indian National Congress as distinguished from the
dominion status demanded by constitutional moderates.

PUROHITA. Priest of the Brahmin class entitled to conduct
puja or other religious rites.

PURU. An Aryan tribe in Vedic times.

PURUSHA-CHARITA   see   HEMACHANDRA

PURUSHAPURA.   Ancient name for modern Peshawar; capital of the Kushan kings.

PURVA.   (In Jainism) canon containing the teachings of
Mahavira.

PURVA MIMAMSA.   Also known as Karma Mimamsa or
Jnana Mimamsa.   A school of Hindu philosophy that
emphasized the ethical rather than speculative side of
the Vedas.   It provides detailed texts for interpreting
Vedic rites and ceremonies.   It emphasized right action
as a means of liberation.   Its principal exponents were
Jaimini, author of Mimamsa Sutras, Sabara, author of
Bhasya, Prabhakara, commentator on the Bhasya, and
Kumarila Bhatta, author of Slokavarttika and Tantra-
varttika.

PUSHYABHUTI.   Dynasty founded at Thaneswar in the sixth
century by Pushyabhuti.   It consisted of four kings of
whom Harshavardhana was the most famous: Pushyabhuti, Prabhakaravardhana, Rajyavardhana (605), and
Harshavardhana (606).

PUSHYAMITRAS.   Warlike tribe in Gupta times.

PUSHYAMITRA SUNGA.   Founder of the Sunga Dynasty who
killed Brihadratha, the last Maurya king, to ascend the
throne and rule for 38 years.   He performed an asvamedha after rolling back invasions of Indo-Greeks
and Orossans.   He was a Brahmin who patronized orthodox Hinduism which had fallen into disarray under
Asoka.

- Q -

QADIAN.   A heretic Muslim sect founded by Mirza Ghulam
Ahmad (1839-1908) in Qadian, a town in the Punjab.

QASI.   A Muslim judge appointed under Muslim rulers to
administer civil and criminal law according to the
Sharia.   In the Mughal administration he was also the
judicial assistant to the governor.   In British India he
was employed as a legal adviser on Muslim law, customs, and calendar.

QASIM BARID.   Founder in 1487 of the Barid Shahi Dynasty
of Bidar; sultan of Bidar (1487-1504).   He was originally a minister of the Bahmani sultan Mahmud Shah.

QAWALI.   Muslim devotional song invented by Amir Khusrav.

QUILON.   Town and port in Kerala known in ancient times
as Kollam, one of the greatest centers of Indian trade
with western Asia in ancient and medieval times.   According to extant Syrian chronicles three Syrian Christian missionaries came to Quilon in 823 and received
permission from king Shakirbirti to build a church.   The
Kollam Era dates from 824.

QULI QUTB SHAH.   Founder of the Qutb Shahi Dynasty of
Golkonda.   A protégé of Muhammad Gawan and governor
of Golkonda, he proclaimed independence in 1518 and
ruled until 1543.

QUTB MINAR.   Literally, the turret of Qutb.   It is disputed
whether it was named after the first sultan of Delhi,
Qutb-ud-din Aibak, who began its construction, or a
Muslim saint of the same name.   It was completed by
Sultan Iltutmish in 1232 in a suburb of Delhi and sur-
vives as a fine example of Muslim architecture.

QUTB SHAHI.   Dynasty founded by Quli Qutb Shah in 1518
in Golkonda, the eastern province of the Bahmani Empire.   The dynasty ruled until 1687 and consisted of
eight kings:

Quli Qutb Shah (1518)	Muhammad Quli Qutb Shah
Jamshid (1543)	(1580)
Subhan Quli (1550)	Muhammad Qutb Shah (1612)
Ibrahim (1550)	Abdullah (1626)
	Abdul Hasan Qutb Shah (1672)

QUTB-UD-DIN AIBAK.   First sultan of Delhi (1206-10).   A
protégé of Shihab-ud-din Muhammad Ghori, he was entrusted by his master with the task of furthering his
conquests after the Second Battle of Tarain in 1192.
In 1193 Qutb-ud-din occupied Delhi and during the next
ten years carried Muslim arms into Kanauj, Gwalior,
Anhilwara, Ajmer, and Kalanjar.   He succeeded Ghori
in 1206 and ruled until 1210.   He is believed to have
begun the building of Qutb Minar.

QUTB-UD-DIN MUBARAK.   Last sultan of the Khalji Dynasty (1316-20).

- R -

RABANASTRANA   see   SARANGI

RABI.   Crop sown after the rains and harvested in the following spring or early summer, as wheat, barley,
gram, linseed, tobacco, onion, carrot, turnip, etc.

RADHA.   Region of western Bengal comprising the districts
of Burdwan, Hooghly, and part of Birbhum.   The Rad-
hiya Brahmins are natives of this region.

RADHAKRISHNAN, SARVEPALLI. 1888-1975. Second President or rashtrapati of India (1962-67).   Eminent Hindu
philosopher; vice chancellor of Benares Hindu University
(1939-48); Spalding Professor of Eastern Religions at
Oxford University (1936-39); author of The History of
Indian Philosophy and other books.

RADHANATH   see   ORIYA

RAFI-UD-DARAJAT.   16th Mughal emperor of Delhi set up
in 1719 by the Sayyid Brothers; deposed after a short
rule of few months.

RAFI-UD-DAULAH.   17th Mughal emperor of Delhi set up
in 1719 by the Sayyid Brothers to succeed his brother
Rafi-ud-darajat.   He was also deposed after a short
while.

RAGA.   Literally, tint.   Class of melodies in Indian music
that create a specific emotional mood with their own
characteristic signature.   A raga consists of a combina-
tion or sequence of certain fixed notes which may last
for several hours and may include the musician's own
embellishments and grace notes.   The principal ragas
are six in number and are called janaka or father ragas.
Each janaka raga has five wives called raginis.   Each
ragini has six sons called putras.   The family of ragas
thus consists of 216 members.   Each raga has a particular season and a particular time of night or day or
god or sage associated with it.   Some are ascribed
magical powers.   The major ragas are: Bhairava,
Bhupali, Dipaka, Hammira, Hillola, Kausika, Kedara,
Lalita, Malla, Malkos, Megha, Nata, Panchama, Pillu,
Purvi, Sriraga, Surati, Todi, Varali, Vasanta, Vela-
vali, Vibhasa, and Yamani.

RAGHOBA   see   RAGHUNATH RAO

RAGHUJI BHONSLA.   Founder around 1730 of the Bhonsla
   Dynasty of Nagpur; leader of the Maratha confederacy
   whose greatest achievement was compelling Nawab Alivardi Khan to cede part of Orissa to him.   See also
   BHONSLA.

RAGHUNATH RAO (also, Raghoba).   Second son of Peshwa
   Baji Rao I; opposed the accession of his nephews Madhav Rao and Narayan Rao and was an accessory to the
   murder of the latter; ascended the throne in 1773 but
   was deposed by a party led by Nana Fadnavis who proclaimed allegiance to the posthumous son of Narayan
   Rao; attempted to regain power by concluding the Treaty
   of Surat with the English in 1775 which led to the First
   Anglo-Maratha War; retired after the English finally
   gave up his cause by the Treaty of Salbai in 1783.

RAGMALA.   Literally, rosary of ragas.   Miniature paintings of ragas and raginis expressing the mood assigned
   to each.

RAHDARI.   Internal transit duty abolished by Lord Cornwallis in 1789.

RAHMAT KHAN, HAFIZ.   Rohilla leader and ruler of Rohilkhand; defeated and killed in the Battle of Miranpur
   Katra by the combined armies of the East India Company and the Nawab of Oudh in 1774.

RAI.   A title denoting a prince; bestowed by Mughal emperors on Hindu civil officers of high rank.

RAICHUR.   Fortified town in the Raichur doab between the
   Krishna and the Tungabhadra whose possession was con-
   tested by Vijayanagar kings and Bahmani sultans.

RAIDAS (also, Ravidas or Rohidas).   c1430.   A chamar or
   cobbler and disciple of Ramananda who became one of
   the greatest bhagats or saints of the Vaishnavite revival.

RAIGARH.   Fortress in Maharashtra built by Shivaji in
   which he was crowned in 1674; caputred by Aurangzeb
   in 1689-90.

RAJ.   (1) A kingdom ruled by a raja; (2) sovereignty or
   paramount power.

RAJA.   A king or ruler of royal lineage.

RAJADHIRAJA I.   Chola king (1044-1054).   His reign was marked by hostilities with the Chalukyas.   In one of these encounters Rajadhiraja was killed at Koppam in 1054.

RAJAGOPALACHARI, CHAKRAVARTI.   1879-1974.   Indian statesman and first Indian-born governor general of India (1948-50); prime minister of Madras Presidency (1937-39); chief minister of Madras state (1952-54); founder of the right-wing Swatantra Party; author of many books on Hinduism.

RAJAGRIHA.   Ancient name for the town of Rajgir built by king Bimbisara in the sixth century; site of the First Buddhist Council.

RAJANYA.   Literally, warrior princes.   Name applied to the Kshattriya caste in Asokan edicts.

RAJARAJA THE GREAT.   958-1012.   Celebrated Chola king (985-1012) whose dominions included the whole of Tamil country, Mysore, Kerala, Orissa, and Ceylon which he conquered in 1005 after a victorious naval campaign.

RAJA RAM.   Second son of Shivaji and Maratha ruler from 1689 to 1700.   He carried on a war of attrition against Aurangzeb first from his fort at Jinjee and later from Satara.

RAJASEKHARA.   Sanskrit and Prakrit dramatist and poet who flourished around 900 in the court of the Pratihara kings of Kanauj; author of the Prakrit classic Karpura-Manjeri and three Sanskrit dramas Balaramayana, Prachandapandava, and Viddhashalabhanjika.

RAJASTHAN.   State in the Union of India comprising the former princely states of Rajputana.   Capital: Jaipur.

RAJASTHANI.   Language of Rajasthan including five dialects: Marwari, Jaipuri, Malvi, Mewari, and Udaipuri.

RAJASTHANI SCHOOL.   School of miniature painting which flourished from 1550 until 1850 under the patronage of Rajput princes.   Portraits were the long suit of this school.

RAJATARANGINI.   Literally, Stream of Kings.   Sanskrit
chronicle of the kings of Kashmir written in the 12th
century by Kalhana.

RAJENDRA I. Chola king (1012-44). His victorious armies
conquered lower Burma, Andaman and Nicobar Islands,
and reached the bank of the Ganges after defeating Mahipala, king of Bengal. To celebrate his victories he assumed the title of Gangai Konda and built a new capital
city named Gangai Konda Cholapuram.

RAJENDRA III   see KULOTTUNGA I

RAJMAHAL.   A Dravidian language spoken in Bihar and
Bengal.

RAJPRAMUKH.   Title bestowed on Indian maharajas who
served as heads of regional groups of native states.

RAJPUTANA.   Region in NW India ruled in pre-Muslim times
by various Hindu clans such as Chalukyas, Rashtrakutas,
Rathors, Chauhans, Solankis, Sesodiyas, and Kachchh-
wahas. Successfully resisted Muslim inroads by acknowledging the suzerainty of Delhi rulers especially
after the Battle of Khanua in 1526 in which Babur defeated Rana Sangram Singha of Mewar. Gained British
protection against plundering Maratha raids in early
18th century.   Under British rule the region consisted
of 23 princely states including Bikaner, Jaipur, Jodhpur,
Udaipur, and Jaisalmer.

RAJPUTS.   Warlike Indian people inhabiting Rajputana believed to have descended from foreign invaders of India
including the Huns, Sakas, and Gurjaras. They were
later admitted to the Kshattriya caste. They were divided into 36 clans of whom the most prominent were
Gurjara-Pratiharas, Chauhans, Chalukyas, Chandellas,
Tomaras, Kalachuris, and Rashtrakutas.

RAJUKA.   Title of the magistrate in the administration of
Asoka; referred to in Asokan edicts.

RAJYA SABHA.   Council of State; upper house of the Indian
Parliament.

RAMA (or Ramachandra).   Hero of the epic Ramayana; regarded by Hindus as the seventh avatar of Vishnu.

RAMACHARITAMANASA.   Literally, the Pool of Rama's
    Life.   Story of Rama's life written in Awadhi (Hindi)
    by Tulsi Das.

RAMAKRISHNA PARAMAHAMSA.   1834-1886.   Bengali-born
    Hindu spiritual leader whose inspired fervor attracted
    to him a vast following including Swami Vivekananda.
    He tried to modernize Vedantist philosophy.   The social
    dimensions of his teachings are reflected in the work of
    Ramakrishna Mission, an international missionary or-
    ganization.

RAMAN, CHANDRASEKHARA VENKATA.   1888-1973.   In-
    dian scientist.   Awarded Nobel prize for physics in
    1930 for researches in the molecular structure of light
    that led to the discovery of Raman's Effect.   Founded
    the Raman Institute in Bangalore.

RAMANAND.   An exponent of the Bhakti cult who lived in
    the 14th century.   He traveled all over India preaching
    his doctrines among all castes.   Among his later dis-
    ciples was Kabir.

RAMANUJA.   Hindu philosopher and Vaishnavite sage of the
    12th century who lived and taught in Mysore and Sriran-
    gam.   His monistic doctrines were a modified form of
    advaita known as visishtadvaita.   He is said to have
    founded over 700 monasteries and converted the Hoysala
    king Bittiga to the Vaishnava faith.

RAMA'S BRIDGE.   Series of shoals between NW Ceyon and
    SE India believed by Hindus to be the remains of a cause-
    way built by Rama in order that he might cross from
    India to Ceylon to rescue his wife Sita but which may
    actually be the submerged portions of an isthmus that
    once connected the island with the mainland.

RAMAYANA.   One of the two sacred epics of the Hindus
    ascribed to the sage Valmiki of the second century
    B. C.   It consists of 24,000 couplets divided into seven
    books describing the life and exploits of Rama or Rama-
    chandra, the seventh avatar of Vishnu.   It was at first
    handed down orally and variously modified when reduced
    to writing.   There are at least four distinct recensions,
    each following a different arrangement.

[1]RAMDAS.   fl. 1600.   Celebrated Hindustani musician at the
    court of Shah Jahan.

²RAMDAS see MARATHI

RAM MOHAN ROY, Raja. 1772-1833. Theistical religious
reformer whose lifelong opposition to superstition and
idolatory led to the formation at Calcutta in 1816 of the
Atmiya Sabha, precursor of the Brahma Sabha and the
Brahma Samaj. He was also a linguist and scholar
who spoke Sanskrit, Pali, Hebrew, Arabic, and Greek.
He was given the title of Raja by the Mughal emperor
Akbar II whose cause he pleaded before the British government. In politics he was a moderate constitutional-
ist who protested inequities in the judicial and tax systems. He emigrated to England in 1831 where he died
two years later.

RAMNAGAR, BATTLE OF. Battle in 1848 between the English and the Sikhs during the course of the Second Sikh
War which ended inconclusively.

RAMNARAYAN (surname: Tarkaratna). 1822-86. Bengali
dramatist; author of Kulin-Kula-Sarbbasva, the first
modern Bengali play (1854).

RAMRAJYA. Literally, the kingdom of Rama. Ideal Hindu
polity envisaged by Mahatma Gandhi based on the ancient Vedic ideals of the age of Ramayana.

RANA. Title held by Rajput princes in central and western
India.

RANADE, MADHAV GOVINDA. 1852-1904. Indian scholar
and social reformer; one of the founders of the Deccan
Education Society and an active member of the Prarthana Samaj and the Indian National Congress; author of
many works on economics and social history.

RANI. Queen of a raja.

RANJIT SINGH. 1780-1839. Founder and maharaja of the
largest Sikh kingdom in the Punjab. A leader of the
Sukercheria misl, he began his career by occupying
Lahore in 1799 and was acknowledged as governor of
Lahore by Zaman Shah, the Afghan ruler. He organized
his army with the aid of French officers and united the
trans-Sutlej misls, occupied Amritsar in 1805, and reduced Jammu to a tributary state. He attempted to establish a pan-Sikh state by extending his power beyond

the Sutlej and occupying Ludhiana. Here he came into
conflict with the British and was forced to yield both
Jammu and Ludhiana under the Treaty of Amritsar in
1809.   But he continued his course of expansion in the
north where he added to his dominions Kangra in 1811,
Attock in 1813, Multan in 1818, Kashmir in 1819, and
Peshawar in 1834.   His treaty of perpetual friendship
with the British was renewed in 1831.

RANOJI SINDHIA. d. 1750. Founder of the Sindhia Dynasty
    (ruled from 1761-1750); lieutenant of Peshwa Baji Rao I
    who was placed in control of the Malwa region with
    capital at Gwalior.

RAO. A title denoting a chief or prince, used especially
    by the Marathas.

RASARATNAKARA   see   2NAGARJUNA

RASHTRAKUTA.   Dynasty founded by Dantivarman I some-
    time in the seventh century in the Deccan with Nasik
    as the capital.   Its period of power and glory began with
    the reign of Dantivarman II or Dantidurga who ruled
    from 754 to 768.   The eleventh king Amoghavarsha
    transferred the capital to Manyakheta or Malkhed.   The
    last king Indra IV was overthrown by Taila or Tailapa
    II in 973.   The Rashtrakuta dynasty consisted of 20
    kings:

Dantivarman I	Krishna II (877)
Indra I	Indra III (915)
Govinda I	Amoghavarsha II (917)
Karka I	Govinda IV (918)
Indra II	Amoghavarsha III or
Dantivarman II	Vaddiga (934)
(Dantidurga) (754)	Krishna III (939)
Krishna I (768)	Khottiga (968)
Govinda II (783)	Karka II or Amoghavar-
Dhruva	sha IV (972)
Govinda III (793)	Indra IV (973)
Amoghavarsha I (814)	

RASHTRAPATI.   Title of the president of India elected by
    an electoral college.   There have been five rashtrapatis
    since India became a republic in 1950:

Rajendra Prasad	V. V. Giri
S. Radhakrishnan	Fakhruddin Ali
Zakir Hussain	Ahmed

RASHTRIYA.   A deputy or high commissioner in Maurya
     times.

RASO.   Chronicles of Rajasthani bards, who were known as
     charans or bhats, containing the semi-legendary exploits
     of the Rajputs.

RATHA.   Chariot of war in the Hindu army of Vedic times.

RATHOR (also, Gahadwala).   A Rajput tribe of the solar
     line of Marwar, Jodhpur, and Bikaner.   (The Rathor
     were sun worshippers and claimed (like the Japanese
     imperial family) to have descended from the sun.)

RATNAKARAN   see   HARAVIJAYA

RATTI (or, rati).   The basic monetary unit of Mauryan
     times.   From Sanskrit raktika, a weight of 1.83 gr.

RAYA.   Title held by the Hindu sovereigns of Vijayanagar.

RAZIYA.   Full name: Raziyyat-ud-din.   Sultana of the
     Slave Dynasty and the only woman ruler of Delhi (1236-
     40); daughter of Iltutmish.   Her sex was resented by
     the nobles who led a revolt under Altuniya, the governor
     of Sind.   She was deposed but Raziya tried to save her
     life by marrying Altuniya.   The nobles however pursued
     her and killed both Raziya and Altuniya in 1240.

READING, Lord.   Full name: Rufus Daniel Isaacs.   1860-
     1935.   Viceroy and governor general of India (1921-25).
     Administration marked by nationalist agitation and the
     application of the Government of India Act of 1919.

RED FORT.   Fort built on the site of the present Qutb
     Mosque by Anangapala, the Tomara king, in the 11th
     century.   So called because it was built of red sand-
     stone.

RED SHIRT MOVEMENT.   Militant separatist movement of
     the Pathans of North-West Frontier Province founded
     in 1930 by Abdul Gaffar Khan known also as "the Fron-
     tier Gandhi."   Its goal was the formation of a state
     known as Pakhtoonistan.   The demand was muted after
     the formation of Pakistan but the movement has not en-
     tirely been suppressed.

REGULATING ACT.   Act of British Parliament, 1773, plac-
ing the administration of the Company's territories in
India under parliamentary supervision.   The administration of Bengal was vested in the governor general in
council who had also control in matters of war and peace
over the presidencies of Madras and Bombay each of
which was administered by a governor in council.   The
Act also established the supreme court at Calcutta.

REIS.   A small coin of Portuguese origin in use in western
India in the 17th and 18th centuries and definitely until
1834; worth 1/25 of an anna or 1/400 of a rupee.

RENNELL, JAMES.   1742-1830.   Geographer in the service
of East India Company; surveyor general of Bengal and
father of Indian geography; author of Memoir of a Map
of Hindustan.

REPUBLIC DAY.   National day celebrated on January 26 to
mark the establishment of the Republic of India on January 26, 1950.

RESIDENT.   (1) (In earlier usage) chief of the Company's
commercial establishment in the provinces or chief of
a district.
    (2) Representative of the Crown and Paramount Power
in a native state.

RIG VEDA.   Literally, hymns of knowledge.   The oldest of
the four Vedas; believed to have been compiled between
2500 and 500 B.C.   Divided into four parts: Samhita,
Brahmana, Aranyaka, and Upanishads.   The Samhita
contains 1017 shuktas or hymns in ten mandalas or
books.

RIPON, Lord.   Full name: George Frederick Samuel Rob-
inson.   1827-1909.   Viceroy and governor general of
India (1880-84).   One of the most liberal and popular
British rulers.   His reforms included: complete free
trade, increase in the agencies of local government as
district boards and tahsil boards, repeal of the Vernacular Press Act, improvement in primary and secondary
school education, betterment of conditions of work in
factories, and the abolition of discriminatory clauses
in the Ilbert Bill which restricted the rights of Indian
judges to try Europeans.

RISALA. A troop in a regiment of irregular cavalry commanded by a risaladar.

RISHI. A Hindu sage, patriarch, or mage possessed of extraordinary spiritual power and wisdom. Rishis generally lived in jungles either alone or with a group of
disciples and the place where they lived was known as
an ashram. Seven kinds of rishis are distinguished in
the Puranas: 1) Prajapati: term applied to the ten sons
of Brahma. 2) Brahma-rishi (also called Dvija-rishi
or Twice-Born rishis): term applied to the founders of
Brahmin gotras or gens and hence sometimes called
gotrakaras or family-makers. Listed in the Puranas as
Agastya, Angiras, Atri, Bharadvaja, Bhrigu, Jamadag-
ni, Kanva, Kasyapa, Pulaha, Kratu, and Gautama. 3)
Devarishi: term applied to the rishis who are ranked
with the Gods. Markandeya was considered a devarishi.
4) Saptarishi: term applied to the rishis who were
identified with the seven stars of the Great Bear--
Kasyapa, Atri, Vasishtha, Visvamitra, Gotama, Jama-
dagni, and Bharadvaja. 5) Maharishi (literally, great
sage; also, paramarishi or the supreme sage): term
applied to rishis who have attained ultimate wisdom.
6) Srutarishi (literally, a sage who has heard divine
wisdom): term applied to rishis to whom knowledge of
the Vedas was directly handed down by gods or maha-
rishis. 7) Rajarishi: philosopher kings, such as Janaka, Bhangasvana, and Dhruva.
    Rishis are important in Hinduism not only as founders
of Brahmin stock but as founders of Vedic schools and
authors of Puranas and Vedas. Valmiki is believed to
have written the Ramayana and Vyasa the Mahabharata.
They also appear in Sanskrit literature as wonder-work-
ers and contenders with the gods.

ROE, Sir THOMAS. 1580/1-1644. English diplomat. Ambassador of King James I at the court of Emperor
Jahangir (1615-18).

ROHILKHAND. Region and former kingdom between the
Ganges and the Kumaon Hills named after the Afghan
tribe of Rohillas who conquered it in 1740. The territory was annexed to Oudh in 1774 after the Battle of
Miranpur Katra and was in turn ceded to the British
in 1801. It now forms a division of Uttar Pradesh with
headquarters at Bareilly.

RONG   see   LEPCHA

ROPE TRICK.   One of the most famous tricks attributed to
    Indian jugglers by which a coil of rope unwinds itself
    into a stiff pole at the tip of which the juggler stands
    like a stylite.

ROWLATT ACTS.   Acts passed in 1919 vesting the govern-
    ment of India with extraconstitutional powers to deal
    with subversive and violent nationalist movements.
    They provided for stricter restrictions over freedom
    of the press, summary trials of political prisoners, im-
    prisonment of suspects for long periods without bringing
    them to trial, and suspension of habeas corpus rights.

ROYAL ASIATIC SOCIETY OF BENGAL   see   ASIATIC
    SOCIETY ...

RUDRADAMAN.   Powerful Saka satrap of Saurashtra whose
    dominions included Saurashtra, Malwa, Kutch, Sind,
    Konkan, and the whole of western India with capital at
    Ujjain.   The period of his rule is believed to be from
    128 to 150.

RUHELA.   Dynasty of Rohilla kings founded by Muhammad
    Ruhela Ali in 1744.   The main event in the history of
    the dynasty was the Rohilla War in which Hafiz Rahamat
    Khan, successor of Ruhela Ali, was defeated and killed
    at the Battle of Miranpur Katra in 1774.   Faizullah
    Khan, son of Rahamat Khan, was however granted pos-
    session of Rampur and his descendants came to be
    known as the Nawabs of Rampur.

RUKN-UD-DIN.   Sultan of the Slave Dynasty; son and suc-
    cessor of Iltutmish who occupied the throne of Delhi
    for a few months in 1236.

RUKN-UD-DIN IBRAHIM.   Sultan of the Khalji Dynasty; son
    of Jalal-ud-din Khalji who was proclaimed emperor on
    the murder of his father in 1296; deposed after a short
    rule of four months by Ala-ud-din Khalji.

RUPEE.   Standard Indian monetary unit introduced by Sher
    Shah in 1542 as a silver coin of 175 to 178 grams.
    The East India Company adopted the system and the
    first British rupee was minted at Bombay in 1677.   Four
    different rupees were current in the three presidencies

in the 17th and 18th centuries: sicca, bhari, Farrukha-
bad, and Benares. In 1818 the rupee was made the
official coin of the Empire. Now worth 21 cents.

RYOT (also, raiyat). Peasant or cultivator considered as a
unit of the land tenure system.

RYOTWARI. System of land tenure under which revenue is
collected directly from the ryots or peasants on the
basis of 30-year settlements. Under this system the
government received one half of the produce.

- S -

SAADAT KHAN. Founder of the dynasty of the Nawabs of
Oudh; Mughal governor of Oudh who declared himself
independent in 1724 and ruled until 1739.

SABARA. Primitive tribe mentioned in the Puranas and
Epics; sometimes identified with the Subari or Sabari
noted in Pliny and Ptolemy.

SABHA. Council, especially a council of elders or representatives.

SABUKTIGIN. Amir of Ghazni, Afghanistan (977-997). He
was a slave of Alptigin who carved out an independent
kingdom with Ghazni as its capital in 962. Sabuktigin
ascended the throne in 977 and founded the Ghaznavid
Dynasty which lasted until 1186. He was the first Central Asian Muslim ruler to turn his attention to India
and in 989 he inflicted a crushing defeat on a league of
Hindu princes led by Jaipal, king of the Punjab, and
Dhanga, the Chandella king, at Ghuzuk, near the Kurram
Valley. This victory paved the way for the invasions
of India by his son Sultan Mahmud.

SACHIVA. Ministerial position in the cabinet of Shivaji in
charge of correspondence and records.

SADADARSHANA. Collective name for the six systems of
Hindu philosophy: Nyaya by Gautama, Vaiseshika by
Kanada, Samkhya by Kapila, Patanjali or Yoga by Patanjali, Purva-Mimamsa by Jaimini, and Uttara-Mimamsa
or Brahmasutra by Badarayana or Vyasa.

SADHU. A holy man who has renounced the world and attained spiritual enlightenment through severe tapas or
ascetic practices.

SADHU-BHASA   see   BENGALI

SADR. (1) Literally, supreme.   The chief seat of government as distinguished from the provincial or district
headquarters.
(2) Mughal official in charge of religious endowments
and wakfs in a pargana.

SADR AMIN.   Title of a class of civil judges created under
the East India Company.

SADR DIWANI ADALAT.   Court established at Calcutta in
1772 by Warren Hastings to hear appeals in civil cases.
It was presided over by the governor general and two
members of the council.   The adalats were later
merged with the High Court at Calcutta.

SADR NIZAMAT ADALAT.   Court established in 1772 by
Warren Hastings at Calcutta to hear criminal cases.

SADR-US-SADR.   Literally, chief of chiefs.   Title of the
principal law officer under Muslim rulers.

SAGAULI, TREATY OF.   Treaty in 1815 ending the Anglo-
Nepali War of 1814-15.

SAHITYA AKADEMI.   National academy of Indian letters
founded in 1954 for the development of Indian literature,
research in Indian languages and literature, publication
of literary works and the promotion of exchanges with
other countries in the field of literature.   The Akademi's
general council consists of one representative of each
of the 17 languages of India along with nominees of central and state governments and representatives of universities.   Publishes Indian Literature, Sanskrita Pra-
tibha, and Monthly News Bulletin.

SAHITYADARPANA.   Also called the Mirror of Poetry; a
15th-century work on poetics of unknown authorship.
See also PRAKRIT.

SAHU.   Grandson of Shivaji and son of Shambuji.   After the
capture and murder of his father in 1689 by Aurangzeb,

Sahu was taken to the Mughal court as a minor. He was released by Emperor Bahadur Shah in 1707 and returned to assume the throne which had been occupied from 1689 to 1700 by his uncle Rajaram and from 1700 by his aunt Tara Bai. He owed his throne to Balaji Viswanath whom he appointed as his peshwa. Baji Rao I and Balaji Rao also served him as peshwas and their increasing power made them the virtual rulers of the empire. Sahu died in 1749.

SAISUNAGA. Dynasty founded by a king of the same name who ruled over Magadha in the seventh century B. C. The line consisted of ten kings according to some historians and six according to Buddhist texts. Two of the kings, Bimbisara and Ajatasatru, were famous for their conquests. It was overthrown in 362 B. C. by Mahapadma, founder of the Nanda Dynasty.

SAIVA SIDDHANTA. A school of Saivism which flourished in South India. Its devotional literature was written in Tamil between the seventh and tenth centuries and is known collectively as Tirumurai. It consists of 11 books of hymns by 63 nayanars or teachers.

SAIVISM. Hindu sect devoted to the worship of Siva and his symbols. It has a large following in South India. Saivite scriptures are collectively known as Siva-agama.

SAKA ERA. Era established by Kanishka dated from 78.

SAKAS. Central Asian nomads, related to modern Yakuts, who invaded India in several waves in second century B. C. Their leaders assumed the title of Satraps or Great Satraps and ruled Ujjain until 388.

SAKUNTALA see KALIDAS

SAKYA-MUNI. Literally, the sage of the Sakya tribe; one of the titles bestowed on Gautama Buddha.

SAKYAS. Tribe who inhabited the Nepalese Terai in the sixth century B. C. Gautama Buddha was the son of Sakya chief Suddhodhana of Kapilavastu.

SALABAT JANG. Nizam of Hyderabad (1751-1761). Succeeded to the throne on the death of Muzaffar Jang. He cultivated the alliance of the French East India

Company to whom he granted the district of Northern
Circars in return for the presence of a French regiment in Hyderabad under Marquis de Bussy. But with
the recall of Bussy in 1758 and the capture of Masuli-
patam by the English he forsook the French and accepted British protection. He suffered humiliation at
the hands of the Marathas in the Battle of Udgir in 1760
and was forced to make peace by surrendering territory.
He was assassinated in 1761.

SALBAI, TREATY OF. Treaty in 1782 between Mahadaji
Sindhia and the East India Company concluding the First
Maratha War. Under the terms of the treaty the English
were allowed to retain Salsette in return for disavowing
Raghunath Rao (i. e. , Raghoba) and acknowledging Madhav
Rao Narayan as the peshwa.

SALIM CHISTI, SHAIKH. Muslim saint who lived in Sikri
near Agra probably in the latter half of the 16th century. Emperor Akbar credited him with great powers
after the birth of three princes in answer to a prayer
for male heirs. Akbar named his eldest son Salim after
the saint and built the city of Sikri (later Fatehpur Sikri) in his honor.

SALT MARCH. March by Mahatma Gandhi and his followers
from Sabarmati Ashram to Dandi on the coast to distill
salt from sea water, an act prohibited by law; part of
the Civil Disobedience movement.

SALUVA. Dynasty of Vijayanagar kings founded by Saluva
Narasimha, a feudatory chief of Chandragiri, who overthrew Praudhadeva, the last king of the Sangama Dynasty in 1486. The line ruled until 1503 when it was
overthrown in turn by Vira Narasimha.

SAMANNA-PHALA-SUTTA see AJIVIKAS

SAMAR TARANGA see ORIYA

SAMATATA. One of the pratyantas or frontier states in
eastern India mentioned in Samudragupta's Allahabad
Pillar.

SAMAVAHARA. (In Sanskrit drama) play generally in three
acts dealing with the supernatural.

SAMA VEDA.   One of the four Vedas consisting of 1549 hymns including Chhandogya Upanishad and Jaiminiya Brahmana.

SAMHITA.   (In Sanskrit literature) the final text of a work.

SAMHITAS.   Supplements to the Veda written in verse; they are generally classed as revelations.

SAMITI.   General assembly attended by elders and princes.

SAMKHYA.   The oldest of the six orthodox systems of Hindu philosophy founded by the sage Kapila, author of Samkhya Pravacana Sutra, in the sixth century B. C.   The oldest systematic exposition of Samkhya is the Samkhya karika written by Isvara Krishna in the third century.   Early Samkhya postulates a dualism of soul and matter and was essentially atheistic; in medieval times monism and theism were introduced into the system.

SAMRAT.   Title assumed by ancient Hindu emperors connoting their universal overlordship.

SAMS-UD-DIN.   Original name: Shah Mirza or Mir.   An adventurer who founded the dynasty of the Muslim sultans of Kashmir after overthrowing the last Hindu raja in 1346.   He ruled until 1349.

SAMS-UD-DIN MUZAFFAR SHAH.   Ruler of Bengal (1490-93).   Original name: Sidi Badr.   He was an Abyssinian slave who rose in the service of Nasir-ud-din Mahmud II of the Iliyas Dynasty of Bengal.   In 1490 he usurped the throne after assassinating his master and assumed the title of Sams-ud-din Muzaffar Shah.   His three-year rule was marked by acts of fiendish tyranny and was ended when his minister Ala-ud-din Husain Shah led the nobles in a successful revolt.

SAMUDRAGUPTA.   The second emperor of the Gupta Dynasty (330-380).   He extended his dominions by subjugating Samatata, Davaka, Kamarupa, Nepal, Kartripura, Malwa, the Sakas, and the Kushans.   He led an expedition to the south and reduced to submission all the kings of the Deccan.   His empire covered the whole of Aryavarta and he performed the asvamedha to celebrate his imperium.   His conquests are recorded in the Allahabad Pillar.

SAMUGARH, BATTLE OF.   Battle in 1658 between Prince
     Dara and his two younger brothers, Aurangzeb and
     Murad, in which Dara was defeated.

SAMVAT (or samvatsara).   Any one year of the Vikrama
     Era, which began in 58 B. C.

SAN.   Any one year of the Bengali and Vilayati Eras estab-
     lished by the Emperor Akbar.   The former is used in
     Bengal and the latter in the Deccan.

SANAD.   A patent of deed by royal authority granting privi-
     lege, office, or right.

SANAI.   Airblown musical instrument resembling the oboe
     about a foot long with seven holes; believed to be of
     Persian origin.

SANGA (also, Sangramasinha or Sangram Singha).   The
     Rana of Mewar (1509-29) who led a great confederacy
     of Rajput chiefs against Babur but was defeated at the
     Battle of Khanua   in 1527.

SANGAMA.   Dynasty of Vijayanagar kings founded by San-
     gama, father of Harihara and Bukka, in the 14th cen-
     tury.   The line consisted of ten kings:
     Sangama   Deva Raya I (1406)
     Harihara I (1339)   Vijaya Bukka or Vira Vijaya
     Bukka I (1354)   (1422)
     Harihara II (1379)   Deva Raya II (1422)
     Bukka II (1406)   Mallikarjuna (1446)
                                  Virupaksha II (1465)

SANGEET NATAK AKADEMI.   Organization founded at New
     Delhi in 1953 under the auspices of the government of
     India to promote the development of the performing
     arts: dancing, drama, and music.   It documents folk
     performing arts, maintains a museum of musical instru-
     ments, coordinates activities of regional and state
     academies, offers financial aid to dance, drama, and
     music institutions, conducts national festivals, seminars,
     and competitions, and awards prizes in the fields of its
     concern.   Publishes Sangeet Natak.

SANGHA.   (1) A religious congregation.
            (2) The Buddhist Church, especially the order of

monks established by Gautama Buddha.

SANGITA SUDHA see DIKSHITAR, GOVIND

SANKARACHARYA. Hindu monist philosopher and religious
teacher of the eighth century and exponent of the advaita
philosophy. He established four maths or monasteries
which still survive as centers of Hindu orthodoxy: at
Sringeri in Mysore, Dwaraka in Kathiawar, Puri in
Orissa, and Badrinath in the Himalayas. His commentaries on the Upanishads and Bhagavad Gita form
the basis of the advaita philosophy.

SANKARADEVA. Vaishnava reformer in Assam who was
patronized by king Nara Narayan of Cooch-Behar.

SANKHA. Conch shell used in temple rituals and in battle
to summon troops.

SANNYASIN. A mendicant who has entered the last of the
four stages of spiritual perfection.

SANSKRIT. Sacred language of Hinduism written in Devanagiri script; belongs to the Indic branch of the Indo-
Iranian subfamily of Indo-European languages. Its
earlier form was known as Vedic. It was spoken about
the fourth century B. C. as standard court language but
was later supplanted by the Prakrits. Its form and
usage was codified by the grammarian Panini in his
treatise Ashtadhyayi.

SANTAL. A Kolarian aboriginal tribe living in Chota Nagpur
and West Bengal in an area now known as Santal Pradesh.

SANTALI. Language spoken by the Santal tribe.

SAQI, MUHAMMAD see MAASIR-I-ALAMGIRI

SARADA. Script which came into use in NW India from the
ninth century. It includes the following variants: Tak-
kari or Tankri, the parent of Dogri, Chameali, and
Kului; Sindhi; Landa or Bania of Punjab, and Multani,
a variety of Landa; and Gurmukhi, in which the scriptures of the Sikhs are written.

SARANGI. Nonfretted stringed musical instrument derived

from the ancient rabanastrana used for playing a form
of music known as lahra or wave.

SARDAR. (1) A military chief or headman of a group; (2)
by extension, title assumed by certain Sikh families.

SARDESHMUKH. The chief deshmukh in the Maratha administration.

SARDESHMUKHI. Tax equal to one-tenth of revenue levied
on non-Maratha lands conquered by Maratha arms.

SARFARAZ KHAN see ALIVARDI KHAN

SARIRASTHANA see SUSRUTA

SARKAR. (1) (also, circar). Administrative unit of the
empire of Sher Shah; subdivision of a suba or province
under Akbar; usually a revenue district.
     (2) The government as a whole.

SARNATH. Town near Varanasi where Gautama Buddha delivered his first sermon; site of the famous stone pillar
with the lion capital erected by Asoka.

SAROD. Musical instrument with four strings popular in
Bengal; believed to be of Persian origin.

SAROJINI NAIDU. 1879-1949. Hindu nationalist and poet;
first woman president of the Indian National Congress;
author of The Golden Threshold, The Bird of Time, and
The Broken Wing.

SARVODAYA. A populist political ideology with socialist
overtones formulated by Jayaprakash Narain in 1947.

SASANA. (In ancient India) an ordinance or edict of administrative character.

SASANKA. King of Bengal who ruled from 606 or 619 to
637 from his capital at Karnasuvarna. His rule was
marked by hostilities with the Maukharis of Kanauj and
the kings of Thaneswar and Kamarupa. Hiuen Tsang
portrays him as a persecutor of Buddhists.

SATAKA. (In Sanskrit literature) a collection of 100 stanzas.

SATARA. (1) Town in Maharashtra; former capital of Maratha Empire under Sahu.
   (2) Former native state that was annexed to the British Raj under the Doctrine of Lapse in 1848.

SATA SASTRA see [1]NAGARJUNA

SATAVAHANA. Dynasty founded by Simuka in about 60 B. C. after overthrowing the Sunga-Kanvas. It ruled over a kingdom lying between the Godavari and the Krishna Rivers known as Andhra. For this reason it is also known as the Andhra Dynasty. The line consisted of 30 kings who ruled for 400 years. The greatest king of the line was Satakarni I whose capital was Pratisthana (modern Paithan). He celebrated the asvamedha to signalize his undisputed sovereignty.

SATI. Former Hindu custom of immolation of surviving wives on the funeral pyres of husbands; abolished under Lord William Bentinck in 1829.

SATRAPS (also, Kshatrapas). Pre-Kushan Saka kings who ruled areas of northern India. Divided into three main groups: Kapisi in Afghanistan, Taxila in Punjab, and Mathura in Uttar Pradesh.

SATSAI see BIHARILAL

SATTAN[AR] see MANIMEKALAI

SATTASAI see MAHARASHTRI

SATYAGRAHA. Sustained application of nonviolent moral force for the removal of social and political inequities. First introduced in 1894 in South Africa by Mahatma Gandhi, who later refined the technique to include passive resistance, fasting, civil disobedience, and noncooperation.

SAURASENI. A Prakrit dialect used in Sanskrit plays as the speech of the common people. It is the parent of Western Hindi and Punjabi and the language of the Digambara Jain scriptures.

SAURASHTRA. (1) Former state of the Union of India comprising most of the Kathiawar Peninsula formed in 1948 by the union of 22 natives states with capital at Rajkot.

(2) (Also, Khatri, Patanuli).   Gujarati with a slight
addition of South Indian words to its vocabulary.

SAURASHTRI.   A lesser Prakrit with Scythian intermixture.

SAYER.   Variable and arbitrary imposts consisting of tolls,
license fees, duties on merchandise, and tax on houses
and bazars.

SAYYID.   Fourth dynasty of the Delhi Sultanate founded in
1414 by Khizr Khan.   The line consisted of four kings
who ruled Delhi until 1451:   Khizr Khan (1414), Muizz-
ud-din Mubarak (1421), Muhammad Shah (1434), and
Ala-ud-din Alam Shah (1445).

SAYYID AHMED KHAN, Sir.   1815-1898.   Muslim leader
and educator; founder in 1875 of the Anglo-Oriental
College at Aligarh which in 1920 became the Aligarh
Muslim University.

SAYYID ALI, MIR   see   DASTAN-I-AMIR HAMZAL

SAYYID ALI ABDUS SAMAD   see   MUGHAL SCHOOL

SAYYID ALI TABA-TABA   see   BURHAM-I-MAASIR

SAYYID BROTHERS.   Barha Sayyid Husain Ali and Barha
Sayyid Hasan Ali Abdullah, two brothers who were king-
makers at the court of Delhi from 1713 to 1720.   They
helped Farrukhsiyar to depose his uncle Jahandar Shah
and obtain the throne but subsequently blinded and deposed him in 1719.   They imposed four more puppet
sovereigns during the course of the next seven months
but their power was cut short by Emperor Muhammad
Shah who had Abdullah put to death.

SCHEDULED CASTE.   (Also, depressed caste).   Official
term for untouchable Hindu caste.

SEER (also, ser).   A unit of weight in widespread use in
modern India equal officially to 2.057 lbs.   Like all
Indian measures it varies in different parts of the
country from over 3 lbs. in north India to 8 oz. in
Malabar.   The Regulation Act of 1833 established the
seer as a standard unit of weight for the whole of India.
It was superseded by the adoption of the metric system
in the 1960s.

[1]SENA.   In the Hindu army of Vedic times, a regiment led
by a senapati or senani consisting of 225 elephants, 225
chariots, 675 horses, and 1125 infantry soldiers.

[2]SENA.   Dynasty founded by Samantasena that ruled Bengal
from 1095 until 1245 with its capital at Vijayapura.   Its
greatest rulers were Vijaya Sena, Ballal Sena, Lakshmana Sena, Vishvarupa Sena, and Keshava Sena.   They
were noted as patrons of learning.

SENANI (also, senapati).   Commander of a Hindu army in
Vedic times.

SENAPATI.   The commander in chief of a Hindu army in
Vedic times.

SENIOR MERCHANT.   Designation of the seniormost category of East India Company's civil service.

SEPOY.   Term for foot soldier in the British Indian Army,
used from the 1750s.   From Persian sipahi, meaning
soldiery.

SEPOY MUTINY.   Mutiny of sepoys or Indian native soldiers
that broke out in Meerut in 1857 and spread like a con-
flagration throughout north India.   The immediate cause
was the introduction of the Enfield Rifle which offended
the religious sentiments of Hindus and Muslims because
it required the use of greased cartridges.   The disaf-
fection was fanned by dispossessed Indian rulers and the
social upheaval caused by the assimilation of Western
and nontraditional ideas and practices.   The mutineers
were ill-organized and they had no unity of purpose.
Only a few leaders--such as Tantia Topi, Nana Sahib,
and the Rani of Jhansi--emerged to provide them a
focus of loyalty.
    Their early successes included the capture of Meerut
and Delhi where they proclaimed Bahadur Shah II as
emperor.   The other centers of outbreak were Oudh,
Rohilkhand, Nasirabad in Rajasthan, Nimach in Gwalior,
Bareilly, Lucknow, Varanasi, Kanpur, and Bundelkhand.
With the help of the loyal Sikhs, Gurkhas, and South
Indians the British quickly broke the back of the Mutiny.
Delhi was recaptured and Kanpur, Lucknow, and Gwalior
were relieved.
    Led by brilliant generals such as Sir Colin Campbell,
Sir Hugh Rose, Sir Henry Havelock, John Nicholson, and

Sir James Outram, the British finally stamped out the
Mutiny. On July 8, 1858, Lord Canning, the governor
general, announced the end of the Mutiny and the re-
storation of peace. The same year witnessed the transfer of power from the East India Company to the Crown.

SER   see SEER

SERVANTS OF INDIA SOCIETY. Organization founded in
   Poona in 1905 to train Indians in public service and to
   promote by constitutional means political, economic, and
   social progress. Publishes the daily Hitavada.

SESODIYAS (also, Guhilas). A Rajput clan based in Mewar.

SETT. A North Indian Hindu merchant or banker corresponding to the South Indian chetty or shetti. From
   Sanskrit sreshtha, best or chief.

SETUBANDHAM see MAHARASHTRI

SHADAKSHARADEVA see KANARESE

SHAH ALAM II (or Alam Shah II). Original name: Mirza
   Abdullah Ali Gohar. The 23rd Mughal emperor (1759-
   1806). During his reign Delhi was invaded by Ahmad
   Shah Abdali after the Third Battle of Panipat in 1761.
   He was also defeated by the East India Company at the
   Battle of Buxar in 1764 and forced to grant the Company
   the right of Diwani or collection of revenues in Bengal,
   Bihar, and Orissa. He was a puppet in the hands of
   the Marathas until the conclusion of the Second Anglo-
   Maratha War of 1803-05 when he accepted the protection
   of the East India Company and became its pensioner.

SHAH-BANDAR. Title of the harbor master and head of
   customs.

SHAH JAHAN. Full name: Khurram Shihab-ud-din Muhammad. 1592-1666. Sixth Mughal emperor (1628-58); son
   of Jahangir who ascended the throne after disposing of
   his brother Shahryar. In 1648 he transferred his capital
   to Delhi and founded the town of Shahjahanabad. He lost
   the province of Kandahar in 1653 but extended his dominions by annexing Ahmadnagar and subjugating Bijapur and
   Golkonda. His reign is generally regarded as the golden
   age of Muslim architecture in India. Among his

buildings are: the Pearl Mosque at Agra, the Jumma Masjid and the palace at Delhi containing the Dewan-i-Am and the Diwan-i-Khas, and the celebrated Taj Mahal which he built in memory of his wife Arjumand Bano Begum or Mumtaz Mahal. In 1658 the war of succession among his four sons resulted in the victory of Aurangzeb who crowned himself emperor after imprisoning his father. Shah Jahan spent the last years of his life as a prisoner and died in 1666.

SHAIKH MUHAMMAD see MARATHI

SHAISTA KHAN.   Uncle of Emperor of Aurangzeb. He was appointed governor of the Deccan in 1660 but notably failed to contain or capture Shivaji. He was transferred as governor of Bengal, a post he held with conspicuous success for 30 years. During his administration the French were granted the site for a factory at Chandernagore.   He also suppressed the Portuguese pirates and seized Chittagong from the king of Arakan. He died in 1694.

SHAKTI.   Female counterpart of the Hindu deity embodying the feminine aspect of cosmic energy. The worship of Shakti is especially associated with the cult of Siva and occurs variously in myths as Durga, Parvati, Uma, and many others, all being names for the mother goddess of India, Devi. Worshipers of Shakti, who are especially numerous in Bengal, are known as shaktas.

SHAKUNTALA. Famous Sanskrit drama of Kalidas.   Its plot is built around a heroine of the same name.   It was first translated by Sir William Jones in 1789 and did much to arouse interest in ancient Indian drama.

SHAMBUJI. Son and successor of Shivaji (1680-89).   He resisted Aurangzeb successfully for nine years but was taken by surprise at Sangameshwar and executed.

SHANAN. A Panchama class of Tamil Nadu primarily engaged as toddy tappers.

SHANKARA see ADVAITA

SHANWAR TELLIS see BENI ISRAEL

SHARIAT-ULLA, HAJI. Muslim leader who founded the

Faraidhi movement for reforming Islam in the early
decades of the 19th century.   The movement was cen-
tered in Faridpur in east Bengal.

SHARQI.   Dynasty founded by Malik Sarvar, also known as
Khwaja-i-Jahan, who had been appointed Malik-ush-
Sharq by Sultan Nasir-ud-din.   This dynasty ruled Jaun-
pur for 85 years until overthrown by Sultan Bahlol Lodi.
Its most famous ruler was Ibrahim who built the Atala
Masjid in 1408.   The dynasty consisted of six rulers:
Khwaja-i-Jahan (1394)   Mahmud (1436)
Mubarak (1399)   Muhammad (1458)
Ibrahim (1402)   Husain (1458)

SHASTRA.   Any of certain Hindu sacred books constituting
the sources of dharma.

SHASTRI.   A person versed in a shastra or department of
religious knowledge; often used as a title.

SHASTRI, LAL BAHADUR.   1904-66.   Second prime minister of India (1964-66).   Frail and unostentatious leader
whose administration was marked by a war with Pakistan over Kashmir.

SHAUKAT ALI, MAULANA.   Indian Muslim leader of the
Khilafat Movement of 1919-20 along with his brother
Mohammed Ali.   He later joined the Indian National
Congress but left it to espouse the Muslim League.

SHERISTADAR.   Head ministerial officer of a court whose
duty it is to receive plaints and see that they are in
proper form and duly stamped.   Properly register-
keeper, from Sanskrit, sarishta register.

SHER SHAH.   Original name: Farid Khan; also known as
Sher Khan Sur.   1472-1545.   Founder of the Sur Dynasty
and the emperor of India (1539-45).   Son of a petty
jagirdar in Bihar, he became a soldier of fortune in the
service of the Lohani king who gave him the title of
Sher Khan for killing a tiger singlehandedly.   In 1533
he defeated Mahmud Shah, king of Bengal, at the Battle
of Surajgarh and became ruler of Bihar.   Emperor
Humayun led a large army to punish him but was himself defeated at the Battle of Chaunsa in 1539.   Sher
Khan now proclaimed himself ruler of eastern India with
the title of Sher Shah.

Sher Shah defeated Humayun again in 1540 at the
Battle of Bilgram and marched to Delhi and occupied
the imperial city.   He followed this victory by over-
running Punjab and Malwa in 1542 and Sind, Multan,
and Marwar in 1544.   He was killed in the siege of
Kalinjar in 1545.   Sher Shah was also an able and in-
novative administrator who introduced many military and
financial reforms.   He divided his empire into 47 units
known as sarkars each subdivided into parganas; reformed the currency on the ratio of 54 copper coins to
the silver tanka or rupeya; improved communications by
building trunk roads; reorganized the police system; and
brought the army under imperial control by introducing
direct recruitment and cash payments.

SHIA.   Minority Islam sect (mainly Irani).   See also SUNNI.

SHIBBAR.   A coastal vessel from 100 to 300 tons used in
the Malabar trade.

SHIKARA.   (1) Spiral top of a South Indian temple.
(2) Long, narrow boat with a peak at each end.

SHIKARI. A big game hunter; applied also to game hunting.

SHIVAJI.   1627-80.   Founder of the Maratha Empire and
chhatrapati (1674-80).   Son of a petty official in Bijapur,
Shivaji began his career at the age of 19 by capturing
the forts of Torna, Raigarh, Chakan, Singhagarh, Purandahar, Kalyan, and Javli.   His loosely organized band
of guerrillas soon became such a menace that the sultan
of Bijapur sent a large army against him under Afzal
Khan; the army was defeated in a pitched battle and its
commander murdered in a face-to-face encounter.   Now
Shivaji began a long war of attrition combining craft and
arms against Aurangzeb and repulsed the imperial army
under Shaista Khan.   In 1665 he made peace by the
Treaty of Purandahar under which he surrendered 23
forts keeping only 12.   He was compelled to go to the
emperor's court at Agra but managed to escape in 1666.
He resumed hostilities in 1670.   Four years later he
crowned himself chhatrapati or emperor with great pomp
at Raigarh.   By the time of his death in 1680 he was
the undisputed ruler of the west coast of India from
Belgaum to the Tungabhadra River.

SHORE, Sir JOHN.   Governor general of India (1793-98).

He enforced the reforms of Lord Cornwallis and adopted a hands-off policy toward native states. However, he compelled Oudh in 1795 to cede Allahabad to the Company.

SHRENI.   (In ancient India) a craft guild.

SHUJA-UD-DIN   see   ALIVARDI KHAN

SICCA.   Newly minted rupees which were at a premium over those worn by use.   It was allowed to be used in Bengal by the Act of 1833 but was officially abolished in 1836. From Persian sikka, a coining die.

SIDDHANTA SIROMANI   see   BHASKARACHARYA

SIDDHA-SILA.   (In Jainism) heavenly abode of those attaining salvation, equivalent to Hindu moksha.

SIDI.   Any of the Muslim soldiers of fortune of African descent in the service of the sultans of the Deccan or in the Mughal navy.

SIHBANDI.   Irregular soldiery or militia employed for revenue and police duties.

[1]SIKANDER SHAH.   Real name: Nizam Khan.   Second sultan of the Lodi Dynasty (1489-1517) who managed to maintain order and civil peace in the empire by curbing the powers of the provincial governors and jagirdars.

[2]SIKANDER SHAH.   Fifth and last ruler of the Sur Dynasty who was defeated by Humayun at the Battle of Sirhind in 1555 and forced to flee to Bengal.

SIKHS.   Followers of a religion founded by Guru Nanak about 1500 as a casteless and priestless sect based on monotheism and brotherhood.   Guru Nanak was succeeded by nine Gurus: Angad, Amardas, Ramdas, Arjan, Har Govind, Har Rai, Har Kishan, Tej Bahadur, and Govind Singh.   Under these chiefs the Sikhs were organized into a military and political force collectively called the Khalsa or "portion of God" while every member received the surname of Singh, a name derived from Sanskrit sinha meaning lion.
        Guru Ramdas built the Golden Temple at Amritsar on a site donated by Akbar.   Guru Arjan compiled the Adi

Granth and introduced a tithing system and appointed masnads or agents as collectors. He was executed by Emperor Jahangir. Guru Har Govind and Guru Tej Bahadur turned Sikhs into a militant body implacably hostile to the Mughals; the latter guru became a martyr when he was beheaded by Aurangzeb for not accepting Islam. The last guru Govind Singh organized the Sikhs into a Khalsa, a tightly knit band of disciplined warriors. He struggled with the Mughals for 30 years and then accepted a command in the imperial army. He fell at the hands of an Afghan assassin in 1708, appointing no successor and declaring the Adi Granth to be the future guru.

The leadership now passed into the hands of an ascetic named Banda. Under him the Sikhs were almost annihilated by the army of Farrukhsiyar. Banda himself was captured and tortured to death in 1716 along with 740 companions. After Banda's death the Akalis or the "worshipers of the eternal" became the guardians of the sanctuary at Amritsar while the Gurmata held supreme authority. By 1773 with the decline of Mughal power the Sikhs became an independent force divided into 12 misls or confederacies. Ranjit Singh, the leader of the Sukerchakia misl made himself master of the trans-Sutlej misls and transformed the Sikhs from a sect into a people. The political history of the Sikhs ended in 1849 when the English annexed the Punjab.

SIKH WARS. First Sikh War (1845-46). Consisted of four battles in which the English under Sir Hugh Gough defeated the Sikhs at Mudki, Ferozshah, Aliwal, and Sobraon. Concluded by the Treaty of Lahore by which the Sikhs gave up Kashmir.

Second Sikh War (1848-49). Began with the killing of two British officers at Multan in 1848. A drawn battle at Chillianwala was followed by a decisive British victory at Gujarat. The Sikh dominions were annexed to the British Raj and Dalip Singh, the son of Ranjit Singh, was deposed and exiled on pension.

SIKKIM. State in the Himalaya region; from 1890-1975 a protectorate of India ruled by chogyals or maharajas. Of the population about 75% are Nepalese and the remainder Lepchas and Bhutias. The principal administrative officer and the heads of important departments were Indian civil servants. Now a state in the Indian Union. Capital: Gangtok.

SILAHDAR.   Maratha cavalryman who supplied his own equip-
ment and horses.   Distinguished from bargir.

SILAPPADIGARAM   see   ILANGO

SIMLA.   Hill town in Punjab and former summer capital of
the Indian Empire; came under British occupation after
the Gurkha War of 1815-16.   Elevation, 7166 ft.

SIMON COMMISSION.   Commission appointed in 1927 with
Sir John Simon as chairman to inquire into the working
of the Government of India Act of 1919.   Its report,
published in 1930, recommended legislative autonomy
only in the provinces.   The Commission as well as the
Report were boycotted by the Indian National Congress.

SIMUKA.   Founder of the Satavahana Dynasty which ruled
Andhra in the second century B. C.

SIND.   Region of the Indus Valley below the Jhelum River;
site of the ancient Indus Valley Civilization.   Conquered
by Alexander the Great who turned homeward after reaching the city of Patala.   It was later part of the Maurya
and Gupta Empires.   It was conquered from its Hindu
rulers by the Arabs in 711.   In 1176 the Afghans
wrested it from the Arabs and though parts of Sind
seceded it was rejoined to the Mughal Empire under
Akbar.   Sind again became independent under the Amirs.
In 1842 Sir Charles Napier led an expedition that brought
the rule of the Amirs to an end and Sind into the British
Empire.   It was part of Bombay Presidency until 1936
when it became a separate province.   Now a state in
Pakistan with Karachi as its capital.

SINDHI.   Language related to Lahnda spoken in Sind.

SINDHIA.   Maratha dynasty of Gwalior founded by Ranoji
Sindhia, a lieutenant of Peshwa Baji Rao I.   Under
Ranoji's son, Mahadaji, the Sindhias became a power to
be reckoned with in India and the protectors of Emperor
Shah Alam II.   Mahadaji's son, Daulat Rao, suffered
serious reverses in the Second Maratha War and was
forced by the Treaty of Surji Arjangaon to cede all
territories between the Ganges and the Yamuna.   The
line consisted of seven rulers:

Ranoji (d. 1750)   Mahadaji (1761)
Madhava Rao or   Daulat Rao (1794)

Jankoji Rao (1827)   Madhava Rao II (1886)
Jayaji Rao (1843)   Jivaji Rao (1925)

SINDHU. Sanskritic form of Indus.

SINGNAD. Whistle made of horn used by mendicants.

SIPAHSALAR. Title of Persian origin applied to the commander-in-chief of an army, introduced into India by
the later Mughals.

SIRAJ-UD-DAULAH. 1728-57. Nawab of Bengal (1756-57).
Soon after his accession he came into conflict with the
English; seized their settlement at Calcutta where he
placed the English merchants and their families in the
infamous Black Hole. The English under Robert Clive
recaptured Calcutta and emboldened by the Nawab's disaffected courtiers offered battle and defeated him at the
Battle of Plassey in 1757. Siraj-ud-daulah was captured and beheaded.

SIRMAURI. A Pahari dialect spoken in parts of Punjab.

SISUNAGA. Founder of a dynasty of Magadhan kings in the
seventh century B. C.

SITABALDI, BATTLE OF. Battle in 1817 between the Bhonsla Raja Appa Sahib and the British during the course
of the Third Maratha War in which the former was defeated.

SITAR. Nonfretted musical instrument with three or more
strings invented by Amir Khusrav.

SIVA. Third god of the Hindu triad regarded in later mythology as the destroyer with Brahma as the creator and
Vishnu as the preserver. He is a development of the
Vedic storm god Rudra who was also known by the
epithet Shiva meaning auspicious. There are more than
1000 names for Siva, of which Mahadeva is the most
frequent. His cult was popularized by Sankaracharya
and he is especially worshiped at Varanasi.

SIVA-AGAMA see SAIVISM

SIWALIK HILLS. Outer range of tertiary hills that run
parallel to the Himalayas separated from it by valleys
known as duns.

SIYAR-UL-MUTAQHERIN   see   GHULAM HOSSAIN

SKANDAGUPTA.   The last Gupta emperor, who ascended
the throne in 455 and ruled until 468.   His reign was
marked by incessant wars with the Huns and the Pushyamitras.

SLAVE.   Dynasty founded by Qutb-ud-din Aibak in 1206
which ruled the Delhi Sultanate until 1290; so called because Qutb-ud-din was a Turki slave of Shihab-ud-din
(or Muizz-ud-din) Muhammad Ghori who rose from the
ranks by merit and succeeded to the throne on his
master's death.   The line consisted of ten kings:

Qutb-ud-din Aibak (1206)	Muizz-ud-din Bahram
Aram (1210)	(1240)
Shams-ud-din Iltutmish	Ala-ud-din Masud (1242)
(1211)	Nasir-ud-din Mahmud
Rukn-ud-din Firoz Shah	(1246)
(1236)	Ghiyas-ud-din Balban
Raziyat-ud-din (1236)	(1266)
	Muizz-ud-din Kaiqubad
	(1287)

SLEEMAN, Sir WILLIAM.   East India Company official who
was charged with the suppression of thuggee; resident
in Oudh (1848-54); author of Rambles and Recollections
of an Indian Official.

SOBRAON, BATTLE OF.   Battle in 1846 between the Sikhs
and the British during the course of the First Sikh War
in which the Sikhs were defeated.

SODASAJANAPADA.   Collective name of the 16 states that
comprised India in ancient times:

Anga (East Bihar)	Kuru (Thaneswar and Delhi)
Magadha (South Bihar)	Panchala (Bareilly and
Kashi (Varanasi)	Badaun)
Koshala (Oudh)	Matsya (Jaipur)
Vriji (North Bihar)	Surasena (Mathura)
Malla (Gorakhpur)	Asmaka (Godavari)
Chedi (Bundelkhand)	Avanti (Malwa)
Vatsa (Allahabad)	Gandhara (Peshawar)
	Kamboja (Kashmir)

SOLANKI.   Dynasty (961-1297) founded by Mularaja I with
his capital at Anhilvad or Anahilavada.   The Solankis
were related to the Chalukyas of the Gurjara stock.

Bhima I, Siddharaja, Kumarapala, and Virdhavala were
the most important rulers of this dynasty. They were
Jains by faith and great patrons of art and architecture.

SOLINGER, BATTLE OF. Battle in 1781 between Haider
Ali and the British during the course of the Second Mysore War in which Haider Ali was defeated.

SOMAPURA. Medieval university founded in Rajshahi district in Bangladesh by Devapala in 820. It was destroyed
in 1050.

SOMESWARA I. Chalukya king of Kalyani (1041-1072). He
founded Kalyani as his capital. He defeated the Chola
king Rajadhiraja at the Battle of Koppam around 1152
but was later defeated by the Chola kings Rajendradeva
and Virarajendra.

SOMNATH. Town in Gujarat on the Kathiawar coast; site of
an ancient Siva temple which was destroyed by Sultan
Mahmud of Ghazni in 1024.

SOWCAR see MARWARI

SRAVASTI. Town on the Rapti River in Uttar Pradesh;
capital of the ancient kingdom of Koshala.

SRENI. (In ancient India) an assembly of craftsmen.

SRIDHARA see VAISESHIKA

SRINATHA see TELUGU

SRINGA. Airblown musical instrument made of animal horn
related to the ancient kahala.

STEPHENS, THOMAS see MARATHI

STHANAKAVASI. Jain sect that rejects idol worship.

STOTRA. (In Sanskrit literature) a hymn of praise.

STUPA. Buddhist monumental building consisting of a
hemispherical solid dome of earth, stone, and brick.
On the dome is a small square structure called the
harmika or pedestal which is covered by a chhatra or
umbrella. Under the harmika is the sacred relic of the

Buddha or his disciples. The dome of the stupa is sur-
rounded by a pradikshana-patha or a processional path
for pilgrims. The stupa is enclosed by a stone railing
called vriti. On the four sides of the vriti are four
ornamental gateways called torana. From Prakrit
thupa or tope.

SUBA. A province of the Mughal empire under a subadar.
Akbar divided his empire into 15 subas: Kabul, Lahore
including Kashmir, Multan including Sind, Delhi, Agra,
Oudh, Allahabad, Ajmer, Ahmadabad, Malwa, Bihar,
Bengal including Orissa, Khandesh, Berar, and Ahmad-
nagar.

SUDDHI MOVEMENT see DAYANANDA SARASWATI

SUDRA. The last and the lowest of the Hindu castes comprising the menial professions.

SUDRAKA. Sanskrit dramatist of the sixth century; author
of Mrichchhakatika or Little Clay Cart.

SUKAPHA see AHOMS

SUKETI. A dialect of Pahari spoken in Suket.

SULAIMAN. Arab merchant and traveler who visited India
in the ninth century and left an account of the Rashtrakuta kingdom.

SULTANATE OF DELHI. Collective name for the five dynasties that ruled Delhi and northern India from 1206
until 1526: Slave (1206-90), Khalji (1290-1320), Tughluq (1321-1413), Sayyid (1414-50), and Lodi (1450-1526).

SUNDARA, JADAVARMAN see PANDYA

SUNDERBANS. Tract of intersecting creeks and channels,
swampy islands, and jungles which constitute the
Gangetic Delta near the Bay of Bengal.

SUNGA. Magadhan dynasty founded by Pushyamitra in 185
after overthrowing the last Maurya king Brihadratha.
The dynasty was in power for 112 years. Pushyamitra
celebrated his conquests with two asvamedhas.

SUNNI. Orthodox majority sect of Islam.

SUR. Imperial dynasty founded by Sher Shah Sur in 1540 after the defeat of Humayun. It ruled the Delhi Empire until the Second Battle of Panipat in 1556 and consisted of five rulers: Sher Shah (1540), Islam or Salim Shah (1545), Mubariz Khan Muhammad Adil Shah (1554), Ibrahim Shah (1555), and Ahmad Khan Sikandar Shah (1555).

SURA. Dynasty founded by Adisura which ruled Bengal until the 11th century.

SURAT. Town and port in Gujarat; site of an English factory established in 1608-9 and chief English settlement on the west coast until 1687. It was part of the independent kingdom of Gujarat until 1573 when it was taken by Akbar and annexed to the Mughal Empire.

SURAVALI see SURDAS

SURDAS. 1483-1563. Blind bard of Agra considered one of the greatest Hindi poets; author of Sur-Sagar and Suravali, both lyrical works on devotional themes.

SURI. Title of a Jain religious leader.

SURJI-ARJUNGAON, TREATY OF. Treaty in 1803 between the British and Daulat Rao Sindhia by which the latter ceded the doab between the Ganges and the Yamuna and all his territories in the Deccan and Gujarat.

SURNOBAT. Officer in the Maratha Army.

SUR-SAGAR see SURDAS

SURVEY OF INDIA. Map record and issue office at Hathibarkala, Dehra Dun, engaged in detailed mapping of river basins and preparation of topographical maps.

SUSRUTA. Medical writer of the fourth century; author of Sarirasthana, a systematic compendium of Indian medical lore.

SUTA. (In ancient India) court bard and royal herald whose duty was to preserve the genealogy of kings and sages. The heroic ballads that he composed and sang were known as chariya-kavya.

SUTRA. Literally, a thread or string so called because the

collection was a string of rules. Body of Hindu sacred
writings dealing with rituals, custom, and law. Divided
into srauta (sacrificial rituals), grihya (household rituals), and dharma (social and legal usage). A fourth
group treated of magic and astronomy.

SUTTAPITAKA   see   JATAKAS

SVETAMBARA. Literally, those having white garments.
 One of the two important Jain sects, whose members
 wear white clothes. Their scriptures, known as agamas, are written in a Prakrit dialect called Ardha
 Magadhi.

SWADESHI. Literally, of one's own country. Political
 movement launched in Bengal in 1905 to boycott foreign
 goods, particularly Lancashire textiles imported into
 India paying nominal or no duty. It was developed by
 Mahatma Gandhi to include a campaign for economic
 self sufficiency and promotion of cottage industries.

SWAMI. Title of the spiritual preceptor of a cult or religious order.

SWARAJ. (1) Literally, one's own rule. Political autonomy
 as the goal of the Indian nationalist movement.
  (2) An impost levied on conquered territories by the
 Marathas.

SWARAJ PARTY. Political party founded by Pandit Motilal
 Nehru, Chittaranjan Das, and N. C. Kelkar as a moderate alternative to the Indian National Congress.

SWASTIKA. Literally, it is well. Ancient Hindu symbol of
 good luck; also called fire cross or solar cross.

SWAT. State in North-West Frontier Province under the
 rule in the 19th century of chiefs known as akhoonds.
 The most famous of these akhoonds was Abdul Ghafur
 (1835-77), who was often mistakenly called the Sultan
 of Swat.

SWATANTRA. Rightwing political party founded in the 1950s
 by a group led by C. Rajagopalachari dedicated to free
 enterprise and traditionalism. It was dominant for brief
 periods in Gujarat and Orissa.

SYRIAN CHRISTIANS. Christian community of Kerala whose origin is traced to the proto-Christians converted by the Apostle St. Thomas in the first century of the Christian era. So called because they were in communion with the Nestorian Church until the arrival of the Portuguese in the 15th century. The majority of the Syrian Christians belong to the Uniat (Catholic) and Jacobite (Monophysite) Churches. A small Nestorian community survives in Trichur.

- T -

TABAQAT-I-AKBARI. History of the reign of Emperor Akbar written by Nizam-ud-din Ahmad.

TABAQAT-I-NASIRI. History of the early sultans of Delhi up to the time of Nasir-ud-din written by Minhaj-i-Siraj.

TABLA. Drum of Persian origin played by both hands on one end.

TAGORE, ABANINDRANATH. 1871-1951. Noted Bengali artist and founder of the Indian Society of Oriental Arts.

TAGORE, DEVENDRANATH. 1817-1905. Son of Dwarakanath; leader of the Brahma Samaj and founder of the literary journal Tattvabodhini Patrika in 1843; bore the title of Prince and Maharshi.

TAGORE, DWARAKANATH. 1794-1846. Founder of the Tagore family of Jorasanko; banker, philanthropist and leader of the Brahmo Samaj; bore the title of Prince; died in London in 1846.

TAGORE, RABINDRANATH. 1861-1941. Indian poet and playwright; son of Devendranath; awarded the Nobel Prize for Literature in 1912; established in 1901 school at Santiniketan which developed into a university called Visva-Bharati; set to music over 3000 songs; author of about 60 works of which the best-known are: Gitanjali, The Gardener, The Crescent Moon, Chitra, Sadhana, Songs of Kabir, Fruit Gathering, Stray Birds, Hungry Stones, Nationalism, Lover's Gift, Parrot's Training, The Wreck, Gora, The Home and the World, Red Oleander, Glimpses of Bengal, The Religion of Man, Mashi, Broken Ties, The Post Office, and Creative Unity.

TAHSILDAR.   Chief revenue officer of a tahsil or subdivision of a district.

TAILA (or Tailapa).   Founder of the second Chalukya Dynasty of Kalyani.   In 973 he overthrew the last Rashtrakuta king Indra IV.

TAJ MAHAL.   Marble mausoleum erected near Agra by Emperor Shah Jahan over the tomb of his queen Mumtaz Mahal.   It is believed to have been designed by an architect named Ustad I'sa.   The construction began in 1632 and was finished 21 years later at a cost of 5 million rupees.   The structure crowned by a pointed and slightly bulbous dome is regarded as one of the wonders of the world.

TAJ-UL-MA'ASIR   see   HASAN-UN-NIZAMI

TALAM.   Small finger cymbal played with one hand for marking time in a dance.

TALI.   Ornament of gold engraved with the likeness of a goddess and suspended by a consecrated string of many fine yellow threads, tied by a Brahmin around the neck of his wife at the time of the marriage ceremony.

TALIKOTA, BATTLE OF.   Battle in 1565 between Ramaraja, king of Vijayanagar, and the combined armies of the sultans of Ahmadnagar, Bijapur, and Golkonda in which Vijayanagar was defeated.   The battle marked the extinction of the famous Hindu kingdom.

TALUK.   (1) A subdivision of a district presided over by a tahsildar.
    (2) An estate in Uttar Pradesh owned by two or more landlords known as talukdars.

TALUKDAR.   (1) Government official in charge of the revenues of a taluk.
    (2) Proprietor of a taluk consisting of several villages either as sole owner or as principal landholder.

TALUKDARI.   System of land tenure in Uttar Pradesh under which talukdars were recognized by the government as owners of land responsible for the payment and collection of revenue and its payment into the treasury.   Unlike the zamindari system, talukdari was not a permanent settlement.

TALWAR.   A short and curved saber.

TAMBURA.   Popular nonfretted musical instrument with four strings.

TAMIL.   South Indian language belonging to the Tamil-Kurukh branch of the Dravidian family; name derived from Damila, an anaryan tribe who lived in prehistoric times. The development of Tamil was fostered by the three great Sangams or literary academies and early Tamil writing is known as Sangam literature. Tolkappiyam belonging to the second Sangam is the earliest extant Tamil work; it is a grammar of Tamil by a Jain writer. The first great poetic work in Tamil is the Kural by Tiruvalluvar.   Tiruvalluvar's sister Avvaiyar was also a poet.   Other Tamil classics include Naladiyar, a poetic work of which only 400 verses are extant, Chintamani, a romantic epic, Ilango's Silappadigaram, Kamban's Ramayana, Tirumurai--an anthology of Saivite hymns, and Prabandham, an anthology of Vaishnavite hymns.   In the early 18th century Father Constanzio Beschi, an Italian Jesuit, published Tembavani containing a Tamil translation of Old and New Testament stories under his assumed name of Viramamunivar.   Among modern Tamil writers Subramanya Bharati is the most famous.

TAMILAZHAKAM.   Land of the Tamil-speaking people of Dravidian stock coextensive with modern Tamil Nadu.

TAMIL NADU.   State in the Indian Union comprising Tamil-speaking areas of the Madras Presidency and four taluks of the old Travancore-Cochin state.   Capital: Madras.

TAMRALIPTI.   Ancient town and port in Midnapore district in West Bengal in the fifth century; now known as Tamluk.

TANKA.   A gold or silver coin of Turkish origin introduced by the Delhi Sultanate into India in the 11th century.   It was the principal monetary unit in India during the 13th and 14th centuries.   It continued to be current on the west coast until Portuguese times.

TANSEN.   1550-1610.   Celebrated Hindustani classical musician and court musician to Man Singh of Gwalior and Emperor Akbar.   He was born a Hindu but brought up as a Muslim.   He developed the dhrupad.

TANTIA TOPI. 1819-1859. Leader in the Sepoy Mutiny
and lieutenant of Nana Sahib; organized the capture of
Kanpur and Gwalior; responsible for the Kanpur massacre; defeated in successive battles by Sir Colin Campbell and Sir Hugh Rose; fled to the jungles of Rajasthan;
captured by Sir Robert Napier's forces and hanged.

TANTRAS. Writings of the Sakta and Saivite sects and of
certain Buddhist schools. The Hindu Tantras comprise
64 books compiled in the sixth and seventh centuries
and ascribed to Dattatreya. The Tantras deal with the
attainment of power, worship of the gods, and union
with the supreme spirit with the aid of magic, amulets,
secret rites, and occult symbols. They also provide
modes of worshiping the female deities or shaktis.

TANTRISM. Saivite sect which follows the occult rites
prescribed in Dattatreya's Tantras; divided into the
right-handed sect, so called because it follows the ancient Vedic ritual, and the left-handed sect which con-
centrates on the worship of the female aspects of the
deities known as shaktis. Tantrists make use of man-
tras or spells, magic, amulets, and symbols for the
attainment of their spiritual ends. Tantrism spread its
influence into Buddhism where it gained a considerable
following.

TAPAL. Mail service in South India corresponding to dak
in North India.

TAPPA see KHYAL

TARA. A small silver coin current in South India at the
time of the arrival of the Portuguese.

TARAF. A province of the Bahmani Empire considered as
a unit of administration.

TARAIN, BATTLE OF. (1) First Battle of Tarain in 1191
between Prithviraj, the Chauhan king of Delhi and Ajmer, and Shihab-ud-din Muhammad Ghori in which the
latter was defeated.
    (2) Second Battle of Tarain in 1192 between the same
combatants in which the Afghan invader avenged his
earlier defeat and killed Prithviraj. This battle opened
the gates of Hindustan to the Muslims.

TARIKH-I-ALAI   see   KHUSRAV, AMIR

TARIKH-I-FIRISHTA   see   FIRISHTA

TARIKH-I-FIROZ SHAHI   see   BARANI

TATA.   Stringed musical instrument played with a bow.

TAXILA (also, Takshasila).   Ancient city near modern
    Rawalpindi in Pakistan; capital of king Ambi at the
    time of the invasion of India by Alexander the Great.
    It was a center of medical studies and a military
    stronghold in Mauryan, Indo-Greek, and Kushan times
    and was the seat of a viceroy under Asoka.   It lost its
    eminence under Muslim rule.

TEJ BAHADUR.   Ninth guru (1664-1675) of the Sikhs; son
    of Guru Har Govind; incurred imperial displeasure un-
    der Aurangzeb and was imprisoned and offered a choice
    between death and conversion to Islam.   Preferred
    death and was beheaded in 1675.   Revered by the Sikhs
    as a martyr.

TELENGANA.   Region in Andhra Pradesh comprising the
    districts of Hyderabad, Medak, Nizamabad, Karimnagar,
    Warangal, Khammam, Nalgonda, and Mahbubnagar.

TELUGU.   A Dravidian language spoken in Andhra Pradesh.
    Its literature goes back to the 11th century.   Its great-
    est writers include Nanniah (1022-63), translator of the
    first three cantos of Mahabharata into Telugu in champu
    style; Tikkanna (1220-1300) who completed Nanniah's
    translation, Errapragada (1280-1350); Atharvana (1240-
    1310), author of the first Telugu grammar; Srinatha
    (1375-1450), the first great Telugu poet; Potana, 15th-
    century writer of devotional hymns; Paddana, 16th-cen-
    tury poet laureate; Tenali Ramakrishna, satirist;
    Kumari Molla (1509-30), woman poet; and Vemana 16th-
    century writer and social critic.

TERAI.   Belt of marshy jungle land which runs along the
    foot of the Himalayas.

THAKUR.   Term of respect used in addressing Rajput nobles.

THAMBURAN (feminine: thamburatti).   Title assumed by the
    Nairs of Malabar and Saiva monks in Tamil Nadu.   It
    is also used by some royal families in Malabar.

THANA. A police station under a thanadar. Originally the
   term meant a fortified post with its garrison.

THANESWAR. Ancient city near modern Delhi between Ambala and Karnal. The name is derived from Sthanes-
   wara and is rich in religious meaning. It was the
   capital of the Pushyabhuti Dynasty which ruled over
   Malwa, northwest Punjab, and part of Rajasthan. Six
   of the most decisive battles in Indian history were
   fought near Thaneswar: the Battle of Kurukshetra, the
   two Battles of Tarain, and the three Battles of Panipat.

THANJAVUR. Town in Tamil Nadu on the Cauvery River;
   former capital of the Rajas of Thanjavur. The Great
   Temple of Thanjavur is a stately structure dating from
   the 11th century. From the temple an avenue of columns
   leads to the bull shrine containing a colossal bull statue.

THEOSOPHICAL SOCIETY. International society founded in
   1875 with headquarters at Adyar, Madras, for the promotion of the study of comparative religion and the occult. Its library consists of over 17,000 palm-leaf and
   paper manuscripts. Publishes The Theosophist.

THIYA see IZHAVA

THOMAS, St. (also, Didymus). Disciple of Christ and
   Apostle of India and Parthia; arrived in India around
   A. D. 51. Evangelized Kerala and was martyred at
   Mylapore near Madras.

"THREE GEMS" (Pampa, Ponna, Ranna) see KANARESE

THUGS (also, Phansigars). Hindu religious brotherhood of
   marauding robbers who generally strangled their victims
   as offerings to their goddess. They are found as early
   as the mid-12th century. They murdered affluent travelers and at the end of an expedition the loot was divided among the members of the band after a portion
   had been offered to the goddess Kali. Initiates to the
   order were sworn to secrecy with dire threats in case
   of violation. The sect was suppressed by Lord William
   Bentinck with the help of Sir William Sleeman during
   the period from 1829 to 1836.

THUMRI. A lively and plastic mixture of khyal and tappa
   suitable for pantomime and dance.

TILAK, BAL GANGADHAR. 1857-1920. Indian extremist
   nationalist leader and Marathi scholar. In 1907 along
   with Bepin Pal and Lala Lajpat Rai he organized an extremist group in the Indian National Congress demanding
   Purna Swaraj which led to the foundation of the Home
   Rule League in 1916. To expound his revolutionary
   ideology he founded the journals Kesari and Mahratta.
   He was imprisoned several times for sedition and subversion. A social and religious conservative he founded
   the Deccan Education Society for promoting popular education.

TIMUR (also, Timur-i-lang, Tamerlane). 1336-1405. Invaded India in 1398; defeated Sultan Mahmud Shah and
   occupied and plundered Delhi for 15 days. He returned
   home leaving a mountain of 80,000 skulls heaped upon
   the capital city and a legacy of famine, anarchy, and
   pestilence from which the country took years to recover.

TIPU SULTAN. 1749-1799. Ruler of Mysore (1783-99).
   He pursued a policy of implacable hostility toward the
   English and conducted the Second, Third, and Fourth
   Mysore Wars. The Second ended indecisively; the
   Third ended in a humiliating treaty by which he had to
   cede half his kingdom; and the fourth ended in his death
   before the walls of Seringapatam which fell to the Eng-
   lish in 1799.

TIRTHANKARA. Literally, bridge-finder. A Jain saint
   considered as a mode of crossing the dark waters of
   life.

TIRUCHIRAPALLY. Anglicized name: Trichinopoly. Town
   on the Cauvery River in Tamil Nadu; site of two famous
   sieges by the French in the 18th century; noted for its
   picturesque fortress atop a large rock hill.

TIRUMALA. Hindu ruler who usurped the Vijayanagar
   throne in 1565 and founded the Aravidu or Karnata
   Dynasty.

TIRUMURAI see SAIVA SIDDHANTA

TIRUVALLUVAR see KURAL

TODA. (1) A pastoral and polyandrous tribe in Nilgiri Hills.
   (2) A Dravidian language spoken by the Todas.

TODAR MAL, Raja. Revenue minister under Akbar; devised one of the earliest revenue settlements based on uniform measurement of land, classification according to fertility, and a fixed assessment, usually one-third of the produce, collected direct from the ryot.

TOL. Sanskrit school in classical times in which the students instead of paying fees to the teacher or adhyapakas (usually a Brahmin), were fed and clothed as well as taught by them. It was considered the dharma or ritual obligation of a Brahmin to impart a knowledge of the shastras to the young and it was an act of irreverence to accept a fee in return. The teachers were perhaps supported by the community at large through donations.

TOLA. A unit of weight established by the Regulation Act of 1833 as equal to 180 grams or 1/80 of a seer.

TOLKAPPIYAM   see   TAMIL

TOMARA. Rajput clan who lived in the area near Delhi. The town of Delhi was founded by a Tomara chief named Anangapal.

TONGA. A light and small two-wheeled vehicle.

TORAMANA. Hun chief who established a kingdom in Malwa around 500 and ruled over Central India with the title of Maharajadhiraja.

TRANQUEBAR. Seaport on the Bay of Bengal in Tamil Nadu; site of a Dutch settlement until 1845.

TRAVANCORE. Former native state in SW India ruled by a Hindu dynasty founded by Martanda Varma in the 18th century. The name is derived from Tiru-vidan-kodu, a small village south of Trivandrum from which the ruling family came.

TRIKANDA   see   AMARA SINGHA

TRIPITAKA. Literally, Three Baskets (because the palm leaves on which they were written were kept in baskets). Collection of Buddhist writings embodying Buddha's teachings and oral traditions. It consists of Sutta or sermons and parables of the Buddha, Vinaya or rules of discipline for the Sangha, and Abhidhamma or an

analysis of metaphysics and doctrines. The Sutta is di-
vided again into five nikayas, one of which contains the
Dhammapada, Thera and Therigathas and Jatakas. The
Vinaya similarly has three subdivisions--Suttabibhanga,
Parivara, and Khandaka--while Abhidhamma has seven
of which Dhammasangini is one.

TRIPURA. State of the Indian Union between Bangladesh
and Lushai Hill tract. Capital: Agartala.

TRI-RATNA. Literally, three jewels. The three cardinal
principles of Jainism: right faith, right knowledge, and
right conduct.

TRIVANDRUM. Capital of Kerala and former capital of
Travancore state; named after its principal Hindu deity
Ananda Padmanabhan.

TRIVENI. Confluence of the three holy rivers, Ganges,
Yamuna, and (the invisible) Saraswati at Allahabad.

TUGHLUQ. The third dynasty of the Sultanate of Delhi
founded in 1320 by Ghiyas-ud-din Tughluq Shah I by
overthrowing Sultan Nasir-ud-din Khusrav, last king of
the Khalji Dynasty. The dynasty yielded to the Sayyids
in 1414. The line consisted of nine rulers:

Ghiyas-ud-din Tughluq Shah I (1320)	Abu Bakr (1389)
Muhammad Ibn Tughluq (1325)	Nasir-ud-din Muhammad Shah (1390)
Firoz Shah (1351)	Ala-ud-din Sikander or Humayun Khan (1394)
Ghiyas-ud-din Tughluq II (1388)	Nusrat Shah (1394)
	Mahmud Shah (1394)

TUGHLUQNAMAH see KHUSRAV, AMIR

TUKARAM. 1607-49. Maharashtrian saint and poet whose
religious hymns and teachings influenced Shivaji.

TUKAROI, BATTLE OF. Battle in 1575 between the Mughal
Army led by Munim Khan and Daud Khan, the Afghan
king of Bengal, in which the latter was defeated.

TULLAL see MALAYALAM

TULSI DAS. c1532-1623. Hindu mystic and poet. His principal work is the Ramacharitamanasa, a version of

Ramayana in Awadhi, the literary dialect of Eastern
Hindi. He is also the author of five other longer works
consisting of hymns, prayers, and devotional histories,
all dealing with Rama. He also traveled throughout
India preaching bhakti.

TULU. A Dravidian language spoken in Canara.

TULUVA. Dynasty founded in 1473 by Narasa Nayaka that
ruled Vijayanagar until the Battle of Talikota in 1565.
The line consisted of seven kings of whom Krishnadeva
was the greatest:

Narasa Nayaka (1473)	Venkata I (1542)
Vira Narasimha (1505)	Sadashiva (1542)
Krishnadeva Raya (1508)	Rama Raya (1542)
Achyuta Raya (1530)	

TUNGABHADRA. River in the Deccan that rises in the
Western Ghats and joins the Krishna near Kurnool.

TURUSHKA-DANDA. Impost levied by King Govindachandra
of Kanauj to meet the expenses of war with Muslim invaders in the 12th century.

TWENTY-FOUR PERGANAS. District Comprising Calcutta and environs ceded to the British by Mir Jafar in
1757.

TYAGARAJA. 1767-1847. Celebrated South Indian musician
known for his devotional songs in Telugu; exponent of
ganamarga or way of salvation through devotional music.
His kirtans and ragas were sung in honor of Rama.

- U -

UDAIPUR, TREATY OF. Treaty in 1818 between the Rana
of Udaipur and the Company by which the Rana accepted
the status of a protected state under the Paramount
Power.

UDGIR, BATTLE OF. Battle in 1760 between the Marathas
led by Sadasiva Rao Bhao and the Nizam in which the
Nizam was defeated.

UJJAIN (also, Avantika). City on the Sipra River in Malwa
considered one of the seven sacred Hindu cities; capital

in the seventh century of the kingdom of Avanti or Malwa.   It was under the Saka Satraps until the fifth century when Chandragupta II recovered it and made it his
capital.   The city is the locale of Kalidas' Meghaduta.

ULAK.   A large baggage boat with planks laid edge to edge
and fastened with iron clamps.

ULLALAH.   A Panchama class of Malabar who were both
untouchable and unseeable, i. e. their very sight was
considered pollution.

UMARA.   Collective title applied to the higher officials of
the Mughal court.

UMARKOT (also, Amarkot).   Small Rajput feudatory state
near the Sind border, noted as the birthplace of Akbar.

UNITED EAST INDIA COMPANY OF THE NETHERLANDS.
Formed in 1602 through the merger of several small
trading companies.   It received from the state a monop-
oly of the trade on the further side of the strait of
Magellan and of the Cape of Good Hope, including the
right of making treaties and alliances, building forts,
and employing soldiers.   It established settlements at
Pulicat and Machilipatnam on the east coast, Surat on
the west coast, and Chinsurah in Bengal.   All these settlements were abandoned to the English during the Revolutionary War which broke out in 1791.

UNITED PROVINCES OF AGRA AND OUDH.   Former province in the British Raj formed in 1902 consisting of
Northwest Provinces and Oudh which had been united in
1877 under one administrative head as lieutenant governor
of Northwest Provinces and chief commissioner of Oudh.
Name changed to Uttar Pradesh in 1947.

UPADHYAYA.   Reciter and teacher of sastras considered to
rank below an acharya.

UPAGUPTA.   Buddhist monk who converted Asoka to Buddhism.

UPANGA.   Collection of treatises, such as the philosophical
systems of nyaya and mimamsa.

UPANISHADS.   Literally, sitting close to, in the sense of a

group sitting around a teacher.   Philosophical treatises
or metaphysical commentaries attached to the Brahmanas
which provide the underpinnings of Vedic religion.   The
oldest Upanishad is believed to antedate 500 B. C.   They
are written partly in prose and partly in verse.   Over
100 texts are grouped under the term Upanishads.   The
12 most important are Aitareya and Kausitaki in Rig
Veda; Chhandogya and Kena in Sama Veda; and Tait-
tiria, Katha, Svetsvatara, Brihadaranyaka, Isha, Pras-
na, Manduka, and Mandukya in Yajur Veda.

UPARIKA.   Governor of a province or bhukti of the Gupta
     Empire.

UPAVEDAS.   Four minor Vedas that relate to arts and sci-
     ences: Ayurveda (medicine), Dhanurveda (archery),
     Gandharvaveda (music), and Shilpa-shastra (art and
     architecture).

URDU.   Properly: zaban-i-urdu or camp language.   Form
     of Hindustani using Arabic and Persian loan words and
     the Arabic alphabet.

UTPALA.   Dynasty founded in 855 by Anantivarman which
     ruled Kashmir until 939.

UTTARACHARITA see BHAVABHUTI

UTTAR PRADESH.   State of the Indian Union comprising the
     former United Provinces and the states of Rampur,
     Benares, and Tehri-Garhwal.   The state has 11 admin-
     istrative divisions and 54 districts.   Capital: Lucknow.

- V -

VAGABHATA.   Buddhist physician and medical writer (610-
     650); author of Ashtanga-samgraha.

VAHIN.   In the Hindu army of Vedic times, a battalion led
     by a vahinpati consisting of 81 elephants, 81 chariots,
     243 horses, and 405 foot soldiers.

VAISALI.   Ancient city on the north bank of the Ganges in
     Muzaffar district in Bihar; capital of the kingdom of
     Lichchhavis.

VAISESHIKA.   One of the six orthodox systems of Hindu
    philosophy founded in the third century B. C. by Kanada,
    author of Vaiseshika Sutra.   Vaiseshika assumed the
    universe to be composed of atoms and strives to ex-
    plain the world of experience by rational means.   The
    system was further developed by Prasastapada, author
    of Padarthadharmasamgraha in the fourth century and
    Sridhara, author of Nyayakandali in the tenth century.
    Nyaya and Vaiseshika systems merged in medieval
    times.

VAISHNAVISM.   Monistic Hindu theology preached by Nim-
    barka in the north, Ramanuja (fl. 12th century) in the
    south, Madhva in Canara, and Vallabha in Gujarat and
    Mathura.   It began to emerge as a major force in
    Hinduism around the 12th century.   It was popularized
    by a host of mystics and poets such as Ramananda (fl.
    14th century), Kabir, Sri Chaitanya (fl. 15th century),
    Sankaradeva, Jayadeva, Vidyapati, Chandidas, Mirabai,
    Tulsi Das, and Kirtivasa.   It is today still one of the
    principal sects in Hinduism.

VAISYA.   The third caste or varna in the Hindu caste sys-
    tem constituted by traders and farmers.

VAJAPEYA.   A one-day Vedic ritual in which animals in-
    cluding the cow were sacrificed to the Maruts or the
    storm gods.   The number 17 played an occult role in
    this sacrifice.   It was performed by 17 priests with 17
    invocations and 17 chants and the number of animals
    slain was also 17.   Each guest was given 17 cups of
    soma, or wine, to drink and the ritual culminated in a
    race of 17 chariots.

VAKATAKA.   Dynasty founded in the fourth century by Pra-
    varasena I which ruled Central India until the seventh
    century.   The kingdom was divided on the death of the
    founder between his two sons.

VAKIL.   Under the Sultans of Delhi, the highest ceremonial
    officer at the court.   Under the Mughals, prime minis-
    ter directly responsible to the emperor.

VAKYA-SASTRA   see   MIMAMSA

VALABHI.   (1) City, now known as Wala, in Kathiawar; a
    center of Buddhist learning in the time of Hiuen Tsang.

(2) Kingdom founded in the fifth century by Dronosimha of the Maitraka Rajput clan in eastern Kathiawar.   A branch of the dynasty was established in western Malwa.   The kingdom was overthrown by the Arabs
in the eighth century.

VALLABHACHARYA. 1479-1531. Vaishnavite saint. Born
in a Brahmin family in Andhra, Vallabhacharya lived in
Varanasi and Mathura. He claimed that Krishna manifested himself to him at Mathura. He gained a large
following in North India and Gujarat. He held that
since the created and the creator are one, the body
should be worshiped and indulged. His system is therefore called Pushti-Marga or the Abundant Path. It is
also characterized as Sudh-Advaita or pure monism.

VALMIKI.   Poet and rishi who is believed to have written
the epic Ramayana. He is represented as taking part
in some of the scenes, as when he receives the banished
Sita in his hermitage.

VANAVASI.   Also, Jayanti, Vaijayanti. Ancient city on the
upper Tungabhadra; capital of the Kadambas from the
third to the sixth century.

VANDEMATARAM.   Literally, Hail to the Motherland.
Anthem of the Indian nationalist movement composed by
Bankim Chandra Chatterji.

VANGA.   Region comprising eastern and central Bengal in
ancient times.

VANNAN.   A Panchama class of Tamil Nadu primarily engaged as launderers.

VARAHA.   A gold coin current in the medieval kingdoms of
the Deccan related to the dinar.

VARAHAMIHIRA.   505-87. Indian astronomer and mathematician; author of Brihat-samhita and Hora-sastra.

VARANASI.   Also known as Benares or Kasi. City on the
northern bank of the Ganges between the Varuna and the
Ashi; one of the seven sacred cities of the Hindus.
First mentioned in the Atharva Veda as the capital of
the kingdom of Kasi. Gautama Buddha delivered his
first sermon in this city. In 1775 the local Hindu ruler

Chait Singh made a treaty with the East India Company and accepted its suzerainty. In 1781 Chait Singh was deposed and the principality was annexed to the British dominions. As a place of pilgrimage Varanasi is famous for its temple of Viswanath. In 1669 Aurangzeb destroyed the original temple and built a mosque on its site. The present temple was rebuilt in later times. The city is also famous for its silk brocades and its Hindu University.

VARENDRA. Name by which north Bengal was known in ancient times.

VARNA. Any of the four main castes into which Hindu society is divided. From Sanskrit varna, color.

VARTHEMA, LUDOVICO DI. Italian traveler who visited Gujarat in the 16th century and left an account of the kingdom under Sultan Mahmud Begath.

VARTIKKA see KATYAYANA

VARUNA. Literally, the encompasser of the universe. The creator and the supreme god in the Rig Veda to whom belongs especially the sky, the waters, the night, and the west.

VASAVA. 1125-1170. Founder of the Lingayet or Vira Saiva sect; minister in the reign of Bijjala Kalachurya of Kalyani.

VASUDEVA. Founder of the Kanva Dynasty of Pataliputra who ascended the throne after the assassination of the last Sunga king Devabhuti or Devabhumi in 73 B.C. The dynasty consisted of four kings who ruled until Simuka overthrew the last king, Susarman, in 28 B.C. and established the Satavahana Dynasty.

VASUMITRA. Buddhist author and polemicist who presided over the Buddhist church council held in the time of Kanishka in the first or second century; author of Mahavibhasa Sastra.

VATAPI see BADAMI

VAYU PURANA. One of the 18 Puranas containing genealogical lists of Vedic kings.

VAZIR.   Under the Sultans of Delhi, the prime minister in
    charge of general and revenue administration.   Under
    the Mughals, revenue and finance minister under the
    vakil.

VEDANGAS.   Supplements to the Vedas dealing with siksha
    (phonetics), kalpa (religious ritual), vyakarna (gram-
    mar), chhanda (meter), nirukta (etymology), and
    jyotisha (astrology).

VEDANTA.   Literally, the goal of the Vedas.   The most
    famous of the six systems of Hindu philosophy which
    seek to explain the laws of the universe, the practical
    application of these laws, and the identification of the
    individual with reality.   It was founded by Badarayana
    sometime between 500 and 200 B. C.   Of the three
    schools into which Vedanta developed, the monism of
    Sankaracharya is the best known and the most deeply
    rooted.   It presents Brahma as the creator of the cos-
    mos, at once transcendent and immanent.   The second
    school of interpretation came about 300 years later
    when Ramanuja expounded a qualified monism.   The
    third school of Madhva in the 12th century posits a
    complete duality.

VEDAS.   Collections of Hindu sacred writings including
    hymns, prayers, ritualistic instructions, philosophy,
    mythology, and holy lore.   The Vedas comprise some
    100 books in all but the four principal ones are: Rig
    Veda, Sama Veda, Yajur Veda, and Atharva Veda.
    Each Veda is divided further into four parts: Samhita
    or collected hymns, Brahmanas or directions for sacri-
    ficial rites, Aranyakas or speculative texts for recluses
    in forests, and Upanishads or philosophical discourses.
    The Vedas were originally meant to be learned by rote
    and are therefore also called sruti.

VEDIC.   Language of the Vedas from which Sanskrit is de-
    rived.   It is believed to be related to Avestan.

VELLALA.   A Panchama class of Tamil Nadu primarily en-
    gaged as agriculturists.

VELLORE.   Town in Tamil Nadu near Madras; site of a
    sepoy mutiny in 1806 which was suppressed with ease.

VENGI   Kingdom between the Godavari and the Krishna

rivers ruled by the Pallavas when it was conquered by
Samudragupta in the fourth century B. C.   In 611 it fell
to the Chalukya king Pulakeshin II who set up his
brother Kubja Vishnuvardhana as viceroy with a capital
at Pishtapura, the modern Pithapuram.   In 615 Vishnuvardhana declared his independence and founded the
dynasty of Eastern Chalukyas which ruled for over four
centuries until 1070.

VENKATA   see   ARAVIDU

VENKATAMAKHIN.   c1680.   Karnataka musician called the
Panini of Music; inventor of the Janaka-Mela system of
raga scales.

SRI VENKATESWARA UNIVERSITY ORIENTAL RESEARCH
INSTITUTE.   Institution founded in Tirupati, Andhra
Pradesh, in 1939 for the promotion of Indological
studies.   Publishes a Journal, Glossary of Indian Philosophical Terms, Bharata Kosa, and other treatises.

VENU   see   BANSRI

VICEROY.   Title and office created by the Government of
India Act of 1858.   Earl Canning was the first and Lord
Linlithgow the 20th and last.   The names of acting
viceroys are given within parentheses:

Earl Canning (1858)   Earl Curzon (1899)
Earl of Elgin (1862)   (Lord Ampthill 1904)
(Sir Robert Napier 1863)   Earl Curzon (reappointed
(Sir William T. Denison   1904)
   1863)   Earl of Minto (1905)
Lord Lawrence (1864)   Lord Hardinge (1910)
Earl of Mayo (1869)   Lord Chelmsford (1916)
(Sir John Strachey 1872)   Earl of Reading (1921)
(Lord Napier 1872)   (Lord Lytton II 1925)
Earl of Northbrook (1872)   Earl of Reading (1925)
Earl of Lytton I (1876)   Lord Irwin (1926)
Marquess of Ripon (1880)   (Lord Goschen 1929)
Earl of Dufferin (1884)   Earl of Willingdon (1931)
Marquess of Lansdowne   (Sir George Stanley 1934)
   (1888)   Marquess of Linlithgow
Earl of Elgin II (1894)   (1936)

VICTORIA MEMORIAL.   Grandiose monument erected by
Lord Curzon in the Calcutta maidan in honor of Queen
Victoria.

VIDARBHA.   Ancient name for modern Berar.

VIDDHASHALABHANJIKA   see   RAJASEKHARA

VIDHAN PARISHAD.   The legislative council of a state
legislature.

VIDHAN SABHA.   The legislative assembly of a state legislature.

VIDYASAGAR, Pandit ISWARCHANDRA.   1820-91.   Sanskrit
and Bengali writer, social reformer, and educationist
considered as the father of Bengali prose literature.
Of his many works the best known is Betal-Panchavimsati.   He also encouraged the spread and assimilation
of Western culture and ideas.

VIHARA.   A Buddhist monastery; originally the hall where
the monks met and later extended to the whole building
and to the attached shrine.

VIJAYANAGAR.   (1) Former city in the Deccan now in ruins;
capital of the Vijayanagar Empire sacked and destroyed
by Muslim victors after the Battle of Talikota in 1565.
In 1443 Abdur Razzak described its grandeur: "The
city is such that the eye has not seen nor the ear heard
of any place resembling it upon the earth. "
    (2) Former Hindu kingdom in the Deccan founded
about 1336 by Harihara and Bukka, sons of Sangama.
The kingdom was ruled by three dynasties: Sangama (up
to 1485), Saluva (1485-1503), and Tuluva of which Krishnadeva Raya was the third king.   At its zenith the kingdom extended from the Bay of Bengal to the Arabian
Sea and included modern Tamil Nadu, Mysore, and
Andhra Pradesh.

VIJNANESWARA.   Hindu jurist who lived in Kalyani during
the reign of the Chalukya king Vikramaditya; author of
Mitakshara, a treatise on the law of succession.

VIJNAPTI MAITRAKA   see   DHARMAPALA

VIKRAMADITYA-CHARITA   see   BILHANA

VIKRAMA ERA.   Also Sa-nanda (or Sri-Nripa) Vikrama
Samvat or Malava Era.   Hindu era dated from 58 B. C.

VIKRAMANKA-CHALUKYA ERA.   Era established by the
Chalukya king Vikramanka to mark his accession in
1076.

VIKRAMASILA.   Tantrik university founded in 810 by the
Pala king Dharmapala.   Its most famous teacher was
Atisha.   It was destroyed by Ikhtiyar-ud-din Muhammad
Khalji in 1198.

VIKRAMORVASI see KALIDAS

VINA.   The Indian lute believed to be the oldest Indian musical instrument still in use.   It has seven strings, a
curved neck, and two large gourds which are resonating
chambers.

VINDHYA.   System of mountains and hills in central India
extending east to west across Madhya Pradesh for about
350 miles.   They form part of the boundary of the
Deccan.

VIRA NARASIMHA.   King of Vijayanagar (1505-1509).   He
was the son of Narasa Nayaka, a Taluva chief and crown
regent in the service of the Saluva king, Immadi Narasimha.   Immadi Narasimha was a minor and a virtual
prisoner in the hands of the regent.   On the death of
Narasa Nayaka, Vira Narasimha became the regent in
1503.   Two years later he had Immadi Narasimha killed
and proclaimed himself king.   During his short reign
Vira Narasimha proved himself to be a strong and cap-
able ruler.

VISAKHADATTA.   Sanskrit dramatist of the Gupta age; author of Mudrarakshasa.

VISHAKHAPATNAM.   Port on the Andhra coast; site of an
English settlement in the 18th century.

VISHAYA (also, mandala).   A division of a bhukti or administrative province in the Gupta Empire, corresponding
to a modern district.

VISHNU.   One of the three principals gods of the Hindu
pantheon, regarded as the preserver.   His preserving
and restoring power is believed to have been manifested
in ten avatars, of which Rama and Krishna are specially
honored and worshiped.

VISHNU PURANA.   One of the 18 Puranas which treats of
cosmogony, genealogies of gods and patriarchs of the
human race, and dynastic lines.

VISHVESHVARANAND VEDIC RESEARCH INSTITUTE.   Institution founded at Hoshiarpur in 1903 for the promotion
of Indological studies.   Publishes Vishva Jyoti, Vishva
Sanskritam, Vishveshvaranand Indological Journal, and
VVRI News Bulletin.

VISS.   A unit of weight in South India equal to 1/8 of a
maund or 3 lb. 2 oz.

VITHI.   (In Sanskrit drama) one-act romantic play.

VIVEKANANDA, SWAMI.   Original name: Narendranath
Dutta.   1863-1902.   Disciple of Ramakrishna Parama-
hamsa and missionary; gained fame as Hindu delegate
to the Parliament of Religions at Chicago in 1893; organized the Ramakrishna Mission with branches in India
and abroad for the propagation of Vedanta; author of
many books on philosophy and religion.

VOPADEVA   see BHAGAVATA PURANA

VRACHADI.   A lesser Prakrit spoken in NW India from
which Lahnda, Sindhi, Kashmiri are derived.

VRIJJIS.   Ancient tribe, also known as Lichchhavis, who inhabited a region in Muzaffarpur district in Bihar with
capital at Vaisali; noted for a republican form of government.

VYASA (or Vyasadeva).   Sage to whom is attributed the
Mahabharata, the 18 Puranas, Bhagavad Gita, and
Vedanta Sutra.

VYAYOGA.   (In Sanskrit drama) a heroic play with military
spectacle.

- W - X -

WANDIWASH, BATTLE OF.   Battle in 1760 between the
Company forces led by Sir Eyre Coote and the French
Army led by Count de Lally in which the French were
defeated.

WANG-HIUEN-TSE.   Chinese Buddhist pilgrim and envoy
    who visited India three times: 643, 646-47, and 657.

WARANGAL.   (1) City in Andhra Pradesh; capital of the
    kingdom of Warangal.
    (2) Former kingdom in the Deccan ruled by the Kaka-
    tiya Dynasty which was destroyed by Alauddin Khalji in
    the 13th century.

WAVELL, Lord ARCHIBALD.   1883-1950.   Governor gen-
    eral and Crown representative (1943-47).   Administration
    marked by communal tensions and nationalist militancy
    during the "Quit India" campaign of 1944.   Presided
    over the formation of an interim Congress-led govern-
    ment at the center.

WAZIRI.   Warlike Afghan tribe inhabiting the North-West
    Frontier Province.

WELLESLEY, Marquis; Earl of Mornington.   Full name:
    Richard Colley Wellesley.   1760-1842.   Governor gen-
    eral of India (1798-1805).   He made British power
    supreme in India.   His policy of subsidiary alliances
    was designed to reduce native states into harmless ap-
    pendages of the Paramount Power.   He destroyed Tipu
    Sultan's power in Mysore and forced the Maratha chiefs
    to cede large areas in central India, Malwa, Gujarat,
    and Delhi after the Second Maratha War.   He also an-
    nexed the Carnatic, Thanjavur, and Oudh and thus made
    the Company the undisputed master of the subcontinent
    outside Sind and the Punjab.

WELLINGDON, Lord.   Full name: Freeman Freeman-
    Thomas.   1865-1941.   Viceroy and governor general of
    India (1931-35).   Administration marked by retreat from
    the policy of conciliation initiated by his predecessor,
    Lord Irwin.   He put down the Civil Disobedience Move-
    ment.

WEST BENGAL.   State of the Indian Union comprising the
    western districts of the former Bengal presidency, the
    former state of Cooch-Behar, and the former French
    possession of Chandernagore.   The state has two divi-
    sions under which there are 15 districts.   Capital: Cal-
    cutta.

WESTERN HINDI.   Regional form of Hindi including three

dialects: Dakhni or Southern, Kanauji and Bundelhi,
Hindvi and Braj Bhasha.

WHITE MUTINY.   Mutiny by English soldiers protesting
against the reduction of their batta and allowances by
Lord Clive, governor of Bengal.   It was easily suppressed.

WOOD, Sir CHARLES.   President of the Board of Control
(1854-58).   His report of 1854 formulated the education
policy of the government of India; it led to the introduction of an English model of graded schools, colleges,
and universities.   Wood also emphasized the secular
character of education and the role of regional languages.
One immediate result of the report was the foundation
of the universities of Calcutta, Bombay, and Madras.

WRITER.   Designation of the juniormost category of East
India Company's civil service during the period from
the first to the fifth year of service.

XAVIER, St. FRANCIS.   1506-1552.   Jesuit missionary
called Apostle to the Indies.   Sent by John III of Portu-
gal to Goa and preached there in 1542.   He labored in
western and southern India, Malacca, the Moluccas,
and Japan; died on a small island near Macao but his
remains are interred in Goa.   He was canonized in
1622.

- Y -

YADAVA.   Dynasty founded in 1191 by Bhillama with Devagiri as capital.   It was in power until 1318 when its
last ruler was defeated by the sultan of Delhi and beheaded.

YADU.   A tribe who inhabited western India in Vedic times.

YAJNAVALKYA.   Rishi who lived in the time of Janaka of
Mithila; believed to have compiled a few minor texts of
the 100 or so texts of the Upanishads.

YAJUR VEDA.   One of the 18 Vedas concerned with sacrificial prayers, rites, and rituals.   Divided into Black
Yajur Veda and White Yajur Veda.

YAMA (also, Dharma-raja).   Vedic god of the underworld.
Yama and his sister Yami are portrayed in the Rig Veda
as the first human pair and Yama as the first man to
die.

YAMUNA (also, Jumna).   River in north India, chief tributary
of the Ganges.   It rises in the Himalayas and joins the
Ganges near Allahabad.   On its banks are Delhi, Agra,
and Allahabad.   Length, 860 miles.

YASODHARMAN.   King of Malwa whose greatest exploit was
the defeat of the Hun king Mihiragula in 528.   No pre-
cise dates have been assigned to Yasodharman but he
is believed to have lived in the sixth century.   Inscriptions on two columns of victory that he erected at Mandasor describe him as a powerful monarch whose dominions extended from the Himalayas to Kerala and from
Brahmaputra to the Arabian Sea.

YAUDHEYAS.   Warrior tribe mentioned in the Allahabad
Pillar inscription of Samudragupta as living in the Sutlej Valley.   They had a republican form of government.

YAVANAS.   From Yauna or Ionia.   Hindu term for Greeks;
later applied by extension to all Westerners.

YOGA.   One of the six orthodox systems of Hindu philosophy
founded by the sage Yajnavalkya and later codified by
Patanjali in Yoga-sutra in the second century B. C.   It
shares many common tenets with the Samkhya school.
The system is divided into karma (work) yoga, bhakti
(faith) yoga, jnana (knowledge) yoga, mantra (spells)
yoga, laya yoga through the activation of the chakras
or centers of the body, hatha yoga, and raja yoga, the
last two stressing physical culture.

YOGACHARYA BHUMI SHASTRA   see   ASANGA

YOJANA.   A unit of distance in ancient India equal to (according to Fa-hien) seven miles.

YUAN CHWANG   see   HIUEN TSANG

YUGA.   One of the four ages of mankind: Krita yuga, Treta
yuga, Dvapara yuga, and Kali yuga.   The four yugas
make one maha-yuga equal to 4,320,000 solar years.
Two thousand maha-yugas or 8,640,000,000 years make

261   Yusuf

a kalpa or one Day of Brahma the creator. At the end
of each maha-yuga the world is destroyed by fire and
water in an event known as the laya or dissolution.
Kali yuga, the present age, began at midnight February
17 3102 B. C. at the time of the accession of Parikshit,
son of Abhimanyu, to the throne of Hastinapura. It has
427,000 more years to go before another dissolution.

YUSUF ADIL KHAN (or Shah). Founder of the Adil Shahi
Dynasty of Bijapur; a Turkish slave of Muhammad Gawan who rose by merit to become governor of Bijapur.
He declared his independence in 1490 and ruled until
1510.

YUVARAJA (or yuvamaharaja). Properly the title of the
eldest son of a raja or heir apparent; also applied to a
young prince associated with his father in the government of the realm.

- Z -

ZABT. System of land revenue assessment.

[1]ZAFAR KHAN. Original name: Hasan. Founder of the
Bahmani Empire. Began career in the service of Sultan
Muhammad Tughluq; declared himself as an independent
ruler in 1347 with Gulbarga as capital taking the title of
Abul-Muzaffar Ala-ud-din Bahman Shah. Since Zafar
Khan claimed descent from the Persian hero Bahman
his dynasty came to be known as Bahmani. At his
death in 1358 his kingdom extended from Pengenga in
the north to Krishna in the south and from Daulatabad
in the west to Bhongir in the east.

[2]ZAFAR KHAN. Founder of the independent Muslim dynasty
of Gujarat; appointed as governor of Gujarat in 1391 by
Muhammad Shah Tughluq; proclaimed his independence in
1396 and ruled until 1411. Later he assumed the title
of Muzaffar. He also overran Malwa and set up his
brother Nusrat as king there.

ZAKAT. Tax, usually 2 per cent of income earmarked for
public charity, levied on Muslim subjects by Muslim
rulers.

ZAMINDARI. System of land tenure under which zamindars

were recognized as owners of land on condition that they pay into the treasury by a fixed date every year the annual rent which was fixed at 90 per cent of the estimated revenue collected from the peasants.   This was the basis of the Permanent Settlement.

ZAMORIN.   Title of the Hindu raja of Calicut or Kozhikode. From Sanskrit samundri, sea-king.

ZENANA.   Part of a house set aside for women in a Muslim home.

ZILLA.   Literally, a rib.   A district as an administrative unit in British India.

BIBLIOGRAPHY

Abul Fazl. Ain-i-Akbari. 3 vols. Calcutta: Royal Asiatic Society of Bengal, 1873-96.

_____. Akbar Namah. 3 vols. Calcutta: Royal Asiatic Society of Bengal, 1897-1921.

Agrawala, Vasudeva S. India as Known to Panini. Lucknow: Prithvi Prakashan, 1963.

Ahmad, Muhammad Aziz. The Early Turkish Empire of Delhi. Lahore: Muhammad Ashraf, 1949.

Akbar, Muhammad. The Punjab Under the Mughals. Lahore: Ripon Press, 1948.

Al Biruni. Alberuni's India. 2 vols. London: Trubner, 1910.

Albuquerque, Alfonso de. The Commentaries of Albuquerque. 4 vols. London: Hakluyt Society, 1875-84.

Alexander, Horace G. New Citizens of India. London: Oxford University Press, 1951.

Ali, Yusuf. Nawabs of Bengal. Calcutta: Asiatic Society of Bengal, 1952.

Allan, John, T. W. Haig, H. H. Dodwell, and R. R. Sethi. The Cambridge Shorter History of India. Delhi: S. Chand, 1958.

Altekar, Anand Sadashiv. Education in Ancient India. Varanasi: Nand Kishore, 1951.

_____. The Rashtrakutas and Their Times. Poona: Oriental Book Agency, 1934.

Bibliography   264

_____ . State and Government in Ancient India.   Varanasi: Motilal Banarsidass, 1959.

Anand, Mulk Raj. Story of India.   Thompson, Conn. : Interculture, 1958.

Anandaranga Pillai. Private Diary of Ananda Ranga Pillai.
12 vols. Madras: Superintendent Government Printing,
1904-28.

Archer, William G. The Loves of Krishna.   London:
George Allen & Unwin, 1957.

Arnold, Edwin. The Marquess of Dalhousie's Administration of British India. 2 vols. London: Saunders,
Otley, 1862-65.

Arokiaswami, M. The Kongu Country. Madras: University of Madras, 1956.

_____ and T. M. Royappa. The Modern Economic History of India. Madras: S. Devotta, 1955.

Aspinall, Arthur. Cornwallis in Bengal. Manchester, England: Manchester University Press, 1931.

Auboyer, J. Daily Life in Ancient India. New York: Macmillan, 1965.

Azad, Maulana Abul Kalam. India Wins Freedom. New
York: Asia Publishing House, 1960.

Babur. Memoirs of Babur. 2 vols. London: Luzac, 1922.

Baden-Powell, B. H. The Indian Village Community. New
Haven, Conn. : Human Relations Area Files, 1958.

_____ . Land Systems of British India. 3 vols. London:
Clarendon Press, 1892.

Bahadur, Lal. The Muslim League. Agra: Agra Book
Store, 1954.

Balakrishna, R. Shivaji the Great. New York: Asia Publishing House, 1962.

Balfour, Edward G.   Cyclopedia of India and of Eastern and
    Southern Asia. 3 vols. New York: International Pub-
    lications Service, 1968 (reprint).

Balfour, Elizabeth.   History of Lord Lytton's Indian Admin-
    istration, 1876-1880. London: Longmans, 1899.

Ballhatchet, Kenneth.   Social Policy and Social Change in
    Western India. London: Oxford University Press, 1957.

Banerjea, Surendranath.   A Nation in the Making: Being the
    Reminiscences of Fifty Years of Public Life.   London:
    Oxford University Press, 1925.

Banerjee, Anil C.   Guru Nanak and His Times.   Columbia,
    Mo.: South Asia Books, 1971.

_____.   The Rajput States and the East India Company.
    Calcutta: A. Mukherjee, 1951.

Banerjee, S. K.   Humayun Badshah.   2 vols. London:
    Oxford University Press, 1938.

Banerji, Projesh.   Dance of India. Allahabad: Kitabistan,
    1947.

Banerji, Rakhal Das.   History of Orissa.   2 vols.   Cal-
    cutta: Susil Gupta, 1956.

Bapat, Purushottam V.   2500 Years of Buddhism.   Delhi:
    Publications Division, 1956.

Barbosa, Duarte.   The Book of Duarte Barbosa.   2 vols.
    London: Hakluyt Society, 1918-21.

Barnett, Lionel D.   Antiquities of India: An Account of the
    History and Culture of Ancient Hindustan.   Mystic,
    Conn.: Verry, 1964.

_____.   Hindu Gods and Heroes.   London: J. Murray,
    1922.

Barooah, Nirode K.   David Scott in North-East India: A
    Study in British Paternalism.   Mystic, Conn.: Verry,
    1970.

Barth, Auguste.   Religions of India.   Varanasi: Chowkhamba
    Sanskrit Studies, 1963 (reprint).

Basak, Radha Govinda. The History of North-Eastern India. London: Kegal Paul Trench Trubner, 1934.

Basham, Arthur Llewellyn. The Wonder That Was India. New York: Grove Press, 1959.

Beaglehole, T. H. Thomas Munro and the Development of Administrative Policy in Madras. New York: Cambridge University Press, 1966.

Beal, Samuel, trans. Chinese Accounts of India. Calcutta: Susil Gupta, 1957.

_____. Travels of Fa-Hian and Sung Yun. London: Trubner, 1869.

Beals, Alan R., and J. T. Hitchcock. Field Guide to India. Washington, D. C.: National Academy of Sciences, 1960.

Beny, Roloff and Aubrey Menen. India. New York: McGraw, 1969.

Bernard, Theos. Hindu Philosophy. New York: Philosophical Library, 1947.

Bernier, Francois. Travels in the Moghul Empire. London: Oxford University Press, 1934.

Bernstein, Henry T. Steamboats on the Ganges. Bombay: Orient Longmans, 1960.

Bhandarkar, Ramakrishna G. Early History of the Deccan. Calcutta: Susil Gupta, 1957.

Bhardwaj, Surinder M. Hindu Places of Pilgrimage in India: A Study in Cultural Geography. Berkeley: University of California Press, 1973.

Bhatia, B. M. Famines in India. New York: Asia Publishing House, 1963.

Bhatia, Krishan. Indira: A Biography of Prime Minister Gandhi. New York: Praeger, 1974.

Bhattacharya, Sachchidananda. A Dictionary of Indian History. New York: Braziller, 1967.

Bhattacharyya, Haridas, ed. The Cultural Heritage of India.
4 vols. Calcutta: Institute of Culture, 1953-61.

Bhushan, Jamila Brij. Indian Jewelry. Bombay: Taraporevala, 1954.

Biardeau, Madeleine. India. New York: Viking, 1960.

Binyon, Lawrence. Akbar. London: Nelson Press, 1939.

Biswas, Atreyi. The Political History of the Hunas in India. Columbia, Mo.: South Asia Books, 1973.

Blunt, Edward. The I. C. S.: The Indian Civil Service.
London: Faber & Faber, 1937.

Bose, N. S. History of the Candellas of Jejakabhukti. Calcutta: Firma K. K. Mukhopadhyay, 1956.

_____. The Indian Awakening and Bengal. Calcutta:
Firma K. L. Mukhopadhyay, 1960.

_____. The Indian National Movement: An Outline.
Thompson, Conn.: Interculture, 1965.

Bose, Subhas Chandra. Netaji's Life and Writings. 2 vols.
Calcutta: Thacker Spink, 1948.

Boulger, Demetrius. Lord William Bentinck. Oxford:
Clarendon Press, 1897.

Bourke-White, Margaret. Half-Way to Freedom. New
York: Simon & Schuster, 1949.

Bowers, Faubion. The Dance in India. New York: Columbia University Press, 1953.

Bradshaw, John. Sir Thomas Munro and the British of
Madras Presidency. Oxford: Clarendon Press, 1894.

Brecher, Michael. The Struggle for Kashmir. New York:
Oxford University Press, 1953.

_____. Nehru: A Political Biography. London: Oxford
University Press, 1959.

Brown, C. J. The Coins of India. London: Oxford University Press, 1922.

Brown, D. M. The Nationalist Movement: Indian Political
Thought from Manu to Gandhi. Berkeley: University of
California Press, 1961.

_____ . The White Umbrella: Indian Political Thought
from Manu to Gandhi. Berkeley: University of California Press, 1953.

Brown, Hilton. The Sahibs. London: W. Hodge, 1948.

Brown, Leslie W. The Indian Christians of St. Thomas.
Cambridge: Cambridge University Press, 1956.

Brown, Percy. Indian Architecture. Bombay: Taraporevala, 1956.

Buchanan, Francis H. Journey from Madras Through the
Countries of Mysore, Canara, and Malabar. 3 vols.
New York: AMS Press, 1807 (reprint).

Buckland, Charles E. Dictionary of Indian Biography. London: Swan Sonnenschein, 1906.

Burgess, James. A Chronology of Indian History: Medieval
and Modern. Portland, Ore.: International Scholarly
Book Services, 1973.

Burnell, John. Bombay in the Days of Queen Anne. London: Hakluyt Society, 1933.

Busteed, Henry E. Echoes from Old Calcutta. London:
Thacker, 1908.

Campbell-Johnson, Alan. Mission with Mountbatten. New
York: Dutton, 1953.

Carstairs, G. Morris. The Twice-Born: A Study of a
Community of High Caste Hindus. Bloomington: Indiana
University Press, 1958.

Chacko, George K. India: Toward an Understanding. New
Haven, Conn.: College and University Press, 1959.

Chaitanya, Krishna. A New History of Sanskrit Literature.
New York: Asia Publishing House, 1962.

Chaladar, Haran C. Social Life in Ancient India. Calcutta: Susil Gupta, 1954.

Chand, Tara. History of the Freedom Movement in India. 3 vols. Delhi: Publications Division, 1961.

Chanda, Asok. Indian Administration. London: Allen & Unwin, 1958.

Chatterjee, Satischandra, and D. M. Datta. An Introduction to Indian Philosophy. Calcutta: University of Calcutta, 1954.

Chatterji, Suniti Kumar. Languages and Literatures of Modern India. Calcutta: Bengal Publishers, 1963.

Chattopadhyaya, Sudhaker. Early History of North India. Calcutta: Progressive Publishers, 1958.

_____. The Sakas in India. Santiniketan: Viswa Bharati, 1955.

Chaudhuri, Nirad C. Autobiography of an Unknown Indian. New York: Macmillan, 1951.

_____. Intellectual in India. Mystic, Conn.: Verry, 1970.

Chaudhuri, Sashi B. Civil Disturbances During the British Rule in India, 1765-1857. Calcutta: World Press, 1955.

Chavarria-Aguilar, Oscar L. Traditional India. Englewood Cliffs, N. J.: Prentice-Hall, 1964.

Chirol, Valentine. India. London: E Benn, 1926.

_____. Indian Unrest. London: Macmillan, 1910.

Chopra, Pran Nath. Some Aspects of Society and Culture During the Mughal Age. Agra: S. L. Agarwala, 1955.

_____. Uncertain India: A Political Profile of Two Decades of Freedom. Cambridge, Mass.: M. I. T. Press, 1969.

_____. Who's Who of Indian Martyrs. 2 vols. Columbia, Mo.: South Asia Books, 1971-72.

Cohn, Bernard. India: The Social Anthropology of a Civilization. Englewood Cliffs, N.J.: Prentice-Hall, 1971.

Commissariat, M. Sorabshah. A History of Gujarat. 3 vols. Bombay: Orient Longmans, 1938-57.

Correia-Alfonso, John. Jesuit Letters and Indian History, 1542-1773. New York: Oxford University Press, 1969.

Cosmas "Indicopleustes". Topographia Christiana. London: Hakluyt Society, 1897.

Crane, Robert. The History of India: Its Study and Interpretation. Washington, D.C.: Service Center for Teachers of History, 1958.

Crooke, W. The North-Western Provinces of India: Their History, Ethnology and Administration. New York: Oxford University Press, 1973 (reprint).

Cumming, John, ed. Revealing India's Past. London: India Society, 1939.

Cunningham, Alexander. The Ancient Geography of India. Calcutta: Chuckervertty Chatterjee, 1924.

Cunningham, Joseph D. A History of the Sikhs. Delhi: S. Chand, 1955.

Curzon, George N. British Government in India. 2 vols. London: Cassell, 1925.

Dalton, Edward T. Tribal History of Eastern India. New York: International Publications Service, 1974 (reprint).

Daniélou, Alain. Northern Indian Music. 2 vols. London: C. Johnson and Halcyon Press, 1949; 1954.

Danvers, Frederick C. The Portuguese in India. 2 vols. London: W. H. Allen, 1894.

Das, Harihar. The Norris Embassy to Aurangzeb. Calcutta: Firma K. L. Mukhopadhyay, 1959.

Das, Santosh Kumar. The Education System of the Ancient Hindus. Calcutta: S. K. Das, 1930.

Das Gupta, Anil Chandra, ed. The Days of John Company. Calcutta: Superintendent Government Printing, 1959.

Dasgupta, Surendra Nath. Hindu Mysticism. New York: Ungar, 1959.

_____. A History of Indian Philosophy. 5 vols. Cambridge: Cambridge University Press, 1922-55.

Datta, Kalinkinkar. The Dutch in Bengal and Bihar. Patna: University of Patna, 1948.

Davids, Thomas W. Rhys. Buddhist India. Calcutta: Susil Gupta, 1957.

Davies, Alfred M. Clive of Plassey. New York: Scribner's, 1939.

DeBary, William T., et al. Sources of Indian Tradition. New York: Columbia University Press, 1958.

Derrett, J. Duncan M. The Hoysalas: A Medieval Indian Royal Family. London: Oxford University Press, 1957.

Deshpande, Pandurang G. Gandhiana: A Bibliography of Gandhian Literature. Ahmadabad: Navajivan, 1948.

De Souza, J. P. and C. M. Kulkarni, eds. Historiography in Indian Languages. Columbia, Mo.: South Asia Books, 1972.

Dey, Nundolal. The Geographical Dictionary of Ancient and Medieval India. London: Luzac, 1927.

Dhanapala, D. B. Eminent Indians. Bombay: Nalanda, 1947.

Dikshiter, V. R. Ramachandra. Gupta Polity. Madras: University of Madras, 1952.

_____. Mauryan Polity. Madras: University of Madras, 1953.

_____. Pre-Historic South India. Madras: University of Madras, 1951.

_____. War in Ancient India. Madras: Macmillan, 1948.

Diver, Katherine H. Royal India. Freeport, N. Y. : Books for Libraries, 1942.

D'Mello, Ralph. Rhythms of India. Thompson, Conn. : Interculture, 1971.

Dodwell, Henry H. Dupleix and Clive: The Beginning of an Empire. London: Methuen, 1920.

_____. The Nabobs of Madras. London: Williams & Norgate, 1926.

_____, ed. The Cambridge History of India. 6 vols. Cambridge: Cambridge University Press, 1922-53.

Dowson, John A. A Classical Dictionary of Hindu Mythology, and Religion, Geography, History, and Literature. London: Routledge & Kegan Paul, 1961 (reprint).

Dubois, Jean A. Hindu Manners, Customs and Ceremonies. Oxford: Clarendon Press, 1928.

Duff, James G. History of the Mahrattas. 2 vols. London: Oxford University Press, 1921.

Duff, Mabel C. Chronology of Indian History from the Earliest Times to the Beginning of the 16th Century. Portland, Ore. : International Scholarly Book Services, 1973.

Du Jarric, Father Pierre. Akbar and the Jesuits. New York: Harper, 1926.

Dutt, Romesh C. The Economic History of India Under Early British Rule. Delhi: Ministry of Information, 1960.

_____. A History of Civilization in Ancient India. 2 vols. Columbia, Mo. : South Asia Books, 1972 (reprint).

Edwardes, Michael. British India, 1772-1947: A Survey of the Nature and Effects of Alien Rule. New York: Taplinger, 1968.

_____ . Glorious Sahibs: The Romantic as Empire Builder, 1799-1838. New York: Taplinger, 1969.

_____ . The Necessary Hell. London: Cassell, 1958.

_____ . The Orchid House: Splendours and Miseries of the Kings of Oudh, 1827-1857. London: Casell, 1960.

_____ . Plassey: The Founding of an Empire. New York: Taplinger, 1970.

Edwardes, Stephen M. Babur, Diarist and Despot. London: A. M. Philpot, 1926.

_____ and H. L. O. Garrett. Mughal Rule in India. Delhi: S. Chand, 1956.

Elliot, Henry M. , ed. A History of India as Told by Its Own Historians. 31 vols. Calcutta: Susil Gupta, 1952-59 (reprint).

Elwin, Verrier. The Tribal Art of Middle India. Bombay: Oxford University Press, 1951.

Embree, Ainslee T. Charles Grant and British Rule in India. New York: Columbia University Press, 1962.

Erskine, William. History of India Under the First Two Sovereigns of the House of Taimur: Baber and Humayun. 2 vols. Columbia, Mo. : South Asia Books, 1973 (reprint).

Fabri, Charles. A History of Indian Dress. Calcutta: Orient Longmans, 1961.

_____ . An Introduction to Indian Architecture. New York: Asia Publishing House, 1962.

Farquhar, John Nicol. Modern Religious Movements in India. New York: Macmillan, 1915.

_____ . An Outline of the Religious Literature of India. London: Oxford University Press, 1920.

Faruki, Zahir-un-din. Aurangzeb and his Times. Bombay: Taraporevala, 1935.

Fawcett, Charles, ed. The English Factories in India, 1670-1684. 4 vols. Oxford: Clarendon Press, 1936-55.

Feiling, Keith G. Warren Hastings. London: Macmillan, 1954.

Felton, Monica. I Meet Rajaji. New York: St. Martin's, 1962.

Festivals of India. Thompson, Conn.: Interculture, 1968.

Filliozat, Jean. Political History of India. Calcutta: Susil Gupta, 1957.

Firishta, Muhammad Kasim. History of the Rise of Muhammadan Power in India. Calcutta: Susil Gupta, 1958 (reprint).

Fischel, Walter Joseph. The Jews in India. Jerusalem: Ben Zvi Institute, 1960.

Fischer, Louis. The Life of Mahatma Gandhi. New York: Harper, 1950.

Fitze, Kenneth. Twilight of the Maharajahs. Mystic, Conn.: Verry, 1970.

Forrest, George. The Life of Lord Clive. 2 vols. London: Cassell, 1918.

Forster, E. M. The Hill of Devi. New York: Harcourt, Brace, 1953.

_____. A Passage to India. New York: Harcourt, Brace, 1924.

Foster, William, ed. England's Quest of Eastern Trade. London: A & C Black, 1933.

_____, ed. Early Travels in India. London: Oxford University Press, 1921.

_____. English Factories in India, 1618-1669. 13 vols. Oxford: Clarendon Press, 1906-1927.

Fraser, Robert W. British India. Freeport, N.Y.: Books for Libraries, 1972 (reprint).

_____. Literary History of India. New York: Haskell,
1970 (reprint).

Fryer, John. An Account of East India and Persia. 3 vols.
London: Hakluyt Society, 1909-1915.

Furber, Holden. Indian Governor Generalship. Cambridge,
Mass. : Harvard University Press, 1953.

_____. John Company at Work. Cambridge, Mass. :
Harvard University Press, 1948.

Gaer, Joseph. The Fables of India. Boston: Little,
Brown, 1955.

Gandhi, Mohandas Karamchand. An Autobiography; or, The
Story of My Experiments with Truth. Boston: Beacon
Press, 1957.

_____. The Collected Works of Mahatma Gandhi. Delhi:
Publications Division, 1958- .

_____. The Gandhi Reader. Edited by H. A. Jack.
Bloomington: Indiana University Press, 1956.

_____. Hind Swaraj; or, Indian Home Rule. Ahmadabad:
Navajivan, 1946.

_____. Mahatma Gandhi: His Own Story. Edited by
C. F. Andrews. New York: Macmillan, 1930.

Ganguly, D. C. History of the Paramara Dynasty. Dacca:
Dacca University, 1943.

Gargi, Balwant. Theatre in India. New York: Theatre
Arts, 1962.

Garratt, Geoffrey T. , ed. The Legacy of India. London:
Oxford University Press, 1962.

Garrett, John A. A Classical Dictionary of India. New
York: International Publications Service, 1971 (reprint).

Gascoigne, Bambur. Great Moghuls. New York: Harper,
1971.

Gazetteer of India. 2 vols. New Delhi: Ministry of Education, 1974.

Ghoshal, Upendra Nath. History of Indian Political Ideas: The Ancient Period and the Period of Transition to the Middle Ages. New York: Oxford University Press, 1959.

_____. Studies in Indian History and Culture. Bombay: Orient Longmans, 1957.

Ghurye, Govind S. Indian Costume. Bombay: Popular Book Depot, 1951.

Giles, Herbert A. The Travels of Fa-Hsien. London: Routledge & Kegan Paul, 1956.

Godden, Jon, and Rumer Godden. Siva's Pigeons: An Experience of India. New York: Viking, 1972.

Goetz, Herman. India: Five Thousand Years of Indian Art. New York: Crown, 1959.

Gokhale, B. G. Ancient India: History and Culture. New York: Asia Publishing House, 1960.

_____. The Indian View of History. Bombay: Asia Publishing House, 1961.

Golant, William. The Long Afternoon: British India. New York: St. Martin's, 1975.

Gopal, Ram. British Rule in India: An Assessment. New York: Asia Publishing House, 1963.

_____. How the British Occupied Bengal. New York: Asian Publishing House, 1962.

_____. Indian Muslims: A Political History. New York: Asia Publishing House, 1959.

_____. Lokamanya Tilak. Bombay: Asia Publishing House, 1956.

Gopal, Sarvepalli. British Policy in India, 1858-1905. New York: Cambridge University Press, 1966.

_____ . The Vice-Royalty of Lord Ripon, 1880-1884. London: Oxford University Press, 1953.

Gopalan, R. History of the Pallavas of Kanchi. Madras: University of Madras, 1928.

Gordon, Leonard A. Bengal: The Nationalist Movement, 1876-1940. New York: Columbia University Press, 1974.

_____ and Barbara S. Miller. Syllabus of Indian Civilization. New York: Columbia University Press, 1971.

Grenard, Fernand. Baber, First of the Mughals. New York: R. M. McBride, 1930.

Grey, C. European Adventurers of Northern India, 1785-1849. Columbia, Mo.: South Asia Books, 1970.

Grierson, George A. Linguistic Survey of India. 11 vols. Calcutta: Central Publications Branch, 1903-1928.

Griffin, Lepel. Ranjit Singh. Oxford: Clarendon Press, 1911.

Griffiths, Percival J. The British Impact on India. London: Macdonald, 1952.

_____ . Modern India. London: Benn, 1962.

Gupta, Brijen K. India in English Fiction, 1800-1970: An Annotated Bibliography. Metuchen, N.J.: Scarecrow Press, 1973.

_____ . Sirajuddaullah and the East India Company, 1756-1757. Leiden: E. J. Brill, 1962.

Gupta, Hari Ram. History of the Sikhs. 3 vols. Lahore, Pakistan: Minerva Book Shop, 1939-1944.

Gwyer, Maurice, and A. Appadorai, eds. Speeches and Documents on the Indian Constitution, 1921-47. 2 vols. New York: Oxford University Press, 1957.

Habibullah, A. B. M. The Foundation of Muslim Rule in India. Allahabad: Central Book Dept., 1961.

Haq, Syed Moinul. A Short History of the Sultanate of Delhi. Karachi, Pakistan: H. M. Said, 1956.

Hardy, Peter. Historians of Medieval India. London: Luzac, 1960.

_____. Muslims of British India. New York: Cambridge University Press, 1973.

Harrison, Selig. India: The Most Dangerous Decade. Princeton, N. J. : Princeton University Press, 1960.

Hartmann, Horst. Political Parties in India. New York: International Publications Service, 1974.

Havell, Ernest B. Ancient and Medieval Architecture of India: A Study of Indo-Aryan Civilization. Mystic, Conn. : Verry, 1972 (reprint).

_____. The History of Aryan Rule in India. New York: International Publications Service, 1972 (reprint).

Hawkridge, Emma. Indian Gods and Kings: The Story of a Living Past. Freeport, N. Y. : Books for Libraries, 1935 (reprint).

Hayavadana Rao, Conjeevaram. History of Mysore, 1399-1799. 3 vols. Bangalore: Superintendent Government Printing, 1943-1946.

Hazari (pseud. of Marcus Abraham Malik). Untouchable: The Autobiography of an Indian Outcaste. New York: Praeger, 1969.

Heathcote, T. A. The Indian Army, 1822-1922. New York: Hippocrene Books, 1974.

Heimsath, C. H. , and S. Mansingh. A Diplomatic History of Modern India. Mystic, Conn. : Verry, 1971.

Hiriyanna, Mysore. Outlines of Indian Philosophy. London: Allen & Unwin, 1949.

Hobbs, Lisa. India, India. New York: McGraw, 1967.

Hopkins, Edward Washburn. Ethics of India. New Haven, Conn. : Yale University Press, 1924.

_____. Religions of India. Mystic, Conn.: Verry, 1970.

Houlton, M. I. India, Land and People. New York: International Publications Service, 1974.

Hukkerikar, R. S., ed. Karnataka Darshana. Bombay: Popular Book Depot, 1955.

Humphreys, Christmas. A Popular Dictionary of Buddhism. London: Arco Publications, 1962.

Hunter, William W. A History of British India. 2 vols. London: Longmans, 1899-1900.

_____. The Marquess of Dalhousie. London: Oxford University Press, 1905.

Husain, Agha Mahdi. The Rise and Fall of Muhammad-bin Tughluq. London: Luzac, 1938.

Husain, Yusaf. Glimpses of Medieval Indian Culture. Bombay: Asia Publishing House, 1957.

Husaini, Abdul Qadir. Bahman Shah. Calcutta: Firma K. L. Mukhopadhyay, 1959.

Hutchins, F. Illusion of Permanence: British Imperialism in India. Princeton, N.J.: Princeton University Press, 1967.

Hutchinson, Lester. European Freebooters in Mogul India. New York: Asia Publishing House, 1964.

Huttenback, Robert A. British Relations with Sind, 1799-1843: An Anatomy of Imperialism. Berkeley: University of California Press, 1962.

Hutton, John H. Caste in India. Bombay: Oxford University Press, 1961.

Ibn Batuta. Ibn Batuta's Travels. 3 vols. London: Hakluyt Society, 1929-1962.

Ilbert, Courtenay P. Government of India. New York: Barnes and Noble, 1974.

Imlah, Albert H. Lord Ellenborough. London: Oxford University Press, 1939.

Imperial Gazetteer of India. 26 vols. Oxford, England: Clarendon Press, 1907-1909.

India: A Reference Annual. New Delhi: Ministry of Information, Annual.

Indian Institute of Public Administration. The Organization of the Government of India. Bombay: Asia Publishing House, 1958.

Ingham, Kenneth. Reformers in India, 1793-1833. Cambridge, England: Cambridge University Press, 1956.

Irvine, William. The Army of the Indian Mughals. New Delhi: Eurasia Publishing House, 1962 (reprint).

_____. Later Moguls. 2 vols. Calcutta: M. C. Sarkar, 1921-1922.

Iyengar, P. T. Srinivasa. History of the Tamils. Madras: C. Commeraswamy Naidu, 1929.

Jackson, Abraham K. History of India. 9 vols. New York: AMS Press, 1907 (reprint).

Jaffar, S. M. The Mughal Empire from Babur to Aurangzeb. Peshawar, Pakistan: S. M. Sadiq Khan, 1936.

Jagganarayanan, S. India Under Nehru. Mystic, Conn. : Verry, 1968.

Jahangir. Memoirs of Jahangir. 2 vols. London: Royal Asiatic Society, 1909-1914.

Jayaswal, K. P. Hindu Polity: A Constitutional History of India in Hindu Times. Bangalore: Bangalore Printing and Publishing, 1955.

_____. History of India, A. D. 150-350. Lahore, Pakistan: Motilal Banarsidass, 1933.

Jindal, K. B. A History of Hindi Literature. Allahabad: Kitab Mahal, 1955.

281   Bibliography

Jolly, Julius. Hindu Law and Custom. Calcutta: Greater India Society, 1928.

Jones, M. E. Monckton. Warren Hastings in Bengal, 1772-1774. Oxford, England: Clarendon Press, 1918.

Joshi, Baburao. Understanding Indian Music. New York: Asia Publishing House, 1963.

Joshi, Gulabbhai N. Constitution of India. Mystic, Conn.: Verry, 1966.

Judd, Denis. The British Raj. New York: Putnam, 1973.

Kabir, Humayun. Indian Heritage. New York: Asia Publishing House, 1972.

Kaegi, Adolf. Life in Ancient India. Calcutta: Susil Gupta, 1950.

Kalhana. Rajatarangini. London: A Probsthain, 1935.

Kanakasabhai, V. The Tamils Eighteen Hundred Years Ago. Tirunelveli: South India Saiva Siddhanta Works Publishing Society, 1956.

Kapur, Anup C. Constitutional History of India, 1765-1970. Mystic, Conn.: Verry, 1970.

Karim, Abdul. Social History of the Muslims in Bengal. Dacca: Asiatic Society of Pakistan, 1959.

Karmarkar, A. P. A Cultural History of the Karnataka. Dharwar: Karnataka Vidyanardhaka Sangha, 1947.

Kautilya. Arthasastra. Translated by R. Ramasastry. Mysore: Sri Raghuveer Printing Press, 1956.

Kaye, John W., and G. B. Malleson. History of the Indian Mutiny. 6 vols. London: Longmans, 1897-98.

Keay, Frank E. A History of Education in India and Pakistan. London: Oxford University Press, 1959.

_____. A History of Hindi Literature. Calcutta: YMCA Publishing House, 1960.

Keene, H. G. Hindustan Under the Free Lances, 1770-1820. New York: Barnes & Noble, 1972.

Keith, Arthur B. A Constitutional History of India, 1600-1935. London: Methuen, 1936.

_____. A History of Sanskrit Literature. London: Oxford University Press, 1953.

_____. The Sanskrit Drama. Oxford, England: Clarendon Press, 1924.

Khan, Mohibbul Hasan. History of Tipu Sultan. Calcutta: Bibliophile, 1951.

Khan, Yusuf Husain. The First Nizam. New York: Asia Publishing House, 1962.

Kincaid, Charles A., and R. B. Parasnis. A History of the Maratha People. 3 vols. London: Oxford University Press, 1931.

Kling, Blair. The Blue Mutiny. Berkeley: University of California Press, 1966.

Kohli, P. A Short History of Akbar. Delhi: S. Chand, 1949.

Kosambi, Damodar D. An Introduction to the Study of Indian History. Bombay: Popular Book Depot, 1956.

Kramrisch, Stella. The Art of India Through the Ages. New York: · Phaidon, 1954.

Kripalani, Krishna R. Tagore. New York: Grove Press, 1962.

Krishna, Bal. Commercial Relations Between India and England. London: Routledge & Kegan Paul, 1924.

Krishnaswami Aiyangar, Sakottai. South India and Her Muhammadan Invaders. London: Oxford University Press, 1921.

Kulkarni, V. B. India and Pakistan: A Historical Survey of Hindu-Muslim Relations. New York: International Publications Service, 1974.

Kurian, George B. T. Dictionary of Indian English. Madras: Indian Universities Press, 1966.

Lach, Donald F. India in the Eyes of Europe in the Sixteenth Century. Chicago: University of Chicago Press, 1965.

Ladendorf, Janice M. Revolt in India, 1857-58. New York: International Publications Service, 1966.

Lahiri, Mohan R. The Annexation of Assam. Calcutta: General Printers, 1955.

Lajpat Rai, Lala. The Arya Samaj. London: Longmans, 1915.

_____. Young India, An Interpretation and a History of the Nationalist Movement from Within. New York: B. W. Huebsch, 1917.

Lal, Kanwar. Holy Cities of India. Delhi: Asia Press, 1961.

Lal, S. K. History of the Khaljis. Allahabad: Indian Press, 1950.

Lamb, Alastair. McMahon Line: A Study in the Relations Between India, China, and Tibet, 1904-1914. 2 vols. Toronto: University of Toronto Press, 1966.

Lamb, Beatrice. India: A World in Transition. New York: Praeger, 1963.

Lambrick, Hugh T. Sir Charles Napier and Sind. Oxford: Clarendon Press, 1952.

Lane-Poole, Stanley. Aurangzeb. Delhi: S. Chand, 1957 (reprint).

_____. Babar. Delhi: S. Chand, 1957 (reprint).

_____. Medieval India Under Muhammadan Rule. 2 vols. Calcutta: Susil Gupta, 1951.

_____, ed. Medieval India from Contemporary Sources. Bombay: K & J Cooper, 1920.

Law, Bimala C.   Historical Geography of Ancient India.
Paris: Société Asiatique de Paris, 1954.

_____ . Tribes in Ancient India.   Poona: Bhandarkar
Oriental Research Institute, 1943.

Leasor, James.   The Red Fort.   New York: Harcourt,
Brace, 1957.

Lee-Warner, William.   Life of the Marquis of Dalhousie.
2 vols. London: Macmillan, 1904.

_____ . The Native States of India.   London: Macmillan,
1910.

Locke, John C. , ed.   The First Englishmen in India.   London: George Routledge, 1930.

Lohuizen, Jan van.   The Dutch East India Company and Mysore.   The Hague: N. Nijhoff, 1961.

Lord, John.   Maharajahs.   New York: Random House, 1971.

Lovett, Verney.   A History of the Indian Nationalist Movement.   Columbia, Mo. : South Asia Books, 1972.

Lumby, Esmond W. R.   The Transfer of Power in India,
1945-47.   New York: Praeger, 1954.

Lyall, Alfred C.   The Rise and Expansion of British Dominion in India.   London: John Murray, 1910.

Lyon, Jean.   Just Half a World Away.   New York: Crowell,
1954.

Mabbet, Ian W.   A Short History of India.   New York:
Praeger, 1970.

McCrindle, John W.   Ancient India as Described by Megasthenes and Arrian.   London: Trubner, 1877.

_____ . Ancient India as Described by Ptolemy.   Calcutta:
Chuckervertty, Chatterjee, 1927.

_____ . The Invasion of India by Alexander the Great.
Westminster, England: A Constable, 1896.

McDermott, Robert A. , and V. S. Naravane, eds. The Spirit of Modern India. New York: Crowell, 1974.

Macdonnell, Arthur A. A History of Sanskrit Literature. London: W. Heinemann, 1905.

_____. India's Past. Varanasi: Motilal Banarsidass, 1956 (reprint).

_____. Vedic Mythology. Strassbourg: Trubner, 1897.

Maclagen, Edward D. The Jesuits and the Great Mogul. London: Burns, Oates & Washbourne, 1932.

Mahadevan, T. M. P. Outlines of Hinduism. Bombay: Chetana, 1960.

Mahalingam, T. V. Administration and Social Life under Vijayanagar. Madras: Madras University, 1940.

Mahajan, Vidya D. Muslim Rule in India. Mystic, Conn.: Verry, 1965.

Mahar, Michael J. India: A Critical Bibliography. Tucson: University of Arizona Press, 1964.

Mahtab, Harekrushna. The History of Orissa. Lucknow: Lucknow University, 1957.

Major, Richard H. , ed. India in the Fifteenth Century. London: Hakluyt Society, 1857.

Majumdar, Asoke Kumar. The Chalukyas of Gujarat. Bombay: Bharatiya Vidya Bhavan, 1956.

Majumdar, Bimal Kanti. The Military System in Ancient India. Calcutta: Firma K. L. Mukhopadhyay, 1960.

Majumdar, Dhirendranath. Races and Cultures of India. New York: Asia Publishing House, 1961.

Majumdar, Manjulal, ed. The Historical and Cultural Chronology of Gujarat. Baroda: M. S. University of Baroda, 1960.

Majumdar, Ramesh C. , ed. Ancient India. Delhi: Motilal Banarsidass, 1960.

_____. The History and Culture of the Indian People. 10 vols. Bombay: Bharatiya Vidya Bhavan, 1951-1960.

_____. History of the Freedom Movement in India, 1919-1945. Mystic, Conn.: Verry, 1963.

_____. The Sepoy Mutiny and the Revolt of 1857. Calcutta: Firma K. L. Mukhopadhyay, 1957.

_____, ed. The Classical Accounts of India. Calcutta: Firma K. L. Mukhopadhyay, 1960.

_____, H. C. Raychaudhuri, and K. K. Datta. An Advanced History of India. London: Macmillan, 1948.

_____, and Jadunath Sarkar. The History of Bengal. 2 vols. Vol. 1 Dacca: Dacca University, 1943; Vol. 2 Calcutta: Calcutta University, 1948.

Malcolm, John. A Memoir of Central India. 2 vols. London: Parbury, Allen, 1832.

Malleson, George B. The Decisive Battles of India. Portland, Ore.: International Scholarly Book Services, 1974.

_____. History of the French in India. London: W. H. Allen, 1893.

Manrique, Sebastian. The Travels of Sebastian Manrique. 2 vols. London: Hakluyt Society, 1926-27.

Manucci, Niccolò. Storia do Mogor; or, Mogul India. 4 vols. London: John Murray, 1906-08.

Marshall, Sir John H. A Guide to Taxila. Cambridge: Cambridge University Press, 1961.

_____. Mohenjo-Daro and the Indus Civilization. 3 vols. London: A. Probsthain, 1931.

Martineau, Alfred A. Bussy in the Deccan. Pondicherry: Bibliothèque Publique, 1941.

Mason, Philip. The Men Who Ruled India, by Philip Woodruff [pseud.]. 2 vols. New York: St. Martin's, 1954.

Masson-Oursel, Paul, Wilman Grabowska, and P. Stern.

287   Bibliography

Ancient India and Indian Civilization. London: Kegan
Paul Trench Trubner, 1934.

Mayer, Adrian C. Land and Society in Malabar. Bombay:
Oxford University Press, 1952.

Mayo, Katherine. Mother India. New York: Harcourt,
Brace, 1927.

Meherally, Yusuf. Leaders of India. 2 vols. Bombay:
Padma, 1942.

Mehta, Rustam J. The Handicrafts and Industrial Arts of
India. Bombay: Taraporevala, 1960.

Mehta, Ved. Portrait of India. New York: Farrar,
Straus, 1970.

Menon, K. P. S. Many Worlds: An Autobiography. New
York: Oxford University Press, 1965.

Menon, V. P. The Story of the Integration of the Indian
States. New York: Macmillan, 1956.

_____. The Transfer of Power in India. Princeton,
N. J. : Princeton University Press, 1957.

Mersey, Clive B. Viceroys and Governor Generals of India,
1757-1947. London: John Murray, 1949.

Metcalf, T. R. Modern India: An Interpretative Anthology.
New York: Macmillan, 1971.

Mill, James. History of British India. 10 vols. London:
J. Madden, 1858.

Minakshi, Cadambi. Administration and Social Life Under
the Pallavas. Madras: Madras University, 1938.

Mishra, Vibhuti B. Gurjara Pratiharas and their Times.
Mystic, Conn. : Verry, 1966.

Misra, Satish Chandra. Rise of Muslim Power in Gujarat.
New York: Asia Publishing House, 1963.

Mitchell, J. F. North-East Frontier of India. Mystic,
Conn. : Verry, 1973.

Mitra, Sisir Kumar.   Early Rulers of Khajuraho.   Calcutta:
     Firma K. L. Mukhopadhyay, 1958.

_____.   Evolution of India: Its Meaning.   Thompson,
     Conn. :   Interculture, 1968.

Mohan, Jag, ed.   Twenty-Five Years of Indian Independence.
     Portland, Ore. :   International Scholarly Book Services,
     1973.

Monserrate, Antonio.   The Commentary of Father Monser-
     rate.   London: Oxford University Press, 1922.

Montague, Edwin S.   An Indian Diary.   London: W. Heine-
     mann, 1930.

Mookerjee, Girija K.   History of Indian National Congress.
     New York: International Publications Service, 1974.

Mookerji, Radha Kumud.   Ancient Indian Education.   London:
     Macmillan, 1951.

_____.   Asoka.   London: Macmillan, 1955.

_____.   Chandragupta Maurya and His Times.   Delhi:
     Motilal Banarsidass, 1960.

_____.   The Gupta Empire.   Bombay: Hind Kitabs, 1959.

_____.   Harsha.   New York: Oxford University Press,
     1925.

_____.   Men and Thought in Ancient India.   Bombay:
     Hind Kitabs, 1957.

Moon, Penderel.   Divide and Quit.   Berkeley: University of
     California Press, 1962.

_____.   Gandhi and Modern India.   New York: Norton,
     1969.

_____.   Strangers in India.   New York: Reynal & Hitch-
     cock, 1945.

_____.   Warren Hastings and British India.   New York:
     Collier, 1962.

Moraes, Frank R. India Today. New York: Macmillan,
1960.

_____. Jawaharlal Nehru: A Biography. New York:
Macmillan, 1956.

_____. Witness to an Era. New York: Holt, 1971.

_____, and Edward Howe. John Kenneth Galbraith Intro-
duces India. New York: McGraw, 1974.

Moraes, G. M. History of Christianity in India from Early
Times to St. Francis Xavier. New York: Asia Publishing House, 1964.

Moreland, William H. From Akbar to Aurangzeb. London:
Macmillan, 1923.

_____. India at the Death of Akbar. London: Macmil-
lan, 1920.

_____, ed. Relations of Golconda in the Early 17th Cen-
tury. London: Hakluyt Society, 1931.

_____, and A. C. Chatterjee. A Short History of India.
London: Longmans, 1957.

_____, and P. Geyl. Jahangir's India. Columbia, Mo. :
South Asia Books, 1972.

Morison, John Lyle. Lawrence of Lucknow, 1806-1857:
The Life of Sir Henry Lawrence. London: George Bell,
1934.

Morris-Jones, Wyndraeth H. Government and Politics of
India. New York: Hillary, 1971.

_____. Parliament in India. Philadelphia: University of
Pennsylvania Press, 1957.

Mosley, Leonard. Curfew on Olympus: The Last Days of
British Rule in India. New York: Asia Publishing
House, 1961.

Muir, Ramsey. Making of British India, 1756-1858. New
York: Oxford University Press, 1969.

Mujeeb, M.   Islamic Influence on Indian Society.   Mystic,
      Conn. :   Verry, 1972.

Muller, F. Max.   The Six Systems of Indian Philosophy.
      London: Longmans, 1919.

Mundy, Peter.   The Travels of Peter Mundy.   5 vols.
      London: Hakluyt Society, 1907-36.

Munshi, K. M.   Gujarat and Its Literature.   Bombay:
      Bharatiya Vidya Bhavan, 1954.

Murray, Stark.   India, Which Century?   New York: Inter-
      national Publications Service, 1967.

Nag, Jamuna.   Raja Rammohun Roy: India's Great Religious
      Reformer.   Columbia, Mo. :   South Asia Books, 1972.

Nair, Pyarelal.   Mahatma Gandhi--The Last Phase.   2 vols.
      Ahmadabad: Navajivan, 1956-58.

Nambiar, O. K.   Kunjalis: Admirals of Calicut.   New York:
      Asia Publishing House, 1963.

Nanda, Bal Ram.   Mahatma Gandhi: A Biography.   Boston:
      Beacon, 1959.

_____. The Nehrus, Motilal and Jawaharlal.   New York:
      John Day, 1962.

_____, and V. C. Joshi, eds.   Studies in Modern Indian
      History.   New York: Kennikat, 1972.

Narain, A. K.   The Indo-Greeks.   Oxford: Clarendon
      Press, 1957.

Natarajan, S.   A Century of Social Reform in India.   Bom-
      bay: Asia Publishing House, 1963.

_____. A History of the Press in India.   New York:
      Asia Publishing House, 1963.

Nehru, Jawaharlal.   A Bunch of Old Letters.   Bombay:
      Asia Publishing House, 1960.

_____. The Discovery of India.   New York: John Day,
      1946.

_____ . Independence and After: A Collection of Speeches,
1946-1949. New York: John Day, 1950.

_____ . Toward Freedom: The Autobiography of Jawaharlal Nehru. Boston: Beacon Press, 1958.

_____ . The Unity of India: Collected Writings, 1937-40.
New York: John Day, 1948.

The New History of the Indian People. 2 vols. Lahore,
Pakistan: Motilal Banarsidass, 1946.

Nilakanta Sastri, K. A. The Colas. 2 vols. Madras:
University of Madras, 1955.

_____ . History of India. 3 vols. Madras: S. Viswana-
than, 1950-2.

_____ . A History of South India. London: Oxford University Press, 1958.

_____ . The Pandyan Kingdom. London: Luzac, 1929.

_____ . The Sangam: Its Cult and Cultures. Thompson,
Conn. : Interculture, 1974.

_____ , ed. A Comprehensive History of India. 12 vols.
Bombay: Orient Longmans, 1957.

Niyogi, Roma. The History of the Gahadvala Dynasty. Calcutta: Oriental Book Agency, 1959.

Oaten, Edward F. European Travellers in India During the
15th, 16th and 17th Centuries. London: Kegan Paul
Trench Trubner, 1909.

O'Malley, Lewis S. S. Indian Caste Customs. Cambridge,
England: Cambridge University Press, 1932.

_____ . The Indian Civil Service, 1601-1930. London:
John Murray, 1931.

_____ . Popular Hinduism: The Religion of the Masses.
New York: Johnson Reprint, 1971 (reprint).

_____ , ed. Modern India and the West. London: Oxford
University Press, 1941.

Bibliography   292

Oswell, G. D. , ed. Sketches of Rulers of India. 3 vols.
Columbia, Mo. : South Asia Books, 1972.

Owen, Sidney J. The Fall of the Mogul Empire. Varanasi:
Chowkhamba Sanskrit Studies, 1960 (reprint).

Pal, Bipin Chandra. Memories of My Life and Times. 2
vols. Calcutta: Modern Book Agency, 1932-51.

Pal, Dharma. Administration of Sir John Lawrence in India,
1864-1869. Simla: Minerva Book Shop, 1952.

Palande, Manohar R. Introduction to the Indian Constitution.
New York: Oxford University Press, 1956.

Pandey, Raj Bali. Vikramaditya of Ujjayini. Varanasi:
Shatadala Prakashana, 1951.

Pandey, Swadh Bihari. The First Afghan Empire in India.
Calcutta: Bookland, 1956.

Panikkar, Kavalam M. The Foundations of New India.
London: George Allen & Unwin, 1963.

_____. Geographical Factors in Indian History. Bombay:
Bharatiya Vidya Bhavan, 1959.

_____. A History of Kerala. Annamalainagar: Anna-
malai University, 1960.

_____. Malabar and the Dutch. Bombay: Taraporevala,
1931.

_____. Studies in Indian History. New York: Asia Pub-
lishing House, 1968.

_____. A Survey of Indian History. Bombay: Asia Pub-
lishing House, 1962.

Pargiter, Frederick E. Ancient Historical Tradition. London: Oxford University Press, 1922.

Parikh, Narahari D. Sardar Vallabhbhai Patel. 2 vols.
Ahmadabad: Navajivan, 1953-56.

Park, Richard L. India's Political System. Englewood
Cliffs, N. J. : Prentice-Hall, 1968.

Pathak, V. S. Ancient Historians of India: A Study of His-
    torical Biographies. New York: Asia Publishing House,
    1966.

Pattabhi Sitaramayya, Bhogaraju. History of the Indian Na-
    tional Congress. 2 vols. Bombay: Padma, 1946-47.

Pelsaert, Francisco. Jahangir's India, The Remonstrantie
    of F. Pelsaert. Cambridge, England: W. Heffer, 1925.

Petech, Luciano. Northern India According to the Shui-
    Ching-Chu. Rome: Istituto Italiano per Medio ed Es-
    tremo Oriente, 1950.

Philips, Cyril H. The East India Company, 1784-1834.
    Manchester, England: Manchester University Press,
    1961.

_____. Historians of India, Pakistan, and Ceylon. Lon-
    don: Oxford University Press, 1961.

_____. India. New York: Hutchinson's University Li-
    brary, 1949.

_____, ed. The Evolution of India and Pakistan, 1858-
    1947. London: Oxford University Press, 1962.

_____, ed. Handbook of Oriental History. London:
    Royal Historical Society, 1951.

Piggott, Stuart. Prehistoric India. Harmondsworth, Eng-
    land: Penguin Books, 1961.

_____. Some Ancient Cities of India. London: Oxford
    University Press, 1945.

Pires, Edward A. The Maukharis. Madras: B. G. Paul,
    1934.

Polier, Antoine L. Shah Alam II and His Court. Calcutta:
    S. C. Sarkar, 1947.

Poonen, T. I. A Survey of the Rise of the Dutch Power in
    Malabar. Trivandrum: University of Travancore Press,
    1948.

Popley, Herbert A. The Music of India. Calcutta: YMCA
    Publishing House, 1950.

Prasad, Beni. History of Jahangir. London: Oxford University Press, 1930.

Prasad, G. K. Bureaucracy in India: A Sociological Study. Mystic, Conn.: Verry, 1974.

Prasad, Ishwari. History of Medieval India. Allahabad: Indian Press, 1933.

_____. India in the Eighteenth Century. Columbia, Mo.: South Asia Books, 1973.

_____. The Life and Times of Humayun. Bombay: Orient Longmans, 1956.

Prasad, Rajendra. At the Feet of Mahatma Gandhi. New York: Asia Publishing House, 1961.

_____. Autobiography. Bombay: Asia Publishing House, 1957.

_____. India Divided. Bombay: Hind Kitabs, 1946.

_____. Satyagraha in Champaran. Ahmadabad: Navajivan, 1949.

Prasad, Ram. Early English Travellers in India. Mystic, Conn.: Verry, 1965.

Prinsep, Henry T. History of the Military and Political Transactions in India During the Administration of the Marquess of Hastings. New York: Barnes & Noble, 1972 (reprint).

Puri, Baij Nath. The History of the Gurjara-Pratiharas. Bombay: Hind Kitabs, 1957.

_____. India Under the Kushanas. New York: Paragon, 1965.

Pylee, M. V. Constitutional Government in India. New York: Asia Publishing House, 1959.

Qanungo, Kalika Ranja. Dara Shukoh. Calcutta: S. C. Sarkar, 1952.

_____. Studies in Rajput History. Delhi: S. Chand, 1960.

Radhakrishnan, Sarvepalli. Indian Philosophy. 2 vols. London: George Allen & Unwin, 1958.

_____, and C. A. Moore. Our Heritage. Thompson, Conn.: Interculture, 1974.

_____ and _____. A Sourcebook in Indian Philosophy. Princeton, N. J.: Princeton University Press, 1957.

Rahim, Muhammad. History of the Afghans in India. Karachi: Pakistan Publishing House, 1961.

Raja, P. K. S. Medieval Kerala. Annamalainagar: Annamalai University, 1953.

Raju, Poola Tirupati. Telugu Literature. Bombay: International Book House, 1944.

Ramana Rao, M. V. A Short History of the Indian National Congress. Delhi: S. Chand, 1959.

Rama Rau, Shanta. Home to India. New York: Harper, 1945.

_____. This Is India. New York: Harper, 1954.

Ramasastry, R. The Origin of the Devanagiri Alphabet. New York: International Publications Service, 1974.

Ram Gopal and Serozh Dadachanji. Indian Dancing. London: Phoenix House, 1951.

Rammohun Roy, Raja. The English Works of Raja Rammohun Roy. 3 vols. Edited by K. Nag and D. Burman. Calcutta: Sadharan Brahmo Samaj, 1945-51.

Rao, B. S. India's Freedom Movement: Some Notable Figures. New York: Kennikat, 1972.

Rao, Bhaskara. Rudyard Kipling's India. Norman: University of Oklahoma Press, 1967.

Rao, M. Rama. Glimpses of Dekkan History. Calcutta: Orient Longmans, 1951.

Rapson, E. J.   Sources of Indian History.   New York:
    Ares, 1974.

Rawlinson, Hugh G.   The British Achievement in India.
    London: W. Hodge, 1948.

_____. Concise History of the Indian People.   New York:
    Oxford University Press, 1950.

_____. India: A Short Cultural History.   New York:
    Praeger, 1952.

_____. Intercourse Between India and the Western World.
    Cambridge, England: Cambridge University Press,
    1926.

Ray, H. C.   The Dynastic History of Northern India.   2
    vols. Calcutta: Calcutta University Press, 1931-36.

Ray, Sunil Chandra.   Early History and Culture of Kashmir.
    New Delhi: Munshi Lal Manohar Lal, 1957.

Raychaudhuri, Hemchandra.   Political History of Ancient In-
    dia. Calcutta: University of Calcutta, 1953.

Raychaudhuri, Rapan.   Jan Company in Coromandel, 1605-
    1690. The Hague: M. Nijhoff, 1962.

Reed, Stanley.   The India I Knew, 1897-1947.   London:
    Odhams, 1952.

Renou, Louis.   The Civilization of Ancient India.   Calcutta:
    Susil Gupta, 1959.

_____. Religions of Ancient India.   New York: DeGraff,
    1953 (reprint).

Reynolds, Reginald.   White Sahibs in India.   New York:
    John Day, 1937.

Rice, Edward P.   A History of Kanarese Literature.   Cal-
    cutta: Thacker, Spink, 1915.

Roberts, Paul E.   India Under Wellesley.   London: G. Bell,
    1929.

_____, and T. G. P. Spear.   History of British India.
    London: Oxford University Press, 1952.

Roe, Sir Thomas. The Embassy of Sir Thomas Roe in In-
    dia. Edited by William Foster. London: Oxford Uni-
    versity Press, 1926.

Ronaldshay, Earl of. The Life of Lord Curzon. 3 vols.
    London: E. Benn, 1928.

Rowland, Benjamin. The Art and Architecture of India.
    Baltimore: Penguin, 1956.

Roy, Jyotirmoy. History of Manipur. Calcutta: Firma K.
    L. Mukhopadhyay, 1958.

Roy, M. P. Origin, Growth and Suppression of the Pindaris.
    New York: International Publications Service, 1974.

Roy Choudhury, Makhanlal. The Din-i-Ilahi. Calcutta:
    University of Calcutta, 1941.

_____. The State and Religion in Mughal India. Calcutta:
    Indian Publishing Society, 1951.

Ruthnaswamy, Mariadas. Some Influences That Made the
    British Administrative System in India. London: Luzac,
    1939.

Saksena, Benarsi Prasad. History of Shah Jahan. Allaha-
    bad: Central Book Dept., 1962.

Saksena, Ram Babu. A History of Urdu Literature. Alla-
    habad: Ram Narain Lal, 1940.

Saletore, Bhasker Anand. Social and Political Life in the
    Vijayanagar Empire. 2 vols. Madras: B. G. Paul,
    1934.

Saletore, Rajaram N. Life in the Gupta Age. Bombay:
    Popular Book Depot, 1943.

Saraswati, S. K. A Survey of Indian Sculpture. Calcutta:
    Firma K. L. Mukhopadhyay, 1957.

Sardesai, Govind S. A New History of the Marathas. 3
    vols. Bombay: Phoenix Publications, 1948-56.

Sarkar, Jadunath. Fall of the Mughal Empire. 4 vols.
    Calcutta: M. C. Sarkar, 1932-50.

_____. History of Aurangzeb. 5 vols. Calcutta: M.
C. Sarkar, 1912-25.

_____. The India of Aurangzeb. Calcutta: Bose Broth-
ers, 1901.

_____. Military History of India. Calcutta: M. C.
Sarkar, 1960.

_____. Mughal Administration. Calcutta: M. C. Sar-
kar, 1952.

_____. Shivaji and His Times. Calcutta: M. C. Sarkar,
1961.

_____. A Short History of Aurangzeb. Calcutta: M. C.
Sarkar, 1962.

Satin, Nora. India in Modern English Fiction. New York:
Norwood Editions, 1973.

Saxena, K. M. The Military System of India, 1850-1900.
Columbia, Mo.: South Asia Books, 1974.

Schoff, Wilfred H., trans. The Periplus of the Erythraen
Sea. New York: Longmans, 1912.

Schweitzer, Albert. Indian Thought and Its Development.
Boston: Beacon, 1957.

Sen, Dinesh Chandra. History of Bengali Language and Literature. Calcutta: University of Calcutta, 1954.

Sen, Gertrude Emerson. The Pageant of India's History.
New York: Longmans, 1948.

_____. Voiceless India. New York: John Day, 1944.

Sen, S. P. The French in India, 1763-1816. Mystic, Conn.:
Verry, 1972.

_____. Historians and Historiography in Modern India.
Columbia: South Asia Books, 1973.

_____, ed. Dictionary of National Biography. 4 vols.
Columbia: South Asia Books, 1974.

Sen, Sukumar. History of Bengali Literature. New Delhi: Sahiya Akademi, 1960.

Sen, Surendra Nath. Eighteen Fifty Seven. New Delhi: Ministry of Information, 1957.

_____. Indian Travels of Careri and Thevanot. Delhi: National Archives, 1949.

Sencourt, Robert. India in English Literature. New York: Kennikat, 1970.

Sewell, Robert. A Forgotten Empire. London: Swan Sonnenschein, 1924.

Shafaat Ahmad Khan. Sources of the History of British India in the 17th Century. Totowa, N. J. : Rowman & Littlefield, 1974.

Shafer, Robert. Ethnography of Ancient India. Weisbaden: Otto Harassowitz, 1954.

Sharma, B. N. Social and Cultural History of Northern India c1000-1200 A. D. New York: Humanities, 1972.

Sharma, Chandradhar. Indian Philosophy: A Critical Survey. New York: Barnes & Noble, 1962.

Sharma, Dasharatha. Early Chauhan Dynasties. Delhi: S. Chand, 1959.

Sharma, H. D. Indian Reference Sources. Portland, Ore. : International Scholarly Book Services, 1972.

Sharma, Jagdish Saran. Encyclopedia of India's Struggle for Freedom. Columbia, Mo. : South Asia Books, 1971.

_____. Indian National Congress: A Descriptive Bibliography of India's Struggle for Freedom. Delhi: S. Chand, 1959.

_____. Jawaharlal Nehru: A Descriptive Bibliography. Delhi: S. Chand, 1955.

_____. Mahatma Gandhi: A Descriptive Bibliography. Delhi: S. Chand, 1955.

Bibliography   300

_____. The National Biographical Dictionary of India. New York: International Publications Service, 1972.

_____. The National Geographical Dictionary of India. New York: International Publications Service, 1972.

Sharma, Sri Ram. A Bibliography of Mughal India. Bombay: Karnatak Publishing House, 1942.

_____. The Crescent in India. Bombay: Hind Kitabs, 1954.

Shastri, Gaurinath. A Concise History of Classical Sanskrit Literature. Calcutta: Oxford University Press, 1960.

Shelat, Jayendra M. Akbar. Bombay: Bharatiya Vidya Bhavan, 1959.

Sheppard, Eric W. Coote Bahadur. London: W. Laurie, 1956.

Sherwani, Harun Khan. The Bahmanis of the Deccan. London: Luzac, 1953.

_____. History of the Qutb Shahi Dynasty. Columbia, Mo.: South Asia Books, 1974.

Singh, Iqbal. Rammohun Roy. New York: Asia Publishing House, 1958.

Singh, Kushwant. History of the Sikhs, 1469-1839. Princeton, N. J.: Princeton University Press, 1963.

_____. Ranjit Singh, Maharajah of the Punjab. London: Allen & Unwin, 1962.

_____. The Sikhs. London: Allen & Unwin, 1953.

Sinha, B. P. The Decline of the Kingdom of Magadha. Patna: Motilal Banarsidass, 1954.

Sinha, Jadunath. A History of Indian Philosophy. 2 vols. Calcutta: Central Book Agency, 1952-56.

Sinha, Narendra K. Haider Ali. Calcutta: A. Mukherjee, 1959.

_____. Ranjit Singh. Calcutta: University of Calcutta, 1933.

_____. Rise of the Sikh Power. Calcutta: University of Calcutta, 1946.

Sircar, Dinesh Chandra. Indian Epigraphy. Mystic, Conn.: Verry, 1965.

_____. Successors of the Satavahanas. Calcutta: University of Calcutta, 1939.

Sleeman, William H. Rambles and Recollections of an Indian Official. London: Oxford University Press, 1915.

Smith, Morton. Dates and Dynasties in Earliest India. Mystic, Conn.: Verry, 1973.

Smith, Vincent A. Akbar the Great Mogul. Delhi: S. Chand, 1958 (reprint).

_____. Asoka, the Buddhist Emperor of India. Delhi: S. Chand, 1957 (reprint).

_____. Early History of India. Oxford: Clarendon Press, 1958.

_____. History of Fine Art in India and Ceylon. Bombay: Taraporevala, 1962 (reprint).

_____. The Oxford History of India. Oxford: Clarendon Press, 1958.

Smith, Wilfred C. Modern Islam in India: A Social Analysis. London: Victor Gollancz, 1946.

Spate, Oskar H., and A. T. Learmonth. India and Pakistan: A General and Regional Geography. New York: Barnes & Noble, 1967.

Spear, Thomas George Percival. India: A Modern History. Ann Arbor: University of Michigan Press, 1961.

_____. The Nabobs. London: Oxford University Press, 1963.

_____. Twilight of the Mughals. Cambridge, England: Cambridge University Press, 1951.

Srinivasan, C. K. Baji Rao I--The Great Peshwa. New
    York: Asia Publishing House, 1962.

Srivastava, Ashirbadi Lal. The First Two Nawabs of Oudh.
    Agra: Shiv Lal Agarwala, 1954.

_____. History of India, 1000-1707 A. D. Mystic, Conn. :
    Verry, 1964.

_____. The Mughal Empire. Agra: Shiv Lal Agarwala,
    1957.

_____. A Short History of Akbar. Agra: Shiv Lal Agar-
    wala, 1957.

_____. The Sultanate of Delhi. Agra: Shiv Lal Agar-
    wala, 1953.

Stevenson, Margaret Sinclair. The Heart of Jainism. Lon-
    don: Oxford University Press, 1915.

Subba Rao, G. Indian Words in English. Oxford: Claren-
    don Press, 1954.

Subramanian, N. History of Tamilnad to A. D. 1336.
    Thompson, Conn. : Interculture, 1974.

Sutton, S. C. A Guide to the India Office Library. London:
    H. M. Stationery Office, 1952.

Swaminathan, K. D. The Nayakas of Ikkeri. Madras: P.
    Varadachary, 1957.

Tandon, P. D. Leaders of Modern India. Bombay: Vora,
    1955.

Tandon, Prakash. Beyond Punjab: A Sequel to the Punjabi
    Century. Berkeley: University of California Press,
    1971.

Taraporevala, V. D. B. , and D. N. Marshall. Mughal
    Bibliography. Bombay: New Book Company, 1962.

Tavernier, J. B. Travels in India. 2 vols. London: Ox-
    ford University Press, 1925.

Taylor, Philip Meadows. Confessions of a Thug. London: Oxford University Press, 1933.

Tendulkar, Dinanath G. Mahatma: Life of Mohandas Karamchand Gandhi. 8 vols. Delhi: Publications Division, 1960-63.

Tennyson, Hallam. India's Walking Saint: The Story of Vinoba Bhave. Garden City, N. Y.: Doubleday, 1955.

Thakkar, Amritlal V. Tribes of India. 2 vols. Delhi: Bharatiya Adimajati Sevak Sangh, 1950-51.

Thapar, Romila. Ancient India. Thompson: Interculture, 1969.

_____. Asoka and the Decline of the Mauryas. London: Oxford University Press, 1961.

_____. History of India. Baltimore: Penguin, 1964.

_____. Medieval India. Thompson: Interculture, 1970.

Thomas, Paul. Epics, Myths and Legends of India. Bombay: Taraporevala, 1961.

_____. Hindu Religion, Customs, and Manners. Bombay: Taraporevala, 1960.

Thompson, Edward J. Life of Charles, Lord Metcalfe. London: Faber & Faber, 1937.

_____. The Making of the Indian Princes. London: Oxford University Press, 1944.

_____. Suttee. New York: Finch Press, 1928 (reprint).

_____, and G. T. Garratt. Rise and Fulfilment of British Rule in India. Allahabad: Central Book Depot, 1958 (reprint).

Thurston, Edgar, and K. Rangachari. Castes and Tribes of Southern India. 7 vols. New York: Johnson, 1909 (reprint).

Tilak, Lakshmibai. I Follow After: An Autobiography. Madras: Oxford University Press, 1950.

Tod, James.   Annals and Antiquities of Rajasthan.   2 vols.
    Routledge & Kegan Paul, 1957.

Tripathi, Ram Prasad.   Rise and Fall of the Mughal Em-
    pire.   Allahabad: Central Book Dept. , 1956.

Tripathi, Rama S.   History of Kanauj to the Moslem Con-
    quest.   Mystic, Conn. :   Verry, 1964.

Trotter, Lionel J.   Warren Hastings.   Mystic, Conn. :
    Verry, 1962.

Vaidya, C. V.   History of Medieval Hindu India.   3 vols.
    Poona: Oriental Book Agency, 1921.

Vaiyapuri Pillai, S.   History of Tamil Language and Litera-
    ture.   Madras: New Century Book House, 1956.

Valle, Pietro della.   The Travels of Pietro della Valle in
    India.   2 vols.   London: Hakluyt Society, 1892.

Varthema, Ludovico di.   Travels.   London: Hakluyt Soci-
    ety, 1863.

Venkataramanayya, N.   The Eastern Chalukyas of Vengi.
    Madras: University of Madras, 1950.

Venkatarangaiya, M.   Local Government in India.   Columbia,
    Mo. :   South Asia Books, 1969.

Verma, D. C.   History of Bijapur.   Columbia, Mo. :   South
    Asia Books, 1974.

Viswanatham, K.   India in English Fiction.   New York: In-
    ternational Publications Service, 1971.

Walker, Benjamin.   The Hindu World.   2 vols.   New York:
    Praeger, 1968.

Wallbank, Thomas W.   A Short History of India and Pakistan.
    New York: Mentor, 1958.

Warder, A. K.   An Introduction to Indian Historiography.
    New York: Humanities, 1972.

Warmington, E. H.   The Commerce Between the Roman Empire and India. New York: Octagon, 1974.

Watson, Francis A.   A Concise History of India.   New York: Scribner's, 1974.

Watters, Thomas, trans.   On Yuan Chwang's Travels in India. 2 vols. London: Royal Asiatic Society, 1904-05.

Weber, Max.   The Religion of India, the Sociology of Hinduism and Buddhism. Glencoe, N. Y. : Free Press, 1958.

Wells, Henry W.   The Classical Drama of India.   New York: Asia Publishing House, 1963.

Wheeler, James T. , and M. Macmillan.   European Travellers in India. Calcutta: Susil Gupta, 1956.

Wheeler, Mortimer.   Early India and Pakistan.   New York: Praeger, 1959.

_____. Indus Civilization.   New York: Cambridge University Press, 1968.

Whiteway, Richard S.   The Rise of Portuguese Power in India. Westminster, England: A. Constable, 1899.

Williams, Rushbrook L.   An Empire Builder of the 16th Century. Delhi: S. Chand, 1962.

_____. A Handbook for Travellers in India.   New York: Barnes & Noble, 1973.

Wilson, H. H.   Glossary of Judicial and Revenue Terms.   Mystic, Conn. : Verry, 1968.

Wilson, Horace R.   Religious Sects of the Hindus.   Calcutta: Susil Gupta, 1958 (reprint).

Winstedt, Richard O. , ed.   Indian Art.   New York: Philosophical Library, 1948.

Winternitz, Maurice.   History of Indian Literature.   2 vols. Calcutta: University of Calcutta, 1927-33.

Wiser, William H. , and Charlotte V.   Behind Mud Walls, 1930-60.   Berkeley: University of California Press, 1963.

Wolpert, Stanley. India. Englewood Cliffs, N. J. : Prentice-Hall, 1965.

———. Tilak and Gokhale: Revolution and Reform in the Making of Modern India. Berkeley: University of California Press, 1962.

Woodruff, Philip see Philip Mason

Woytinsky, Wladimir S. India: The Awakening Giant. Millwood, N. Y. : Kraus, 1969.

Yasin, Mohammad. A Social History of Islamic India. Lucknow: Upper India Publishing House, 1968.

Yazdani, Ghulam, ed. The Early History of the Deccan. 2 vols. London: Oxford University Press, 1960.

Yeats-Brown, Francis. Lives of a Bengal Lancer. New York: Popular Library.

Zimand, Savel. Living India. Freeport, N. Y. : Books for Libraries, 1972.

Zimmer, Heinrich R. The Art of India. 2 vols. New York: Pantheon, 1955.

———. Hindu Medicine. Baltimore: Johns Hopkins University Press, 1948.

———. Myths and Symbols in Indian Art and Civilization. New York: Pantheon, 1946.

———. Philosophies of India. New York: Meridian, 1956.

Zinkin, Taya. Caste Today. London: Oxford University Press, 1962.

———. India. New York: Walker, 1966.

———. India Changes. London: Oxford University Press, 1958.

Zulfiqar, Ali Khan. Sher Shah Suri. Lahore, Pakistan: Civil and Military Gazette, 1925.

MAP OF INDIA

Main Political Divisions

Cease Fire Line
JAMMU & KASHMIR
Srinagar ✪
PUNJAB ✪
Chandigarh✪ Simla
HIMACHAL PRADESH
HARYANA
DELHI
Delhi
Jaipur ✪
UTTAR PRADESH
Lucknow ✪
RAJASTHAN
Patna ✪
SIKKIM
Gangtok✪
ARUNACHAL PRADESH
ASSAM
NAGALAND
✪Kohima
Shillong✪
MEGHALAYA
✪Imphal
MANIPUR
Gandinagar
✪
GUJARAT
Bhopal ✪
MADHYA PRADESH
BIHAR
W.
BENGAL
✪
Agartala
TRIPURA
Aizawl
MIZORAM
Calcutta
ORISSA
Diu Daman
Dadra & Nagar Aveli
MAHARASHTRA
Bombay
Bhubaneswar ✪
Hyderabad ✪
KARNATAKA
ANDHRA PRADESH
Panaji ✪
GOA
Bangalore ✪
Madras ✪
LAKSHADWEEP
TAMIL NADU
PONDICHERRY
Kawarathy ✪
KERALA
✪ Trivandrum
ANDAMAN AND NICOBAR ISLANDS
✪ Port Blair
R C K